We Need to Talk About Heidegger

LITERARY AND CULTURAL THEORY

General Editor
Wojciech H. Kalaga

VOLUME 55

PETER LANG

Justin Michael Battin / German A. Duarte (eds.)

We Need to Talk About Heidegger

Essays Situating Martin Heidegger in
Contemporary Media Studies

PETER LANG

Bibliographic Information published by the Deutsche Nationalbibliothek
The Deutsche Nationalbibliothek lists this publication in the Deutsche
Nationalbibliografie; detailed bibliographic data is available online at
http://dnb.d-nb.de.

Library of Congress Cataloging-in-Publication Data
A CIP catalog record for this book has been applied for at the Library of Congress.

This publication was financially supported by the Institute of English
Cultures and Literatures at the University of Silesia in Katowice.

Printed by CPI books GmbH, Leck

ISBN 978-3-631-75067-4 (Print)
E-ISBN 978-3-631-76052-9 (E-PDF)
E-ISBN 978-3-631-76053-6 (EPUB)
E-ISBN 978-3-631-76054-3 (MOBI)
DOI 10.3726/b14331

Contents

Justin Michael Battin and German A. Duarte
Martin Heidegger and Media Studies 7

German A. Duarte
Introducing the Fractal Character of *Dasein* in the Digital Age 21

Georgios Tsadgis
The Manual: Heidegger and Fundamental *Oto-chiero-logy* I 53

Justin Michael Battin
Ereignis and *Lichtung* in the Production of a Galaxy Far Far Away 73

Eve Forrest and Leighton Evans
Feeling Photography: Exploring Care, Attunement, and
Dwelling through the Work of Andre Kertész 101

Camilo Salazar Prince
Self-Understanding in the Age of the Selfie: Kierkegaard, Dreyfus,
and Heidegger on Social Networks 117

Heidi Herzogenrath-Amelung
Speaking the Unspeakable: Heidegger and Social Media's
'Mouseclick Solidarity' 151

Dimitra V. Pavlakou
Thinking Architecture through Heidegger's Views 169

Tony Richards
Take a Wander in My Shoes: Of Zombeing, Twombs, and
Equipmentality 185

Sascha Rashof
Heidegger's Topology in the World/s of Ubiquitious Computing 211

Philippe Theophanidis
A Decisive Mediation: Heidegger, Media Studies, and Ethics 233

6   Contents

Pieter Lemmens
From Ontology to Organology: Heidegger and Stiegler on the Danger
and Ambiguity of Technology and Technical Media 279

Author Biographies 309

Justin Michael Battin and German A. Duarte

Martin Heidegger and Media Studies

Media studies, much like critical theory, attempts to understand the effects of mass media on societies and to draw links between issues of representation, media artifacts, and, to echo Adorno, the culture industries, often with the intent of elucidating its potential as a hegemonic force. In 2007, David Morley suggested that the research output distributed under the designation of media studies had gradually become too idealist and exclusively concentrated on *media* itself, as both content and a dispositive.[1] In his view, a non-media-centric form of media studies must emerge in order to return the discipline to, in his own words, "its full range of classical concerns."[2] Inspired by the time-space compression that has come to epitomize our contemporary social, economic, and political context, Morley suggested that a new paradigm for the discipline was needed, one that "attends more closely to its material as well as its symbolic dimensions."[3] Following this framework, Shaun Moores argues that media studies has become too captivated with symbolic representation and cognitive interpretation as its primary means of investigation,[4] and echoes Morley's call for more inclusive form of the discipline, one that seeks to engage with a diverse collection of discourses circulating across the social sciences. This solicitation for a materialist intervention unveiled an opening to allow what we feel was Heidegger's inevitable entry into the discipline.

Considering that Heidegger often regarded as being one of the most relevant philosophers of the twentieth century, it is no surprise that he has already penetrated several fields of inquiry, namely cultural geography, social anthropology, and sociology, yet his oeuvre has yet to directly gain significant traction in the field of media studies. His absence could potentially be due to the field being spread, in part, out of two schools of thought, the Frankfurt School and Birmingham School, each of which strove to investigate myriad cultural and

---

1 Morley, M., 2007, *Media, Modernity and Technology: The Geography of the New*, London: Routledge.

2 Morley, M., 2009, "For a Materialist, Non-media-centric Media Studies." *Television and New Media* Vol. 10, No. 1, pp. 114–116.

3 *Ibid.*

4 Moores, S., 2013, "We Find Our Way About: Everyday Media Use and Inhabitant Knowledge." *Mobilities* Vol. 10, No. 1, pp. 17–35.

social issues via a rigorous reassessment of Marx. Each school was particularly
interested in utilizing this renewed appreciation of Marxism in order to question
the perpetuation of different inequalities across the commodity-driven, con-
sumerist, post-industrial societies that solidly emerged following the conclusion
of World War II and that initiated the transformation of capitalism into a force
towards the production of meaning, the production of imaginary. Although
media studies have become more open to varied forms of investigation, the
discipline still heavily relies upon these roots. Somewhat paradoxically, despite
Heidegger rarely being mentioned or called upon, those within the media
studies discipline frequently draw from a cadre of thinkers whom have openly
professed the fundamental importance of Heidegger with regards to the development of their own thought. Hannah Arendt, Pierre Bourdieu, Michel Foucault,
Jacques Derrida, Herbert Marcuse and Bernard Stiegler are merely a few of the
more notable examples. It is our position that if the media studies discipline is
to revitalize its interdisciplinary roots, specifically to grapple with contemporary
phenomena, identified by Krajina, Moores, and Morley as the linked mobilities
of information, people and commodities, the articulation of material and virtual geographies, and the meaningfulness of everyday, embodied practices, then
Heidegger must be warranted a place.[5]

The question of Heidegger's value and place within the discipline has been
tackled directly via Paul Taylor and David Gunkel in their recent *Heidegger and
the Media* (2014). In their view, Media Studies and Communication Studies
urgently need to take distance from the evaluation of the adequacy of a representation to the 'primary' reality. Instead, as noted by them, "more systematic
attention is required to the ways in which the means of available communication
participate in the uncovering and revealing of what is."[6] As noted by the authors,
following in the footsteps of Carey, this means a change in the paradigm that
would bring to the field of studies a different approach. In their words:

'How do we do this? What are the differences between these forms? What are the historical and comparative variations in them? How do changes in communication technology influence what we can concretely create and apprehend? How do groups in

5   Krajina, Z., S. Moores, D. Morley, 2014, "Non-media-centric Media Studies: A
     Cross-generational Conversation" in Sage Online Vol. 17, No. 6, pp. 682–700. Date
     Accessed: 5 December, 2017. Accessible from: http://journals.sagepub.com/doi/
     abs/10.1177/1367549414526733.
6   Gunkel, D.J. and P.A. Taylor, 2014, *Heidegger and the Media*, Cambridge: Polity
     Press, p. 89.

society struggle over the definition of what is real?' (Carey, in Gunkel and Taylor, 2014, p. 89).

In their view, Heidegger offers a decidedly fresh path to break away from the representation the discipline often relies upon. In many ways, it has become an anchor of sorts – providing a suitable foundation but prohibiting it from venturing into new territories. In addition, as remarked by Gunkel and Taylor, Heidegger's analysis of the technological context could represent a fundamental theoretical tool that not only allows for us to better comprehend the condition of being in our digital media context, but above all, his philosophy allows us to highlight, and hopefully to avoid, a technological deterministic view. Indeed, as Gunkel and Taylor noted – through a remarkable comparative analysis, from which similarities and divergences between Heidegger and McLuhan's theories emerge – the question of technology must return to the centre of the field of Media and Communication Studies through the concept of *Dasein*. In fact, the equation that Gunkel and Taylor propose (T = τ + λ) reconstructs the etymological dimension of the Greek word τέχνη (*technē*), and highlights the essence of technology (**T**), which is the sum of τέχνη and λόγος (*logos*). This interesting equation re-establishes technology's fundamental relationship with λόγος, "the originary dimension of language that lays open the way to the being of things."[7] Consequently, by proposing this understanding of the technological component, and its indispensable relationship with the *logos*, the authors advocate for a Heideggerian basis in the arduous task of analyzing our current digital media condition. In fact, by recognizing the presence of the *logos* as inherent in the conception of technology, our understanding of technology acquires a different dimension in which technology is no longer understood as an 'extension' – or as a prosthesis added onto human faculties – but is instead seen as a projection or as an extension of *Dasein*.

It should be stated, also, that Taylor and Gunkel are not exclusive in their advocating of Heidegger. Friedrich Kittler, in particular, emphatically argued that only through Heidegger could a philosophical consciousness for technical media emerge. Moreover, in the mid-1990s, Paddy Scannell relied heavily on Heidegger's thought to offer phenomenological insights into the dual sense of place that manifests while watching television. More recently, Shaun Moores has taken a Dreyfus-infused approach to Heidegger in order to raise awareness to the rather mundane and often overlooked tangible character of our daily media use, specifically to counter arguments that have disembodied online presence.

---

7   *Ibid.*, p. 166.

Based on the aforementioned authors, it should be apparent that Heidegger does have a meaningful place in media studies, especially if one takes into account some fundamental convergences between Heidegger's comprehension of media technologies and Marshall McLuhan's theories, several of which have become cornerstones for the study of media.

In an attempt to build on the pathway laid down by these authors, this collection's main aim is to shed additional light upon the value Heidegger's philosophy may potentially add to contemporary media studies. Arguably, even if not referenced directly, Heidegger is a philosopher whose work pervades various media-related academic texts. Whether these investigations centre technological development, media practices, textual analysis, or embark with a political dimension, it is possible to trace and demonstrate the presence of a Heideggerian voice, echoing in the conceptual space of such texts. Therefore, the authors contributing to the volume collectively adopt the hypothesis of Heidegger-as-a-father-figure, whose influence, albeit indirect, is omnipresent in the intellectual substrate underlying many of present-day approaches to media studies. Our goal, thus, is to showcase a collection of complementary chapters that reveal the role Heidegger plays in media studies as well as elucidate new paths to which one can take by employing an explicit Heideggerian lens. Following the release of the Heidegger's controversial *Black Notebooks* and the subsequent calls to abandon the philosopher,[8] this book seeks to demonstrate why Heidegger, rather than be pushed aside and shunned by media studies practitioners, ought to be embraced and further incorporated into the discipline, as he offers unique, and often innovative, pathways to address, and ultimately understand, our daily engagements with media-related phenomena.

Chapter Summaries

I Introducing the Fractal Character of Dasein in the Digital Age

This opening chapter investigates the way in which the development of non-Euclidean geometries, particularly topology, contributed to the dissolving of both the Cartesian dualism thought-extension and the Cartesian *cogito*. After a brief survey on the main theories that posited the existence of a topologic condition (e.g. Bergson's *devenir*, Poincaré's *Analisis Situs* and Whitehead's concrescence

---

8   Fuchs, C., 2015, "Martin Heidegger's Anti-Semitism: Philosophy of Technology and the Media in the Light of the Black Notebooks. Implications for the Reception of Heidegger in Media and Communication Studies." tripleC Vol. 13, No. 1, pp. 55–78.

and bifurcation), the chapter suggests to understand the Heideggerian *Dasein* as the culmination of a process that recognizes existence under topological terms. It is to say, the Heideggerian *Dasein*, in this chapter, is seen as a notion that displays a topological conception of the subject, which no longer represents the centre of the experience, a phenomenon that was already *in nuce* in Bergson, Poincaré, and Whitehead's theories.

Particular attention has been given to the technological context in which these theories were developed. In this chapter, The Second Industrial Revolution is analyzed as a decisive phase of industrialization that represents the exaltation of fragmentation and seriality (e.g. interchangeable parts and the production line). However, after this initial stage, the Second Industrial Revolution transformed the machine into an autonomous form of praxis and determined the end of fragmentation and seriality as an *episteme*, replacing it by an incessant flux derived from electric technology. Starting from the recognition of this phenomenon, the chapter seeks to highlight the implications that emerged from the disappearance of the seriality that characterized the shift from one technological context to another. The investigation is built on the acknowledgment of the topologic nature of the Heideggerian *Dasein* and, through it, the chapter also deals with fundamental Heideggerian concepts, contextualizing them into our digital technological milieu. Particular interest is given to Heidegger's understanding of technology, to the ways in which media technologies affect distances in space and time and the way modern technologies became instruments of reification of every form of information, placing the thing and thingness the middle of the philosophical thinking. To conclude, the chapter proposes an analysis of Heidegger's oeuvre as a fundamental work from which new insights into the media condition – and into a possible current post-media condition – can emerge.

II The Manual: Heidegger and Fundamental *Oto-chiero-logy* I

This second chapter examines the function of the hand in Heidegger's thought. The hand is more than a literary-theoretical trope. It points to the absent corporeality of *Dasein*, enabling a reconsideration of the notions of *mediality*—the total apparatus of mediation in the countless ways it conditions phenomenality and communication—and *epochality*—the unity of diverse theoretical figurations which define a given historic time. The hand, severed and singular, outlines the exceptionality of the human as a being of monstration, a sign which, through the use of the hand, signifies in turn.

This chapter follows closely this manual labour, which is constituted by the metaphysical proximity of the hand to *logos* in order to demonstrate the way in which this monstration—at once technology and inscription—announces from the outset an infinite danger. Profoundly attentive to this danger, Heidegger seeks the possibility of salvation in the exceptionality of the human hand, an exceptionality defined through a strenuous balancing act on the limits of technology. Accordingly, Heidegger outlines how the proper use of the hand, the use of a pen or a hammer, a tool or a machine, is threatened by the mere 'mechanism' of the typewriter. Nietzsche meets Heidegger at this juncture from the future. Through Derrida and Kittler, this chapter unravels the suppositions that support and limit the thought of Heidegger to show the constitutive technicity of thought, to call for a reinvention of the theoretical-corporeal hand, and re-signify the moment at which an epoch witnesses the closure of itself.

III *Ereignis* and *Lichtung* in the Production of a Galaxy Far Far Away

This chapter draws links between *Ereignis* and *Lichtung*, two concepts that regularly appear in Heidegger's post-*Being and Time* output, in order to demonstrate how our living in being is made most evident to human beings when they engage with *things* in such a way that can illuminate their *thingly* nature. A human being's meaningful and skillful engagement with things should prompt their temporal deliverance into a world that matters to them, where the nuances of their being-there unveils itself in a rather deliberate way. Moreover, such use of things should unveil the unique role human beings play in the manifestation of that world via their own motivational, pre-reflective, and improvised activities. The primary reason for focusing on and linking these two Heideggerian ideas is because they, when considered together, offer a path to revise within our everyday experience how immersive worlds not only become inhabitable and meaningful to human beings in a temporal fashion, but also how such immersive worlds can offer new avenues and levels of richness where human beings can revitalize a sense of individual creativity and their belongness with being.

A significant amount of Heidegger's late work explicitly explored how the potential for such an understanding of human being had gradually begun to fade from possibility, as human beings had too often begun to move about in everyday life and attempt to inflict their will on things and environments for the sake of efficiency, thus removing the potential for hearing and responding to being's call. Humans had, in Heidegger's estimation, become engulfed in a state of enframing (*Das Gestell*). As Dreyfus suggests, accepting a world with *Das Gestell* as its foundation has sparked our being closed off from improvisation, individual exploration and creativity, and the benefits that manifest when working together alongside diverse and meaningful things.

To illustrate this connection, this chapter specifically draws from the production processes of Disney's *Star Wars*, three films that have been heralded for their return to a more tangible, traditional form of filmmaking, as well as a reliance on practices that both encourage and unveil the interconnected fabric between human beings, things, and worlds.

IV Feeling Photography: Exploring Care, Attunement, and Dwelling through the Work of Andre Kertész

This chapter questions the difference between a photographer and someone who merely carries a camera. For some, the difference is redundant: the continuing visual turn in the 21st century that has encouraged making photographs so ubiquitous has led to a world where we are all image takers. Advances in technology mean that most people have some form of image taking device with them at all times. However, just as access to a paintbrush does not make everyone an artist, the label of photographer denotes more than just access to technology. Using Heidegger's concept of *attunement*, the authors argue that being a photographer goes beyond taking images. It is being alert to the sensibilities that the camera enables and makes visible: it is a particular worldview. Heidegger describes how technological orientation to the world (*Gestell* or *Enframing*) affects the possibility of an *attunement* with things that allows for a poetic revealing of entities, and reveals entities as resource. In photographic terms, such a worldview would be illustrated by screenic images that are used to accrue social capital. A poetic revealing of entities emerges from an event (*Ereingis*) where the key elements of world are gathered by a thing and *Dasein* can understand the world and other entities through taking things into care. In this case, we posit that some practices of photography can allow for a poetic revealing of the world (free from *Gestell*). This is a coming-forth of entities, making these entities visible within the image.

To illustrate this attunement and poetic revealing of everyday life, we consider the work of Andre Kertész. Kertész was a hugely prolific photographer throughout his life although he believed his work never received the merit it deserved, when he was alive. The images of Kertész reveal much about his position and view on the world, showing a deep attunement to the places he inhabited both in Europe and later in America. They detail an unflinching, surreal and curious gaze an understanding of the entities in the world. Kertész's use of the camera and his being-in-the-world were clearly deeply entangled going far beyond simple image taking.

Heidegger's original project was to understand being. Through the work of André Kertész this chapter argues that this understanding of being through photography is dependent upon proper dwelling in the world, and that dwelling is a relationship to things that allows for continued everyday elegiac encounters. Dwelling needs to be understood in reference not only to things but also to *Dasein's* taking up of things into care. *Dasein's* engagement with things is part of the clearing (*Lichtung*) away of ontheology and assessment of being *as* being. The clearing is the ground for *Dasein's* understanding of the world and other entities, but *Dasein's* access to that clearing is through its use of things in a manner that allows for the revealing of place to occur. In the context of Kertész's practices and orientations with the camera, the authors argue it is the manner of use that is illustrative of *Dasein's* attunement or dwelling and that the camera affords the visibility of entities as entities.

V Self-Understanding in the Age of the Selfie: Kierkegaard, Dreyfus, and Heidegger on Social Networks

This chapter draws on Hubert Dreyfus, Kierkegaard, and Heidegger to explore the self and its relationship to commitment and focal practices in the enframing, technological age, an era demarcated by an individual and cultural nihilistic leveling. The author explores how the understanding of self of the age of the selfie is no longer made intelligible to us as a self, but rather as an embodied self entangled with an online self that manifests as flexible, dynamic, and highly ordered, often for the sake of efficiency and, in some instances, for the accruement of social capital, both of which have significantly impacted a person's engagement with focal practices and unconditional commitments.

Rather than hastily shun social networks, however, human beings must discover and allow for *Gelassenheit*, or releasement, as doing so will permit human beings to further understand the ordering power of social networks. This unique releasement towards social networks will equally permit an opening for human beings to find ways in which social networks both enable and sustain focal practices and commitments by harboring the power they have to *gather*, to connect us with both telepresent others and ourselves.

Among the most pressing tasks in the contemporary world is a human's responsibility to discover how to engage with the omnipresent virtual landscape in such a way that allows for social networks to sustain and encourage unconditional commitments and enable focal practices that resist the efficiency of the technological epoch, and thus open a free relation with social networks and, by consequence, escape the cultural and individual leveling of contemporary nihilism. If human beings begin to approach social networks in the same vein as Heidegger has done with the Heidelberg Bridge, as locations brought about by a temporal gathering, then they can learn to regard them as divergent but interconnecting technological paths that, if experienced appropriately, will enable the embodied self to merge with the online self in a manner that encourages unconditional (virtual) commitments that can unveil, or open up, the world to our highest potentiality of being.

VI Speaking the Unspeakable: Heidegger and Social Media's 'Mouseclick Solidarity'

In this chapter, the author acknowledges that philosophy is not a popular approach for thinking about technology and the social. The fast paced environment of social media studies especially makes philosophy look slow moving, sluggish, and out of touch. Philosophy, Marx famously wrote in his famous *Theses on Feuerbach*, has only ever interpreted the world – what counts is to change it. And social media have become almost synonymous with social change since the Arab Spring, which has widely been hailed as a 'social media revolution'.

Martin Heidegger took on Marx's complaint head on, countering that in order to change the world, one would first need to interpret it correctly. This chapter seeks to challenge the dominant narrative of social media as engines of social change, arguing that instead they pose acute examples of the extent to which not only social life, but the critical human mind, that faculty on which the Enlightenment built its hopes, are increasingly enframed by instrumentality. Heidegger's critique of technology is often misread as a Luddite attack on all technological modernity, and a passionate plea to return to pre-technological forms of life. As this chapter will show, however, Heidegger's concept of *Das Gestell* offers a critical perspective on the impacts of technological mediation that goes beyond the typical utopian/dystopian dichotomy. While social media have widely been hyped as ushering in a communications revolution, rupturing established hierarchies, and creating democracies bottom-up, Heidegger's conceptual framework allows us to see how the freedom promised by social media continues to be technologically enframed.

This chapter considers Twitter as an example of technological enframing, and problematizes the 'quick fix' solution to democratic action that Twitter promises, and highlights how the Tweet encourages what Heidegger refers to as the 'privileging of the correct over the true'. A number of instances will be discussed where it emerges how Twitter, while seemingly challenging established power hierarchies, in fact serves to reinforce these. Thus, rather than being the 'terrifying abstraction', as which it has often been criticized, Heidegger's *Das Gestell* offers a sophisticated mechanism for addressing how the digital matrix reduces

the complexity of human being-in-the world to a technologized parody of itself.
It is a strength, not a weakness, that it operates at the level of the abstract, as this
allows us to address the unifying features of modern information & communication technologies, rather than being caught up in its specificities.

VII Thinking Architecture through Heidegger's Views

This chapter explores how philosophy and architecture have engaged in a continuous and open dialogue, one which finds its roots deep in the history of both
fields of knowledge. Philosophy investigates the boundaries of human thought,
posing questions and seeking for answers that often transcend a human being's
cognitive abilities. It places architecture as a creative praxis in its intellectual
dimension. Architecture not only addresses what is directly perceived through
the human eye, but also challenges emotions which are triggered through real-
life experience. The answers to questions like what is architecture and how man
dwells should be sought in architecture's substance as a praxis. These kinds of
concerns emerge under the philosophical contemplations of the human being,
the relationship between human being and cosmos, and the place of human
beings in the world.

According to Heidegger man dwells by spanning the *on the earth* and the
beneath the sky. The original admission of dwelling is the result of *poiēsis* that
constitutes the primal form of building. Via *poiēsis*, the statement "man dwells
in that he builds" is given its proper sense. Man does not dwell in that he merely
establishes his stay on the earth beneath the sky, by cultivating the land and
simultaneously raising buildings. Authentic building occurs so far as there are
poets to take the measure for architecture, the structure of dwelling. "It's about
creating emotional space" the architect Peter Zumthor mentions, recalling how
he once asked his students to design a house without form. It is pertinent that
we ask how is the mystery of place (*topos*) approached as far as it concerns the
invisible aspects of its phenomena. In addition, which is the real space, the one
that we see and experience every day or the one that emerges in our consciousness taking its own shape and geometry? Moreover, should we equally question
its boundaries?

In this philosophical context that it becomes meaningful to focus on the
interplay between architecture and cinema. Both arts seek the relationship
between the past and the present. Using memory as a tool they are under a continuous confrontation with time. The investigation of "the notion of boundary"
constitutes the centre of their references. Architecture, being restricted to follow
the rules that the art of building imposes, derives often its visions from cinema's

transcendences. In *Cinematic Language* Andrei Tarkovsky argues that it is time which ultimately dictates editing techniques. Rhythm is at the core of the *poetic film*. He believes that the main characteristic of poetic film is the process of "sculpting in time" as opposed to Eisenstein montage of attractions. This idea, introduces the art of filming as the representation of distinctive currents of time, conveyed in the shot by its internal rhythm. In general, the issue of time is posed as a boundary/border which is reflected in every creative manifestation, seen from all its aspects, even from its existential one. It is about a new narration, one in pursuit of *aletheia* (unconcealment), truth as conceived by Heidegger.

VIII Take a Wander in My Shoes: Of Zombeing, Twombs, and Equipmentality

In this chapter, the author posits how the zombie, just as the animal was famously for Heidegger, is poor in world. Humans are the only entity under the sun, according to Heidegger, who exist with being and thus are bestowed with the art or comportment of being-there or *Da-sein*. What happens however when the human goes rogue, when its mentality and its ability to deal or cope with equipment, and thus to have equipmentality, disappears? S/he devolves into an it, loses their name, and becomes simply a zombie. Zombies, as some surviving scientists will typically point out within the genre, lose their cerebral cortex and become aimless eating machines, flesh machines. They may carry guns but cannot any longer comport themselves towards them, but yet they also then swarm the planet as contagious human insects making the equipmental totalities that they once, as *Dasein* occupied, fall apart. Ethernet cables no longer carry data within a post/industrial complex but retreat to becoming mere strangulation things for the few surviving *Dasein*. Equipmental structures no longer circulate and carry being toward one another but become short-term hand-to-mouth devices. Such is the poverty of equipmental being within the zombie realm that unites humans and zombies.

But what of the equipmental function of those partaking of those seemingly worlds? What of the zombie text itself as equipment for environmental coping? What is this world for those watching these dead men walking who have lost their heads? These de-pictions (non-representational) comport a losing of our heads also. The govern-mental terminal *for-the-sake-of-which* structures have melted away in the age of a liquidic mutable modernity and so the sense of solidly emplaced equipment finds residence within these abandoned audio-visual housings. We take residence or we dis-placedly dwell within these de-govern-mental structures and we do not in any way merely observe a representational space. In the last episode of *Fear The Walking Dead*, the *Walking Dead* spinoff, two very different characters, now thrown together and given temporary reflective shelter towards the end of this summative episode, exclaim similar sentiments at the encroaching de-worlding that the "zombie virus" will all-too-shortly entail: one, a heroin addict says "I feel like rest of the world is catching up with me" whilst a taught-owning character of economic means state that "the only way to survive in a mad world is to embrace the madness. The directedness of equipment and of equipmentality's terminal *for-the-sake-of-which* in a liquidic and neoliberal universe, gives way to a more dispersed de-dwelling and so the world of the zombie, itself, provides an avatarial performative and forms an integral component within our own equipmental coping.

IX Heidegger's Topology in the World/s of Ubiquitous Computing

Within media studies, as well as outside, Heidegger's philosophy has primarily been considered from a temporal point of view, especially his early work, apart from some exceptions. This is partly due to the intention of *Being and Time*, at the time, which was to critique the Western tradition of metaphysics in order to develop more *processual* notions of beings through Being. However, in a world where technics has become accelerated to the point of pervasiveness, i.e. *Das Gesell* has been completed and thus differentiated itself into multiplicities of sub-'*Ge-Stelle*', the need for a different reading is pressing.

This chapter explores Heidegger's ontology through a techno-*platial* framework across (a selection of) his works. By considering Heidegger as one of the most important theorists of place [*topos*] in recent philosophical history, this essay aims to show the significance of his topo-logy for contemporary media studies by focusing on the conceptions of Being-in(-the-World), Thingliness, *Techné*, Dwelling, *Entwurf* ['Design'] and Being-with. The evolution of these concepts will be traced from his early thought, in which platiality was secondary to temporality, through to his late philosophy after the well recognized turn, where he put more emphasis on the *places* of Being, in order to close the phenomenological circle. This essay explicitly tries to distinguish itself from a spatial reading, since the realm of space is rather universal, while conceptions of place offer more contemporary affordances within (a) globalised world order/s. Apart from considering Heidegger's topology as a useful vehicle to think highly mediated worlds, this essay will furthermore point out the limitations of his late modern technical thought.

X A Decisive Mediation: Heidegger, Media Studies, and Ethics

The first part of this chapter casts the problem of defining "media" and "media studies" as an epistemological problem. In doing so, it shows how a common way to borrow from Heidegger's work in media studies is often done through reference to modern communication technologies. This being a relatively recent and rather specialized extension of the idea of *medium*, the chapter shows Heidegger's influence in the nascent field of media studies to be neither straightforward, nor clearly established. Turning more specifically to Heidegger, the chapter then outlines the well-documented, although more complicated problem of his involvement with Nazism and anti-Semitism. This is cast as a political problem. While some have argued that Heidegger's grave political commitments contaminated parts of, or all his thought, the chapter argues that this is no reason for media studies to steer away from it. Going back to the emergence of the fields of communication and media studies, it shows how the epistemological was and remain entangled with the political. While banning Heidegger is ultimately ineffective regarding the nature of the problems he got involved with (for getting rid of him does not spare us of the issues he got involved with), sidestepping this involvement clearly is not responsible either. The chapter finally suggests instead that both the epistemological and the political problems require an ethical engagement. In conclusion, the chapter outlines how such an ethical engagement is of special concern for media studies for it can be cast as a process of mediation.

XI From Ontology to Organology: Heidegger and Stiegler on the Danger and Ambiguity of Technology and Technical Media

This closing chapter discusses the views on (media) technology in its relation to the human condition of Martin Heidegger and Bernard Stiegler, focusing particularly on their respective understandings of what Heidegger has first theorized in 1949–50 as the danger and the ambiguity of technology, i.e., of technology's essence. Although Stiegler acknowledges the power of Heidegger's ontological or more precisely onto-historical understanding of technology as enframing and likewise emphasizes the danger and ambiguity inherent in technology's essence, he contests Heidegger's famous claim that the essence of technology is nothing technological. On the contrary, and through a move that in some sense reverses the transcendental conditionality of being with respect to beings or the onto-logical in relation to the ontic consequently maintained by Heidegger, Stiegler shows that the essence of technology is technical in the ontic and thus empirical sense after all, and that it is concrete (media) technologies that constitute Dasein's openness to being and profoundly condition its understanding of being. For

Stiegler, in contrast to Heidegger, the 'free essence' of man does not exist without an intimate and original coupling with concrete technical media. Dasein as the being capable of questioning both its own being and the being of other beings can in his opinion not exist without a relation to concrete (media) technologies.

Interpreting (media) technologies as technical organs coupled with and transductively evolving in an intimate relation with the psychic and somatic organs of human beings and supporting as such social organizations, Stiegler replaces Heidegger's ontological or onto-historical view of technology with an ontico-ontological one or in his terms an organological view that assigns to (media) technologies in their concrete empirical-accidental nature an ontological effectiveness or constitutivity. This entails an ontico-ontological re-interpretation of Heidegger's notions of the danger and ambiguity of technology in terms of a pharmacology that considers (media) technologies as simultaneously – and irreducibly – supportive and undermining or in his terminology as both toxic and curative for human existence. And instead of calling for a quietist response to technology's danger in terms of releasement, as in the case of Heidegger, he proposes an active technopolitics and noopolitics of media understood as a positive pharmacotherapy.

Bibliography

Fuchs, C., 2015, "Martin Heidegger's Anti-Semitism: Philosophy of Technology and the Media in the Light of the Black Notebooks. Implications for the Reception of Heidegger in Media and Communication Studies." tripleC Vol. 13, No. 1, pp. 55–78.

Gunkel, D. and P. Taylor,2014, *Heidegger and the Media*, Cambridge: Polity Press.

Krajina, Z., S. Moores, D. Morley, 2014. "Non-media-centric Media Studies: A Cross-generational Conversation" Sage Online Vol. 17, No. 6, pp. 682–700. Date Accessed: 5 December 2017. Accessible from: http://journals.sagepub.com/doi/abs/10.1177/1367549414526733

Moores, S., 2013. "We Find Our Way About: Everyday Media Use and Inhabitant Knowledge." *Mobilities* Vol. 10, No. 1, pp. 17–35.

Morley, M., 2007, *Media, Modernity and Technology: The Geography of the New*, London: Routledge.

Morley, M. 2009, "For a Materialist, Non-media-centric Media Studies." *Television and New Media* Vol. 10, No. 1, pp. 114–116.

German A. Duarte

Introducing the Fractal Character of *Dasein* in the Digital Age

1 Toward a topologic condition

In the nineteenth century, the emergence of a new paradigm was concretized through Henri Bergson's notion of *devenir*. In fact, through this concept, it was possible to recognize every form of existence in movement, the same movement through which reality develops itself.[1] According to Bergson, this incessant movement concerns everything: it concerns the subject and its psychological experience, as well as the extension, the latter also embraced by a continuous progression. Movement concerns everything, and consequently, every single entity is traversed by a progression that eliminates the existence of enclosed systems, which only exist in the human intellect, which finds in inert and isolated objects the convenience for their understanding.[2] Like a film camera, the human mind exerts an "act of order" through the generation of fixed states of reality. In other words, the human mind takes snapshots in order to substitute with images the continuous mutation of reality.[3]

Through the acknowledgment of *devenir*, Bergson postulated that objects are simultaneity; they are in continuous change and it is only through the subject's consciousness that extension is organized, serialized, and fixed in intelligible images: objects become moments.[4] To use Bergson's concept, the human mind "fabricates", that is to say, it exerts an isolation of assembled parts around the action.[5] Accordingly, fabrication isolates nature and natural phenomena. Thus, fabrication means a limit, a paradigm through which humankind organizes everything by applying a preordained system based on a series of pre-ordained

---

1 H. Bergson, *La pensée et le mouvant*, Paris, PUF, 1934, p. 218.
2 H. Bergson, *L'évolution créatrice*, Paris, PUF, 1907, p. 10.
3 *Ibid.*, pp. 187–272.
4 It is important to remember that the etymology of the word 'moment' encapsulates Bergson's analysis. In fact, the word 'moment', which determines a brief portion of time, finds its direct etymon in the Latin *momentum*, which means movement, motion, alteration or change.
5 Bergson, *L'évolution créatrice*, p. 93.

effects already contained in the cause.[6] In opposition to fabrication, Bergson theorizes organization, which represents a desirable human capacity through which humankind could liberate itself from the Newtonian Clockwork Universe. By means of organization, according to Bergson, science could avoid the understanding of living organisms and reality as assembled parts deriving from a mechanical view.

An analogous human limit was criticized by Poincaré, who found the same human limitation personified by the notion of dimension, which is, according to him, an instinctive concept built by our ancestors or somehow implanted in our childhood.[7] According to him, by developing a different notion of dimension, humankind could build a new order that allows the conception of new forms of relation between elements. In fact, Poincaré, during the development of the *Analysis Situs*, noted that the imposition of the three-dimensional Euclidean space generates a cognitive limitation because it pre-organizes human being's natural perception. The limit, in this case, was clearly inherited from Euclid's *Elements*, from which derived the understanding of space as a "container of elements."[8]

Poincaré's analysis situs and topology represented the decisive loss of the imperative three dimensions. Thanks to Poincaré's analysis situs, the space decisively loses its connotation as a 'three dimensional container of elements' and starts to be understood as a composition that responds to movements and forms derived from a complex thought.[9] That is the reason why, for Poincaré, the development of the analysis situs represented an "urgent human need." By means of the development and improvement of the analysis situs, humankind acquires an instrument that finally enables us to discover the 'hyperspace', an instrument able to 'replace' human senses.[10]

While Bergson attempted to highlight this problematic by using the notion of fabrication to oppose the notion of organization, Poincaré proposed the analysis of situation as a theory that allows the understanding of the space as a continuous

---

6   D. Kreps, *Bergson, Complexity and Creative Emergence*, New York, Palgrave Macmillan, 2015, p. 56.

7   H. Poincaré, *Science et méthode*, Paris, Flammarion, 1908, p. 121.

8   *Ibid.*, p. 39.

9   On this subject see, Günzel S. "Raum – Topographie – Topologie", in: S. Günzel (Ed.,) *Topologie. Zur Raumbeschreibung in den Kultur- und Medienwissenschaften*, Bielefeld, Transcript Verlag, 2007, pp. 13–29. And also J. Dieudonné, *A History of Algebraic and Differential Topology 1900–1960*, Boston, Birkhäuser, 1989.

10 Poincaré, *Science et méthode*, p. 40.

form derived by infinite relationships. The space that emerges from the analysis of situation displays a multidimensional nature that is exclusively generated by relationships, which implies a series of continuous transformations of the whole. As one can see, both authors, by recognizing an immanent movement that pervades every entity—a *devenir* that traverses objects and subjects—postulate the inexistence of enclosed systems and the understanding of space as a pure set of relationships.

*It is in Bergson's *Essai sur les données immédiates de la conscience* (1889) where the thoughts on an immanent movement emerged as an instrument to hypothesize the dissolution of the Cartesian dualism thought–extension. Indeed, Bergson theorizes that objects are in continuous change, movements that embrace both thought and extension, and consequently, extension no longer represents a simply form of exteriority, but an entity that finds its existence through movement which is shared by the subject.[11] This hypothesis proposes the inexistence of isolated systems, but above all, it incentivises the understanding of the extension as mobility, as a set of continuous mutations whose existence resides in both movement and relationships.[12]

*The inexistence of isolated systems and the comprehension of space as a set of relationships, founded on the acknowledgement of *devenir*, requires the dissolution of the dualism thought–extension and places the phenomenological approach in a first plane.[13] In fact, the new conception of space, materialized by topology, generated the necessity to understand the subject's presence in a reality conceived as topological, that is to say, a reality shaped by relationships between everything. A witness of this necessity could be the direction that Whitehead's oeuvre progressively took. In fact, from his important works on mathematics, algebra and axioms of projective geometry, he turned his interests toward logic and phenomenology. As a contemporary of Bergson and Poincaré, Whitehead also highlighted a limit that hampers the human mind in its comprehension of the inexistence of isolated systems.

---

11 H.W. Carr. *Henri Bergson: The Philosophy of Change*, London, T. Nelson & Sons, 1919, p. 14.

12 See, M.-L. Heuser, "Die Anfänge der Topologie in Mathematik und Naturphilosophie", in: S. Günzel (Hrsg.), Topologie. Zur Raumbeschreibung in den Kultur- und Medienwissenschaften, Bielefeld, 2007, pp. 181–200.

13 Topology, as noted by Malpas, is "an attempt to think the place of thinking" (p. 45). Consequently, it is possible to affirm that topology is essentially phenomenological. On this subject, see, J. Malpas, *Heidegger and the Thinking of Place. Explorations in the Topology of Being*, Cambridge, MA, MIT Press, 2012.

Whitehead was concerned with the human act of "bifurcation", through which the human mind isolates natural phenomena.[14] In fact, for Whitehead, the impossibility to understand the natural character of the existence as a present moment—a *movimentum*, in which the existence means the temporal establishment of relationships, and, consequently, in which no enclosed system can exist—derives from an act of bifurcation through which humankind isolates, organizes, substitutes, but above all, divides the object from a perceiving subject. The problematic that Bergson, Poincaré and Whitehead wanted to overcome could be summarized as humankind's impossibility of conceiving existence as concrescence. In fact, through this concept of Whitehead's, it is possible to recognize the associative character of the extension. Accordingly, extension would be understood as an open entity that forms open sets of entities.[15] Whitehead's notion implies, at the same time, a topological conception of the subject, which no longer represents the centre of the experience and consequently transforms the egological understanding of it.[16]

2 *Wohnen* in the topological space

Bergson's *devenir* established a common entity, a force that traverses objects and subjects. The recognition of this immanent force that dissolves the idea of the existence of enclosed systems imposed a new understanding of the space, which took form through the development of Topology. In such a space, which acquires the character of a continuum built by variations and relations, the subject becomes an interconnected entity defined by momentary relations of togetherness. In addition, as postulated by one of the most prominent characteristics of the topological space, the space is not a 'container' of objects and subjects; space is a pure set of relationships, it is the domain of interrelatedness. Thus, when one thinks on the subject's presence in the topological space, one designates its momentary presence as *In-der-Welt-sein*, which implies to live, *habitare* or *wohnen*. This condition was proposed by Merleau-Ponty in 1945 in *Phénoménologie de la perception* in these words:

> "Space is not the milieu (real or logical) in which things are arranged, but it is the means by which the position of things become possible. That is to say, instead of imagining it as a kind of ether in which all things derive, or instead of conceiving it as an abstraction

14 A.N. Whitehead, *The Concept of Nature*, Cambridge, Cambridge University Press, 1964, p 21.
15 A.N. Whitehead, *Science and the Modern World*, New York, Pelican, 1948, pp. 50–57.
16 X. Verley, "Whitehead et la subjectivité". *Les Études Philosophiques*, 4, 2002, pp. 511–525.

of a common character to them, one must think of it as the universal power of their connections." (My translation)[17]

Following this framework, the subject is able to possess, by regionalizing it, a part of the world. In fact, as subjects, "(…) we belong to the world, we are not just in the world" (My translation).[18]

In the frame of topology, *res extensa* becomes, in this way, a continuous form and consequently, 'in' this space; we cannot 'place' a subject, due to its topologic nature. The topological nature of the space imposes a different understanding of the preposition. The preposition 'in' does not indicate only an extended relation 'in' space that subjects have to each other with regard to their location in a particular space. This transformation is clearly presented by Heidegger. In his words: "By this 'in' we mean the relation of being which two beings extended 'in' space to each other relating to their place in that space" (My translation).[19] Nor does the preposition 'in' designate a spatial '*ineinander*' of things objectively present; it would be more a preposition that designates the being as *momentum*, of 'being-together-with' in the sense of 'being absorbed' 'in' the world. In Heidegger's words: "The 'Being at' the world, in the sense of becoming absorbed in the world, is an existential-ness, which is grounded in being-in" (My translation).[20]

The subject's presence as an entity absorbed in the world, displays some interesting analogies with Leibniz' theories, in which he posits that the essence of every entity resides in its capacity to be absorbed, to link itself with the whole.[21]

---

17 "L'espace n'est pas le milieu (réel ou logique) dans lequel se disposent les choses, mais le moyen par lequel la position des choses devient possible. C'est-à-dire qu'au lieu de l'imaginer comme une sorte d'éther dans lequel baignent toutes les choses ou de le concevoir abstraitement comme un caractère qui leur soit commun, nous devons le penser comme la puissance universelle de leurs connexions." M. Merleau-Ponty, *Phénoménologie de la perception*, Paris, Gallimard, 1945, p. 281.

18 "(…) nous sommes au monde, et non pas seulement dans le monde." *Ibid.*, p. 520.

19 "Wir meinen mit dem »in« das Seinsverhältnis zweier »im« Raum ausgedehnter Seienden zueinander in Bezug auf ihren Ort in diesem Raum." M. Heidegger, *Sein und Zeit*, Tübingen, Max Niemeyer Verlag, 1967, p. 54.

20 "Das »Sein bei« der Welt, in dem noch näher auszulegenden Sinne des Aufgehens in der Welt, ist ein im In-Sein fundiertes Existenzial." M. Heidegger, *Sein und Zeit*, p. 54.

21 See, Leibniz, G.W. *Nouveaux essais sur l'entendement humain / Neue Abhandlungen über den menschlichen Verstand* In: G.W. Leibniz, Philosophische Schriften Band 3.1 and 3.2, W. Von Engelhardt – HH. Holz (Eds.,) Frankfurt am Main, Suhrkamp, 1996 (1765). Conversely to Newton's conception of space, in which space and time is a single entity that has its own properties and that represents an open field without limits in which atoms are arranged and governed by gravity, for Leibniz, space does not represent an independent entity. In fact, the world is constructed, according to

Consequently, for Leibniz, existence implies a *momentum* of connection with the whole, a *mens momentanea*, which is an arrangement (*accommodement*) among every created thing where everything is linked or absorbed with everything else.

Leibniz' theories clearly represent the foundations of the future Topology. In fact, since Leibniz' theories, one recognizes movement as the product of the infinite relationships that, at the same time, radically transform the nature of the object. Being part of a constant and infinite set of relations, the object becomes functional. That is to say, it is no longer defined by its essential form but by its functionality in the whole. Indeed, an object is no longer an object when it is placed in a continuum, i.e. it does not imply a spatial mould, a relationship of form to matter. The object implies the notion of temporal modulation in which the continuous variations of matter generate a continuous development of form.[22] In addition, in this dynamic and flexible *accommodement*, the centre does not refer to a point of view; it is the point of view that refers to the centre.[23]

This new nature of the space emerged, as already noted, from Leibniz theories, especially when he understood the introduction of algebra into the world of geometrical figures as the possibility to develop a new axiomatization differing from that of Euclid's *Elements*. In fact, Leibniz developed new definitions—axioms— that departed from Euclid's system. By distancing himself from Euclid's *notiones communes*, Leibniz constructed different families of curves that allowed him to theorize the fundamental notions of the future topology, for example, place— understood as locations of parts—nearness, congruence, homogeneity, variability, and similarity. These notions transform the nature of geometric objects, and, consequently, enabled him to conceive the space as a set of relationships

---

him, through the relations between entities. These relations are explained through the existence of the Monad. Consequently, while for Newtown's conception of space there can exist an empty space—because space is totally independent of the object 'in it contained'—for Leibniz, empty space is inconceivable, because it is created through relationships. In addition, the concept of monad not only implies the negation of the existence of vacui, as noted by Poser, it also imposes some negations. In his words: "Von der Einfachheit der Monaden abgesehen beruhen auch die folgenden auf Negationen: Unteilbarkeit, Unzerstörbarkeit, Figurlosigkeit, Zeitlosigkeit, Unbeeinflussbarkeit und Fensterlosigkeit." Poser H. "Innere Prinzipen und Hierarchie der Monaden (§§ 9-9, 82 f.)", in: H. Busche (Ed.) *Gottfried Wilhelm Leibniz Monadologie* (Klassiker Auslegen Band 34), Berlin, Akademie Verlag, 2009, p. 81.

22 G. Deleuze, *Le Pli. Leibniz et le baroque*, Paris, Les Éditions de Minuit, 1988, p. 27.
23 See, M. Serres, *Le système de Leibniz et ses modèles mathématiques*, Paris, PUF, 1968.

between objects, relationships between spaces, between points whose links determine movement.[24]

3 When subject[25] and object differ from *Dasein*

"Sobald aber das »Phänomen des Welterkennens« selbst erfaßt wurde, geriet es auch schon in eine »äußerliche«, formale Auslegung. Der Index dafür ist die heute noch übliche Ansetzung von Erkennen als einer »Beziehung zwischen Subjekt und Objekt«, die so viel »Wahrheit« als Leerheit in sich birgt. Subjekt und Objekt decken sich aber nicht etwa mit Dasein und Welt."[26]

The new character of the object, the *objectil*, implies the transformation of the subject, which is no longer a sub-ject but a *superject*.[27] In fact, the subject is no longer *subiectum*, that is to say, an entity submitted. *Devenir*, which absorbs the objects into a continuum, modifying it and building it only though relationships and variations, transforms the subject into a point of view on a site. In fact, the object, recognized as *objectil*, follows a group of transformations; it is a site. In its turn, the subject is a point of view because it allows the recognition of the passage from one form to another. Thus, the *superject*, through the relationships with the infinite series of the *objectil*, determines a point of view, a situs. In other words, the *superject* is a witness and, at the same time, a part of the *objectil*'s dynamics, of a series of metamorphoses—i.e. of its passage from form to form[28]—that not only

---

24 See M.-L. Heuser, "Die Anfänge der Topologie in Mathematik und Naturphilosophie", in: S. Günzel (Hrsg.), *Topologie. Zur Raumbeschreibung in den Kultur- und Medienwissenschaften*, Bielefeld, 2007, pp. 181–200.

25 It is important to remember that this philosophical term displays a very complex history because its meaning sometimes was antithetical to its original meaning. Its etymology is usually found in the Latin word *subiectum*, which is in turn a translation of the Greek word ὑποκείμενον, which designates all that 'underlies' or 'submits'. Consequently, the Latin *subiectum* also defines 'substance' and 'hypostasis', terms through which one designates reality. That is the reason why, since early scholasticism '*esse subiective*' has defined the existing reality, while '*esse obiective*' defines human thought. As one can note, these meanings are completely in opposition to the modern meaning of subject and object.

26 M. Heidegger, *Sein und Zeit*, p. 60. "But as soon as the "phenomenon of knowing the world" was grasped, it was already interpreted in an "external" formal way. The proof for this is the still prevalent interpretation of knowledge as a "relation between subject and object" which contains as much "truth" as vacuity. However, subject and object do not coincide with Dasein and World" (My translation).

27 G. Deleuze, *Le Pli. Leibniz et le baroque*, Paris, Les Éditions de Minuit, 1988, p. 27.

28 Ibid., p. 27.

highlights the flexible nature of the object, but also determines the dissolution of the Cartesian dualism thought–extension. Above all, as noted by Heidegger, the dissolution of the Cartesian dualism also implies the dissolution of his *cogito*, and, consequently, it imposes an attempt to define the concept of being.[29] In fact, *cogito sum* must be related to the subject itself, a subject that is related to the world.[30] In Heidegger's words:

> "If "cogito sum" serves as the point of departure of the existential analytic, then it requires not only an inversion, but also a new ontological and phenomenal confirmation of its content. Then, the first statement is "sum" in the sense of I-am-in-a-world. As such being, "I am" in the possibility of being towards various forms of behavior (cogitationes) as way of being together with inner-worldly beings. Descartes, contrarily, says: cogitationes are present and a ego is present as a worldless res cogitans." (My translation)[31]

It is possible to suppose that the dissolution of the Cartesian *cogito* is related to the development of topology, which represented a violent departure from the space built by the Greek tradition[32] and designated a space created by series of relationships that determine movement. The space became a continuous form that displays a spatial character that is determined by three main phenomena: generation (*Erzeugen*), positioning (*Setzen*) and bonding (*Verknüpfen*). In this framework, as theorized by Hermann Grassmann, *devenir* represents a generating phenomenon (*Erzeugen*) that obliges the recognition of the position (*Setzen*) of entities and their direct relationship (*Verknüpfen*) with the whole set. Such recognition allows the analysis of the character of a given entity only through its relationship with the others in the set.[33] Consequently, neither objects

---

29 See, Heidegger, *Sein und Zeit*, p. 2.
30 Merleau-Ponty, *Phénoménologie de la perception*, Chap. *Le cogito*.
31 "Sollte das »cogito sum« als Ausgang der existenzialen Analytik des Daseins dienen, dann bedarf es nicht nur der Umkehrung, sondern einer neuen ontologisch-phänomenalen Bewährung seines Gehalts. Die erste Aussage ist dann: »sum« und zwar in dem Sinne: ich-bin-in-einer-Welt. Als so Seiendes »bin ich« in der Seinsmöglichkeit zu verschiedenen Verhaltungen (cogitationes) als Weisen des Seins bei innerweltlichem Seienden. *Descartes* dagegen sagt: cogitationes sind vorhanden, darin ist ein ego mit vorhanden als weltlose res cogitans." Heidegger, *Sein und Zeit*, p. 211.
32 See, M. Serres, *Les origines de la géométrie*, Paris, Flammarion, 1993, p. 21.
33 That is to say, geometry assigns meaning to the objects. Therefore, the object itself is totally irrelevant. What is important is the meaning granted to the object. See, H. Grassmann, *Die Ausdehnungslehre von 1844: oder Die Lineale Ausdehnungslehre, ein neuer Zweig der Mathematik*, Leipzig, Otto Wigand, 1844. Also see, A.N. Kolmogorov and A.P Yushkevich, *Mathematics of the 19th Century. Geometry Analytic Function Theory*, Basel, Springer, 1996.

nor subjects in such a space determine an objective presence; instead they determine a set of relationships that defines existence exclusively as co-existential (*Mitsein*). Following this framework, the subject is absorbed by a reality conceived as mobility and its being-in implies a generating phenomenon (*Erzeugen*) that forms a topological space, a series of relationships (*Verknüpfens*) or regions established by positioning (*Setzen*). Therefore, in the space designed by Topology, the subject cannot be conceived as an objective presence in a three-dimensional space; its existence 'in' the topological space is exclusively a coexistence (*Mitdasein*) whose experience (*erlebt*) in the environment-world (*Umwelt*) is compulsorily a shared world (*Mitwelt*).

At this point, it is possible to see more clearly the fundamental role played by Heidegger's *Sein und Zeit* in the culmination of the processes that hypothesized existence under topological terms, a process that, as already noted, presents a complex and articulated conceptual structure that embraces different scientific fields and that is rooted in the development of non-Euclidean geometries. However, this long and complex process manifests some clear and common concepts that became highly present during the second half of the nineteenth century. These shared concepts, as already noted, was a culmination of the dissolving of Cartesian dualism and, in its turn, the dissolving of *cogito*. We can see, for example, that a main problematic shared by Bergson, Poincaré and Whitehead was the human limitation in conceiving the inexistence of isolated systems, an impossibility that derived, for Bergson, from the human act of fabrication, for Poincaré, form the three-dimensionality of the space derived by Euclid's axioms, and, for Whitehead, from the phenomenon of bifurcation. To accept the inexistence of isolated systems means to conceive existence in topologic terms. Thus, it also means to conceive being not as something apart and aside of beings, but, as noted by Malpas, "being and beings belong together."[34]

The question that emerges at this point is why, during the nineteenth century, this problematic became an urgency for humankind. The answer to this question, in my opinion, might be found in a technological context—especially in the media context—that found its maximal expression in the representative media (e.g. photo-chemical media) like photography and cinematography, the same technological context that progressively transformed the machine into an autonomous form of praxis.[35]

---

34 J. Malpas, *Heidegger and the Thinking of Place*, p. 40.
35 See, M. Heidegger, *Die Zeit des Weltbildes* (1950), p. 69. (In: M. Heidegger, *Gesamtausgabe I. Abteilung: Veröffentliche Schriften 1914–1970*, Band 5, *Holzwege*, Frankfurt am Main, Vittorio Klostermann, 1977).

4 The medium is the space

Even though the term *Dasein* had already been used by some important authors during the nineteenth century—e.g. Hegel, Jaspers, and Feuerbach—it gained a particular relevance with Heidegger's *Sein und Zeit*. In my opinion, the term took form as the culmination of the development of Topology and the necessity of understanding the presence of the subject in the space designed by this new theory. This new understanding of the space arose from the doubts generated by the non-probability of Euclid's Fifth Postulate: the Postulate of Parallels. Although the non-demonstrability of that postulate emerged with the very first commentators on Euclid's *Elements*—e.g. Ptolemy, Proclus, and Posidonius—it was not until the second half of the nineteen century that one started to conceive reality under topological notions, that is to say, under a concrete non-Euclidean thought. It would be legitimate to affirm that the delineation of the Heideggerian *Dasein* started to take form during the Second Industrial Revolution, during the rapid phase of industrialization that took place from the last third of the nineteen century and that culminated with the murderous tyranny of the speed—marvellously declaimed in Marinetti's Manifesto of Futurism in 1909— accomplished in a climax of seriality by the Vickers machine gun, the decisive technological factor of the First World War.

The Second Industrial Revolution represented the exaltation of fragmentation and seriality rooted in the alphabetic system that, by combining letters (γραμμάτων τε συνθέσεις), as expressed by Aeschylus, became the "creative mother of the Muse's arts" (460). In fact, the effective power of the Greek alphabet is both fragmentation and combination (σύνθεσις), which allowed the atomizing and fragmenting of language to its most essential and indivisible particle: the phoneme. The Greek alphabet, mother of the Muse's arts, rapidly became the tool for the classification of reality on which western philosophy was founded.[36] The alphabet imposed fragmentation as an episteme, and, during the Second Industrial Revolution, within this technological context, the fragmentation found an expression in manufacturing through the interchangeable parts and the production line conceptualized by Frederick Winslow Taylor in 1911 for the sake of the scientific management.

The increasing use of machinery in industrial production placed the subject in front of new forms of fragmentation, and, consequently, in front of a seriality that generated certain metaphysical issues. As noted by Deleuze in his early

---

36 See, D. De Kerckhove, *Dall'alfabeto a Internet. L'homme "littéré": alfabetizzazione, cultura, tecnologia*, Milano, Mimesis, 2008.

works, our cognition is incessantly extracting little differences, variations and modifications because it is constantly facing mechanical repetitions, series that characterize a well-defined technological context.[37]

The subject faces an arduous task to find, in the seriality imposed by the technological context, the instant—the present—through which the being is aware of the existence.[38] Consequently, the understanding of difference—which implies at the same time the analysis of resemblance—and repetition allows us to comprehend the way in which the human mind 'fabricates' a mobile reality.[39] As noted by Deleuze, from seriality emerges a phenomenon of resemblance, which plays a fundamental role in western culture because it represents an instrument of order, an episteme that sets in motion the structure of symbols, allowing the development of complex concepts and representations.[40] The subject, facing repetition, exerts a contractile power.[41] As noted by Hume, "(…) repetition neither discovers nor causes anything in the object, but has an influence only in the mind, by that customary transition it produces."[42] Following Hume's examples, Deleuze posits that the subject plays an active role in the constitution of seriality. This assertion not only supposes, as claimed by Bergson, that perception is never a mere contact between the spirit and the present object, but also that, facing seriality, the subject, through a contractile power, exerts a synthesis of time, by means of which the subject exists.

From this special experience that the subject undergoes when dealing with seriality emerges the question of the abstraction of the subject from the object, a similar abstraction that the subject undergoes through action (*Handlung*) and that abstracts the subject from its life-world (*Lebenswelt*). As noted by Flusser, action (*Handlung*) places the subject outside of itself. That is to say, action means ecstasy (Heidegger's *Ekstase*), through which present time is generated,[43] and, at the same time, action is the means by which the subject regionalizes, or informs, the three-dimensional reality of the grasped objects. In Flusser's words: "This

---

37 See, G. Deleuze, *Différence et répétition*, Paris, PUF, 1968.

38 G. Bachelard, *L'intuition de l'instant*, Paris, Stock, 1931, p. 14.

39 Deleuze, *Différence et répétition*, p. 32.

40 M. Foucault, *Les mots et les choses*, Paris, Gallimard, 1966, p. 32.

41 G. Deleuze, *Différence et répétition*, p. 96.

42 D. Hume, *A Treatise of Human Nature*, Oxford, Oxford University Press, 2000, p. 105.

43 Note that for Bergson repetition can also only be developed through abstraction. Thus, for Bergson, repetition is a product of the human intellect, a product that derives from a mobile reality. Bergson, *L'évolution créatrice*, pp. 45–46.

universe of objects can then be transformed, "informed" by the subject" (My translation).[44]

Following this framework, it is possible to affirm that that human beings are world-forming, and in this process of 'information', language actively participates. As noted by Malpas: "Such world-formation, which nevertheless stands in an intimate relation to the essence of language understood as *logos*, has its ground in the original opening of the world as a whole that enables the accessibility to things in order that they can be grasped as thus and so, and in order that statement and assertion about them can be possible."[45] The continuous process of formation, in the topologic approach, could be identified by the delineation of a region, a localized structure in which human beings, as noted by Malpas, are brought into an encounter with themselves, and with the world.[46] In this continuous process of information Bergsonian *devenir* becomes an interesting tool of analysis. As noted by him, *devenir* is infinitely diverse, and human cognition—as well as language—artificially extracts from *devenir* a unique representation of it.[47] According to Bergson, the subject, through its intellect, its *logos* (λόγος), extracts from *devenir* moments that display an immobile nature, moments that are serialized, and, consequently, become intelligible—become space, territory. It would be possible to affirm that the subject's abstraction is mediated by λόγος, or, as remarked by Heidegger, by language, which is the house of being in which man ek-sist: "Rather, language is the house of being in which man ek-sists by dwelling, in that he belongs to the truth of being, guarding it" (My translation).[48] Additionally, mediation, which can be exerted by language or media technologies, is the vector of disclosure (*Erschlossenheit*) of the subject that is constantly informing or regionalizing its *Umwelt*. As one might suppose, this continuous act of regionalizing, or informing, becomes explicit in the face of repetition, of serialized objects, which is the reason why the development of the film camera

---

44 "Dieses Universum der Objekte kann nun von Subjekt umgeformt 'informiert' werden." V. Flusser, *Ins universum der Technischen Bilder*, Göttingen, European Photography, 1996, p. 12.
45 Malpas, *Heidegger and the Thinking of Place*, p. 129.
46 *Ibid.*, p. 203.
47 Bergson, *L'évolution créatrice*, p. 304.
48 "Vielmehr ist die Sprache das Haus des Seins, darin wohnend der Mensch ek-sistiert, indem er der Wahrheit des Seins, sie hütend, gehört." M. Heidegger, *Brief über den »Humanismus«*, (1946), p. 164. (In: M. Heidegger, *Gesamtausgabe I. Abteilung: Veröffentlichte Schriften 1914–1970*, Band 9, *Wegmarken*, Frankfurt am Main, Vittorio Klostermann, 1976).

allowed and encouraged further reflections on the effects that seriality have on the perceiving subject.

As already noted, the Second Industrial Revolution founded its conceptual basis on serializing, fractioning and assembling with the speed of machines. It is through this logic that one can see Marey's experiences with the use of the *fusil photographique*.[49] It is not a coincidence that at the same time that photographic technology, through Marey's *fusil photographique*, acquired its temporal extension, Bergson, in his fundamental work *Essai sur les données immediates de la conscience*, published in 1889, a couple of years after Marey's technological inventions, and a few years before the imminent improvement and not so imminent acquisition of cinematography as a social practice, analysed the nature of time and movement and introduced the fundamental Eleatic arguments against motion into a technological context that had begun to conceive the cinematographic image. In that work, Bergson highlighted that the subject's understanding of movement is a juxtaposition of the intensive feeling of mobility and the extensive representation of a covered space.[50] From this analysis on the human perception of movement derives the conclusion that the covered space is past, and movement is present, because it is an action, and like all actions, it cannot be divided.[51] Consequently, Bergson concludes, human perception attributes to movement the divisibility of space, forgetting that it is impossible to divide an action. Through this juxtaposition, which corresponds to the foundation of Zeno's paradoxes, the subject projects an act (movement) to the space, divides it, and serializes it.

> "On the one hand, indeed, we attribute to movement the same divisibility of the covered space, forgetting that we can divide a thing, but we cannot divide an act – and on the other hand, we use to project this same act of division on the space, we use to apply the line traveled by the mobile, we use to solidify it (…)." (My translation)[52]

It is interesting to note that by introducing the Eleatic question—a question that emerged from Parmenides' thoughts on motionlessness (ἀτρεμής) while

---

49 See, E.J. Marey, *La machine animale, locomotion terrestre et aérienne*, Paris, Germer Baillière, 1873.

50 H. Bergson, *Essai sur les données immédiates de la conscience*, Paris, PUF, 1889, p. 83.

51 G. Deleuze, *Cinéma 1. L'image-mouvement*, Paris, Les éditions de minuit, 1983, p. 9.

52 "D'une part, en effet, nous attribuons au mouvement la divisibilité même de l'espace qu'il parcourt, oubliant qu'on peut bien diviser une chose, mais non pas un acte – et d'autre part nous habituons à projeter cet acte lui-même dans l'espace, à l'appliquer le long de la ligne que le mobile parcourt, à le solidifier (…)." Bergson, *Essai sur les données immédiates de la conscience*, pp. 83–84.

dealing with the concept of reality/truth (ἀλήθεια)—to the technological context, Bergson highlights the impossibility to reconstruct movement by means
of positions in the space, or, as noted by Deleuze, by means of instants 'in' time.
That is to say, Bergson affirms that it is impossible to reconstruct time like the
cinematographic camera does, by means of 'coupes immobiles':

> "You only make this reconstruction by joining to positions, or to instants, the abstract
> idea of succession, of mechanical time, homogeneous and universal, transferred from
> space, the same for all movements." (My translation)[53]

However, some years later, with the influence of Lumière's invention, when film
narratives started a "dynamization of space and, accordingly, spatialization of
time,"[54] especially through the filmic experiments of the Brighton School (e.g.
Geroge Albert Smith, and James Williamson) that resulted in editing and
montage, Bergson fell into a reverie on the cinematographic reconstruction
of movement. In L'évolution créatrice, published in 1907, Bergson analyzed,
through cinematographic mechanisms, human perception of movement. That
is to say, he understood movement through coupes immobiles. According to
Bergson, by simulating human senses, the film camera simulates human intellect and human language. That is to say, the house of being in which man ek-sists
by dwelling acquired the serialized extension of the cinematographic camera.
Further, as one might suppose, from this analogy, one starts to comprehend the
subject through the mechanism of cinematography, as is clear in the following
words from Bergson: "Whether it is thinking on devenir, or expressing it, or even
perceiving it, we just activate a sort of interior film camera. We could summarize
all the above by positing that the mechanism of our usual knowledge displays a
cinematographic nature." (My translation)[55]

The introduction of the Eleatic question into a technological context strongly
influenced by visual media, especially by photo-chemical media of representation, allowed the highlighting of the way in which the subject hides the inner

---

53 "Cette reconstruction, vous ne la faites qu'en joignant aux positions ou aux instants
    l'idée abstraite d'une succession, d'un temps mécanique, homogène, universel et
    décalqué de l'espace, le même pour tous les mouvements." Deleuze, Cinéma 1. p. 9.
54 E. Panofsky, "Style and Medium in the Motion Pictures", p. 71, in: A.D. Vacche, (Ed.)
    The Visual Turn. Classical Film Theory and Art History, New Brunswick, Rutgers
    University Press, 2003, pp. 69–84.
55 "Qu'il s'agisse de penser le devenir, ou de l'exprimer, ou même de le percevoir, nous ne
    faisons guère autre chose qu'actionner une espèce de cinématographe intérieur. On
    résumerait donc tout ce qui précède en disant que le mécanisme de notre connaissance
    usuelle est de nature cinématographique." Bergson, L'évolution créatrice, p. 305.

devenir of things, that is to say, the way in which the subject tends to inhabit an exterior reality in which movement is artificially reconstructed by the intellect. This last phenomenon is exemplified in Bergson's analysis of memory, in which he posits that in the continuous reconstruction of *devenir* the power of the instant corresponds to a kind of photographic *hic et nunc*, and memory represents an act of grouping around the past. That is to say, it is the human capacity to break loose of the present in order to bring into the seriality a memory of the past.[56] Thus, Bergson places perception into the present and memory into the past because perception moves memory into an earlier time. Following Bergson's logic, 'my present' (*mon présent*) is a perception of my immediate past and also a determination of the immediate future, an analogous operation to that exerted by the cinematographic camera.[57] As one can see, time is, in such way, conceived as a seriality in which the subject can bring into its continuous present some past event that has already gone by.

It is at this point that Heidegger's theories begin radically to distance themselves from Bergson. Bergson's concept of *devenir* as the immanent entity that traverses everything tends to place time into the space, and Heidegger starts to distance himself from this assertion with the introduction of *Sein und Zeit*. In fact, Heidegger proposes some fundamental differences between temporal (*zeitlich*) beings (natural processes and historical events) and atemporal (*unzeitlich*) beings (spatial and numerical relations), and by arguing that temporal means being in time,[58] he separates regions of being.[59] It is possible to see in this last assertion that the division of time, contrary to the division developed by Bergson, represents a form of abstraction that allows the subject to *exist*, it is to say, to abstract itself from the tyrannical seriality of the technological context. In fact, from this assertion emerges the concept of temporality of being (*Temporalität des Seins*) aimed at separating the regions of the being—aimed

---

56 H. Bergson, *Matière et mémoire. Essai sur la relation du corps à l'esprit*, Paris, PUF, 1896, Chap. III. *De la survivance des images. La mémoire et l'esprit*, pp. 276–315.

57 *Ibidem*.

58 "»Zeitlich« besagt hier jeweils soviel wie »in der Zeit« seiend, eine Bestimmung, die freilich auch noch dunkel genug ist (…)" Heidegger, *Sein und Zeit*, p. 18. ""Temporal" here means as much as being "in time," a definition that, of course, is still obscure enough" (My translation).

59 "Das Faktum besteht: Zeit, im Sinne von »in der Zeit sein«, fungiert als Kriterium der Scheidung von Seinsregionen." Heidegger, *Sein und Zeit*, p. 18. "The fact is that time, in the sense of "being in time," functions as a criterion for separating the regions of being" (My translation).

at understanding being in time, a necessity in a technological context strongly marked by electronic technologies.

5 Replacing the alphabetic νῦν (now) for the video-electronic ἀεί (ever, unceasing)

The rupture with seriality exerted by Heideggerian thought had been developing since the first phenomenological approach to the question of time.[60] From the phenomenological approach, which displays a topologic character, emerged the fundamental difference between experienced time and objectivized time, the latter, as already noted, transforming *devenir* into objective states, into a series that we commonly know as past, present, and future. Nevertheless, these states are different in the subjective sphere, wherein the objective seriality, following Husserl, becomes *praesentatio, retentio* and *protentio,*[61] conditions to regionalizing *tempora* through which seriality is replaced by a notion of flux. Following this framework, *praesentatio* (now) has implicit an arrival from *retentio,* which implies the direction toward *protentio.* However, in the flux, one cannot design chronological series that the subject alters from its present time. Indeed, *tempora* do not represent states, but ecstasies. In Heidegger's words:

> "Temporalizing does not mean "succession" of ecstasies. The future is *not later* than having-been, which in its turn, it is *not earlier* than the present. Temporality temporalizes itself as a future that makes present, in the process of having-been. The Disclosedness of the There and the fundamental existential possibilities of *Da-sein,* authenticity and inauthenticity, are grounded in temporality." (My translation)[62]

The absence of states determines the notion of flux, which emerges from recognizing these *tempora* and that can be better understood when contrasting the understanding of memory generated within a serial view, to the understanding of memory within the *tempora* as flux. While for Bergson, influenced by the cinematographic camera, as explicit in *L'évolution créatrice,* movement derived

---

60 See, E. Severino, *Studi di filosofia della prassi,* Milano, Adelfi, 1984 (1962), Una tesi capitale di Husserl, pp. 63–68.

61 See, E. Husserl, *Zur Phänomenologie des Inneren Zeitbewusstseins (1893–1917),* Husserliana: Edmund Husserl, Gesammelte Werke, Band 10, Berlin, Springer, 1966.

62 "Die Zeitigung bedeutet kein »Nacheinander« der Ekstasen. Die Zukunft ist *nicht später* als die Gewesenheit und diese *nicht früher* als die Gegenwart. Zeitlichkeit zeitig sich als gewesende-gegenwärtigende Zukunft. Die Erschlossenheit des Da und die existenziellen Grundmöglichkeiten des Daseins, Eigentlichkeit und Uneigentlichkeit, sind in der Zeitlichkeit fundiert." Heidegger, *Sein und Zeit,* p. 350.

from series of immobile states articulated with abstract movement, under the
phenomenological approach proposed by Heidegger, temporality (*Zeitlichkeit*)
is a flux (*gewesende-gegenwärtigende Zukunft*), a conjunction alien to a serial
view. For Bergson, memory is a human act analogous to putting an image into
focus in a photographic camera; within the flux, memory is a conjunction, a
recovery into the flux, a flux that is not 'built' by states but by ecstasies. Again, for
Bergson, movement and time find their concrete image in the photo-chemical
mechanism of representative media; for Heidegger it is analogous to the temporality of video-electronic images: it meets the figure of the rhizome presented
by Deleuze–Guattari in their oeuvre *Mille Plateaux*. In fact, as a rhizome, the
temporality proposed by Heidegger dissolves the arborescent being (*être*) and
replaces it with the conjunction 'and... and... and...'

> "A rhizome has no beginning or end, it is always in the middle, between things, inter-being,
> *intermezzo*. The tree is filiation, while the rhizome is alliance, only alliance. The tree imposes
> the verb "to be," but the fabric of the rhizome is the conjunction, "and... and... and..."
> There is in this conjunction enough force to shake and to uproot the verb "to be." Where are
> you going? Where are you coming from? What are you heading for? These are very useless
> questions. Making a clean slate, starting or beginning again from ground zero, looking
> for a beginning or a foundation – all imply a false conception of journey and movement
> (methodical, educational, initiatory, symbolic...)." (My translation)[63]

The notion of conjunction is absent in seriality because conjunction is foreign to
the structure; it does not define points or positions in the space, it is foreign to
one-to-one correspondences between points. Conjunction develops lines, like a
rhizome, it creates "Lines of segmentation, of stratification, as dimensions, but
also lines of flight or deterritorialization as the maximum dimension according
to which the multiplicity undergoes metamorphosis, changes in nature" (My
translation).[64]

---

63 "Un rhizome ne commence et n'aboutit pas, il est toujours au milieu, entre les choses,
   inter-être, *intermezzo*. L'arbre est filiation, mais le rhizome est alliance, uniquement
   alliance. L'arbre impose le verbe « être », mais le rhizome a pour tissu la conjonction «
   et... et... et... ». Il y a dans cette conjonction assez de force pour secouer et déraciner le
   verbe être. Où allez-vous? d'où partez-vous? où voulez-vous en venir? sont des questions
   bien inutiles. Faire table rase, partir ou repartir à zéro, chercher un commencement,
   ou un fondement, impliquent une fausse conception du voyage et du mouvement
   (méthodique, pédagogique, initiatique, symbolique...)" G. Deleuze and F. Guattari,
   Capitalisme et schizophrénie 2. Mille Plateaux, Paris, Les Éditions de Minuit, 1980, p. 36.
64 "lignes de segmentarité, de stratification, comme dimensions, mais aussi ligne de fuite
   ou de déterritorialisation comme dimension maximale d'après laquelle, en la suivant,
   la multiplicité se métamorphose en changeant nature." *Ibid.*, p. 32.

Devenir dissolves into the flux, it dissolves through the conjunction, through the 'between' (*entre, zwischen*)—it dissolves through the interstice, and, consequently, Bergson's understanding of perception, intellect and language, as analogous 'mechanisms' to the cinematographic machine,[65] is replaced by a different view that is strongly influenced by the notion of flux, by the notion of conjunction that characterizes the video-electronic world, a world that distances itself from the object of reproduction, from the space of localizable points. Like in the rhizome, in the video-electronic context one is not dealing with representations, or produced in-formation, as in the case of the photo-chemical media. Through the flux, one deals with objects that must still be produced, as remarked by Deleuze–Guattari: "The rhizome proceeds by variation, expansion, conquest, capture, offshoots. In contrast to graphic arts, drawing or photography, unlike layers, the rhizome pertains to a map that must be produced, constructed, a map that is always removable, connectable, reversible, modifiable, and that has multiple entryways and exits with its own lines of flight" (My translation).[66]

Video-electronic technology generates a continuum that clearly displays the characteristics of the flux described above. In the flux of video-electronic images, the point—like in the topologic dimension[67]—becomes a methaphorization of space by means of time and, at the same time, a methaphorization of time by means of space. As posited by Engell, in the flux of video-electronic images, the point is a spaceless metaphor for linking the 'something' with the 'other' itself. In his words: "The point is not "something" that could be linked with the "other," but it is the spaceless metaphor of linking "something" with the "other" itself" (My translation).[68] The conjunction is the essence of the video-electronic image and, additionally, in the flux of images, in the conjunction, one deals with variations, with objects that must still be produced, or in Engell's words, with "elements

---

65 Bergson, *L'évolution créatrice*, p. 305.

66 "Le rhizome procède par variation, expansion, conquête, capture, piqûre. A l'opposé du graphisme, du dessin ou de la photo, à l'opposé des calques, le rhizome se rapporte à une carte qui doit être produite, construite, toujours démontable, connectable, renversable, modifiable, à entrées et sorties multiples, avec des lignes de fuite." Deleuze–Guattari, *Capitalisme et schizophrénie 2. Mille Plateaux*, p. 32.

67 Note that since *Sein und Zeit*, temporality for Heidegger, displays a topological character. See, Malpas, *Heidegger and the Thinking of Place*, p. 26.

68 "Der Punkt ist nicht „etwas", das mit „anderem" verknüpft werden könnte, sondern er ist die raumlose Metapher der Verknüpfung des „etwas" mit dem „anderen" selbst." Engell L. "Fernsehen mit Gilles Deleuze", in: O. Fahle and L. Engell (Eds.,) *Der Film Bei Deleuze/Le cinéman selon Deleuze*, Weimar, Bauhaus-Universität/Presses de la Sorbonne Nouvelle, 1999, p. 471.

that just cannot continue to exist" (*Nicht-einfach-vorhanden-bleiben-können*).[69]
* In the flux, there is no past, nor future, there are only projections, and the subject leans toward these *tempora*, regionalizes them because they are not states; they are ecstasies happening in the 'connection of life' (*Zusammenhang des Lebens*).
* In the flux, the subject is in the world, is a project—and, at the same time, a projection—of the world.

The displacement of the representative states of the ecstasy takes our understanding out from the reverie imposed by both representative media and the seriality exalted by the film camera. Ecstasy is the figure of the Second Industrial Revolution, a figure that was eclipsed by the reverie imposed by the cinematographic camera. In fact, it is in the Second Industrial Revolution that one experienced the climax of seriality, of fragmentation, that suddenly disappeared under the influence of electrical power, the electrical flux that, embodied by telegraphy, as noted by McLuhan, externalized our central nervous system to the world. Within the electric age described by McLuhan, Merleau-Ponty's formula acquires consistency: "Le monde est tout au dedans et je suis tout hors de moi."[70]

The phenomenon of a disseminated body—a phenomenon that took form and concretized within post-human theories under the figure of the cyborg[71]—certainly emerged from the shrinking (*einschrumpfen*) of all distances (*Entfernungen*) in time and space brought about by electric communication.[72]
*In the flux of the video-electronic age, distances in time and space shrink. Consequently, like in the topologic space, nearness, closeness or remoteness are notions that enable the recognizing of space as a non-Euclidean space, as a topologic space free from coordinate system because distances and differences cannot be measured by objective Euclidean or Cartesian tools. Instead, closeness and remoteness become experiences, a spatiality experienced and not objective or geometrical.[73] Consequently, Heidegger's topological view allows us to

---

69 *Ibid.*, p. 470.
70 Merleau-Ponty, *Phénoménologie de la perception*, p. 467 "The world is wholly inside, and I am wholly outside myself" (My translation).
71 See A. Caronia, *Il corpo virtuale. Dal corpo robotizzato al corpo disseminato nelle reti*, Padova, Franco Muzzio Editore, 1996, p. 90.
72 See, M. Heidegger, *Das Ding* (1950), p. 157. (In M. Heidegger, *Gesamtausgabe. I. Abteilung: Veröffentliche Schriften 1910-1976*, Band 7. *Vortrage Und Aufsätze*, Frankfurt am Main, Vittorio Klostermann, 2000, pp. 165-188.)
73 See, De Preester H., "Equipment and Existential Spatiality: Heidegger, Cognitive Science and the Prosthetic Subject", in: J. Kiverstein and M. Wheeler (Eds.) *Heidegger and Cognitive Science*, Basingstoke, Palgrave Macmillian, 2012, pp. 276-308.

understand communication in spatial terms—topological or, in our digital context, fractal terms. Indeed, as noted by Heidegger, communication becomes a matter of proximity; it becomes the placing of a region into a region dwelt by another subject. To communicate means to share intimacy, to add dimensions to the spaces dwelt by other subjects, a phenomenon that is exemplified by social media mechanisms. Additionally, by adding dimensions into another subject's regions, one is also sharing different mechanisms of the creation of meaning; one is transforming the subject's space by modifying all the relationships already established in that precise subject's semio-sphere. Paradoxically, as Heidegger remarks in his later works, electronic technologies, by shrinking distances (*Entfernungen*), impede the subject from experiencing nearness. In his words: "However, the hasty removal of all distances brings no nearness; for in nearness does not exist the slightest measure of distance" (My translation).[74] Unable to experience nearness, the subject starts to progressively reduce its skills, to reduce the material experience of its material reality. The subject progressively distances itself from the continuous process of informing the three-dimensional reality of the grasped objects. As an effect of the flux of electronic technology, especially video-electronic media—which can be considered a technology of passage between photo-chemical technologies and digital technologies[75] the subject progressively gets closer to the representation of reality; the subject, by being closer to the flux of electric signals, distances itself from the object, replacing it with an electronic-*Gegenstand*, a phenomenon that embodies one of the primary effects that define the post-modern condition, as theorized by Lyotard. Indeed, as hypothesized by him, immense databases would replace nature, they would be "nature" for the post-modern humankind.[76]

6 The limits of a mediated existence

It is possible to note, since the beginning of McLuhan's *Understanding Media: The extensions of Man* a convergence with Heidegger's analysis. In fact, for both authors, the history of being is a history of the construction and perception of spaces, which derives from dwelling within a precise technological context. Both authors understand the technological component as a system that governs the

---

74 "Allein, das hastige Beseitigen aller Entfernungen bringt keine Nähe; denn Nähe besteht nicht im geringen Maß der Entfernung." Heidegger, *Bremer und Freiburger Vorträge*, p. 3.

75 See, Y. Spielmann, *Video. Das Reflexive Medium*, Frankfurt am Main, Suhrkamp, 2005.

76 J.F. Lyotard, *La condition postmoderne*, Paris, Les Éditions de Minuit, 1979, pp. 84–85.

ways of association, by establishing different distances and durations in the social space. It is also important to note that both also share a common analysis of an imminent different media condition characterized by a centripetal force—contrary to the former media conditions that exerted a centrifugal force embodied by extensions of man—that characterizes electric technology. Indeed, it is possible to see that both are concerned by an imminent transformation of the technological condition that would profoundly affect being. Electric technology transformed, in such a way, the prosthetic status of technology; technology progressively became invasive, and more importantly, autonomous. The centripetal force determines, in my opinion, the departure from the technologies of fragmentation and serialization that we highlighted as heirs of alphabetic logic, the Muse's arts, as narrated in Aeschylus's *Prometheus Bound*. McLuhan announced this departure in the introduction of his fundamental oeuvre:

> "After three thousand years of explosion, by means of fragmentary and mechanical technologies, the Western world is imploding. During the mechanical ages we had extended our bodies in space. Today, after more than a century of electric technology, we have extended our central nervous system itself in a global embrace, abolishing both space and time as far as our planet is concerned. Rapidly, we approach the final phase of the extensions of man—the technological simulation of consciousness, when the creative process of knowing will be collectively and corporately extended to the whole of human society, much as we have already extended our senses and our nerves by the various media."[77]

The world described by McLuhan is a world in which action and reaction occurs at the same time, but, unfortunately, as noted by him, "(…) we continue to think in the old, fragmented space and time patters of the pre-electric age."[78] In this context, like for Heidegger, *durée* disappears, erasing from the subject's presence time patterns, replacing the νῦν (now) with ἀεί (ever, unceasing), a context in which Bergsonian *durée* does not last.[79] There emerges at this point the question of disclosure (*Erschlossenheit*), a Heideggerian concept that, in my opinion, becomes central in the understanding of media because it places the subject, or its experience, in a precise technological context. The concept of disclosure, in our technological condition, on the one hand, obliges us to accept that human experience is always a mediated experience—it can be mediated by language or by media technologies. On the other hand, the concept of disclosure

---

77 M. McLuhan, *Understanding Media. The Extensions of Man*, Cambridge, MA, MIT Press, 1994, pp. 3–4.

78 *Ibid.*, p. 4.

79 G. Dorfles, *Horror Pleni. La (in)civiltà del rumore*, Roma, Castelvecchi, 2008, p. 22.

could allow us to understand the way in which the subject territorializes and dwells in the immaterial world of information. In my opinion, the concept of *Erschlossenheit* becomes central because it is not limited by a deterministic view, and, in consequence, would allow an interesting analysis of the changing spaces in which we dwell in our daily life.

As noted by Kompridis, the concept of disclosure presents two phases. The first determines the imposition of ways to dwell, and derives from the pre-reflective approach to disclosure. The second phase represents a kind of territorialization because disclosure can also be an act of regionalizing dimensions or mechanisms of meaning. In other words, disclosure can present a second-order through which one re-establishes meaning by territorializing the semio-sphere.[80] Thus, disclosing means a way of perceiving, a way of thinking, but also a way of imagining and a way of establishing spaces. It means *wohnen*; it is being in the world.[81]

On the one hand, we have a structured reality mediated by language and certainly by media technologies, which represent mechanisms of structuring reality. In Heidegger's words: "Words, and language are not shells into which things are packed for spoken and written communication. In the word, in language, things first become and are" (My translation).[82] On the other hand, as already noted, following Kompridis' analysis, *Erschlossenheit* displays a second-order that escapes from the deterministic view described above. *Erschlossenheit*, which is certainly exerted through media, is also territorialisation; it also means revealing

---

80 See, N. Kompridis, *Critique and Disclosure. Critical Theory between Past and Future*, MIT Press, Cambridge, MA, 2006.

81 See, H.L. Dreyfus and C. Spinosa, "Further Reflections on Heidegger, Technology and the Everyday", in: N. Kompridis (Ed.,) *Philosophical Romanticism*, New York, Routledge, 2006, pp. 265–281.

82 "(…) die Worte und die Sprache sind keine Hülsen, worin die Dinge nur für den redenden und schreibenden Verkehr verpackt werden. Im Wort, in der Sprache werden und sind erst die Dinge." M. Heidegger, *Einführung in die Metaphysik* (1935), p. 16. (In: M. Heidegger, *Gesamtausgabe. II. Abteilung: Vorlesungen 1923–1944*, Band 40. Frankfurt am Main, Vittorio Klostermann, 1983.) These words, in my opinion, converge with McLuhan's formula "The medium is the message", a formula that clearly affirms that "(…) the personal and social consequences of any medium – that is, of any extension of ourselves – result from the new scale that is introduced into our affairs by each extension of ourselves, or by any new technology." M. McLuhan, *Understanding Media. The Extensions of Man*, Cambridge, MA, MIT Press, 1994, p. 7. Media are not carriers of information, they are information, in its etymological sense, information as formation of the mind, as giving mental form.

mechanisms of creation of meaning. As one can note, the double phase of disclosure is articulated, on the one hand, by informing the world and determining ways to dwell (pre-reflective), and on the other, through a phenomenon of remediation—in which every medium "appropriates the techniques, forms, and social significance of other media and attempts to rival or refashion them in the name of the real."[83]—that allows the territorializing, imaging and re-establishing of meaning in a changing and highly flexible semio-sphere (second-order).

This double articulation of disclosure, as noted above, allows us to understand the subject's experience in a technological context, and, above all, makes the technological component an essential part of *dasein*, because technology, as *Gestell*, reveals the real (ἀλήθεια),[84] and, at the same time, generates vectors of meaning that regionalize or develop *semio-agencements*.[85] In fact, for Heidegger, media are not simply neutral carriers and accumulators of information,[86] but contribute to the creation of the image of reality, because they are active entities in the process of the world's disclosure (*Erschlossenheit*). In this framework, communication cannot be understood as a means of expression but as transformation of the topologic space. Communication means the insertion of a dimension into the semio-sphere. However, in the process of objectification, since the Second Industrial Revolution, the machine has acquired an autonomy that progressively excludes the subject from the transformation and the production of the object, and, consequently, from the creation of *semio-agencements*. The phenomenon of human exclusion from the creation and production of objects described above represents, without a doubt, a radical change that Heidegger remarked during his Bremen Lectures, where the Thing and thingness took an important place in the philosophical debate.

7 Digital *Gegenstände*

In the topologic nature of the world, the subject transforms itself by inhabiting, by a generation (*Erzeugen*) of connections (*Verknüpfen*) that determines its

---

83 J.D Bolter and R. Grusin, *Remediation. Understanding New Media*, Cambridge, MA, MIT Press, 2000, p. 65.

84 See, M. Heidegger, *Die Frage nach der Technik* (1953). (In M. Heidegger, *Gesamtausgabe. I. Abteilung: Veröffentliche Schriften 1910–1976*, Band 7. *Vortrage und Aufsätze*, Frankfurt am Main, Vittorio Klostermann, 2000, pp. 5–36).

85 *Ibid.*, pp. 5–36.

86 On this subject see also, D. De Kerckhove, *Brainframes. Technology, Mind and Business*, Utrecht, VBK, 1991.

position (*Setzen*) through nearness. In this way, technology, as a mediating entity, determines the ways of abstraction of the subject through which the subject establishes a profound and intense relationship with both the instrument and the things. The question that emerges at this point is: How are we establishing this profound relationship with the instrument and the things—a relationship that abstracts the subject and determines its existence, determines *dasein*—in our immaterial digital world?

In the digital era, in our fractal reality, we are continuously dealing with digital-objects, simulacra that are no longer representations. Since the video-electronic age, the effects of nearness produced by this technology seem to have been affecting the materiality of the thing: it seems to distance the object. Consequently, in our digital technological context, the realities that the subject is constantly sharing do not correspond to a material or physical reality. Our daily digital reality is not populated by objects nor by their representations. In our daily digital reality, and since the video-electronic context, things still appear *as things*, yet, as noted by Malpas, things also appear as resource. In addition, technological modernity exerts a modification of time and space that reduces space to a simple location.[87] Within the digital technological context, our space, the space we inhabit, the space we create through infinite relationships, is populated by simulacra, extra-linguistic objects, non-computable objects through which a shared reality is produced.[88] In our digital technological context, the image can no longer imagine the real, because the image corresponds to it,[89] a similar phenomenon highlighted by Heidegger within the former electric age:

> "What is it – a world picture? Certainly a picture of the world. But what does "world" mean here? What does "picture" mean? "World" here stands as designations of beings as a whole. The name is not limited to the cosmos, to nature. The world also includes history. (…) But "world picture" means more than this. We mean the world itself, the world as such, what is, in its entirety, just as it is, formative and binding for us." (My translation)[90]

---

87 Malpas, *Heidegger and the Thinking of Place*, p. 35.
88 See, G.A. Duarte, *Reificación mediática*, Bucaramanga, SIC, 2011.
89 J. Baudrillard, *Le crime parfait*, Paris, Galillée, 1995.
90 Was ist das – ein Weltbild? Offenbar ein Bild von der Welt. Aber was heißt Welt? Was meint da Bild? Welt steht hier als Benennung des Seienden im Ganzen. Der Name ist nicht eingeschränkt auf den Kosmos, die Natur. Zur Welt gehört auch die Geschichte. (…) Doch Weltbild besagt mehr. Wir meinen damit die Welt selbst, sie, das Seiende im Ganzen, so wie es für uns maßgebend und verbindlich ist. Heidegger, *Die Zeit des Weltbildes*, p. 89.

By alienating the human component from the process of revealing the real (ἀλήθεια), and by guiding, through mechanization and digitalization, every activity, media technologies, since the development of video-electronic technologies, have become creators of realities, since many tasks of the process of disclosure dependent on them. Consequently, media technologies moved away from being the mechanism of the representation of the real. In other words, media technologies no longer attempt to re-present the existing object, as was intrinsic in the very nature of the photographic medium. In the video-electronic age, what is perceived as a representation is the product of the mediation–creation of a machine that generates and interprets electrical pulses. Consequently, technology has become fully a part of the creative process of disclosure, meaning that the subject—in this case *subjectum* to the machine—constantly deals with, interacts with, and uses reified objects, non-existing objects that populate its *Umwelt*. As noted by Baudrillard, video-electronic media committed the crime, which was not perfect, apparently. Video-electronic media killed reality, the perfect crime: "meurtre de la réalité. Et de l'extermination d'une illusion—l'illusion vitale, l'illusion radicale du monde."[91] In this context, within the nebula of electrical pulses that forms the flux of the ecstasy of our existence, the rupture with the real happens. A rupture defined by Guy Debord, in *La societé du Spectacle*, "La séparation achavée". Indeed, by re-introducing Heidegger's analysis of *Die Zeit des Weltbildes*, Debord placed the concept of World-picture in a society that found its essence into the immediacy of satellite communication:

> "The whole life of societies, in which the modern conditions of production prevail, is presented as an immense accumulation of spectacles. Everything that was directly lived is now represented in the distance." (My translation)[92]

"Everything that was directly lived is now represented in the distance", affirms Debord. Nevertheless, the process of distancing was *in nuce* in every mediated existence. Since the advent of writing technology, and especially since the Greek alphabet, context has been dislodged from the text.[93] The successive media technologies continued to break the immediate relationship between the subject

---

91 Baudrillard, *Le crime parfait*, p. 10. "the murder of reality and the extermination of an illusion – the vital illusion, the radical illusion of the world" (My translation).

92 "Tout la vie des sociétés dans lesquelles règnent les conditions modernes de production s'annonce comme une immense accumulation de spectacles. Tout ce qui était directement vécu s'est éloigné dans une représentation." G. Debord, *La societé di Spectacle*, Paris, Gallimard, 1992, p. 13.

93 See, De Kerckhove, *Dall'alfabeto a Internet*. 2008.

and its *hic et nunc*.[94] Media technologies placed the subject into a world of representations (photo-chemical media), into images that progressively became independent (video-electronic media), thereafter becoming a whole, becoming the world in its entirety (digital media). Consequently, at a certain moment in the mass media context, shaped by electric technologies, the world became a spectacle, which does not represent "a set of images, but it is a social relation between people that is mediated by images" (My translation).[95]

The mediated existence, exemplified in Heidegger's *Das Wessen der Sprache* through the sentence: "Kein Ding ist, wo das Wort Fehlt",[96] within the late video-electronic era changed to 'no thing is, where the image is lacking'. Following this framework, if we assume that "Der Gegenstand ist das Objekt für das Subjekt,"[97] the question arises, is digital technology reifying all information? Are all imma-terial data the object for the subject that inhabits the digital fractal space? If so, in which way, in the framework of digital-*Gegenstände*,[98] are presence-at-hand (*Vorhandenheit*) and readiness-to-hand (*Zuhandenheit*) expressed? Is it still possible to affirm, as posited by Debord, that our social relation is a relation between people mediated by images—considering that images are no longer representations of an existing reality but complex data expressions that display a multidimensional character, a fractal character that materializes itself through the infinite possibility of combination, through its open hypertextuality and its recursive structure? In other words, in the so-called post-photographic era, are images still mediating the social relation between people? Additionally, if the nearest way of association does not correspond to pure perceptual cogni-tion but to the handling—the use and the taking care of—things (*hantierende, gebrauchende Besorgen*)[99] there emerges, with urgency, the need of a profound

---

94 See, G.W.F Hegel, *Phänomenologie des Geistes*, Frankfurt am Main, Suhrkamp, 2012.
95 "(…) un ensemble d'images, mais un rapport social entre personnes, médiatisé par des images." Debord, *La société du spectacle*, p. 16.
96 M. Heidegger, *Das Wesen der Sprache* (1957/1958), p. 154. (In: M. Heidegger, *Gesamtausgabe. I. Abteilung: Veröffentliche Schriften 1910–1976*, Band 12. *Unterwegs zur Sprache*, Frankfurt am Main, Vittorio Klostermann, 1985, pp. 147–204). "No thing is, where the Word is lacking" (My translation).
97 Heidegger, *Bremer und Freiburger Vorträge*, p. 40. "What stands over against (*der Gegenstand*) is the object for the subject" (My translation).
98 About electronic object, see, L. Wiesing, *Artifizielle Präsenz. Studie zur Philosophie des Bildes*, Frankfurt am Main, Suhrkamp, 2005, especially, *Die Hauptströmungen der gegenwärtigen Philosophie des Bildes*.
99 Heidegger, *Sein und Zeit*, p. 67.

analysis of taking care (*Sorge*) in regard to digital-*Gegenstände*, remembering that it is on *Sorge* that being-in-the-world is based.

These questions could find a point of departure in Heidegger's *The Thing*, a text in which Heidegger presents, in my view, the main problematic of digital media. In fact, during the last century, fundamental media theories have primarily focused on phenomena such as the shrinking of all distances, immediacy, representation, fidelity of representation, and the way in which technology became the realm of revealing truth. In other words, media theories have focused on the ways in which media, as noted by Casetti, constituted the space of negotiation of the relation between natural and artificial.[100] In fact, technology, as noted by Heidegger, sets the way that everything present now presences. [Das Ge-Stell stellt dann die Weise, wie jedes Anwesende jetzt anwest.[101]] Consequently, Enframing (*Ge-stell*) defines the essence of technology [Das Ge-Stell ist das Wesen der Technik.][102] because it determines the conciliation between the natural and the artificial. Nevertheless, the conciliation between natural and artificial fails when technology is no longer a human extension and becomes invasive.[103] This phenomenon is clearly introduced by the figure of the cyborg, which alludes to an extreme proximity between humankind and machine, and denounces the mutations that this proximity would mean to humans.[104] These mutations, described by Caronia in his work *Il Cyborg. Saggio sull'uomo artificiale*, also mean that technology ceases to represent a media entity, and, consequently, the opposition between natural and artificial disappears. The post-media condition, which in my view is characterized by an unmediated existence, is determined by this profound anthropological mutation.[105]

In this essay, we saw the way in which topology represented an instrument for dissolving the established duality object–subject. We saw the way in which some concepts deriving from Topology culminated in Heidegger's *dasein*. As we noted, Heidegger's thoughts conceptualize a topologic nature and placed the subject to inhabit a topological existence. Additionally, as is inevitable, there emerged from these thoughts a profound analysis on the technological

---

100 See, F. Casetti, *L'occhio del Novecento. Cinema, esperienza, modernità*, Milano, Bompiani, 2005.

101 Heidegger, *Bremer und Freiburger Vorträge*, p. 40. "Enframing, then sets the way that everything present now presences" (My translation).

102 *Ibid.*, p. 40. "Enframing is the essence of technology" (My translation).

103 A. Caronia, *Il Cyborg. Saggio sull'uomo artificiale*, Milano, Shake, 2008, p. 106.

104 *Ibid.*, pp. 106–107.

105 R. Eugeni, *La condizione postmediale*, Milano, La Scuola, 2015, p. 45.

condition. Indeed, technology, as *Ge-stell*, places the way that everything present now presences, that is to say, sets in motion the process of disclosure through with the subject meets and interacts with objects and subjects, it is to say, the process that generates, under a particular historical determination, the space.[106] Certainly, as noted by Heidegger, this process places the subject into a historical time, into a technological context, but not only that. Through this analysis, it was also possible to better comprehend the technological context experienced by the subject after the Second Industrial Revolution, especially to better comprehend the video-electronic condition. Nowadays, in my view, Heidegger's extensive work represents a fundamental point of departure for the understanding of the post-media condition. Despite the fact that, for Heidegger, existence is basically a mediated experience, in his later works, he develops some analyses that place under consideration the consistency of things that populate reality in a hypermediatized world in which distances shrink. In addition, the disappearance of distance represented a main concern for him, but it is also possible to see that he was concern by the phenomenon of the exclusion of the human component in a hypertechnological world. As he noted, "We have only purely technical relations" (My translation),[107] and it is through this sentence that one can understand that the disappearance of distance in the mass-media world is also expressed through the disappearance of distance between humankind and technology, a phenomenon that implies a new formulation and analysis of the being. Nevertheless, as we could see in this essay, Heideggerian *dasein* displays the characteristic flexibility of Topology and it could represent the key to understanding the being-in-the-digital-world. Indeed, the topological character of the Heideggerian *dasein* allows to connect the being with its place, as remarked by Malpas, allows connecting of *Sein* with *Da*. In Malpas words, "*Dasein* still encompasses the essence of the human, but it does so precisely because of the way in which the being of the human finds its essence in the being of place–in the belonging together of being and *topos*."[108] Without doubt, Heidegger's oeuvre will represent an instrument for approaching our post-media condition in the near future. In my opinion, Heidegger's oeuvre should return to the centre of

---

106 That is the reason why, for Malpas, the "historical is not opposed by topological, but encompassed by it." In fact, following this framework, under the topologic character of the being, the history of the being represents at the same time a history of the space. Malpas, *Heidegger and the Thinking of Place*, p. 35.

107 "Wir haben nur noch rein technische Verhältniss" M. Heidegger, in Der Spiegel, nr. 23, 31 may, 1976, p. 206.

108 Malpas, *Heidegger and the Thinking of Place*, p. 16.

media analysis. Its exclusion from academic debate would be a serious mistake. It would cause irreparable damage that would draw us away from a better comprehension of our digital condition.

Bibliography

G. Bachelard, *L'intuition de l'instant*, Paris, Stock, 1931.

J. Baudrillard, *Le crime parfait*, Paris, Galillée, 1995.

H. Bergson, *Essai sur les données immédiates de la conscience*, Paris, PUF, 1889.

H. Bergson, *Matière et mémoire. Essai sur la relation du corps à l'esprit*, Paris, PUF, 1896.

H. Bergson, *L'évolution créatrice*, Paris, PUF, 1907.

H. Bergson, *La pensée et le mouvant*, Paris, PUF, 1934.

J.D Bolter and R. Grusin, *Remediation. Understanding New Media*, Cambridge, MA, MIT Press, 2000.

A. Caronia, *Il corpo virtuale. Dal corpo robotizzato al corpo disseminato nelle reti*, Padova, Franco Muzzio Editore, 1996.

A. Caronia, *Il Cyborg. Saggio sull'uomo artificiale*, Milano, Shake, 2008.

H.W. Carr. *Henri Bergson: The Philosophy of Change*, London, T. Nelson & Sons, 1919.

F. Casetti, *L'occhio del Novecento. Cinema, esperienza, modernità*, Milano, Bompiani, 2005.

G. Debord, *La Société du spectacle*, Paris, Gallimard, 1992.

D. De Kerckhove, *Brainframes. Technology, Mind and Business*, Utrecht, VBK, 1991.

D. De Kerckhove, *Dall'alfabeto a Internet. L'homme "littéré": alfabetizzazione, cultura, tecnologia*, Milano, Mimesis, 2008.

G. Deleuze, *Différence et répétition*, Paris, PUF, 1968.

G. Deleuze, *Cinéma 1. L'image-mouvement*, Paris, Les éditions de minuit, 1983.

G. Deleuze, *Le Pli. Leibniz et le baroque*, Paris, Les Éditions de Minuit, 1988.

G. Deleuze and F. Guattari, *Capitalisme et schizophrénie 2. Mille Plateaux*, Paris, Les Éditions de Minuit, 1980.

J. Dieudonné, *A History of Algebraic and Differential Topology 1900–1960*, Boston, Birkhäuser, 1989.

G. Dorfles, *Horror Pleni. La (in)civiltà del rumore*, Roma, Castelvecchi, 2008.

G.A. Duarte, *Reificación mediática*, Bucaramanga, SIC, 2011.

H.L. Dreyfus and C. Spinosa, "Further Reflections on Heidegger, Technology and the Everyday", in: N. Kompridis (Ed.,) *Philosophical Romanticism*, New York, Routledge, 2006, pp. 265–281.

L. Engell, "Fernsehen mit Gilles Deleuze", in: O. Fahle and L. Engell (Eds.,) *Der Film Bei Deleuze / Le cinéman selon Deleuze*, Weimar, Bauhaus-Universität / Presses de la Sorbonne Nouvelle, 1999.

R. Eugeni, *La condizione postmediale*, Milano, La Scuola, 2015.

M. Foucault, *Les mots et les choses*, Paris, Gallimard, 1966.

V. Flusser, *Ins universum der Technischen Bilder*, Göttingen, European Photography, 1996.

S. Günzel, "Raum – Topographie – Topologie", in: S. Günzel (Ed.,) *Topologie. Zur Raumbeschreibung in den Kultur- und Medienwissenschaften*, Bielefeld, Transcript Verlag, 2007, pp. 13–29.

H. Grassmann, *Die Ausdehnungslehre von 1844: oder Die Lineale Ausdehnungslehre, ein neuer Zweig der Mathematik*, Leipzig, Otto Wigand, 1844.

G.W.F Hegel, *Phänomenologie des Geistes*, Frankfurt am Main, Suhrkamp, 2012.

M. Heidegger, *Sein und Zeit*, Tübingen, Max Niemeyer Verlag, 1967.

M. Heidegger, *Brief über den »Humanismus« (1946)*, In M. Heidegger, *Gesamtausgabe I. Abteilung: Veröffentlichte Schriften 1914–1970*, Band 9. *Wegmarken*, Frankfurt am Main, Vittorio Klostermann, 1976.

M. Heidegger, *Die Zeit des Weltbildes (1950)*, In M. Heidegger, *Gesamtausgabe I. Abteilung: Veröffentlichte Schriften 1914–1970*, Band 5. *Holzwege*, Frankfurt am Main, Vittorio Klostermann, 1977.

M. Heidegger, *Einführung in die Metaphysik (1935)*, In M. Heidegger, *Gesamtausgabe. II. Abteilung: Vorlesungen 1923–1944*, Band 40. Frankfurt am Main, Vittorio Klostermann, 1983.

M. Heidegger, *Das Wesen der Sprache (1957/1958)*, In M. Heidegger, *Gesamtausgabe. I. Abteilung: Veröffentliche Schriften 1910–1976*, Band 12. *Unterwegs zur Sprache*, Frankfurt am Main, Vittorio Klostermann, 1985.

M. Heidegger, *Bremer und Freiburger Vorträge (1949)*, In M. Heidegger, *Gesamtausgabe III. Unveröffentlichte Abhandlungen. Vorträge, Gedachtes*, Band 79. Frankfurt am Main, Vittorio Klostermann, 1994.

M. Heidegger, *Das Ding (1950)*, In M. Heidegger, *Gesamtausgabe. I. Abteilung: Veröffentliche Schriften 1910–1976*, Band 7. *Vortrage Und Aufsätze*, Frankfurt am Main, Vittorio Klostermann, 2000.

M. Heidegger, *Die Frage nach der Technik (1953)*, In M. Heidegger, *Gesamtausgabe. I. Abteilung: Veröffentliche Schriften 1910–1976*, Band 7. *Vortrage und Aufsätze*, Frankfurt am Main, Vittorio Klostermann, 2000.

M.-L. Heuser, "Die Anfänge der Topologie in Mathematik und Naturphilosophie", in: S. Günzel (Ed.,) Topologie. Zur Raumbeschreibung in den Kultur- und Medienwissenschaften, Bielefeld, 2007, pp. 181–200.

D. Hume, *A Treatise of Human Nature*, Oxford, Oxford University Press, 2000.

E. Husserl, *Zur Phänomenologie des Inneren Zeitbewusstseins (1893-1917)* In: R. Boehm (Ed.,) *Husserliana: Edmund Husserl, Gesammelte Werke*, Band 10, Berlin, Springer, 1966.

A.N. Kolmogorov and A.P Yushkevich, *Mathematics of the 19th Century. Geometry Analytic Function Theory*, Basel, Springer, 1996.

N. Kompridis, *Critique and Disclosure. Critical Theory between Past and Future*, MIT Press, Cambridge, MA, 2006.

D. Kreps, *Bergson, Complexity and Creative Emergence*, New York, Palgrave Macmillan, 2015.

G.W. Leibniz, *Nouveaux essais sur l'entendement humain / Neue Abhandlungen über den menschlichen Verstand* In: G.W. Leibniz, Philosophische Schriften Band 3.1 and 3.2, W. Von Engelhardt – HH. Holz (Eds.,), Frankfurt am Main, Suhrkamp, 1996 (1765).

J.F. Lyotard, *La condition postmoderne*, Paris, Les Éditions de Minuit, 1979.

J. Malpas, *Heidegger and the Thinking of Place. Explorations in the Topology of Being*, Cambridge, MA, MIT Press, 2012.

E.J. Marey, *La machine animale, locomotion terrestre et aérienne*, Paris, Germer Baillière, 1873.

M. McLuhan, *Understanding Media. The Extensions of Man*, Cambridge, MA, MIT Press, 1994.

M. Merleau-Ponty, *Phénoménologie de la perception*, Paris, Gallimard, 1945.

E. Panofsky, "Style and Medium in the Motion Pictures", in: A.D. Vacche (Ed.,) *The Visual Turn. Classical Film Theory and Art History*, New Brunswick, Rutgers University Press, 2003.

H. Poincaré, *Science et méthode*, Paris, Flammarion, 1908.

H. Poser, "Innere Prinzipen und Hierarchie der Monaden (§§ 9-9, 82 f.)", in: H. Busche (Ed.,) *Gottfried Wilhelm Leibniz Monadologie* (Klassiker Auslegen Band 34), Berlin, Akademie Verlag, 2009.

H. De Preester, "Equipment and Existential Spatiality: Heidegger, Cognitive Science and the Prosthetic Subject," in: J. Kiverstein and M. Wheeler (Eds.,)

Heidegger and Cognitive Science, Basingstoke, Palgrave Macmillian, 2012, pp. 276–308.

M. Serres, *Le système de Leibniz et ses modèles mathématiques*, Paris, PUF, 1968.

M. Serres, *Les origines de la géométrie*, Paris, Flammarion, 1993.

E. Severino, *Studi di filosofía della prassi*, Milano, Adelfi, 1984.

Y. Spielmann, *Video. Das reflexive Medium*, Frankfurt am Main, Suhrkamp, 2005.

X. Verley, "Whitehead et la subjectivité". *Les Études Philosophiques*, 4, 2002, pp. 511–525.

A.N. Whitehead, *Science and the Modern World*, New York, Pelican, 1948.

A.N. Whitehead, *The Concept of Nature*, Cambridge, Cambridge University Press, 1964.

L. Wiesing, *Artifizielle Präsenz. Studie zur Philosophie des Bildes*, Frankfurt am Main, Suhrkamp, 2005.

Georgios Tsadgis

The Manual: Heidegger and Fundamental *Oto-cheiro-logy* I

1 Announcement: *media res* and mediality

One finds a word, a pebble on the shores of civilization, rounded by the waves of language. Along modernity's resplendent esplanade one comes across *media*, a plain word that seems to deflect explanation. Upon taking this pebble in its mouth, the question 'what is?', perhaps philosophy altogether, finds itself at a loss. For, unlike Demosthenes's remedy, the circulation of this pebble from mouth to mouth seems to aggravate rather than relieve the pathology of collective discourse articulation.

One certainly begins *media res*, underway, too late for the transmission of the first broadcast, too early for its reception. From this position, media appears as *mediality*, the between, at once the field of perception or phenomenal space, as much as the phenomenon itself in its phenomenality, and finally, perhaps most importantly, the correlation as well as the conditions of correlation of the two. Accordingly, if one is to speak with Heidegger in a way that Heidegger does not speak, the essence of media emerges as fundamental mediation. The conditions, the exact trajectories and finally the matter and structure of media, in-form this essence, henceforth designated as *mediality*.

Although in late capitalism the signifying horizon of mediality tends to be limited to "what we call after Adorno cultural industries,"[1] this essay probes a deeper stratum of mediality in which the latter appears as the correlation between what Stiegler after Husserl terms primary, secondary and tertiary retentions, that is, in broad strokes, a correlation between perception, memory and mnemotechnics. Thinking through this correlation it becomes possible not only to think *mediality* as the ultimate support of the flection: *the essence of technology is the technology of essence*, but also to perceive *corporeality as the absent heart of this flection*.

Heidegger's reflections on the hand and the ear appear here paramount. They test the limits of corpo-*reality*, setting into relief mediality as re-mediality, a fundamental repetition (*anamnesis* and *hypomnesis*) and a constant pharmacological

1   Bernard Stiegler, *Philosophizing by Accident, Interviews with Élie During*, transl. and ed. Benoît Dillet (Edinburgh: Edinburgh University Press, 2017), pp. 70–71.

administration (poison and remedy). This is then an essay on the hand, *cheir* and *manus* as well as on the ear, *ous* and *auris*, as origins and vanishing points of mediality.

2 A history of monstration and danger

In ecclesiology the *manual* refers to a book of pastoral guidelines for the administration of the sacraments. Never offhand, administration is in practice and principle *of* the hand. It hands out, apportions, metes. It is measured, drawn out in advance. Even where it is free-handed, it's never freehand; rarely is it given a free hand. Lest underhanded corruption wins the upper hand, administrative efficiency depends on a set of rules and functions being at hand: *administration rests on the manual.*

Long after Plato's wondering womb, named hysteria, and long before Kawabata's wondering arm which probes the logic of incorporation, Descartes let another singular body part roam; "endowed with such independence that it could also be considered as a complete substance apart and almost separable,"[2] the bodiless hand, always invisible—for who has *seen* a severed, wondering hand—was now free to administer the economy of all power. It is no surprise perhaps that Adam Smith appears as a regional phenomenon within the hand's gesture, when the whole history of the occident is conceived as the effect of a grasp.

In 1942, as Hitler advances towards Stalingrad, Heidegger prepares an extensive manuscript for a lecture on Anaximander he will never give. In a single stroke its epigraph questions the legitimacy of a return to the Greeks and ventures an answer: "Not because there [was instigated] the inception [*Anfang*] of the occident, but because the occident is what follows that inception of the history of Beyng [*jenes seynsgeschichtlichen Anfangs*]."[3] In-ception, or *An-fang*, is what takes hold not only of a Da-sein, the being-there of thought, but of the epoch of all epochs to come, all times in their timeliness, every imaginable and unimaginable *kairos*.

It begins then with the hand, the hand that seizes the occident and gives the inception. And when Heidegger begins to teach anew, upon the expiration of

---

2   Jacques Derrida, Heidegger's Hand (Geschlecht II), transl. John P. Leavey, Jr. and Elizabeth Rottenberg, in *Psyche, Inventions of the Other*, 2, eds. Peggy Kamuf and Elizabeth Rottenberg (Stanford: Stanford University Press, 2008), pp. 27–62, p. 39.

3   Martin Heidegger, *Der Spruch des Anaximander, Gesamtausgabe, Band 78*, (Frankfurt am Main: Vittorio Klostermann, 2010), p. xxi. My translation; italicized in the original.

the denazification committee's ban from academic teaching, his treatment of the hand will be decisive. On his very first lecture at the University of Freiburg in 1951, his words—at length—resound:

> "We are trying to learn thinking. Perhaps thinking, too, is just something like building a cabinet [*Schrein*]. At any rate, it is a craft, a 'handicraft'. 'Craft' literally means the strength and skill in our hands. The hand is a peculiar thing. In the common view, the hand is part of our bodily organism. But the hand's essence can never be determined, or explained, by its being an organ which can grasp. Apes, too, have organs that can grasp [*Greiforgane*], but they do not have hands. The hand is infinitely different from all grasping organs—paws, claws, or fangs—different by an abyss of essence. Only a being who can speak, that is, think, can have hands and can be handy in achieving works of handicraft.
> But the craft of the hand is richer than we commonly imagine. The hand does not only grasp and catch, or push and pull. The hand reaches and extends, receives and welcomes and not just things: the hand extends itself, and receives its welcome in the hands of others. The hand holds. The hand carries. The hand designs and signs, presumably [*vermutlich*] because man is a sign [*ein Zeichen*]. Two hands fold into one, a gesture meant to carry man into the great oneness. The hand is all this, and this is the true hand-icraft. Everything is rooted here that is commonly known as handicraft, and commonly we go no further. But the hand's gestures run everywhere through language, in their most perfect purity precisely where man speaks by being silent. And only when man speaks, does he think—not the other way around, as metaphysics still believes. Every motion of the hand in every of its works carries itself through the element of thinking, every bearing of the hand bears itself in that element. All the work of the hand is rooted in thinking. Therefore, thinking itself is man's simplest, and for that reason hardest, handiwork [*Handwerk*], if it would be accomplished at its proper time."[4]

After which, no more words about the hand; a strange silence in which the hand of thought must be presumed to work its works. *This* hand that gives and withdraws is monstrous; it is, in Derrida's recasting of Heidegger's words: "monstrosity [*monstrosité*], the proper characteristic of man as the being of monstration. This distinguishes him from every other *Geschlecht*, and above all from the ape." Upon which, Derrida continues: "one cannot talk about the hand without talking about technology."[5]

If, without technology, the hand seems destined to remain empty, destined to fold back upon itself, default its mediality, what of the monstration of the hand that 'designs and signs, presumably because man is a sign'? That same first lecture

4   Martin Heidegger, *What is Called Thinking?*, transl. Fred D. Wieck and J. Glenn Gray (New York: Harper & Row, 1968), pp. 16–17. The German in brackets is my inclusion.
5   Derrida, "Heidegger's Hand", p. 36.

of the course, which would come to be known as *What is Called Thinking?*, closes with Hölderlin's famous stanza from *Mnemosynē*, inscribing the totality of its meaning under the sign of memory:

> "*Ein Zeichen sind wir, deutungslos,*
> *Schmerzlos sind wir, und haben fast*
> *Die Sprache in der Fremde verloren.*"[6]

Hölderlin says and Heidegger repeats—he cites and paraphrases—that man is *presumably* a sign, *ein Zeichen*, in Derrida's translation of choice: *un monstre*. Accordingly, the hand is monstrous because and insofar as man himself, the proper of man, is monstration; insofar as, *man is a monster*. The word is loaded, almost already from the beginning and to the last moment of Derrida's work, over-determined. *Of Grammatology*'s exergue closes with the words:

> "The future can only be anticipated in the form of an absolute danger. It is that which breaks absolutely with constituted normality and can only be proclaimed, presented, as a sort of *monstrosity*. For that future world and for that within it which will have put into question the values of sign, word, and writing, for that which guides our future anterior, there is as yet no exergue."[7]

The future announces itself as *absolute danger*. Which danger is absolute and which monstrosity is accordingly announced by the coming of grammatology? The most direct—and by the same token far from the only—answer is to be found in a series of lectures Heidegger gave in Bremen in 1949.[8] One of the lectures was simply announced as *The Danger*. It was followed by *The Turn*, in which the verse of Hölderlin has a catalytic effect: "But where danger is, grows // The saving power also." These words would find their way, twice, into the reworking of *The Danger* to the seminal essay that *The Question Concerning Technology* was to be.[9]

---

6   Martin Heidegger, *Was Heisst Denken? Gesamtausgabe, Band 8* (Frankfurt am Main: Vittorio Klostermann, 2002a), p. 20. I translate: "We are a sign, meaningless, // Painless we are, and have almost // Lost the language in foreign lands." An alternative translation can be found in: Martin Heidegger, *What is Called Thinking?*, transl. J. Glenn Gray (London: Harper & Row, 1968), p. 18.

7   Jacques Derrida, *Of Grammatology*, transl. Gayatri Chakravorty Spivak (London: The John Hopkins University Press), 1997, p. 5. My emphasis.

8   Martin Heidegger, *Bremen and Freiburg Lectures, Insight Into That Which Is and Basic Principles of Thinking*, transl. Andrew J. Mitchell (Indianapolis: Indiana University Press), 2012a.

9   Martin Heidegger, "The Question Concerning Technology," in *Basic Writings*, transl. David Farrell Krell (San Francisco: Harper, 1993), pp. 307–341, pp. 333, 340.

Already then this outline makes it clear: the absolute danger is the danger of technology, while the monstrosity which will 'put into question the values of sign, word, and writing', emerges as an act of the monstrous hand, destined to undo the monster that man himself is. For Heidegger already in the *Parmenides* seminar of the winter of 1942–3 announced: "Man does not 'have' hands, but the hand holds the essence of man, because the word as the essential realm of the hand is the ground of the essence of man."[10] No sooner does the hand hold the essence of man, than it is able to crush it; all the more forcefully, the more technological the hand becomes. But if everything, including the future, begins with the hand, in the midst of it all one hears about the *word*, the word that is 'the essential realm of the hand'.

First, however, a brief re-turn to the handiwork of thought, the craft of which builds a cabinet. Just like the English shrine, with all its religious connotations, the German *Schrein* comes from the Latin *scrinium* which does not refer to any case or casket, but specifically to a chest of books. At the outset then and as such, the hand of thought builds a library; an archive of the written word. The hand thinks by building a shrine for the word, thought itself is this enshrining, a certain framing. Undoubtedly and unavoidably a grammatology will unfold here its most thorough critique—all is already transparent.

Derrida pauses before undertaking this critique. He offers three 'remarks', which weave together numerous guiding threads of the Heideggerian eminence of the hand. Firstly, the hand signals a certain relation to corporeality, when the body is otherwise absent, at large, in Heidegger. The introduction of the hand is thus a retracting gesture meant to account for an elusive presence, or a restless absence. Secondly, in Heidegger's scheme the hand escapes ontic logic. It refuses to be reduced to a given thing or being, and is thus altogether no object. Accordingly, its work is no *Geschäft*, a practice of utility or utilization of and for profit. Thirdly, this resistance to utility, trade and ultimately business already bespeaks the championing of rustic artisanship, a national socialist tenet which would be suppressed by the historic-pragmatic demands of the Third Reich's war. This tenet became Heidegger's own line of defense against his detractors after the war, the vantage point from which he could devastate with a single stroke both the technological monstrosity that became of the national socialist project, as well as the onset of technological capitalist democracy.[11]

---

10 Martin Heidegger, *Parmenides*, transl. Andre Schuwer and Richard Rojcewicz (Indianapolis: Indiana University Press, 1992), p. 80.

11 Derrida, "Heidegger's Hand", pp. 38–39.

Similarly, Heidegger's dogmatism which establishes "not *some* differences but an absolute oppositional limit"[12] between the human hand and the *Greiforgan* of the ape, would be integral to his critique of organicism and biologism, offering thus significant ideological credit to be cashed against accusations of complicity with a totalitarian politics of 'blood'.[13]

Even such pressing exigencies however offer barely sufficient theoretical justification for the absolute elevation of the human, which establishes an unsupported empirical hierarchy by means of a non-empirical hand, establishing and harboring thus the unthought and unexamined, the silenced and the misguided at the heart of the most exacting thought.[14]

The word for the guiding theoretical prejudice is rather the word itself, *logos*. In the aforementioned key passage of the *Parmenides* seminar Heidegger writes: "Only a being which, like man, 'has' the word (*mythos, logos*), can and must 'have' 'the hand'."[15] Just as in *What is Called Thinking?*, the hand hinges on the word, which it attempts to enshrine and archive. The word however withdraws. We read thus:

> "Whenever man is properly drawing that way, he is thinking—even though he may still be far away from what withdraws, even though the withdrawal may remain as veiled as ever. All through his life and right into his death, Socrates did nothing else than place himself into this draft, this current, and maintain himself in it. This is why he is the purest thinker of the West. This is why he wrote nothing."[16]

The purest thinker is the one who dwells in the receding word, whose hand doesn't write, articulation fusing into a lofty ankylosis. No shrine, no archive—and yet. Heidegger himself rarely mentions Socrates. It is rather always Plato: Plato, the archivist, the collector of Socratic impressions, the Promethean craftsman who manifests the impure essence of man. Plato who inscribes his struggle in a dialogue named *Phaedrus*. Just like Plato's, Heidegger's hand will produce more than a hundred volumes, all the while desiring to cease seizing the pen. The word withdraws, the hand attempts to hold it—the name of this labor is history, the history of Beyng.

---

12 *Ibid.*, p. 41.
13 *Ibid.*, p. 40. Indeed as Farrell Krell notes, "the opposable thumb we take to be in opposition to everything else that lives," misses the Heideggerian position altogether. David Farrell Krell, *Phantoms of the Other, Four Generations of Derrida's Geschlecht* (New York: SUNY Press, 2015), p. 49.
14 Derrida, Heidegger's Hand, pp. 40–41.
15 Heidegger, *Parmenides*, p. 80.
16 Heidegger, *What is Called Thinking?* p. 17.

At the in-ception of this history the hand already operates. Returning to Anaximander, Heidegger is found tracing the *chreōn*, the word that articulates the first sentence of occidental thought, back to the *cheir*, the hand. Accordingly, *chraō* in the verbal form means to handle and at the same time to give to hand, to hand over and thus hand out, for Heidegger to let belong and let into a belonging.[17] This handling is at the same time *a use and a need*, which Heidegger sums up in the translation *Brauch*.

Regarding the understanding of the *chreōn* as *need* [*Not*], Heidegger devotes a considerable amount of thought in his 1942/3 seminar on Anaximander to account for the connotations of coercion [*Zwang*] that echo in the word.[18] If the originary hand coerces at all, its force must be *proper* rather than *brute*, a force that compels one to one's own essence. By the time the short essay *The Saying of Anaximander* is published in 1946 coercion has altogether disappeared. Heidegger will simply write: "in the participial *chrēon*, therefore, there is originarilly no naming of coercion [*Zwang*] or 'must'."[19] For what Heidegger wants to preserve in the hand's *Brauch* is neither a sanctioning nor an ordering, but the preserving of the present in its presence and this as a holding that hands out. An etymological *excursus* is thus undertaken: tracing *brauchen* to *bruchen* and then with a further leap to the Latin *frui*, to fruit. In turn fruition will be understood through enjoyment, where to enjoy (*genießen*) is to have joy in something one needs and uses: "*Frui, bruchen, brauchen, Brauch* means: to hand out something in its own essence and to keep it as thus presencing in the preserving hand."[20]

Accordingly, the *chreōn* is the joyous hand that needs and uses without grasping (*greiffend*). This is why in Heidegger's final lecture, in Zähringen in 1973, the Greeks are said to have no con-cepts [*Be-griffe*]—in their search for a *horismos* they do not take possession.[21] As for the generous hand of *Brauch*, *The*

17 Martin Heidegger, "Der Spruch des Anaximander," in *Holzwege, Gesamtausgabe 5* (Frankfurt am Main: Vittorio Klostermann, 1977a), p. 366. In English: Martin Heidegger, "The Saying of Anaximander," in *Off the Beaten Track* transl. and eds. Julian Young and Kenneth Haynes (Cambridge: Cambridge University Press, 2002b), p. 276.
18 Heidegger, "Der Spruch des Anaximander," pp. 128, 132–133.
19 Heidegger, "Der Spruch des Anaximander, p. 366, my translation. Alternative: Heidegger, "The Saying of Anaximander," p. 276.
20 Heidegger, "Der Spruch des Anaximander," p. 367, my translation. Alternative: Heidegger, "The Saying of Anaximander," p. 277.
21 Martin Heidegger, *Seminare, Gesamtausgabe, Band 15* (Frankfurt am Main: Vittorio Klostermann, 1986), p. 399. In English: Martin Heidegger, *Four Seminars*, transl. Andrew Mitchell and François Raffoul (Indianapolis: Indiana University Press, 2012b), p. 81.

Saying of Anaximander will ultimately ask: "is there salvation? [*Rettung*]?" Its answer is familiar: *only where danger is*. And there is danger only in the oblivion of Being in which the latter turns upon itself. This is the danger of technology. "When however Being in its essence *needs and uses* [*braucht*] the essence of man," then thinking "must poeticize [*dichten*] the enigma of Being" in order to "bring the dawn of thought into proximity of what is to be thought."[22]

3 The singular hand and the typewriter

The history of the hand is accordingly always already a history of monstration and danger, yet this danger grows as technology progressively unfolds its essence. The typewriter signals a decisive moment. In the *Parmenides* seminar, Heidegger writes:

> "It is not accidental that modern man writes 'with' the typewriter and 'dictates' [*diktiert*] (the same word as 'poetize' [*Dichten*]) 'into' a machine. This 'history' of the kinds of writing is one of the main reasons for the increasing destruction of the word. The latter no longer comes and goes by means of the writing hand, the properly acting hand, but by means of the mechanical forces it releases. The typewriter tears writing from the essential realm of the hand, i.e., the realm of the word. The word itself turns into something 'typed'. Where typewriting, on the contrary, is only a transcription and serves to preserve the writing, or turns into print something already written, there it has a proper, though limited, significance. In the time of the first dominance of the typewriter, a letter written on this machine still stood for a breach of good manners. Today a hand-written letter is an antiquated and undesired thing; it disturbs speed reading. Mechanical writing deprives the hand of its rank in the realm of the written word and degrades the word to a means of communication. In addition, mechanical writing provides this 'advantage', that it conceals the handwriting and thereby the character. The typewriter makes everyone look the same."[23]

The typewriter is then first of all guilty of dissimulation (*Verhüllung*), turning the singularity of every longhand into uniform shorthand. It appears strange at first that the thinker of hiddenness and concealment, of the *kryptesthai* and the *lathein*, of *Verdeckung* and *Verbergung*, condemns without second thought the withdrawal at the heart of the phenomenon of the typewriter. The wager becomes clearer however in the language of *Being and Time*, insofar as the typewriter reduces *Da-sein* to *das Man*, the impersonal, homogenous voice of the multitude, of *hoi polloi*. At this juncture, it seems at large that the critique of

---

22 Heidegger, "Der Spruch des Anaximander," p. 373, my translation. Alternative: Heidegger, "The Saying of Anaximander," p. 281.
23 Heidegger, *Parmenides*, pp. 80–81.

culture industry and the media, from Heidegger and Adorno to Baudrillard and beyond has consisted in an effort to understand and account for the existence and behavior of this multitude, in the process reinscribing explicitly or tacitly its Platonic castigation. Stiegler is heir to the same tradition when he sums up a fundamental tenet, a constitutive contest waged by his work: "thinking is a struggle against stupidity, since when it prevails, laziness triumphs. Thinking is to fight one's own laziness. And this fight becomes harder and harder since the media is systematically exploiting and encouraging this laziness."[24] Heidegger thematizes this unthinking at the heart of media as an unthinking of mediality, in effect, an unthinking of the hand.

The typewriter is no less deplored for its irreducible speed-effect. Accelerating the production of texts, it accelerates on the inverse their consumption. Handwriting is thus eschewed as an impediment to speed-reading. Although Heidegger, who in private would confess to being a slow reader, has no time here for the question of speed, a discourse from futurism to accelerationism, along with its counter-discourse, to which Heidegger has contributed more than overtones, has over the last century set the stakes of the question into relief. What is important at this instance for Heidegger is the effect of the typewriter's speed on the hand, namely, the latter's arrest.

The typewriter seems to paralyze the hand, the proper hand, the hand of the word. It thus imperils the essence of man, namely manuscripture, precariously poised between the *Greiforgan* and the typewriter. Can the hand of the word ever be spoken of in the plural? Derrida insists on the question: "Apes have prehensile organs that resemble hands; the man of the typewriter and of technology in general uses two hands. But the man who speaks and the man who writes by hand, as one says, is he not the monster with a single hand?"[25]

William McNeill and David Farrell Krell discover in 1925s *Prolegomena to the History of the Concept of Time* Heidegger's second hand:

> "Dasein is oriented as corporeal, as corporeal it is in each instance its right and left, and that is why the parts of the body are also right and left parts. Accordingly, it belongs to the being of bodily things that they are co-constituted by orientation. There is no such thing as a hand in general. Every hand, or every glove, is a right or a left one, since the glove in use is in its sense designed to go along with bodily movements. Every bodily movement is always an 'I move' and not 'it moves itself', if we disregard certain well-defined organic movements [*sic*]. Thus things like gloves are intrinsically oriented to the right and left but not, say, a thing like the hammer, which I hold in my hand but which

---

24 Stiegler, *Philosophizing by Accident*, p. 78.
25 Derrida, "Heidegger's Hand", p. 50.

does not go along with my self-movement in the strict sense; rather, it is moved by me such that it moves itself. Accordingly, there are also no right and left hammers."[26]

But does this excursion to a lecture that would provide much of the material for *Being and Time* suffice? Is not after all *Being and Time* an unfinished project? And bracketing for the time being the philological apparatus of the *Kehre* with all its cae-suras and breaks, is not Heidegger's path precisely one that undertakes the impos-sible passage from the two hands to such a thing 'as a hand in general'? This seems indeed the only path left once a *Dasein* oriented in everydayness can no longer be probed for the meaning of Being. Orientation in Beyng seems no longer a matter of the hands, while the singular, severed hand appears as the last, vanishing remain of a once celebrated phenomenological corporeality.[27]

Even if the passage is taken in however, questions proliferate. Perhaps a type-writer is operated by *both* hands. But does this make it akin to a hammer? Isn't the pen much closer determined by the significant possibility that it be handled by *either* hand, being thus, pheno-corporeally speaking, non-specific or 'general'? Isn't rather the hand abstract, because and insofar as the pen, just like the hammer, is in fact abstract? Isn't *Being and Time's* striving for concreteness ultimately a mirage, when its every gesture beckons unfailingly to Being?

Again, the hand holds the most concrete answer. In *Being and Time*, the oper-ation of the hand is so pervasive that it becomes unnoticeable: it is merely a *manner of speech*, but this manner is here exemplarily, improperly proper. For this is precisely a speech *of the hand, manuarius*, as Latin would have it; it is the manner of the word itself. Thus, from the outset and fundamentally one discovers beings *either* as being present-at-hand [*Zuhandensein*] or as being ready-to-hand [*Vorhandensein*]. *Being as such* manifests itself, perhaps exhaus-tively, in the hollow of a specific kind of hand. Derrida, for whom the singularity of the Heideggerian hand is of superlative significance, summarizes none-theless the dilemma traversing *Being and Time* in the question: "which hand founds the other?"[28] And yet, even more important perhaps than the fact that

---

26 Martin Heidegger, *Prolegomena to the History of the Concept of Time*, transl. Theodore Kisiel (Bloomington: Indiana University Press, 1985), p. 232.

27 Heidegger will even approach sexuation through the singularity of the *Geschlecht*—race and generation at once—the irreducibly plural reduced to a singularity. Martin Heidegger, "Language in the Poem, A Discussion on Georg Trakl's Poetic Work," in *On the Way to Language*, transl. Peter D. Hertz (London: Harper & Row, 1982), p. 195.

28 Derrida, "Heidegger's Hand," p. 44.

presence-at-hand is grounded in readiness-to-hand,[29] the two hands are never, nowhere plural: one nowhere encounters both at once, existence is nowhere shared. One is led to suppose that the same hand offers Being *in turns*.

Thus Heidegger in the *Fundamental Concepts of Metaphysics* will confine the ape with its two hands, or rather prehensile organs, to a singular mode of being, a being that is poor-in-world (*weltarm*), a captivity called *environment*.[30] On the other hand, the singular hand of man allows him to oscillate between presence-at-hand and readiness-to-hand in order to build worlds (*weltbildend*). Preferably with a singular hammer.

The distance of Heidegger from the thinker who tried to take humanity's values into his hands by 'philosophizing with a hammer', could not be greater at this point. Kittler refers to Nietzsche repeatedly as the 'mechanized philosopher',[31] since "Nietzsche was the first thinker of the West to have a typewriter, of which we have a photograph."[32] The significance of the photographic testimony aside, Nietzsche constitutes a rift in the history of philosophical writing. For his adoption of the typewriter was no less epochal than it was practical. Kittler writes:

> "'Our writing tools are also working on our thoughts', Nietzsche wrote. 'Technology is entrenched in our history', Heidegger said. But the one wrote the sentence about the typewriter on a typewriter, the other described (in a magnificent old German hand) typewriters per se. That is why it was Nietzsche who initiated the transvaluation of all values with his philosophically scandalous sentence about media technology."[33]

29 Martin Heidegger, *Being and Time*, transl. Joan Stambaugh (New York: SUNY, 1996), §15.
30 Martin Heidegger, *Fundamental Concepts of Metaphysics: World, Finitude, Solitude*, transl. William McNeill and Nicholas Walker (Indianapolis: Indiana University Press, 1995), cf. chapters II–V.
31 Friedrich A. Kittler, *Gramophone, Film, Typewriter*, transl. Geoffrey Winthrop-Young and Michael Wutz (Stanford: Stanford University Press, 1999), pp. 200, 205, 292. Kittler even titled one of his essays simply "The Mechanized Philosopher," in *Looking after Nietzsche*, ed. Lawrence A. Rickels (Albany: State Univ. of New York Press, 1990), pp. 195–207.
32 Derrida, "Heidegger's Hand," pp. 35–36. Derrida's lecture is given in March 1985, at the Loyola University Chicago, on the occasion of a colloquium organized by John Sallis—perhaps Kittler whose *Gramophone, Film, Typewriter* was published in 1986 was there. Perhaps he had early access to a manuscript of the lecture. Be it as it may, Derrida's influence on Kittler's moniker for Nietzsche just as much as on the latter's attention to Heidegger's remarks on the typewriter in the *Parmenides* seminar appears decisive—Kittler however remains silent on his sources.
33 Kittler, *Gramophone, Film, Typewriter*, p. 200.

The scandalous sentence, a sentence on mediality, betrayed the technological conditioning of thought. What this meant for Nietzsche, was a change "from arguments to aphorisms, from thoughts to puns, from rhetoric to telegram style."[34] This very same change "designates the turning point at which communications technologies can no longer be related back to humans;"[35] *inscription* is Nietzsche's name for the way in which technology writes itself through the human.

The suspicion that both Nietzsche's adoption of the typewriter and his change of style, were *dictated* by the debilitating onset of his blindness and the general degeneration of his health, is dispelled by T. S. Eliot's testimony. Again Kittler:

> "T. S. Eliot, who will be 'composing' *The Waste Land* 'on the typewriter', 'finds' (no different from Nietzsche) 'that I am sloughing off all my long sentences which I used to dote upon. Short, staccato, like modern French prose'. Instead of 'subtlety', 'the typewriter makes for lucidity', which is, however, nothing but the effect of its technology on style."[36]

The change of Nietzsche's style, his change of the stylus for a typewriter is not merely a medical, but an epochal symptom. It announces an era of wars to be fought with machine-guns, an era of deafening wars. Kittler:

> "The typewriter became a discursive machine-gun. A technology whose basic action not coincidentally consists of strikes and triggers proceeds in automated and discrete steps, as does ammunitions transport in a revolver and a machine-gun, or celluloid transport in a film projector. 'The pen was once mightier than the sword', Otto Burghagen, the first monographer of the typewriter, writes in 1898, 'but where the typewriter rules', he continues, 'Krupp's cannons must remain silent!' "[37]

In light of this exclamation and aside of all that is explicit in the text, the condemnation of the typewriter in the *Parmenides* lectures of 1942/43 appears now as a call for ceasefire, or at least, for a return to the sword. As for the present, even if digital cyber-writing can and even must be thought and assessed as the correlate of bio-chemical warfare, it seems harder than ever to juxtapose their relative strength; it is even harder to imagine what script will overpower the H-bomb.[38]

---

34 *Ibid.*, p. 203.
35 *Ibid.*, p. 211.
36 *Ibid.*, p. 229.
37 *Ibid.*, p. 191.
38 As this essay is being written cyber-attacks and nuclear missiles complement each other perfectly in the grand provocation of North Korea—the former often expropriating the funds for the latter.

Tarrying in the battlefield, the Heideggerian indictment against the typewriter appears as lost cause heroism in its attempt to shield Beyng (the Beyng of History as the History of Beyng) from the epochal onslaught of mediality. It is a desperate gesture—the typewriter denied kinship both to the hammer *and* to the nuclear turbine, being reduced to "an 'intermediate' thing, between a tool and a machine," a mere 'mechanism',[39] lacking altogether a *proper* essence. Although one types with both hands, the product of this mechanism without kind, is anything but a manuscript. Not being a tool, the typewriter never finds itself ready-to-hand, while its product is precluded from the presence of the hand. This third, this non-kind is the true monstrosity. In Heidegger's words:

> "The typewriter is a signless cloud. i.e., a withdrawing concealment in the midst of its very obtrusiveness, and through it the relation of Being to man is transformed. It is in fact signless [*zeichenlos*], not showing itself as to its essence."[40]

In its proliferation of ciphers, the typewriter fails to signify, it fails to produce a single sign. It is the epochal monster that fails to monstrate. Replacing diction with dictation, the typing hand fails to find the word. Being's relation to man is transformed; in truth, transfigured.

It is more than a lost cause. Heidegger has made possible a language in which the rare form *ent-zeihen*, can be heard in *ent-ziehen*, the withdrawing of phenomena, of the word, of Being itself. In the reflexive, *sich ent-zeihen* is a synonym of *sich ent-äußern*, commonly denoting an act of relinquishing or dispossession, but having been transformed through its post-Hegelian reception to an exteriorization which realizes and thus fulfils a thing's essence—*Ent-äußerung* becoming thus destination and destiny.

Heidegger never reaches this destination, never hears the fulfillment at the heart of the exteriorization of the typed word, the fulfillment at the heart of all inscription. From beginning to end, Heidegger's thought remains captive to what Leroi-Gourhan called "the phonetic subordination of the hand,"[41] or in Spivak's translation: "the phonetic confiscation of the hand."[42]

---

39 Heidegger, *Parmenides*, p. 86.
40 Heidegger, *Parmenides*, p. 85.
41 André Leroi-Ghouran, *Gesture and Speech*, transl. Anna Bostock Berger (London: The MIT Press, 1993), p. 404.
42 Derrida, *Of Grammatology*, p. 333.

4 The tool of tools: mnemotechnics and *Gestell*

Manual subordination has a history. The metaphysics of the hand finds itself already articulated in Aristotle:

> "Therefore the soul is like (*hōsper*) the hand. For the hand is an instrument of instruments (*organon esti organōn*) and the intellect (*nous*) a form of forms (*eidos eidōn*) and sensibility (*aisthēsis*) the form of the sensible".[43]

Much, perhaps too much, hinges on this *hōsper*, in this likeness, not of the hand to the soul, but of the soul to the hand. At the outset, both appear to be constituted by a foundational *indetermination*. If form is determination and definition, the form of forms is neither. Similarly the tool of tools is no tool—the hand as tool is useless and where it becomes useful it ceases to be a tool. By being nothing, almost nothing, the soul, just like the hand, becomes everything, almost everything. Through this indetermination, refracted into functional under-determination and semantic over-determination, the metaphysics of the hand opens a history of potentiality and domination.

It is a history dotted with moments of political and technical *emancipation*. The hand of the slave turns against the hand of the master, the hand of the woman against the hand of the man, the hand of humanity against nature, even if and precisely when, the latter is understood as the 'without-hand', i.e. what has no hand in human affairs, what is held, without being able to be held accountable, precisely because it is itself unable to hold—pure, limbless growth. It is always a struggle of hands.

In order to understand this struggle, it is imperative to understand the genitive, the generation of the hand as a tool *of* tools. For Stiegler, this amounts to the task of showing "that *philosophy begins in repressing its own question*,"[44] the question of technics. To ask this question is to return to the responsibility of the self, which *contra* Heidegger "is not alienated but constituted by technics, and made possible by technicity."[45]

As tool of tools, the hand is at the same time connected to memory, mnemotechnics and mediality. "Technics is indissociable from human memory"[46] Stiegler confirms and proceeds to exemplify the manuality of memory with regard to numeration:

---

43 Aristotle, *De Anima*, III, 432a2, my translation.
44 Stiegler, *Philosophizing by Accident*, p. 31.
45 *Ibid.*, p. 49.
46 *Ibid.*, p. 51.

"Numeration, which is first and foremost a motor and corporeal system: a set of gestures that have been learnt at length (to use fingers to count, then abacuses or multiplying tables, and finally the mind) and that have later become embodied under the form of a mental calculation, *in forgetting that it all began with the hands*."[47]

The hand initiates memory and thereby initiates forgetfulness. It presents itself as the origin that forgets itself. For authors such as Geoffrey Bennington, Tracy Colony and Nathan Van Camp this peculiar origin "reaffirms the exceptionality of the human."[48] On the one hand, the hand opens the space of indetermination; on the other, as tool of tools it opens the space of technicity. The one because of the other, yet neither without the other, complicating the manual origin: of humanity, of technicity, of memory. Stiegler:

"Since there is a margin of indetermination in the individual memory, there is neuronal plasticity that makes learning possible. But in human beings, there is a third memory that animals do not have: technics that both supports and constitutes this memory."[49]
And again:
"It is this direct transmission of individual experiences between generations that is forbidden in the animal kingdom, and this is why there is neither an animal 'culture' nor an animal spirit – or, to put it more simply, there is no heredity possible for acquired characters. But if you show me that certain apes have such cultures, I include them in the human world."[50]

This is the peculiarity of the human origin: it is never, nowhere purely human. This is the peculiarity of the mnemonic origin: it never becomes spirit and culture without technics. This is the peculiarity of the technical origin: it is impossible without its manual support. Finally, this is the peculiarity of the origin of the hand, the manual origin itself: it finds itself, always already supported by technics and memory; as such always already a human hand. 'Apes have prehensile organs', but the hand is human.

This 'default of origin', which signifies at the outset and at the very least also a complication of the origin, means that as a tool of tools, despite and precisely because the hand is no tool, it can only be thought of *as* a tool, it can only be approached *from* the tool. The genitive *of* in the expression 'tool of tools', is double, it arrests the hand within the domain of technicity without which it cannot exist. Without tools, the hand cannot be something that is not a tool and yet insofar as

---

47 *Ibid.*, p. 55.
48 Benoît Dillet, "Translator's Introduction: Radiographing Philosophy," in *Philosophizing by Accident*.
49 Stielger, *Philosophizing by Accident*, p. 51.
50 *Ibid.*, p. 51.

there are no tools, the hand certainly cannot be one. Without technicity the hand is neither a tool, nor something other than a tool; it is almost nothing. As soon as the hand becomes technical it is both a tool—the tool of tools—*and* something altogether other; it becomes almost everything. *Technicity is thus the move from double negation to double affirmation.* Not least, with regard to memory. It is through technics that the hand remembers; through technics that it forgets. Through technics the hand exchanges *anamnesis* for *hypomnesis*, gold for silver, presence for exchange itself: commerce and economy. *This* memory will support the technical constellation, the total system of techno-administration, -production and -communication.

This totality Heidegger calls *Gestell*. Translated as enframing, positionality or constellating, *Gestell* is the word that allows Heidegger to think the all-encompassing *apparatus*,[51] while suspending its Marxist legacy. The *Gestell* configures and modulates incessantly the essence of technology, being responsible in equal measure for the gas chambers and for mechanized agriculture—not only for the *eternal Treblinka* of the abattoir, but even for bloodless crop biotechnology. "Everything fits into this frame and there is no outside,"[52] writes Babette Babich. *Il n'y a pas de hors-Gestell*, the apparatus consumes all possible exteriority. It was there before the human figure, it will be there after its contours have been erased from the shores of memory. As long as there is world, be it singular or plural, the apparatus will have operated, for after all, "world and positionality [*Gestell*] are the same [*das Selbe*]."[53]

The pervasiveness of *Gestell* allows a revisit to the badly framed Heideggerian techno-obsolescence, which appears to underpin a forceful neo-Luddism. If the radio transforms the listener into a standing reserve of its medial apparatus, the hammer certainly does this already—from the outset, the tool of tools has set everything into motion. And yet, more important even than the intensification of *manipulation*, is that Heidegger seeks in the same hand, the hand that is clutching ever more tightly its prosthesis (from the remote control to the perpetual smartphone), and a force of resistance. In a moment of rare hope Heidegger seeks in the palm of the hand, the *authenic* hand, the space in

---

51 Georgios Tsadgis, "Love and the Apparatus: on a Hegelian Fragment," in *Can Philosophy Love? Reflections and Encounters*, ed. Todd McGowanforth and Cindy Zeiher (London: Rowman & Littlefield, 2017), pp. 119–131.

52 Babette Babich, "Constellating Technology: Heidegger's Die Gefahr/The Danger," in *The Multidimensionality of Hermeneutic Phenomenology*, ed. Babette Babich and Dimitri Ginev (Frankfurt am Main: Springer, 2014), pp. 153–182, 169.

53 Heidegger, *Bremen and Freiburg Lectures*, p. 49.

which "our inner and real core"[54] might be preserved from the domination of the apparatus. *Proper* use, a use that hearkens the call of Beyng and brings thus one to oneself, to the ownmost or the *propriation of the proper*, opens this space of ex-istance, the impossible exit to the outside of *Gestell*.

Babich points to the inconclusiveness of this hope and seeks to fulfil the quasi-emptiness of its gesture through the *practice* of wabi-sabi, the ancient practice of emptiness, emptiness here as *Gelassenheit*, a practice in which the hand lets go.[55] Whether there is hope or not, practices will have to be discovered, perhaps invented, for invention is the ineluctable destiny of the hand, a destiny that offers the possibility of an epoch.

It is not a call for a new God. Where the *Gestell* exhausts the horizon of *Vorstellung* or representation, it reduces the latter to *Eingleisdenken*, a thought that thinks across a single dimension, a thought therefore that fails to think. The essence of this unthinking thought is calculation, which *be-stells*, orders and requisitions the world, exposing man and nature to the uttermost danger.[56] Against *this* thought the hand operates, patiently, unfailingly. This is the lesson of Heidegger: through and against the latter. No proper is to be restored, no essence to be recovered. But the hand, as long as it is a hand—long after the passage of humanity—will always have one last maneuver.

5 Nearness: the *kairos* of the *cheir*

It seems then that the destiny of the hand is always at hand, always already here, or at least about to arrive, never too far. It is a spatiality that defines a whole epoch. For Warburton, Condillac and Rousseau language begins with a gesture to arrive at last at writing;[57] speech, the mouth and the ear, are here only a duct and a passage, the hand being the true origin and the eye the true destination of language. Accordingly, between the hand of gesture and the hand of writing, the mouth of speech and the ear of hearing are moments of transition. The aural staples itself between the pages of the manual.

The hand initiates the distancing of language, its dispersal, the loss of proximity. The gesture, at arm's length, contains this dispersal within the field of visibility—a

54 Martin Heidegger, *Discourse on Thinking*, transl. J. M. Anderson and E. H. Freund (New York: Harper & Row, 1966), p. 54.
55 Babette Babich, "Heidegger on technology and Gelassenheit: wabi-sabi and the art of Verfallenheit," *AI & Society*, Vol. 32 (2017), pp. 157–166.
56 Heidegger, *Discourse on Thinking*, p. 50.
57 Derrida, *Of Grammatology*, p. 270ff.

corporeal horizon: a gesture is possible, as long as there is a body, a body that sees. Speech, which succeeds gesture, operates across a comparable, albeit perhaps, shorter distance. To the extent that a signal reaches beyond earshot, speech constitutes a partial re-collection of the originary dispersal of the hand. Finally, the writing hand initiates a new epoch. The permanence and mobility of its inscriptions maximize the space of mediality. The movable print, the typewriter, finally the World Wide Web, drive ever further the limits of this spacing. But the decisive has already taken place, the hand has opened the medial space of its beyond.

What is crucial is to maintain in thought the correspondence and thus the responsibility of the eventual singularity of the emergence of writing, its propitious advent or *kairos*, which will set forth a whole epoch *together with* the textual ground in which this advent has taken place. Writing was always already there, yet writing did *also* appear, setting into motion a new epoch. The hand of the writing joins with the hand of gesture: connection and separation.

The *kairos* of the *cheir* deals thus the first and the second distance and between the spacing of each hand, the space of speech. Heidegger occupies this space, he is the thinker who thinks the call of Beyng between the two hands, between an absent arche-writing and the writing of the shrine, and again between presence-at-hand and readiness-to-hand: two times two hands and the transversal *gramme* that cuts across them. All along Heidegger resists the passage to the second hand, attempts to dwell in the first. The hand will for Heidegger signify, if not always the nearness of gesture,[58] certainly the gesture of nearness. As the hand co-ordinates with the eye it defines and measures without measuring *Ent-fernung*, de-stance or dis-stance, a spacing that is always one of proximity. Hand and eye, grasp and look:

> "What is supposedly 'nearest' is by no means that which has the smallest distance 'from us'. What is 'near' lies in that which is in the circle of an average reach, grasp, and look. Since Da-sein is essentially spatial in the manner of de-distancing [*Ent-fernung*], its associations always take place in a 'surrounding world' which is remote from it in a certain leeway."[59]

De-stance is not the metric remove of two points, a uni-*vocal* distance. Between the hand and the eye the call of Being presents itself as the most distant and the most proximal at once. Being is closer than all beings, yet it recedes into the farthest distance.[60] This is for Heidegger the destiny of existence:

---

58 Much would be discovered and understood in collecting the gestural moments of Heidegger's work.

59 Heidegger, *Being and Time*, §23, p. 99.

60 Martin Heidegger, "*Letter on Humanism*," transl. Frank A. Capuzzi and J. Glenn Gray, in *Basic Writings*, ed. David Farrell Krell (New York: Harper and Row, 1977b), pp. 210–211.

"Because man as the one who ek-sists comes to stand in this relation that Being destines (*schickt*) for itself, in that he ecstatically sustains it, that is, in care takes it upon himself, he at first fails to recognize the nearest (das *Nächste*) and attaches himself to the next nearest (*das Übernächste*). He even thinks that this is the nearest. But nearer than the nearest and at the same time for ordinary thinking farther than the farthest is nearness itself: the truth of Being."[61]

To sever the severance of distance, to listen to the call of Being and recover its proximity between the hand of the past and the hand of the future, is for Heidegger the task of thought. We have confronted the *problem* of this task, the onto-theological screen against which Heidegger recasts and reappropriates the whole history of being, re-establishing its suppositions at a deeper ground. The call of Being must thus be heard as a calling into question of two epochs, articulated through the emergence and establishment of the writing hand, *the evasive event of the text*. Having traversed the manual space one must turn to this call, interrupt the coordination of the eye and the hand, in order to examine no more the broken hammer, but the broken screen, the problem or limit of an epoch of a hand, which has only had an ear for itself.

Bibliography

Babich, B. (2014) "Constellating Technology: Heidegger's Die Gefahr/ The Danger," in Babette Babich and Dimitri Ginev's (eds.) *The Multidimensionality of Hermeneutic Phenomenology*. Frankfurt am Main, Germany: Springer, pp. 153–182.

Babich, B. (2017) "Heidegger on Technology and Gelassenheit: Wabi-sabi and the Art of Verfallenheit," in *AI & Society*, Vol. 32, pp. 157–166.

Derrida, J. (1997) *Of Grammatology*. London, UK: The Johns Hopkins University Press.

Derrida, J. (2008) "Heidegger's Hand (Geschlecht II)," in Peggy Kamuf and Elizabeth Rottenberg's (eds.) *Psyche, Inventions of the Other*, 2. Stanford: Stanford University Press, pp. 27–62.

Heidegger, M. (1968) *What is Called Thinking?* New York, NY: Harper & Row.

Heidegger, M. (1977a) "Der Spruch des Anaximander," in *Holzwege, Gesamtausgabe 5*. Frankfurt am Main: Vittorio Klostermann.

Heidegger, M. (1977b) "Letter on Humanism," in David Farrell Krell (ed.) *Basic Writings*. New York, NY: Harper and Row.

---

61 *Ibid.*, pp. 211–212.

Heidegger, M. (1977c) "The Question Concerning Technology," in David Farrell Krell's (ed.) *Basic Writings*. San Francisco, CA: Harper, pp. 307–341.

Heidegger, M. (1982) "Language in the Poem, A Discussion on Georg Trakl's Poetic Work," in *On the Way to Language*, transl. Peter D. Hertz (London: Harper & Row), p. 195.

Heidegger, M. (1985) *Prolegomena to the History of the Concept of Time*. Indianapolis, IN: Indiana University Press.

Heidegger, M. (1986) *Seminare, Gesamtausgabe, Band 15*. Frankfurt am Main: Vittorio Klostermann.

Heidegger, M. (1992) *Parmenides*. Indianapolis, IN: Indiana University Press.

Heidegger, M. (1993) "The Question Concerning Technology," in *Basic Writings*, transl. David Farrell Krell (San Francisco, CA: Harper), pp. 307–341, 333, 340.

Heidegger, M. (1995) *Fundamental Concepts of Metaphysics: World, Finitude, Solitude*. Indianapolis, IN: Indiana University Press.

Heidegger, M. (1996) *Being and Time*. New York, NY: SUNY Press.

Heidegger, M. (2002a) *Was Heisst Denken?, Gesamtausgabe, Band 8*. Frankfurt am Main: Vittorio Klostermann.

Heidegger, M. (2002b) "The Saying of Anaximander," in *Off the Beaten Track* transl. and eds. Julian Young and Kenneth Haynes (Cambridge: Cambridge University Press), p. 276.

Heidegger, M. (2010) *Der Spruch des Anaximander, Gesamtausgabe*, Band 78, Frankfurt am Main: Vittorio Klostermann.

Heidegger, M. (2012a) *Bremen and Freiburg Lectures, Insight Into That Which Is and Basic Principles of Thinking*. Indianapolis, IN: Indiana University Press.

Heidegger, M. (2012b) *Four Seminars*, transl. Andrew Mitchell and François Raffoul (Indianapolis: Indiana University Press), p. 81.

Kittler, F. (1999) *Gramophone, Film, Typewriter*. Stanford, CA: Stanford University Press.

Leroi-Ghouran, A. (1993). *Gesture and Speech*. London, UK: The MIT Press.

Stiegler, B. (2017) *Philosophizing by Accident, Interviews with Élie During*. Edinburgh: Edinburgh University Press, pp. 70–71.

Tsagdis, G. (2017) "Love and the Apparatus: On a Hegelian Fragment," in Todd McGowanforth and Cindy Zeiher's (eds.) *Can Philosophy Love? Reflections and Encounters*. London, UK: Rowman & Littlefield, pp. 119–131.

Justin Michael Battin

Ereignis and *Lichtung* in the Production of a Galaxy Far Far Away

Readers of Heidegger's work will undoubtedly notice numerous criticisms directed at the metaphysical tradition littered throughout. These criticisms show themselves with the most clarity in the essay *"The End of Philosophy and the Task of Thinking"* (1972), a remarkable piece that contains some of Heidegger's sharpest critiques of metaphysics. The critical stance Heidegger adopts throughout this piece proves necessary because of occidental man's ongoing adherence to an identity-within-difference approach; an understanding of the world where, in Heidegger's own words, "the superiority of beings over being has been decided" (1993 [1981], p. 59). This approach has fostered a world where our basic ontology is thus characterized by *the Framework* (*das Gestell*). Heidegger warns that existence both grounded and driven by *the Framework* leads to our treatment of entities – objects and beings like ourselves – as the standing reserve (*Bestand*), stockpile intended to be called upon for technological purposes (see Heidegger 1977b [1956], pp. 287–317). Heidegger bemoans that such a mindset has become omnipresent in all of occidental man's encounters and, due to the overwhelming preoccupation with beings, Being itself is hardly granted a whisper. To counter this dilemma, Heidegger urges us to abandon metaphysics and respond to the call of what is most thought provoking: presence. However, Heidegger's understanding of presence is anything but static. Whereas metaphysically derived presence draws from Descartes' *ego cogito* and is grounded by representational correctness (*orthotēs*), Heidegger's rendition of presence relies on disclosures and openings permissible because of one's situatedness and invested interaction with *things* in the world. When occupied with things and putting them to use in meaningful ways, we have a unique opportunity to find ourselves both being delivered over to being and *belonging* together *with* being (see Heidegger, 1969). This disclosive clearing, or coming into being, made possible through thingly interaction, is characterized by Heidegger as *Lichtung*. Although this specific word translates directly as clearing (as in a clearing in the forest), it can simultaneously be used as opening or lightning of what comes forth into one's phenomenological horizon. In my view, the significance of *Lichtung* shines the most brightly when considered in concert with another Heideggerian term, *Ereignis*, a German word that translates into English as *Event*.

Above all the words used by Heidegger throughout his post *Being and Time* (1962 [1927]) works, perhaps none require more consideration than *Lichtung* and *Ereignis*. In "Letter on Humanism," Heidegger himself even acknowledged that *Ereignis* had been the guiding word of his thinking since 1936 (1998 [1967], p. 241).[1] The reason for such importance is because *Lichtung* as *Ereignis, clearing* as *event*, stands opposed to a disinterested, metaphysical rendition of presence and instead speaks *alētheia*, the Greek word for truth. It ought to be known that Heidegger's interpretation of *alētheia* is not akin to the metaphysical variation of truth, but is rather unconcealment, that which becomes unhidden.[2] Whereas metaphysical truth is predicated on clear subject/object dualisms and conceived "as the correspondence of knowledge with beings, in beings" (Heidegger, 1977c [1972], p. 388), *alētheia* is the open region for everything that becomes present and absent. At first glance, and especially for those new to Heidegger's work, it may appear that the combination of absence and presence inadvertently smuggles in a Cartesian dualism. To counter such a concern, Heidegger notes that *alētheia*, as the open region, encourages an enclosure within disclosure. In his lecture course on Parmenides, Heidegger argues that disclosure is ambiguous. He writes: "at the outset, dis-closure could only say as much as un-veiling, the removing of veiling and the concealment. But disclosure or dis-concealment does not mean the mere removal or elimination of concealment" (Heidegger, 1992 [1982], p. 133). It is crucial to then indicate how the lack of elimination, or descent into oblivion, keeps distinct dualisms or binary oppositions at bay. Rather, the lack of elimination indicates a perpetual murkiness. For an inhabitable world to be disclosed or brought into view at all (and emerge from concealment), Dasein must pull from a set of previously forged relationships lying within the nebulous *alētheia*. The event (*Ereignis*) that is this pulling is grounded by a unique interplay with a specific in-place situatedness and an identification with the world (and the things that populate it) as it becomes disclosed and understood as available. Dasein, as a being who moves with anticipatory awareness (see also Ingold, 2000), is unique in that he possess the capacity to recognize how he achieves varying levels of fluidity with an environment he himself actively helps cultivate. Such

---

1   Heidegger, M. (1998 [1967]) "Letter on Humanism" (pp. 239–276) in William McNeill's (ed.) *Pathmarks*. Cambridge, UK: Cambridge University Press.

2   Heidegger writes: "we must think *alētheia*, unconcealment, as the opening which first grants Being and thinking and their presencing to and for each other. The quiet heart of the opening is the place of stillness from which alone the possibility of the belonging together of Being and thinking, that is, presence and apprehending, can arise at all" (1977c [1972], p. 387).

philosophical jargon may not initially seem so worthwhile in one's everyday busy life; however, I argue that a rediscovery of this distinct association will allow human beings a purview into their own unique affectedness. This specific combination permits us an invitation to come to grips with how we, through our intimate interactivity with things, identify with worlds we innately care for and pre-reflectively yearn to preserve, protect, and nurture.[3] When we, as Dasein, grip an instrument and employ it for a specific undertaking, such as a hammer for craft-making or a camera for taking photographs, we do so as a motivated entity interested in encouraging the ongoing solidification of the worlding world manifesting into our phenomenological horizon.

This chapter will explore how the combination of these two terms allows an avenue to remain free for the essential, to be open to the presencing of presence, specifically by situating them within the productions of *Episode VII: The Force Awakens*, *Episode VIII: The Last Jedi*, and *Rogue One: A Star Wars Story*, the first three outputs of Disney's *Star Wars*. My intent is to explore how *Ereignis* and *Lichtung*, when placed in context with these cinematic productions, offer a suitable route to counter the aforementioned danger of *the Framework*. In this author's opinion, Heidegger's ongoing quest to reinvigorate thinking by rescuing it from the graveyard of metaphysics provides perhaps the most invigorative pathway to recognize Dasein's potentiality, particularly as it concerns creativity and confidence in a world driven by technocracy. In the modern epoch, we are particularly obligated to attend to such a task before, to echo Heidegger, metaphysical thinking eradicates such possibilities. If we are to remember that it is in fact Being that brings beings to into presence, we must return to the ground, to a persistent wrestling with the interplay of unconcealment and concealment, a focus that faded from view with the arrival of Aristotle's taxonomy and his prioritization of beings over being.[4]

---

3   Such is the main argument of Heidegger's seminal essay, *Building Dwelling Thinking* (1977a [1956]).

4   Heidegger, in fact, bemoans that "*alētheia* is named at the beginning of philosophy but afterwards it is not explicitly thought by philosophy. For since Aristotle it became the task of philosophy as metaphysics to think beings ontotheologically" (1977c [1969], p. 388). Among the texts Heidegger suggests we revisit, none possesses more value than Parmenides' poem *On Nature*, an incomplete work that strongly advocates for mortals to trust the traversable opening made possible via *alētheia*, truth conceived as unconcealment, and the Fragment of Anaximander, where being is first named.

1 Living in being (and with *things*): *Ereignis* and *Lichtung*

Any explanation of these two terms must begin with the simple interactions Dasein has with *things*. Fundamental to such analyses is the way one chooses to decipher the word *thing*, as this is a quite a weighty term in Heidegger's vast lexicon. Today the word *thing* is too easily swapped with scientifically infused words like entity or object. Thinking of the term with an explicitly scientific mindset results in losing sight of a thing's fundamental *thingly* nature and thus our neglecting of the association of *Ereignis* and *Lichtung*. As we pre-reflectively move about and perpetually engage with the *things* of the world, it is imperative that we give careful attention to how a thing's *thingly* qualities have nothing to do with identifiable properties like weight, color, or its abilities. Rather than succumb to such disengaged subjectivity (see Taylor, 1995, p. 7) characteristic of meta-physical thinking, we ought to instead consider that the word's original meaning best translates to what we now call *gathering* (see Heidegger, 1971, pp. 163–180). Carol J. White unveils the link between thing and gathering by pointing out how Heidegger, in his explorations of Anaximander, considers the idea *to chreon* as *necessity*, linking it with the phrase that *things* pass in and out of existence by way of necessity. Necessity, in this instance, "is the name for that which unifies or makes a whole of everything that is" (White, 2005, p. 125). White continues by explaining how Heidegger recommends for readers to contemplate necessity in its historical and etymological context, and how this analysis inspires him to connect *chreon* with *he cheir* and *chrao*, two words that refer to "hand" and to "get involved with something," respectively. The purposes of drawing attention to such connections is to emphasize that the feeling of necessity or urgency appears to arise via our recursive practical engagement with things, specifically in ways that are often not of our own making. By this I mean that our being involved with things emerges, in part, by how things solicit us and engage us.

Let us use a nature photographer with a camera to further accentuate the point.[5] When a photographer walks along a path in a dense forest and suddenly

---

5 Consider, also, the carpenter's workshop, an example Heidegger often relied upon. The carpenter pre-reflectively draws upon his embodied understanding of how the individual tools fit together in a equipmental nexus for the purposes of "in-order-to". Heidegger coins this phenomenon as equipmentality. Equipmentality is a pertinent concept to raise here. When Dasein purposefully takes a thing to use in the aforementioned sense of in-order-to, he does so with pre-reflective consideration given to how that specific thing fits with other tools in an equipmental nexus. Such a nexus, when pre-reflectively gathered together and combined with Dasein's particular *Stimmung* (mood), contributes to the unfolding environmental character.

spots with his/her eyes a moment worth capturing, such as a pair of blue jays discreetly resting on a branch, the photographer does not discern whether to grasp the camera-thing and take the photo. Instead, the photographer finds the self involved in an intimate stitching, an event (*Ereignis*) that is being delivered over to a moment exemplified by unmatchable self-confidence, inspiration, and alignment of one's understanding of one's own unique abilities. A seamless flow is reached as the photographer becomes pre-reflectively aware of the actions that must be performed in order to produce a photograph that perfectly captures the moment *as it was felt*. This event is only possible because this photographer has embarked upon this walk armed with a camera, one that he/she merges with because of their previous accounts of recursive interaction and a motivation to employ it for a purposeful act. As a result of this unique ontological conjoining, the photographer pre-reflectively adopts a particular *Stimmung* (mood/state-of-mind), one that instills in him/her the possibility of embracing the world as photographically available. In this instance, the collective assemblage of Dasein and camera gathers the world together in such a way that stimulates a viewpoint where neither the bird nor its environment appear strictly as *bird* and *environment*, but rather as an intimately intertwined medley. The clear metaphysically fueled distinctions between the individual elements fade into obscurity and instead collectively shine in such a way that calls out and elicits, or appeals to, the photographer's pre-reflective know how. When such an intertwining of specific parts becomes realized, as in the moment it becomes felt, it unfolds to the photographer like a clearing in the forest (*Lichtung*) and, by succinctly gathering together, other possible interpretations or avenues for involvement fade away from view.

Should we focus simply on the camera's outward appearance or how it ontically differs from the entities with which it shares a collective relationship, as metaphysics would advocate, then we can never access it explicitly as a *thing*. We should never simply look at a thing's outward appearance or its *eidos* (idea); doing so would, in Heidegger's words, "have already dimmed it down to the uniformity of what is purely present-at-hand" (1962 [1927], p. 177). With the example of the nature photographer provided above, it should be evident that *thingly* qualities are meant to indicate the way that our interactions with a collection of related entities permits the unobtrusive gathering/unfolding of a world (or worlds) suitable for us to become involved with and inhabit. Thingly qualities reveal a specific intertwining of factical motivation and immediate situatedness. In taking a thing and putting it to use, we are thus delivered over to being (*Ereignis*) into a world where a specific *sense of the available* emerges into view within our phenomenological horizon (*Lichtung*).

Let us imagine, briefly, a sound stage being used for the now released film, *Star Wars: Episode VIII*. This stage will inevitably be populated with an assortment of objects: lighting and sound equipment, a plethora of video monitors and cameras (both stationary and mobile), meticulously constructed sets, and a few green screen backgrounds. There will also be a number of skilled practitioners scurrying about, both actors and behind the scenes personnel, all well aware of what ought to be done in order to achieve a successful shoot. It should be evident that each of these individuals, from the camera operator to the sound engineer, have a proficient understanding of the specific instrument under their jurisdiction and how it shares a relationship to other pieces of equipment littered about the set. Like the nature photographer discussed above, these actors and practitioners are immersed in an environment and, provided their flow continues unabated, it is unlikely that they will need to stop to ascertain how to appropriately perform their task or how one piece of equipment meshes with another. When watching them from afar, it becomes apparent that as they move about with motivation, they are engulfed in a state of *toward-which-for-the-sake-of-which*. This phrase, first appearing in Heidegger's *Being and Time*, is meant to indicate how Dasein is perpetually engaged with activities that matter and, equally, whose completion can be envisaged.

Also of note is that the aforementioned practitioners are not simply engaged with the things of the world, but are inherently alongside-others, others that equally possess an understood awareness of how each relies on embodied skillsets to competently fulfill obligations. The film's director, Rian Johnson, if skilled and capable, in particular must have an acquired sense of how these individuals (in addition to their performed tasks) intermesh, as well as the ability to foster and maintain an atmosphere conducive for collaborative productivity. Perhaps more importantly, because Johnson is a being being-alongside-others, he must place his trust in each Dasein co-inhabiting that world to fulfill their own tasks, ones unique to their very own specific situatedness.[6] Johnson, like the surrounding people responsible for specific things and tasks, is likewise in a mode of *being-toward-which-for-the-sake-of-which*. It is at this specific junction

---

6   With this statement I am making reference to the lesser but no less important worlds that form within larger, more comprehensive ones. For instance, although the worlds of lighting and sound are remarkably different from each other, each still offers their own unique contribution to the worlding world as a whole, yet they still remain distinct and somewhat self-contained because of the motivations and practices that ground them. For the world to exist and suture together as a world, an equilibrium across its parts must be pre-reflectively felt by the inhabitants.

that he, as a Dasein, should recognize that prior to assuming the role of Aristotle's *rational animal*, one resolved to map out and justify the creative choices made and explicate how each associates with numerous tasks at hand, is first (and foundationally) living *in* Being and always involved in a variety of meaningful tasks alongside relevant others. If a group of people were to wander on set, they will, if watching attentively, notice the various practitioners rushing about, intermingling and collaborating with their peers. The scene laid out before them is not one of individuals engaged in detached contemplation, but rather of a team spontaneously trudging ahead, pre-reflectively looking toward the inhabitable space of the available (see Dreyfus 1991, pp. 128–140).

It is at this moment that we ought to link Dasein's directional envisioning ahead with *Lichtung* and *Ereignis*, the two terms pertinent to this chapter. While the word *Ereignis* is strictly taken to be as the noun event in English, in German *Ereignis* as event can equally denote an occurrence or a taking place (and thus can assume a verb form). This distinction is imperative to point out because it emphasizes both a temporal dimension and an interactive element. When an event unveils, or takes place, we experience a temporal interplay of our being appropriated by the *da* of Da-sein (*the there* of Da-sein) and, equally, our appropriation of it. This temporal appropriation (as happening) can be understood via how Heidegger positions *the there* (the *da* of Da-sein). In *Being and Time*, Heidegger notes that *the there* should be fragmented into two distinct but connected parts: a here and a yonder. Breaking these down offers us a purview to see, as Heidegger writes, that:

> The 'here' of an 'I-here' is always understood in relation to a 'yonder' ready-to-hand, in the sense of Being towards this 'yonder' – a Being which is de-severant, directional, and concernful. Dasein's existential spatiality, which thus determines its 'location', is itself grounded in Being-in-the-world. The 'yonder' belongs definitely to something encountered within-the-*world*. 'Here' and 'yonder' are possibly only in a 'there' – that is to say, only if there is an entity which has made disclosure a spatiality as the Being of the 'there'. This entity carries its ownmost Being the character of not being closed off. In the expression 'there' we have in view this essential disclosedness. By reason of this disclosedness, this entity, together with the Being-there of the world, is 'there' for itself. (Heidegger, 1962 [1927], p. 171)

This lengthy quote, taken from *Being and Time*, requires unpacking. First, Heidegger's reference to a here and yonder implies that human beings, as Dasein, are always in some way looking ahead or projecting toward the possibilities of their inhabitable world. When human beings confidently engage with the world and the things within it in a meaningful way, they tend to envision precisely both the destination (as an objective) and a traversable path to achieve it. Dreyfus refers to this phenomenon of assured envisioning, the yonder coming into view with clarity, as *fore-having*, defined as a practical disposition that facilitates our understanding of the world prior to any explicit cognitive interpretation (see Wendland, 2014, p. 62).[7] Another way to consider such *fore-having*, as Wrathall describes, is as "a background readiness to act in ways that make sense ... which give unity and coherency to our activities in the world" (Wrathall, 2011, p. 106). As Dreyfus notes, "Dasein dwells in its background familiarity with the available" (Dreyfus, 1991, p. 202). When we, as Dasein, move in the world in conjunction with encountered *things* in the manner that which Heidegger proposes – de-severant, directional, and concernful – what becomes illuminated as available (in the sense of what can foster our continued uninterrupted progression) occurs quite similarly to one's traversing into a clearing in the forest. The temporal happening from the here toward the yonder discloses a number of possible scenarios within view. During this temporal unveiling, all extraneous concerns quickly conceal themselves and fade from possibility. This drawing out, the clearing like unfolding, can only transpire because we always possess some pre-reflective awareness or knowledge of our situatedness – it simply resides in the background and manifests depending on our mood (as *Stimmung*) and existential understanding of our established location.

The second aspect of Heidegger's quote to consider is Dasein designated as being there for itself. In my view, Heidegger means to direct us to how the temporal clearing allows for us to see both the active role we play in disclosing the world and how we are, in fact, invested in maintaining the uninterrupted continuation of that disclosure. In essence, we desire to establish a feeling of continuous at-homeness. In *Being and Time*, Heidegger proposes, rather adamantly, that Dasein must use this temporal disclosure to become a master of its moods (see Heidegger, 1962 [1927], p. 175). This mastery, in Heidegger's view, will allow us to view that we are perpetually being-affected and working to attune ourselves to the unfolding world. Having a sense of one's mood will shine a light on the intimate and immediate relationship they share with *the there*. This emphasis on the here and yonder of *the there*, with regards to both our investment and the necessity of Dasein to master the mood which shapes the progression from here to yonder, demonstrates that what would come to epitomize *Ereignis* was, albeit in a subtle manner, a concern for even the early Heidegger.

---

7   Wendland, A.J. (2014) "Language, Truth, and Logic: Heidegger on the Practical and Historical Grounds of Abstract Thought" (pp. 51–65) in Admir Skodo (ed.) *Other Logics: Alternatives to Formal Logic in the History of Thought and Contemporary Philosophy*. Leiden, Netherlands: Koninklijke Brill NV.

Richard Polt (2005), in drawing specifically from Heidegger's seminal text, *Contributions to Philosophy* (2012 [1989]), outlines seven intertwined facets essential for *Ereignis*: 1) Grounding the there, 2) Inception, 3) Reciprocity, 4) Emergency, 5) Gods, 6) History, and 7) Owndom. The first of these, the grounding of the there, speaks to the when and where of *be-ing* taking place, appropriating its own domain (see Polt, p. 382). This first facet is intended to emphasize the sheer possibility of *things* coming to a state, through the *Lichtung*, where they can be cultivated and questioned by the invested Dasein. The word *Augenblick* might best encapsulate this specific phenomenon, as it translates directly from German to English as *moment*. Both Luther and Kierkegaard characterize *Augenblick* as something critical and opportunistic, thus equating it with the Ancient Greek understanding of the word (*kairos/καιρός*). For Grant, *Augenblick* should be understood as both the moment of performance and the coming forth of time-space, as the two are intricately interlinked[8] (Grant, 2015, p. 213). The word *Augenblick*, thus conceived as critical, performative, and the emergence of time-space, further highlights that it is only through our motivated and necessary engagement with things that the world, as a meaningful, spatiotemporal plane, can be cleared into view.

Inception, the second facet, is the opening up or unfolding of our relationship to *Ereignis*. It is important to clarify that inception should not be understood as a definitive starting point, but rather as an enduring origin capable of unveiling new meanings, hence why Heidegger specifically uses the word *Anfang* rather than *Beginn*, as the former implies an opening whereas the latter implies a commencement or initiation of a process. This specific facet of *Ereignis* hints at our foundational relationship with *alētheia*, the Greek word for truth, described in the opening pages of this chapter as a nebulous space where meanings seem to quietly reside until extracted into view.

Reciprocity, the third facet, points specifically to the intertwined relationship between human being and *being* (as happening); each require the other. Being, according to Polt, "both needs and uses Dasein as its seeker, preserver, and guardian" (Polt, p. 382). From our vantage point, the interactions we have with things can only have meaning for us not simply because we are open to being's taking place and our being appropriated by it, but also because we can become alive to it. Although often unrecognized, human beings strive to embrace and

---

8   Grant, S. (2015) "Heidegger's Augenblick as the moment of Performance" in Grant, NcNeilly, and Veerapen (eds.) *Performance and Temporalisation*. Palgrave Macmillan: London, UK.

acknowledge the spatio-temporal character of their *being-in*. We often exhibit a pre-reflective recognition of moments that ought to be, in colloquial terms, taken advantage of; we then offer utterances about such temporal experiences to others, usually with either exuberance or disappointment. Such instances are particularly important because they offer an opportunity to see how humans, as Dasein, uniquely respond to meaning that does not wholly originate from within the self; in other words, our subjective self does not provide or designate meaning. Heidegger's later writings, specifically, clarify this notion by advocating that Dasein is not the ground for being, but rather a mere site of its disclosure, and the only one to which we have direct unfettered access. The ground of being's disclosure is *Ereignis*; however it requires a human being and his/her experience within the *Lichtung* to make itself apparent.

For the fourth facet, emergency, we should once again turn to Heidegger's interpretation of Anaximander, where he interprets *to chreon* as *necessity*. This interpretation was intended to draw attention to the unification of all that is, a moment that can only occur when one is drawn into action with *things*. As Polt suggests, "all necessity is rooted in urgency; beings emerge as meaningful only in emergencies … when what it means for them to be is called into question" p. 382). *Ereignis*, as the happening of *be-ing*, requires a specific response from us. Should any of us find ourselves compelled to engage as we enter into a mutual appropriation with *things*, we must not simply take the thing and act with it as we often normally do, but equally recognize both the role we play in this appropriation as well as our future potentiality within it. In essence, in emergency, our fundamental role in *Ereignis* manifests into view because we have arrived to such a state where being, and specifically our own, becomes an indisputable issue. Such becomes evident when we are capable of fathoming that we are part and parcel with the unfolding world.

When such an opportunity to recognize our role appears, it is equally because of a temporal meshing of the what Heidegger refers to as the fourfold, a complementary conjoining of earth and sky, mortals and divinities (see Malpas, 2006, pp. 219–230). The last piece of the fourfold, divinities, is yet another facet of *Ereignis*. In Heidegger's conception of the fourfold, the notion of divinities should not be confused with any deities originating from the west, such as the numerous terrestrial gods of Greece or the modern Abrahamic gods, but rather impersonal ones (see Borgmann, 1992, p. 35). Designating these divinities as impersonal is meant to eschew the typical western understanding of world-creating gods and instead point us toward the evanescent energies people feel when they find themselves compelled to engage with things, whether in isolation or in concert with a unified collective. Borgmann uses sports as an example, proclaiming that "a great baseball game ... played in a ballpark that highlights the most beautiful or exciting aspects of the city, can gather people together and focus them on what is best about the season, the community, and themselves" (Borgmann, 1992, p. 135). The divinities, as a distinct fragment of both the four-fold and *Ereignis*, speak to the irresistible force one may find the self swept up in, particularly with a speed, intensity, and remarkable harmony that, upon reflection, often appears unexplainable.

The sixth facet of *Ereignis*, history, should not be interpreted in a traditional framework via the establishment of dates, timelines, and events, but rather the evolution of how Dasein and being ongoingly involve and appropriate the other. As Polt describes, "Be-ing's history must be understood not merely in terms of change but in terms of how we belong (or fail to belong) to a unique dispensation of meaning. The dispensation lays claim to us, and we can succeed or fail in laying claim to it; this dynamic of claiming, or appropriating, is crucial to the happening of being" (2005, p. 382). The facet of history, in my view, provides an ideal segue into the last facet, owndom, which should be understood as the key to which we become ourselves in the most original sense, to which we succeed in laying claim to our destiny with *being*. In owndom, a human being understands the self *as* Dasein, as a temporal entity whose very *being* is an issue. In *owndom*, human beings embrace the world as a world full of potential openings and disclosures capable of traversal by way of their own confident nurturing of them.

Consider, once again, Rian Johnson on the filmmaking set of *Episode VIII*. As he orchestrates a series of shots for a scene and converses with his colleagues over what must be achieved, Johnson, if attuned to the environment in his own unique way, in addition to the things and other people within it, should be able to rely upon his own unique *fore-having* in order to successfully coalesce the distinct parts in order to produce a worthwhile series of shots. If the sequence of shots, once edited together, are intended to elicit an emotional response from the audience, the camera angles, lighting design, and performances of the actors involved ought to collectively allow for the artistry of cinema and the unique talents of each individual to shine at their very best. While a plethora of factors are necessary to consider in the construction of a scene, it should not be forgotten that a single entity, the director, is characteristically responsible for positioning each distinct person in their proper place, whether behind the camera or in front, in order to tap into their skills and obtain the desired result. This director, if capable of achieving such a feat, can only do so because he or she is open to being delivered over to *being*, grounded by an inhabitable location where one can flow freely. One's receptiveness, of course, is a choice that demands recognition; as Heidegger states, "man is essentially this relationship of responding to being, and he is only this … a belonging to Being prevails within man, a belonging which listens to being because it is appropriated to being" (Heidegger, 1969, p. 31).

To conclude this section, in drawing from Polt, it should be apparent that in order for *Ereignis*, as *Ereignis*, to show itself as significant, human beings must be fully engaged and immersed in meaningful activity. Dasein must deal with *things* that gather the world together in an existentially meaningful way, within the *Lichtung*, in order to reveal how such actions, as Malpas argues, act as a unique "sort of unifying and differentiating happening by which things come into presence, by which they come to be" (2006, p. 216). Moreover, within this manifestation, more importantly, such actions reveal "the way in which the givenness of given beings – including ourselves – comes into question for us. This happening is an urgent inception that grounds a site and initiates an age that has its own unique relation to the divine. This event requires Dasein just as much as Dasein requires it" (Polt, 2005, p. 383). With this Heideggerian lens, this chapter will now to pivot to the productions of *The Force Awakens*, *Rogue One*, and *The Last Jedi*.

2 The event of appropriation and engagement with *things*

Of all the discourses surrounding the production of both *Star Wars Episode VII*, *Episode VIII*, and *Rogue One*, Disney's first three feature film outputs following their acquisition of the franchise, perhaps the most prominent of these concerns the saga's professed reliance on traditional filmmaking methods. An abrupt return to this approach was inspired, in part, by the overwhelmingly negative backlash stemming from the overreliance on computer generated images, or CGI, and the ostensible lack of organicness displayed throughout George Lucas' widely panned prequel trilogy. Although no representatives from Lucasfilm or Disney have explicitly confirmed the reason for this production strategy, the immediate intention seems to be the establishment of a link between the original trilogy and the films currently in production.[9] As Myers (2015) demonstrates,

---

9 Over the last several years, even prior to Disney's acquisition of the *Star Wars* property, fan audiences have generally bemoaned the overuse, and in some cases abuse, of CGI, particularly for films with a built-in fan following (Peter Jackson's *The Hobbit* trilogy and Spielberg's fourth film in the *Indiana Jones* saga spring to mind). While these films were unquestionably successful from a financial stance, their collective ratings on both Metacritic and Rotten Tomatoes imply that neither is destined to ever be elevated to the pantheon of great motion pictures.

Disney has, in an effort to showcase the saga's dedication to tangible filmmaking practices, assembled a rather clear advertising campaign, one arranged around a direct central message.

The first featurette for *Episode VII*, produced for the 2015 San Diego Comic Con, opens with a series of shots of different clapboards being pulled away to unveil an on-location setting. Subsequent shots feature images of concept art juxtaposed with corresponding physically-constructed models. The voice of Mark Hamill, the actor who portrays the iconic character of Luke Skywalker, arrives to supplement the images being shown. He proclaims that the sets are real, the effects practical, and that this specific production will rely on evolved technology whilst retaining one foot firmly entrenched in the pre-digital world. As his sentence concludes, an image detailing the interior of a traditional film camera emerges into view. As the camera's gears churn and the ensuing clicking sounds enter into our audial cavities, the message becomes quite apparent: practical sets and tangible film has been revived; those in command have heeded the complaints levied at the prequel trilogy and, subsequently, have opted for the sequel trilogy to be created in a similar vein as the beloved original trilogy. Moreover, and perhaps more importantly, images have been included that position the action of the behinds-the-scenes personnel in concert with activity occurring within the scene itself, thus deliberately showcasing a unique sense of collaboration. From this view, the distinction of being situated on separate sides of the camera seem to take on minimal importance. Rather, the emphasis is on how each individual, regardless of their position, in the sense of both their physical location and production role, are intimately interlinked and fluidly immersed within a flow of collective involvement. Disney is clearly not interested in concealing the elaborate production process and potentially collapsing the cinematic realism of the on-screen *Star Wars* universe. Rather, it appears quite evident that they understand the richness and believability of the on-screen product emerges primarily from a vibrant and immersive behind-the-scenes milieu. This specific notion of collective unity, particularly on tangible sets with restricted green screen exposure, is a theme that continues throughout subsequent featurettes.

In a *Rogue One* featurette, for instance, the director, Gareth Edwards, is frequently presented as moving with the actors during filming. He neither hides behind monitors nor delegates his duties to a member of the production team; rather, he involves himself with his actors and allows himself to become engrossed within their budding performative dynamic. Driven by this involvement, he equally develops a specific attunement to the scene unfolding before him, and is thus capable of making improvised discernible judgments about whether particular aspects of it are working. We, as the audience of this featurette, witness him guiding the actors along, offering immediate feedback as the scene develops. Like Hamill's from the aforementioned featurette, Edwards' voice likewise acts as narration for the unfolding series of images, outlining the benefits of what occurs when intimately involved in the filming of a scene: "your heart is beating, and you're actually in this situation. You get something that you couldn't have planned … this is really where a film crew like this comes into their own" (2016).

Finally, the first featurette for *The Last Jedi*, the most recent *Star Wars* output, opens with brief clips of carpenters working, completed sets, workers pulling ropes, the actors being jovial with each other, and the director orchestrating a shot whilst standing in waist deep water, again demonstrating a continuation of the now established theme. A subsequent featurette, titled *Directing the Last Jedi*, explicitly focuses on the director, Rian Johnson, who stated that when supervising the construction of a new set, it initially appears difficult to imagine how the scene will unfold within it. Upon its completion, however, he declared that "once you show up to film it's overwhelming, at least until you get into the nitty gritty of working on it … and naturally that level of it goes away and you find yourself focused on making the scene work, getting the shots, and then once in a while you're taking a little break, sitting back, and you look around … you get the holy crap moment again. Concentrated works split up by holy craps!" (2017). This final statement, specifically, speaks to the ease by which we handle things and cope with our environment when engulfed within a flow. Furthermore, both the daunting task of supervising an entire production team and managing the enormous expectations of a rather unforgiving fanbase (it's a *Star Wars* movie, after all) seem to take on little importance once Johnson has found his flow. It is only once he takes a break from his directorial duties that his ability to ascertain the enormity of his situation shows itself as possible.

These featurettes, in addition to several others, all intended to support Disney's contributions to the *Star Wars* canon, attempt to link the notion of immersiveness with a person's engagement with tangible sets, props, and characters. For contrast, one should look closely to the experiential remarks of those working on the prequel productions (*Episodes I, II,* and *III*). The featurettes for the prequel films often depict settings of isolated actors dwarfed by a vast sound stage surrounded by little except green screen and partially constructed sets, each intended to be completed via computer animation. In one *Episode II* webisode, Natalie Portman commented that "pretty much every set has blue screen, even if it's out a window or something" (Lucas, 2002a). Her co-star, Hayden Christiansen, echoed this statement, proclaiming that "it's everywhere … I think I've been on one set where there hasn't been any blue screen" (ibid) Before proceeding, it should be known that my intent is not to diminish how these films were produced, as George Lucas' approach to the prequel trilogy was both experimental and groundbreaking. However, when watching these films, both Lucas' prequels and the Disney produced films, it is not terribly difficult to discern the vividness of one and the sterility of the other. To explain, consider what becomes of actors when they are surrounded by an environment composed entirely of green screen instead of rich, organic sets with an abundance of props and activity. When accomplished actors like Ewan McGregor and Natalie Portman, for instance, interacted with characters entirely created through a computer, they were forced to rely primarily on mental calculation in order to produce the desired performance, thus disembodying themselves from their situation and removing the possibility of full fluid immersion. While a stand-in actor may have been physically present and working opposite them, the performance they deliver is of no consequence because it will eventually be replaced via digital means. Any costume, facial gesture, or bodily mannerism provided by that actor will also be replaced. Ewan McGregor, the actor playing Obi-Wan Kenobi, professed the struggle he faced when attempting to perform opposite an inconsequential actor. In his words, this difficulty arose because he knew little of what the character would look like, how it would behave, and what mannerisms it may employ (see Lucas 2005). His confession reveals the unique challenge of engaging in a genuine and satisfactory manner when embodied investment is absent and when one is forced to rely primarily on rational calculation. Acting, very much like our everyday being-in-the-world, involves recognizing and responding to the subtle nuances of that environment. When speaking with another, for instance, facial expressions, gestures, and levels of distance are all considered and responded to accordingly, depending on the context of that situation. Rather than place his actors in environments that encourage immersion through interactivity, George Lucas instead situated them within a completely vapid environment, one that discourages risk taking, lessens possibilities for improvisation, and marginalizes context. As stated by Samuel L. Jackson in a subsequent webisode, "you have no idea what some of these things can look like or some of things will be. So you just kind of, you know, get out there and act like everything's normal" (Lucas, 2002b).

With Disney's *Star Wars*, specifically, what ultimately appears to be taking place is a unique sense of inspiration and satisfaction spurred by an immersive and engaging *being-in* where individuals are able to appropriately situate themselves based on a pre-reflective reading of the multiple interconnected things around them. This pre-reflective situatedness can occur, in part, because each individual inhabiting the set is an indisputable master, someone with a firm grip on their specific task. According to Stuart and Hubert Dreyfus, masters of a specific practice or trade are proficient enough with their profession that they trust their ability to transcend rules; the performer's "repertoire of experienced situations is so vast that normally each specific situation immediately dictates an *intuitively* appropriate action" (Dreyfus and Dreyfus, 1980, p. 12). They continue, stating that:

> The expert is capable of experiencing moments of intense absorption in his work, during which his performance transcends even its usual high level … this masterful performance only takes place when the expert, who no longer needs principles, can cease to pay conscious attention to his performance and can let all the mental energy previously used in monitoring his performance go into producing almost instantaneously the appropriate perspective and its associated action. (ibid)

As we transition from a novice to a master, we rely less on our powers of cognition and instead allow for ourselves to be, in essence, taken or called by the thing(s) before us. Mentioning the stages of skillful acquisition is important for two definitive reasons. First, these stages emphasize the practical richness by which one both obtains and performs abilities. Second, both the learning process itself and the responses to situations that arise are unique to the individual experiencer. Each of these are essential consider for how human beings understand themselves in an involved an immersive *there*. When we, as Dasein, move around the things we interact with on a recursive basis, we may find ourselves being led by those things, guided along in order to attain an ideal relation with them. We take them, handle them, and attempt to employ them such a way that allows us to ascertain an optimal grip on a given situation. Hubert Dreyfus coins this intercorporeal engagement with objects as *skillful coping*.

Skillful coping, the phrase Dreyfus uses to encompass a human being's interactions with tangible things, is meant "to indicate the mostly smooth and unobtrusive responsiveness to circumstances that enable human beings to get around in the world" (Rouse, 2000, p. 8). This responsiveness, like most actions in the world, occurs pre-reflectively and without any explicit mental configuring, and can equally be expressed, by existential phenomenologists in particular, via two crucial concepts: intentional arc and the tendency toward achieving maximal grip, both of which stem form Merleau-Ponty's seminal *Phenomenology of Perception*. The first of these, intentional arc, "names the tight connection between the agent and world, viz. that, as the agent acquires skills, these skills are stored, not as representations in the mind, but as more and more refined dispositions to respond to solicitations of more and more refined perceptions of the current situation" (Dreyfus). The second of these, maximum grip, "names the body's tendency to respond to these solicitations in such a way as to bring the current situation closer to the agent's sense of optimal gestalt" (ibid).

In order for an active agent to attain such a grip via an intentional arc, that individual must often endure an arduous trial and error process, typically under the supervision of a mentor. At the outset of learning any new practice, the student may look upon a thing, like a movie camera for instance, and immediately take note of its various gadgets and ontic properties. The novice may attempt to turn knobs or hold it, unsure of precisely how it should be placed within the context of the body. These initial moments are often distinguished by the novice's uncertainty and hesitancy. More importantly, perhaps, a learner's first encounters with a camera for cinema production often occur under the tutelage of another and are thus free from its commonly understood practical context. The camera in this instance, as a thing, shows itself exclusively as an object of study and the manifesting world coming into view is one of instruction. The novice is then taught a set of rules that must be followed, and is initially prohibited from experimenting beyond a set of enforced parameters. In other words, the learner's *Lichtung*, what is cleared into view, is rather limited and offers little possibility for maneuvering. As Dreyfus points out, however, "the learner obviously not only needs facts but also an understanding of the context in which the facts make sense" (ibid). Such is why instructors tend to gradually incorporate real world scenarios into their lessons, albeit ones that minimize risk and demand little from the student.

Dreyfus proclaims that while such scenarios offer the student an opportunity to recognize new aspects associated with their practice, further involvement is required in order to maximize their abilities. To increase competency and thus expand potential for action, students must take the thing and incorporate it into a situationally appropriate practical context. Such will allow them to encounter risks and encounter unforeseen dilemmas. This scenario, however, is a positive development, specifically because temporary setbacks force the novice to tighten their scope and seek strategies relevant only for a specific task or set of tasks; "as students learn to restrict themselves to only a few of the vast number of possibility relevant features and aspects, understanding and decision making becomes easier ... to avoid mistakes, the competent performer seeks rules and reason procedures to decide which plan or perspective to adopt" (ibid). Engaging with risks, although somewhat frightening and overwhelming, can result in a range of emotions, from euphoria to dissatisfaction or disenchantment, depending on the outcome of the student's choice and action. Positive emotional outcomes, in particular, strengthen skillful responses and, when handling the thing, particularly in real-world scenarios, the learner increasingly relies upon those strategies that have proven successful. Failed ventures are equally as important, as the choices made that fostered this result eventually fade from possibility. To use Heideggerian terms, they cease entering into the performer's phenomenological horizon. Should the performer continue to progress without significant obstruction, "the performer's theory of the skill, represented in rules and principles, will gradually be replaced by situational discriminations, accompanied by associated responses" (ibid). As one progresses from merely being competent to proficient, and then to being a legitimate expert, no decisions need to be made. Rather, experts rely on their embodied knowledge to accomplish their task. Deliberations are rare; "thanks to a vast repertoire of situational discriminations [the performer] sees immediately what to do. Thus, the ability to make more subtle and refined discriminations is what distinguishes the expert from the proficient performer" (ibid). Experts overwhelmingly rely on intuition and appear to have acquired the aforementioned *fore-having*, discussed in the previous section as an embodied confidence that remains in the background until specific situations spur its being cleared into view.

As alluded to with the aforementioned featurettes, a person's confident engagement with *things*, whether they take the form of props, sets, and other production participants, both unveils and delivers them into a world of unparalleled congruency. The words unveiling and delivering, while no doubt interrelated and cooperating in unison, should be approached as two distinct phenomena. As each member of the production toils away and tends to their work, they may, following Rian Johnson's utterances included above, find themselves working in concert with others in order to achieve a similar goal – the successful completion of a shot or the construction of a specific set, for instance. Because they are no doubt accomplished experts of their craft and familiar with how specific technological instruments correlate to their duties, they may simply take such instruments and apply them in ways appropriate for their assignment. However, because they are experts we should be mindful of their ability to make situational discriminations based on pre-reflective readings of their environment. It is this specific point that ought to be considered significant when applying *Ereignis* and *Lichtung* with the sequel productions. Because these films have adopted a traditional style of filmmaking and are allegedly relying less on CGI, at least in those scenes featuring characters interacting with each other, by default the production will be littered with more employees assigned to different on-set roles, particularly those dedicated to special effects and lighting. The reason for drawing attention to these individuals is because their very presence indicates the likelihood for increased activity and, by consequence, further potential for engagement with each other. While this interactive dynamic may seem commonplace, for these specific occurrences the aforementioned situational discriminations take on newfound importance, as they must uniquely account for how each individual's skillset intermeshes with those of their peers.

Consider the role of lighting technician tasked with illuminating a narrow corridor. If this lighting technician can confidently and competently comprehend the cinematographer's intentions, specifically in the sense of knowing what the cinematographer aims to achieve for a specific scene or shot, then this lighting technician should be able to discern how their own distinct skillset can bring out both the best (and most unique) qualities in the components that make up the particular shot; for instance, the actors and their performances, as well as the subtle nuances of the corridor itself. The same scenario can be applied to visual effect supervisors and operators, particularly those of the pyrotechnic and weather variety, as they must be prepared to initiate their effect at a precise moment, and not simply for execution's sake but also so that neither the actors nor other crew members are exposed to any danger. As these individuals begin operating their equipment in concert with others inhabiting the set, each may find themselves being delivered into a world grounded by congruent collaboration for the purposes of completing a designated task. This world is not dependent on the strict following of rules, but rather how motivated and skilled experts of their craft attune themselves to the *things* within their immediate vicinity, such as the various cinema related technologies and the people operating them, in order to foster a sense of camaraderie, togetherness, and trust. To both obtain and nurture this attunement, each individual must, to return to Dreyfus, heavily rely on their own intuition. Actors, for instance, may inadvertently notice something new in another actor's performance or recognize a previously unseen aspect in the setting, an aspect that may have become unveiled due to a particular lighting choice or chosen angle by which the scene will be shot. Upon recognizing this previously unseen quality, the actor may feel compelled to engage with that quality and take a risk of sorts, pre-reflectively altering their own performance into order to seize upon whatever it is they have noticed. From afar the actor may appear to forget that he or she is in fact a performer embodying a role and instead respond in a rather natural, seemingly unplanned way. The American director Stanley Kubrick was particularly infamous for demanding several takes so that he could, in essence, *break* the actors. Kubrick's meticulous style was in part inspired by his desire for the actors to jettison their trained professional behaviors and instead provide a more natural performance, one distinctively in-tune with their immediate surroundings. Kubrick attempted to foster an environment where his actors would stop contemplating their goals for the scene and simply *be*. The primary driver of this deliverance, of course, is that each individual on set, both actors and technicians, have numerous things

to play off of, vivid things from which they can respond. A filmmaking production that is populated with actors in costume, production technicians, tangible props, constructed set pieces, and the execution of practical special effects
provides a unique intertwining of characteristics where those inhabiting the set
can become involved in what surrounds them and make discernible distinctions
about both their interactions and how such interactions drive how each specific *thing* gathers in relation to other *things*. Moreover, involving the self with a
lively and immersive environment surrounded by perpetually gathering things,
what equally emerges is a world of collaboration. In order for the production to
progress smoothly and without interruption, each person must be open to their
environment in such a way that ignites their individual filmmaking instincts.
In other words, within each individual's *Lichtung* emerges not only one's own
potential for engaging with a thing or collection of things, but also how that
potential is interlinked with that of the others on set. Outsiders watching from a
distance should be able to note how each person bounces off the other, and how
each individual response fosters collaborative energies that forms and nurtures
a community of invested individuals. When considering this dynamic, it ought
to come as no surprise that many notable directors tend to regularly reunite with
a small cadre of actors and production crew members as each have, over time,
developed a finely tuned rapport capable of advantageously drawing out and
coalescing each unique skillset.

Secondly, as each individual is delivered over into this collaborative world,
their unique responses should equally unveil their role in both nurturing it into
existence and preserving its continuation, at least until the understood task has
completed. As outlined by Polt, *Ereignis* in the *Contributions* era Heidegger is
intended to stand as a moment where the wording world gathers in such as a
way as to unveil one's future potential aligned with being, where one understands
one's self situated in a congruency that only his or her self has access to (hence
the emphasis on *owndom*). While quantifying whether someone has achieved
a level of recognition is difficult to ascertain, I would certainly proclaim that a
pathway of sorts is at least being embarked upon, as each person interviewed in
the described featurettes characterized their on-set activity as a catalyst for *feeling*
human and recalling familiarity. Regardless of their role, those interviewed
spoke explicitly of how they individually appeared to have achieved a palpable
flow, a state of being that was both satisfactory and rewarding. Moreover, this
flow, upon reflection, seems to have equally sparked an appreciation for the
abundance of tangible materials, such as sets, props, and various filmmaking
devices, as well as for the distinct camaraderie that emerged while working collectively. Although not readily apparent, arriving to this state has occurred only

because these individuals have, to use Heideggerian terms, remained open to being's unveiling and embrace, undoubtedly sparked by the richness of the environment and a familiarity with *things* manifesting almost exclusively as *ready-to-hand*.[10] As the featurettes demonstrate, this embrace can at times provoke a sensation where the performer does not necessarily feel as though he or she has complete control. In fact, when deeply immersed, the performer may indeed feel as though they have been swept away, taken by a difficult to define force. The motivated movements of the body, in particular, seem to occur without any reliance on cognitive thought; the involved participant simply gets on with whatever they have been tasked with doing. In a *Rogue One* featurette called "Living in Star Wars" one of the principal actors proclaims: "we're doing battles and running and chasing, and we're just living the experience. You know, it's a true adventure. We're enjoying the ride in a galaxy far, far away." Of course, these participants are not lacking control; instead, they are merely responding to the unveiled world within which they find themselves situated. As masters of their specific crafts, each draws upon their aforementioned *fore-having* in order to progress without obstruction. By now it should be rather evident that, to again rely on Heidegger's terminology, this distinguishable flow, or congruency, has been attained primarily because of their engagement with known *things* (or a set of *things*) that contribute to the gathering of a meaningful world.

Recognizing this phenomenon as significant, at least for Heidegger, emerges because of a widespread calamity; "a bleak view of the present age" (Polt, 2005, p. 384). *Ereignis* for the *Contributions* era Heidegger is neither recognizable nor accessible in the recursive behaviors that encapsulate one's everyday life; rather, "it is only in a moment of emergency that *be-ing* can emerge" (ibid). In my view, this emergency can and should be applied to the current state of the Hollywood blockbuster, where the increasing reliance on CGI, particularly for the assembly of worlds and characters, has led to a dire state of flaccidness. As expressed in an article from the weekly trade magazine, *Variety*, "the ability to mount enormous battles featuring multiple super-powered characters, however, has become its own trap. And while the results can be visually astounding, the movies regularly feel as lifeless and mechanized as the technology responsible for bringing those visions to fruition" (Lowry, 2015). Ian McKellen, during the filming of the first chapter of Peter Jackson's *The Hobbit* trilogy, spoke rather frankly about the

---

10 *Ready-to-hand* (*Zuhanden*) is a term Heidegger uses to outline how objects show themselves to us in ways that unveil their everyday use. When someone, for instance, picks up a camera, as a familiar object it shows itself as an object for photographing daily life rather than a mechanical instrument with gadgets and ontic properties.

difficulty of being involved in such a production, confessing that he endured isolation and bouts of existential angst during long periods of green-screen-based filming (Pulver, 2013). In his own words, "at the end of the first day, I shed a tear and with my head in my hand and said, 'This is not why I became an actor,' forgetting the mikes were still on!" (Molloy, 2014). He even went so far as to admit that he was not entirely certain of what the film was about throughout filming, as the majority of his scenes were shot with backdrops and opposite characters intended to be added later via digital means! Christopher Nolan, a British director, has frequently acknowledged the benefits of using practical effects and shooting on location, as it allows for the actors, specifically, to properly situate themselves in a perceivable environment. In a promotional article for the 2017 film *Dunkirk*, it was stated that:

> Nolan believes that his job as a director is to try to recreate as closely as possible what it must have been like to be in the thick of battle. It benefits the performances, he said. That meant that when actors like Fionn Whitehead and Harry Styles are hovering under aerial bombardment, they're not doing it in the comfort of a studio. "When those boys are out there on those beaches and explosions are going off, they're going off," said Nolan. "There's no green screen. They're in it" (Lang, 2017).

Based on the above dialogue(s), it is rather apparent that both Nolan and McKellen recognize the connection between an immersive *being-in* and a rich and genuine performance, one that provides satisfaction to the individual performing the role. In an additional *Rogue One* publicity video, numerous participants spoke of their experiences in ways that echo Nolan's description, albeit from the other side of the camera. Among these was an unidentified man who proclaimed: "you'll actually compose shots that, if we were on a green screen set, you just wouldn't have known were available" (unknown speaker, 2016). Such statements, both from Nolan and the unnamed set worker, allude to a particular filmmaking environment as being an immersive and engaging *there*, where the temporal travelling from the here to the yonder shows itself with remarkable clarity, particularly via how it allows for the inspirational manifestation of one's acquired *fore-having* and the confidence to make improvised deviations.

In my view, the steady upswing in the use of practical effects has emerged in part because of a gradual desire to tap into the positive sensations and the productive powers that materialize when we are simply *letting be*. Such practices demonstrate a clear response to a desire for more nuanced productions, one's grounded in practical engagement, where those involved can reside within an open space where what comes forth can, like a clearing in the forest, to do so unobtrusively, yet with an *event* like quality. In Heidegger's view, the altering of one's attitude that accompanies the arrival of a season or a quiet walk in the woods speak to one's situatedness, one's immediate being-there; however I argue that the clearing for *Ereignis* can likewise show itself in a chaotic filmmaking environment, provided those within it have remained open to its taking place, by allowing the self to engage with things in such a way that allows a space for its unveiling. Via an appreciation of our temporal deliverance to *Ereignis*, the taking place of being through its unveiling in our *Lichtung*, we can equally experience *Gelassenheit*, which, according to Dreyfus, is "a serene openness to a possible change in our understanding of being" (1991, p. 339). *Gelassenheit*, as used by Heidegger, implies a mode of dwelling where our interactions with *things* allow for a poetic revealing, one unencumbered by the restrictive, calculative view of technology, where the things emerge fixed as resources to be utilized. Heidegger uses the term to specify a releasement, a letting be or comportment "which enables us to keep open to the meaning hidden in technology" (Heidegger, 1966, p. 55). This specific comportment to the world allows human beings to reach "a new ground and foundation upon which we can stand and endure in the world of technology without being imperiled by it" (ibid). What is needed to counter such a condition, in Heidegger's estimation, is simple, poetic reflection and an openness to being's embrace via *Ereignis*. We must develop a specific attunement to being via our negotiated involvements with the meaningful things around us. These negotiations are imperative for the development and acquisition of unique skills like cooking, sporting, and even different facets of film-making. Because we are spatio-temporal beings capable of improvising and, by consequence, acquiring new knowledge, we are equally capable acquiring the aforementioned (and necessary) *fore-having*. As we acquire such skills and put them to use, specifically in ways that disclose how they matter to us, we increasingly become adept at recognizing how both we and the environment appropriate the other, albeit perhaps not necessarily via dense Heideggerian terms!

3 Conclusion

This chapter has positioned *Ereignis* and *Lichtung*, two of the most essential ideas that emerged in Heidegger's late work, with the productions of Disney's first three *Star Wars* films, in order to argue that our living in Being becomes most apparent when we involve ourselves with *things* in such a way that can illuminate their *thingly* nature. Our engagement with things should prompt our temporal deliverance into a world that matters to us, where our being human shows itself in a rather deliberate way, and where things unveil themselves outside of the restrictive view of technology. Our use of things should disclose the unique role we play in the manifestation of that world via our motivational, pre-reflective, and improvised activities. The primary reason for focusing on and linking these two Heideggerian ideas is because they, when considered together, offer an insightful avenue to shine a light on how immersive worlds not only become inhabitable and meaningful to us in a temporal fashion, but also how such immersive worlds can offer new pathways and levels of richness where human beings can revitalize a sense of individual creativity and their belongness with being.

As Heidegger warns, too often human beings move about in everyday life and attempt to inflict their will on things and environments, removing the potential for hearing and responding to being's call. Accepting a world with *Das Gestell* as its foundation will increasingly lead to our being closed off from off from improvisation, individual exploration and creativity, and the benefits that manifest when working together alongside diverse and meaningful things. The general ambivalence toward cinematic productions that ostensibly lack organicness, those films whose overwhelming reliance on CGI diminishes the interconnected fabric between human beings, things, and worlds, should be contrasted with the celebratory discourses surrounding films like the *Star Wars* sequel trilogy, Christopher Nolan's films, and especially *Mad Max: Fury Road*, an action film nominated for the 2016 Academy Award for Best Picture.

It is equally important to state that this piece has not intended to vilify CGI, as it is indeed a remarkable and often useful tool in cinema today. Pixar, specifically, has built an extensive library of films internationally renowned for their wide appeal, socially conscientious stories, and stunning animation, all via the use of digital means. However, in productions that involve mostly human participants, we should be wary of relying too extensively on digital means for the construction of worlds and characters and instead encourage the proliferation of filmmaking strategies that can foster a sense of togetherness and ignite an attunement to one's own humanity grounded in one's own *being-there*. We should remember that human beings, as Dasein, shine at their very best when taking things and putting them to use alongside others within environments that are capable of stimulating both the unique *fore-having* of individuals, as well the *fore-having* that emerges when those individuals work in unison. If we simply treat things as exploitable resources in order to follow a laid-out plan, regardless of how well orchestrated it is, we will endure a paralyzing closing down of our unique and individual selves. We must, instead, seek avenues where the *Da* of our Dasein can not only manifest into view, but do so in such a way as to unveil its existential importance to us.

Bibliography

Borgmann, A. (1992) *Crossing the Postmodern Divide*. Chicago, IL: University of Chicago Press.

Directing the Last Jedi. YouTube Video. 2:14. 25 Oct 2017. Date accessed: 12 December 2017. Accessible from: https://www.youtube.com/watch?v=gHgBk2fLLHY

Dreyfus, H. (1991) *Being-in-the-World: A Commentary on Heidegger's Being and Time, Division 1*. Cambridge, MA: MIT Press.

Dreyfus, H. (year not given) "A Phenomenology of Skill Acquisition as the Basis for a Merleau-Pontian Non-representationalist Cognitive Science". Date accessed: 12 December 2017. Accessible from: http://www.irafs.org/irafs_1/cd_irafs02/texts/dreyfus.pdf

Dreyfus H. and Dreyfus S. (1980) "A Five-Stage Model of the Mental Activities Involved in Directed Skill Acquisition". Berkeley, CA: Operations Research Center, University of California. Date accessed: 12 December 2017. Accessible from: http://www.dtic.mil/dtic/tr/fulltext/u2/a084551.pdf

Grant, S. (2015) "Heidegger's Augenblick as the Moment of Performance" in Grant, J. NcNeilly, and M. Veerapen (eds.) *Performance and Temporalisation*. Palgrave Macmillan: London, UK; pp. 213–229.

Heidegger, M. (1962 [1927]) *Being and Time*. New York; NY: Harper and Row Publishers.

Heidegger, M. (1966) "Memorial Address" in John M. Anderson (ed.) *Discourse on Thinking*. New York, NY: Harper and Row Publishers; pp. 43–57.

Heidegger, M. (1969) "The Principle of Identity" in Joan Stambaugh (ed.) *Identity and Difference*. Chicago, IL: University of Chicago Press; pp. 21–41.

Heidegger, M. (1971) "The Thing" in Albert Hofstadter (ed.) *Poetry, Language, Thought*. New York, NY: Harper and Row Publishers; pp. 164–180.

Heidegger, M. (1977a [1956] "Building, Dwelling, Thinking" in John David Krell (ed.) *Martin Heidegger: Basic Writings*. San Francisco, CA: Harper and Row Publishers; pp. 319–340.

Heidegger, M. (1977b [1956] "The Question Concerning Technology" in John David Krell (ed.) *Martin Heidegger: Basic Writings*. San Francisco, CA: Harper and Row Publishers; pp. 283–318.

Heidegger, M. (1977c [1969]) "The End of Philosophy and the Task of Thinking" in John David Krell (ed.) *Martin Heidegger: Basic Writings*. San Francisco, CA: Harper and Row Publishers; pp. 369–392.

Heidegger, M. (1992 [1982]) *Parmenides*. Bloomington, IN: Indiana University Press.

Heidegger, M. (1993 [1981]) *Basic Concepts*. Bloomington, IN: Indiana University Press.

Heidegger, M. (1998 [1967]) "Letter on Humanism" in William McNeill (ed.) *Pathmarks*. Cambridge, UK: Cambridge University Press; pp. 239–276.

Heidegger, M. (2012 [1989]) *Contributions to Philosophy (Of the Event)*. Bloomington, IN: Indiana University Press.

Ingold, T. (2000) *The Perception of the Environment: Essays in Livelihood, Dwelling, and Skill*. London, UK: Routledge.

Lang, B. (2017) "Christopher Nolan on Dunkirk: There Was No Green Screen" in Variety; 10 Sept. 2017. Accessible from: http://variety.com/2017/film/news/christopher-nolan-dunkirk-no-green-screen-1202553547/

Lowry, B. (2015) "'Avengers' and the Age of CGI Overkill in Hollywood" in Variety May 4, 2015. Date accessed: 12 December 2017. Accessible from: http://variety.com/2015/film/news/avengers-age-of-ultron-cgi-special-effects-1201487125/

Lucas, G. (2002a) "12 Part Web Documentary: Here We Go Again." *Star Wars Episode II: Attack of the Clones*. Disc 2. Directed by George Lucas, 20th Century Fox.

Lucas, G. (2002b) "12 Part Web Documentary: It's All Magic." *Star Wars Episode II: Attack of the Clones*. Disc 2. Directed by George Lucas, 20th Century Fox.

Lucas, G. (2005) "15 Part Web Documentary: Becoming Obi-Wan." Star Wars Episode III: Revenge of the Sith. Disc 2. Directed by George Lucas. 20th Century Fox.

Malloy, A. (2014) "Ian McKellen on filming The Hobbit 'I had no idea what I was doing'" in The Independent, 5 December 2014. Date accessed: 12 December 2017. Accessible from: https://www.independent.co.uk/arts-entertainment/films/news/ian-mckellen-on-filming-the-hobbit-i-had-no-idea-what-i-was-doing-9905416.html

Malpas, J. (2006) *Heidegger's Topology: Being, Place, World*. Cambridge, MA: MIT Press.

Myers, A. (2015) "A Certain Point of View: Authorship, Authenticity, and Materiality in Behind-the-scenes Discourse for Star Wars: The Force Awakens." Paper presented at the 2015 Society for Cinema and Media Studies Conference, Atlanta, GA, April 2015.

Polt, R. (2005) "Ereignis" in Wrathall, and Dreyfus (eds.) *A Companion to Heidegger*. Malden, MA: Blackwell Publishing; pp. 375–391.

Pulver, A. (2013) "The Hobbit's Gandalf almost prove a greenscreen too far for Ian McKellen" in *The Guardian*, 20 Nov 2013. Date accessed: 12 December

2017. Accessible from: https://www.theguardian.com/film/2013/nov/20/
the-hobbit-gandalf-ian-mckellen-almost-quit-acting

Rogue One: A Star Wars Story Featurette. YouTube Video. 2:04. 17 Nov. 2016.
Date accessed: 12 December 2017. Accessible from: https://www.youtube.
com/watch?v=HSeovXwmOR0

Rogue One: A Star Wars Story – Living in Star Wars. YouTube Video. 1:07. 28
Nov. 2016. Date accessed: 12 December 2017.Accessible from: https://www.
youtube.com/watch?v=Js4ia1g4GMU.

Rouse, J. (2000) "Coping and its Contrasts" in M. Wrathall, and J. Malpas
(eds.) *Heidegger, Coping, and Cognitive Science: Essays in Honor of Hubert
L. Dreyfus* (Vol. 2). Cambridge, MA: MIT Press; pp. 7–28.

Star Wars: The Force Awakens Comic Con Reel. YouTube Video. 3:42. 10 July
2015. Date accessed: 12 December 2017.Accessible From: https://www.
youtube.com/watch?v=CTNJ51ghzdY.

Star Wars: The Last Jedi behind the Scenes. YouTube Video. 2:58. 15 July 2017.
Date accessed: 12 December 2017. Accessible from: https://www.youtube.
com/watch?v=ye6GCY_vqYk.

Taylor, C. (1995) *Philosophical Arguments*. Cambridge, MA: Harvard
University Press.

Wendland, A.J. (2014) "Language, Truth, and Logic: Heidegger on the
Practical and Historical Grounds of Abstract Thought" in Admir Skodo
(ed.) *Other Logics: Alternatives to Formal Logic in the History of Thought
and Contemporary Philosophy*. Leiden, Netherlands: Koninklijke Brill NV;
pp. 51–65.

White, Carol J. (2005) "Heidegger and the Greeks" in M. Wrathall, and
H. Dreyfus (eds.) *A Companion to Heidegger*. Malden, MA: Blackwell
Publishing; pp. 141–155.

Wrathall, M. (2011) *Heidegger and Unconcealment: Truth, Language, and
History*. Cambridge, UK: Cambridge University Press.

Eve Forrest and Leighton Evans

Feeling Photography: Exploring Care, Attunement, and Dwelling through the Work of Andre Kertész

1 Experiencing photography, doing phenomenology

Before approaching a Heideggerian account of photographic practice, it is useful to briefly outline some of the philosophical tropes that have dominated discussions about photography over the last 150 years. These have been less phenomenological and more Cartesian in character, emphasizing the link between 'thinking and seeing, visual perception and certainty'[1]. Descartes was of the belief that sight was the 'noblest of the senses...there is no doubt that inventions which serve to augment its power are among the most useful that there can be'[2]. This led to the photograph representing the positivist ideal of objectivity, a form of absolute truth in everyday life[3]. Although recent scholarship, particularly with the advent of digital photography and the internet, has moved away from this idea[4] the adage of 'not believing something until you see it' still resonates deeply in 21st century, an era characterized by pervasive photography practices[5]. Although photographs were often portrayed as explicit documents of reality this was a self-made myth. At their very inception, images are always a deliberate construction; they are an account of how the photographer wishes to represent or frame the scene in front of the lens.

Framing a scene is more than just optical awareness: 'the essence of the image is to be altogether outside, without intimacy'[6]. By the same association, the photographer has also been seen as a distant and detached observer which is perhaps

---

1   Wylie John, *Landscape* (London: Routledge, 2007), p. 146.

2   Jay Martin, *Downcast Eyes: The Denigration of Vision in Twentieth-century French Thought* (London: University of California Press, 2003), p. 21.

3   Sekula Allan, "The body and the archive". In: *The Contest of Meaning: Critical Histories of Photography*, ed. Richard Bolton (Cambridge, Massachusetts: MIT Press, 1989).

4   Rubenstein Daniel and Katrina Sluis, A Life More Photographic, *Photographies*, Vol 1 (2008), pp. 9–28.

5   Hand, *Ubiquitous Photography*.

6   Blanchot Maurice cited in Roland Barthes *Camera Lucida* (London: Vintage, 1984), p. 106.

the reason that there has been considerably less work centered upon the routine practices of the photographer[7]. The camera acts as a way of separating body and vision, just as it is supposed to temporarily sever the scene from time itself. This means that photographers are viewed as little more than a bundle of talented rods, retinas, and cones, apart from their subject matter and the wider world that surrounds them. These ideas not only jar with a phenomenological under-standing of how everyday life is experienced, they gloss over the many inter-esting and often contradictory facets of being a photographer-in-the world and dwelling inside its environs. Far from being a detached and objective observer, we argue (from a Heideggerian perspective) that the photographer with their camera is fully immersed in the world, fascinated by the stuff and things of everyday life.

2 André Kertész: a life

The subject of this Heideggerian analysis of the photographer is André Kertész. Kertész was born in Hungry in 1894 and was a prolific photographer both in Europe and America. In 1912 his mother bought him a camera, which he taught himself to use, and it accompanied him into his military service in the Austro-Hungarian war. During this time he honed his craft, taking pictures of various scenes and people he found on his travels with the army. Greenough[8] notes that Kertész 'began the war as a novice but emerged four years later... with a more articulated approach and a more nuanced understanding of the medium's power and potential'. In 1918 he trained to be a stockbroker, a career that his lower middle class Jewish family encouraged but one which he had no intention of pur-suing. Instead he continued to take photographs and became actively involved in Hungarian artistic circles, mixing with painters and writers who 'sought to find the roots of a new Hungarian identity'[9] in the aftermath of the war.

By the time he moved to Paris from Budapest in 1925, Kertész was an accom-plished photographer with a refined style. He had a foot in both street and arts practice and a budding reputation. Although he struggled to make a living from his work to begin with, his perseverance led to many acclaimed exhibitions and

---

7   Shove Elizabeth, Martin Hand, Jack Ingram and Matthew Watson, *The Design of Everyday Life* (Oxford: Berg, 2007).

8   Greenough Sarah, "A Hungarian diary: 1894–1925". In: *Andre Kertesz: The Eternal Amateur*, eds. Sarah Greenough, Robert Gurbo and Sarah Kennel (Washington: Washington University Press, 2005), p. 11.

9   Greenough, "A Hungarian diary: 1894–1925", p. 15.

later on wider connections to the new Dadaist circle of artists and writers living in Paris.

Although he later proclaimed to eschew surrealism and instead declare his photography 'absolute realism', his work at this time was unquestionably influenced by the poetry and philosophy of the surrealists who also fully embraced photography as an art form[10]. Increasing tensions in Europe meant that Kertész and his wife were not safe in Paris and they decided to leave France for America in 1936. However he did not settle easily upon arrival in New York and paid work was much harder to find. Kertész struggled to find commissions, permanent contracts or any recognition for over a decade. However in 1947 he was offered a role with Conde Nast to photograph interiors for their magazine Homes and Gardens. Although he felt the job was beneath him, an impoverished Kertész had few options and he accepted the work. He continued at the magazine until 1961 after which he pledged to give up what he termed 'slave work' and instead 'embrace his roots and become an amateur again'[11]. In the twilight of his career Kertész began to get more recognition, which he believed was long overdue. His later resurgence included many major worldwide retrospectives and exhibitions and he worked right up until his death in 1985.

3 The camera, the thing

Our analysis of Kertész's work centers on the use of the camera in revealing entities in the world, and revealing a world of meaning beyond the image. In understanding how a particular orientation to the camera provides the affordance to make visible particular entities in the everyday world, we take a Heideggerian approach to the camera as 'Thing' and how the 'Thing' does work in the world. A useful way of understanding this approach is to consider the contention that we are familiar with objects and places due to our experiences of using them, not by holding them in an intentional manner, or considering them in abstract cognitive ways.

One of the most interesting things about photography practice, when it is done frequently, is the sense of forced serendipity or an expectation of chance encounters that happens in the creation of images. Most photographers carry a camera with them at all times, and by carrying a camera, it begins to alert them to

---

10   Greenough, "A Hungarian diary: 1894–1925", p. 11.
11   Gurbo Robert, "Circle of confusion". In: *Andre Kertesz: The Eternal Amateur*, eds. Sarah Greenough, Robert Gurbo and Sarah Kennel (Washington: Washington University Press, 2005), p. 163.

the imaginative possibilities around them[12]. As photographers begin to use their camera and become interested in the photography of others, they end up seeing the world differently. However, they are purposefully looking for an opportunity to present itself and in doing so they see something where others, who do not habitually use a camera, do not. To think photographically also means to see the world imaginatively and find creativity within everyday life.

To be successful at photography also requires an attunement to the everyday surroundings. There is however an even deeper paradox here regarding photography: in order to see the world and reveal it, there must also be a partial withdrawal in order to see it from a certain distance. With regards to the photographer's engagement with the world, Heidegger explains how Dasein is in the world (that is, how it is involved with the world and the entities in that world) through the concept of *care*. Care is "the structure of Dasein itself"[13] and is both an existential (ontic) and ontological category of Dasein; Dasein necessarily cares for the world through its involvement with equipment or concern and through concern-for others (*Fürsorgen*). Care is part of the structure of Dasein as a thing in itself (ontologically), and existentially is how Dasein is related to the world through its care for the world: "The authentic relation of the world and Dasein is care and meaningfulness"[14].

Therefore, care (taking up of things in use) is how the world becomes meaningful to Dasein. in the context of the photography, care for the camera is how the world 'through the lens' becomes meaningful, and through taking the camera into care this is the possibility (through the orientation to the world through care) of making entities in the world visible. This is because care is concerned with Dasein and other entities that are Dasein (other humans), as well as equipment and things or objects in the world. The understanding that Dasein has is not factual – that is the knowledge derived from empirical or positivist observation that is the method of the empirical sciences – but is instead an understanding rooted in the way Dasein does things. Dasein's understanding of the world does not come from a factual understanding of the world, but instead *knowing how* to live in the world.

---

12 Forrest Eve, "Exploring everyday photographic routines through the habit of noticing". In: *Digital Photography and Everyday Life: Empirical Studies on Material Visual Practices*, eds. Asko Lehmuskallio and Edgar Gomez Cruz (London: Routledge, 2016).

13 Heidegger Martin, *History of the Concept of Time* (Indianapolis: Indiana University Press, 1992), p. 293.

14 Heidegger *History of the Concept of Time*, p. 221.

This explanation of care does not explain what a 'Thing' (in this case, the camera) does with regards to revealing the world. In Heideggerian parlance, when a Thing "things", it draws together elements in the world in a manner (rather than process) Heidegger called the fourfold[15]. The idea of the fourfold – earth, sky, mortals, divinities – is a simple 'oneness' or unity[16] that is how entities in the world exist if an entity has presence in the world as a 'Thing' rather than a simple object. Harman[17] makes much of the unfavorable reception that Heidegger's concept of the fourfold has received from not only critics of Heidegger's philosophy, but also commentators that are favorably disposed.

As a result, many commentaries of Heidegger's philosophy ignore the concept of the fourfold altogether, and other critics are dismissive of the concept as 'pious gibberish'[18]. This may be for a number of reasons: the particularly poetic character of both the writing and the sentiment of the fourfold, the seeming irrelevance of the discussion of multiple essences from a philosopher synonymous with technological essentialism, or just the sheer oddness of the idea itself. Harman[19] insists on interpreting the fourfold in an extension of his interpretation of all being as akin to the as structure of tools, that is in a constant cycle of withdrawal and revealing. Others, in particular Young[20] and Wrathall[21] consider the fourfold as the pivotal aspect of Heidegger's concept of dwelling. Harman's interpretation of withdrawal and revealing is particularly useful to this discussion of making entities visible in the world through photography, as it emphasizes the interplay between visibility and absence in everyday life.

4 Feeling photography

'Seeing is not enough; you have to feel what you photograph' (André Kertész).

To successfully practice photography means balancing withdrawing and revealing as two separate elements, which at first can sound counterintuitive. However, in order to reveal things with photography, there must be at first a

---

15 Heidegger Martin, *Basic Writings* (London: Routledge, 2008), p. 243.
16 Wrathall Mark, *How to Read Heidegger* (New York: W. W. Norton, 2006), p. 112.
17 Harman Graham, *Tool-Being: Heidegger and the Metaphysics of Objects* (London: Open Court, 2002), p. 190.
18 Harman, *Tool-Being: Heidegger and the Metaphysics of Objects*, p. 190.
19 Harman, *Tool-Being: Heidegger and the Metaphysics of Objects*, p. 205.
20 Young Julian, "The Fourfold". In: *The Cambridge Companion to Heidegger (2nd Edition)*, ed. Charles Guignon (Cambridge: Cambridge University Press, 2006).
21 Wrathall, *How to Read Heidegger*.

withdrawal behind the camera. This not the same as detachment: however in
order to see it, photographers need to look and watch the world as it presents
itself to them. If this was not the case, photographers would take pictures of
every single thing that they encountered in the world. The skill of the great photographer is to also know when to tactically reveal and withdraw themselves,
when to be invisible and when to be present behind the camera. André Kertész's
images *Paris, my friend Ernest*[22] from 1932 and *River Walk of Carl Schurz Park*[23]
(1948) both illustrate and demonstrate the interplay between withdrawal and
presence behind the camera.

What makes *Paris, my friend Ernest* such a striking image is Ernest's gaze
directly into the camera, straight down the lens. The photographer has also
shrunk himself to Ernest's size. The boy does not gaze upward, as if he was
looking at an adult he is engaging the photographer as an equal and a friend just
at the title suggests. To get this height, the photographer would have to sit or at
least crouch down to the boy's level. The photographer's presence is telegraphed
into the photograph by Ernest's body language, which is at ease rather than tense.
His elbow on the table, he wears a soft, gentle smile which is not forced, which so
often happens when subjects are forced to be in front of the camera.

Ernest is not the only gaze present is in this photograph. The unnamed girl
briefly looks up from her desk, watching the photographer at work. Due to the
depth of field, her features are less prominent and here again we see the interplay and layering of withdrawal and presence between camera, photographer
and subject. The attention on Ernest sharpens his features, making him the central presence of the image throwing the background out of focus. Had he wanted
to, Kertész could have requested that the girl move when he was taking the picture. However her withdrawn presence in the picture also adds both context and
depth, a boy caught in a moment at school, rather than standing in an empty
classroom. This image demonstrates the subtlety and tactics at work when it
comes to presence and withdrawal with a photographer and their camera. Too
close with the lens and the photographer intimidates their subject and loses the
background. Move too far away both figuratively and literally, the subject loses
interest and their gaze is lost.

River Walk of Carl Schurz Park demonstrates an altogether different immersion
behind the camera and in this scene Kertész is withdrawn to the point of the

---

22 Paris, my friend Ernest (1932), available at http://www.artic.edu/aic/collections/
    artwork/99707
23 River Walk of Carl Schurz Park (1948), available at https://theartstack.com/artist/
    andre-kertesz/river-walk-carl-schurz

landscape passing through him. However it is this withholding that makes the photograph so powerful. Here the urbanites hover in the distance but they also have an unseen presence in the snow underneath the subject's feet, churned up by visitors into grey sludge that echoes the color of the heavy sky. Here the gaze of the main figure in the picture is unseen and he looks away from the camera, unaware or at least unresponsive to its presence. Nonetheless his gaze into the distance draws the eye of the viewer over the curving arc of the empty park benches and into the landscape beyond, where the boat sailing away sits on the very edge of the frame. If *Paris, my friend Ernest* dwells in the presence and warmth of Ernest's gaze, in *River Walk of Carl Schurz Park* it dwells on isolation revealing how the gaze is often avoided in the urban setting.

In drawing on Heidegger's notions of The Thing[24] and care, we are explicitly positioning a type or manner of photography as a practice that is indicative of care and illustrative of this mood or orientation to the camera and world. We also link this care for camera and world to Heidegger's concept of dwelling as a response to a dominant technological worldview[25] (of which, we see the average everyday photograph as an illustrative indicative example) as an explanation of *how* entities are made visible through taking the camera into care to enable 'thinging'. To reiterate, things in the world 'thing'; they perform the function of 'thinging' appropriate to what that thing is and its position in the world. For Harman[26], the thing (when 'thinging') produces a nearness to that thing. This nearness is when the thing produces a specific locale for being based around how that thing operates in the world, that is what its function is, how it gathers the elements and how this is given back to being as a revealing of the thing and its region, therefore providing an existential locale or local world.

The idea of nearness (and how things create nearness) is vital to the under-standing of the gathering or event (*ereignis*) itself and how this gathering is related to dwelling. Malpas[27] argues that distance is the factor by which objects in

24 Heidegger Martin, "*The Thing*", originally delivered as a lecture to the Bayerischen Akademie der Schonen Kunsce, 1950. Translated by Alben Hofstadter in *Poetry Language Thought* (New York: Harper and Row, 1971).

25 Heidegger, Martin. *The Question Concerning Technology, and Other Essays.* New York: Harper Perennial, 1977.

26 Harman Graham, *Heidegger Explained: From Phenomenon to Thing* (London: Open Court, 2007).

27 Malpas Jeff, "Uncovering the space of disclosedness: Heidegger, technology and the problem of spatiality in being and time". In: *Heidegger, Authenticity, and Modernity: Essays in Honour of Hubert L. Dreyfus*, eds. Hubert Dreyfus, Mark Wrathall and Jeff Malpas, (Cambridge, Massachusetts: MIT Press, 2000), p. 218.

a region are near or far (dis-stance). It is this dis-stance, the nearness or farness of an object that decides whether this entity is a 'thing', and secondly whether that thing can perform 'thinging' (with a thing being existentially near in the region or locale). A 'thing' is the critical aspect of a region itself in that without a 'thing', this is no region or locale (and hence the homelessness of man in the technological age).

We dwell by 'attuning' ourselves to the local world, and this 'attunement' is an attuning to a 'thing' or things in that locale[28]. This opens the possibility that different things 'thing' in different ways. Different things will be revealed and withdrawn (and will reveal the local world) in different ways according to their ontic proper-ties. We dwell with things not by exploiting them, not by mastering them and not by subjugating them under our control (as we would if treating things as resource in a technological mode of understanding, enframing in Heidegger's terms). The technological worldview that presents all entities as resources to be used is a danger in itself; the essence of technology being a worldview which frames all entities as resources to be used. Dwelling with things – letting things come-forth as entities with their own essence – is to have a free relationship with technology rather than have the world structured by it. The fundamental character of dwelling is caring for and protecting things[29] and hence 'Being-with things' is to take things into Care and hold them as concern.

In the case of Kertész's use of the camera, we are discussing how the camera (and Kertész's use or manner of use of the camera) reveals entities in a particular way. The character of any 'thing's' 'thinging' is a function of the gathering of *the elements of the fourfold* by that thing. The four elements are *earth, sky, divinities and mortals*, as is their relationship along two axes of earth–sky and mortals–divinities. The inter-section of the four elements is the event. A local world where one can 'dwell' in a free relationship with technology occurs when an everyday thing 'things' and tem-porarily brings things and people into their own appropriation. Here we argue that Kertész's use of the camera in his manner and orientation to the world allows for the attunement to world that reveals in the manner of Kertész's photography.

Each element in this fourfold is simpler than their denotation suggests. The taken-for-granted practices that ground situations and give them significance as situations are *earth*. These practices, such as in Borgmann's[30] example of the

---

28 Evans, *Locative Social Media: Place in the Digital Age*, p. 62.
29 Young, "The fourfold", p. 189.
30 Dreyfus Hubert and Charles Spinoza, *Highway Bridges and Feasts: Heidegger and Borgmann on How to Affirm Technology*, 1997. http://www.focusing.org/apm_papers/dreyfus.html.

family meal, operate to make the gathering significant. For a family, a dining practice is not an option to indulge in eating or not but the basis upon which other options appear[31]. In the case of photographic practice, this would refer to the everyday use of the camera in a particular manner. Heidegger regards this grounding of practices as withdrawn and hidden, whereas *sky* is the revealed or manifest possibilities that arise from the focal situations (such as the family meal) and therefore is explicitly revealed. These are the possibilities for action that are appropriate for that focal gathering or locale in the case of the family meal, discussion of the day and warm conversation would be appropriate[32] while discussion of gory injury and death threats would not be appropriate. The possibilities of action are dictated by the situation which itself is disclosed by the fourfold.

While *earth* and *sky* are linked on one axis of the fourfold, *divinities* and *mortals* are linked on the other axis (and the four elements intersect at the event of revealing). In the context of the fourfold, *divinities* refers to the attunement of being in the situation to an extent that one feels in tune with what is happening and events unfold of their own accord without the need to push this unfolding through action. When a thing 'things' this sense of divinity must be present, although this too will be withdrawn[33]. This is akin to the attunement to dwelling, which should not be thought of as explicit but as the mood in which Dasein is in at that time pre-reflectively. *Mortals* refers to how the thing 'thinging' includes humans but in a specific sense. Obviously, the mortals will be revealed, but also act as disclosers of the thing 'thinging' – and therefore the fourfold – itself, as without humans there would be no meaning to the gathering of the elements. Moreover, the choice of the word mortal is deliberate; the human revealing the thing and fourfold must be mortal in that they are being-toward-death, and therefore accepting of the finitude of Being, as only in this mode of Being can the disclosive way of being be revealed to us[34]. Heidegger also means by mortals an attribute of the way human practices work that causes mortals to understand they have no fixed identity. This understanding is necessary if one is to attune to

---

31 Dreyfus and Spinoza, *Highway Bridges and Feasts: Heidegger and Borgmann on How to Affirm Technology.*

32 Dreyfus and Spinoza, *Highway Bridges and Feasts: Heidegger and Borgmann on How to Affirm Technology.*

33 Harman, *Heidegger Explained: From Phenomenon to Thing*, p. 132.

34 Dreyfus and Spinoza, *Highway Bridges and Feasts: Heidegger and Borgmann on How to Affirm Technology.*

the locale and nature of practices demanded by the thing 'thinging' and the possibilities that are appropriate for that locale[35].

The fourfold is the event of the thing 'thinging': it gathers the four elements, and in doing so it reveals a local world of meaning that is dependent upon the thing. Wrathall[36] surmises Heidegger: we dwell in the fourfold by 'saving the earth, in receiving the sky, in awaiting the divinities and in accompanying the mortals'. In doing this, our being-in-the-world is a dwelling rather than a 'homeless' or lost state. This fourfold way of living – saving, receiving, awaiting and escorting – cannot happen without things, and being-with things in a way that allows the fourfold to both be revealed and to be accepted into everyday being.

5 As above, so below

What can Kertész reveal about the nature of dwelling within everyday life? In *Blois, France*[37] (1930) what is most prominent is the distance between the photographer and the ground below. The framing gives the viewer the same giddy sensation if they were peering over a high ledge, heightened by the blur of the cyclist at the bottom of the image. There is a feeling of falling forward because of the angle of the lens. This is not a birds-eye view of the scene below it is shot from one of Kertész's favorite perspectives: looking downward from an open window or balcony. Staring at the photograph brings more details to the surface. The row of neat cobbles gleaming in the sun, the scrubbed texture of the road that the horse and cart have just travelled across. We see in the far right the image the words 'transmission' on the building, a woman in the shop doorway and different goods on display in the window. A motorcyclist has slowed down in the street, perhaps aware of the horse and the cyclist in front of them, all of which give small clues to when the photograph was taken (1930, in *Blois, France*). There is a sense here of old and new beginning to collide too, of an electronic store and a motorcycle at odds with the slower pace of the horses. The photograph has the feel of an early morning scene, not only because of the quiet street but prompted by the closed shutters of the houses below. There is a satisfying symmetry to the image, from the 'T' shape of the road to the light fanning out and directing the readers gaze straight to the illuminated horse and cart.

---

35 Dreyfus and Spinoza, *Highway Bridges and Feasts: Heidegger and Borgmann on How to Affirm Technology.*

36 Wrathall, *How to Read Heidegger*, p. 113.

37 Blois, France (1930) available at http://www.getty.edu/art/collection/objects/55761/andre-kertesz-carrefour-blois-american-negative-1930-print-later/

It seems that Kertész found comfort in being above the cityscape and it is a perspective that he revisited frequently. In *West 134th Street, New York*[38] (1944), 14 years later, Kertész had moved to New York a place in which he felt isolated and alone. The scene is similar to his image in France, taken from a high aspect. The shadows are long, indicating it is the afternoon, as a lone figure walks along the pavement where several cars are parked. The impression, given the aspect under the bridge and where the vehicles are parked suggests an industrial area of the city, where little happens outside business hours. Gurbo[39] writes that 'early in his career in America, Kertész felt nostalgia, loneliness and a sense of being trapped' all elements that are visible particularly in the tight, claustrophobic framing. Although the photographer finds visual comfort in emptiness there is also a meditative quality to the picture which in part comes from the long arch of the wrought iron bridge bringing to mind an old church window, with the light shining through.

Both *Blois, France* and *West 134th Street, New York* have an additional and powerful orientation because, we would argue, they bring together all elements of the fourfold. There are signs of earth and mortal in the street below, seen in the everyday dirty cobbles and buildings and the people walking amongst them. However there is also an element of sky too, as the viewer sits above to review the streets below them. The divinity comes from the photographer. The scene is not forced or created, it has (to a degree) unfolded in front of his camera and he has captured the optimum moment on film. Without the sun, the texture of the street would be less present, without people the scene would lack a focal point. However what makes the image special is the unusual vantage point. It is a privileged perspective that elevates it from the humble to the divine. It says much about Kertész and his skill as a photographer, to be able to envisage these scenes and how it would look in black and white. Kertész was famously prudent with his film use, often waiting and watching for long periods of time before committing to taking the photograph.

The photographs *River Walk of Carl Schurz Park, Blois, France* and *West 134th Street, New York* show a photographer reveling in the emptiness of the city, taken as an opportunity for self-contemplation. However his cityscapes also show faceless, solitary figures dwelling in the shadows or walking away from the camera. Pictures of such urban isolation could also be read as a visual

---

38 West 134th Street, New York (1944), available at https://www.nga.gov/Collection/art-object-page.110832.html
39 Gurbo, "Circle of confusion", p. 155.

manifestation of the separation felt by Kertész as the eternal émigré in the cities he lived in for most of his life. His photographs 'continued to seek people and things that mirrored his feelings but with a continued separation from his surroundings, observing but not actively participating in the world around him'[40]. Although we would argue that the photographer can never truly be severed from the world, this does highlight the deep phenomenological paradox of photography. In order to see the world through the camera, the photographer must immerse themselves in their environment. However in order to capture its details and create interesting images, the photographer must also step back and have a necessary distance from the scene. Solnit[41] writes that 'photography poses the challenge of finding form and pattern in the stuff that is already out there'. The viewing both these images show the possibility of finding the extraordinary in the prosaic. It allows for the visible yet unseen parts of everyday life rise up to the surface of the picture. The images made by Kertész encourage a kind of 'phenomenological bracketing'[42] and as the viewer looks and holds the photograph, they are brought into one world and retreat from another. Long shadows, pavement markings, iron railings are all banal details, the things of everyday urban life. However under the gaze of Kertész, they are elevated and shake the viewer to attention. Writing about Kertész, Seamon[43] reflects that:

> Kertész's work is significant phenomenologically because it presents sensitive portraits of the way that things and people belong or do not belong to the world in which they find themselves immersed. In one sense, Kertész's photographs are an implicit phenomenological record because they portray the fabric, style and tenor of the lifeworld the ordinary, tacit pattern and elements of life's everydayness, normally taken for granted but given direct scholarly attention in phenomenology.

We would also add to this statement more importantly these images also show the unfolding of movement and space within the urban environment, a meditation on how photographers dwell in the world and skilfully withdraw, engage and reflect to reveal their everyday surroundings.

---

40 Greenough, "A Hungarian diary: 1894–1925", p. 63.
41 Solnit Rebecca, *A Field Guide to Getting Lost* (Edinburgh: Canongate, 2006), p. 144.
42 Seamon David, "Awareness and reunion: A phenomenology of person environment as portrayed in the New York photographs of Andre Kertesz". In: *Place Images in the Media*, ed. Leo E. Zonn (Savage, Maryland: Roman and Littlefield, 1990), pp. 31–61.
43 Seamon, "Awareness and Reunion: A phenomenology of person environment as portrayed in the New York photographs of Andre Kertesz", p. 32.

6 Conclusion

This idea of dwelling being a skill is important as it implies that dwelling is something that is learned and therefore not learned in the technological age. In order to dwell in the technological epoch we would need to relearn the skills that are essential to realize dwelling and therefore reclaiming the essence of man, these skills being the practices that are attuned to the fourfold, no longer treating things as objects and subsequently as resource. Clearly, we position Kertész's use of the camera in the everyday as a particular skill that comes from dwelling and a being-with the thing that allows for the revealing of particular entities. Indeed, to return to Harman's contention on the fourfold, it is the manner of being-with the camera that makes entities in the photographs visible; Kertész's attunement to the thing reveals the world through the lens in a manner that makes these entities visible.

Heidegger holds that different things 'thing' with different modes of revealing[44], and so each thing will gather the elements, or gather to itself, in its own way and manner. Dreyfus and Spinoza[45] outline the possibility of dwelling with technology and a free relationship with technology. If there are local worlds produced by things thinging, then there is logically a multitude of these worlds that could be manifest to humans as things thing in different ways (as they gather in their own way) and that the human passes between these different world as he attunes to different things at different times. This is a potential opening for considering the possibility of a technological thing thinging; if one can be with a technological device that gathers the fourfold in a way then a local world would emerge from its thinging. This world would have a character that may be defined as technological, but that still could be a local world. Dreyfus and Spinoza[46] draw attention to Heidegger's analysis of bridges, and in particular to the autobahn bridge. While this is the modern, technological bridge it still exhibits a kind of gathering, not only a way of linking as many routes as possible (as resource). The sky is manifest as multiple possibilities (going this way or that); the earth is the possibility of these manifest possible routes, and the practices of crossing and encountering the bridge (albeit this is weak compared to the non-technical

---

44 Dreyfus and Spinoza, *Highway Bridges and Feasts: Heidegger and Borgmann on How to Affirm Technology.*

45 Dreyfus and Spinoza, *Highway Bridges and Feasts: Heidegger and Borgmann on How to Affirm Technology.*

46 Dreyfus and Spinoza, *Highway Bridges and Feasts: Heidegger and Borgmann on How to Affirm Technology.*

thing). The divinities would be the being in tune with technological flexibility, and the mortals would of course be the people using the bridge, aware
of its revealing and with the skills appropriate to the world emergent from the
'thinging' of the bridge.

In considering the everyday use of cameras (on smartphones, tablets and
in traditional form) it can be argued that the manner of relationship between
the user and the thing has a substantive effect on the revealing of the world by
the photographers. In the case of Kertész, we see a relationship and use of the
camera that reveals the entities in the world. In the case of the everyday user of
equipment, their relationship to their device will affect the revealing of the world
that their photographs have thanks to how that thing orients and attunes the
user to the local world. Kertész's relationship (through care) is therefore critical
to his world revealing in his art, indeed to his ability to *dwell* with the camera in
a world-revealing moment.

Dwelling is Heidegger's response to the threat of enframing and the holding
all entities in standing reserve[47]. The technological understanding of the world
that is enframing reduces all being (the being of entities and the understanding
of being) down to resource. In such an understanding we can use what we want
with regards to the entities that we encounter in the world, but conversely there
is no reason to do anything as all things are just surface; resources to be used and
consumed but not to be used in any way to further understanding of the world or
in the world. In dwelling, Dasein considers the entities in a locale as meaningful
(not just resource) and hence that environment becomes meaningful.

Kertész's dwelling with the thing, taking thee thing into care in a way that
allows it to gather the elements of the world into a revealing of entities, is how
the photography and art can reveal entities in the world that would otherwise
be withdrawn and hidden. The work shown here is not just an example of fine
photography, but also of how a camera can 'thing' (orient) to the world in a
manner that allows for a revealing of entities rather than a shallow representation of the world.

Bibliography

Barthes, Roland. *Camera Lucida*. London: Vintage, 1984.

Dreyfus, Hubert and Charles Spinoza. "Highway bridges and feasts: Heidegger
and Borgmann on how to affirm technology". http://www.focusing.org/
apm_papers/dreyfus.html. 1997. Last accessed 03 March 2017.

---

47 Wrathall, *How to Read Heidegger*, p. 109.

Evans, Leighton. *Locative Social Media: Place in the Digital Age.*
London: Palgrave, 2015.

Forrest, Eve. "Exploring everyday photographic routines through the habit of
noticing". In: *Digital Photography and Everyday Life: Empirical Studies on
Material Visual Practices*, eds. Asko Lehmuskallio and Edgar Gomez Cruz.
London: Routledge, 2016, pp. 193–208.

Greenough, Sarah. "A Hungarian diary: 1894–1925". In: *Andre Kertesz: The
Eternal Amateur*, eds. Sarah Greenough, Robert Gurbo and Sarah Kennel.
Washington: Washington University Press, 2005, pp. 1–59.

Gurbo, Robert. "Circle of confusion". In: *Andre Kertesz: The Eternal
Amateur*, eds. Sarah Greenough, Robert Gurbo and Sarah Kennel.
Washington: Washington University Press, 2005, pp. 141–191.

Hand, Martin. *Ubiquitous Photography.* Malden: Polity, 2012.

Harman, Graham. *Tool-Being: Heidegger and the Metaphysics of Objects.*
London: Open Court, 2002.

Harman, Graham. *Heidegger Explained: From Phenomenon to Thing (Ideas
Explained).* London: Open Court, 2007.

Heidegger, Martin. *"The Thing"*, originally delivered as a lecture to the
Bayerischen Akademie der Schonen Kunsce, 1950. Translated by Alben
Hofstadter in *Poetry Language Thought.* New York: Harper and Row,
1971.

Heidegger, Martin. *The Question Concerning Technology, and Other Essays.*
New York: Harper Perennial, 1977.

Heidegger, Martin. *History of the Concept of Time.* Indianapolis: Indiana
University Press, 1992.

Heidegger, Martin. *Basic Writings: From Being and Time (1927) to The Task of
Thinking (1964) (Rev. and expanded ed.).* London: Routledge, 2008.

Jay, Martin. *Downcast Eyes: The Denigration of Vision in Twentieth-century
French Thought.* London, University of California Press, 2003.

Malpas, Jeff. "Uncovering the space of disclosedness: Heidegger, technology
and the problem of spatiality in being and time". In: *Heidegger, Authenticity,
and Modernity: Essays in Honour of Hubert L. Dreyfus*, eds. Hubert Dreyfus,
Mark Wrathall and Jeff Malpas. Cambridge, Massachusetts: MIT Press, 2000,
pp. 205–227.

Rubenstein, Daniel and Katrina Sluis. "A Life More Photographic",
Photographies, Vol 1, March 2008, pp. 9–28.

Seamon, David. "Awareness and reunion: A phenomenology of person
environment as portrayed in the New York photographs of Andre Kertesz".

In: *Place Images in the Media*, ed. Leo E. Zonn. Savage, Maryland: Roman and Littlefield, 1990, pp. 31–61.

Sekula, Allan. "The body and the archive". In: *The Contest of Meaning: Critical Histories of Photography*, ed. Richard Bolton. Cambridge: MIT Press, 1989, pp. 342–389.

Shove, Elizabeth, Martin Hand, Jack Ingram and Matthew Watson. *The Design of Everyday Life*. Oxford: Berg, 2007.

Solnit, Rebecca. *A Field Guide to Getting Lost*. Edinburgh: Canongate, 2006.

Wrathall, Mark. *How to Read Heidegger (How to Read)*. New York: W. W. Norton, 2006.

Wylie, John. *Landscape*. London: Routledge, 2007.

Young, Julian. "The fourfold". In: *The Cambridge Companion to Heidegger (2nd Edition)*, ed. Charles Guignon. Cambridge: Cambridge University Press, 2006, pp. 373–392.

Images by Andre Kertesz

Blois, France (1930) available at http://www.getty.edu/art/collection/objects/55761/andre-kertesz-carrefour-blois-american-negative-1930-print-later/ Last Accessed 01 August 2017

Paris, my friend Ernest (1932), available at http://www.artic.edu/aic/collections/artwork/99707 Last Accessed 01 August 2017

River Walk of Carl Schurz Park (1948), available at https://theartstack.com/artist/andre-kertesz/river-walk-carl-schurz Last Accessed 01 August 2017

West 134th Street, New York (1944), available at https://www.nga.gov/Collection/art-object-page.110832.html Last Accessed 01 August 2017

Camilo Salazar Prince

Self-Understanding in the Age of the Selfie: Kierkegaard, Dreyfus, and Heidegger on Social Networks

Before the rise of social networks and the pervasiveness of smart phones, thinking on how everyday life would be if we were to live our lives in the "vast, invisible, interconnected infrastructure" of the internet, philosopher Hubert Dreyfus posed a question: "will it indeed make our lives better? What would be gained and what if anything, would be lost if we were to take leave of our situated bodies in exchange for ubiquitous telepresence in cyberspace?"[1] Fifteen years later, our ubiquitous telepresence in cyberspace is no longer a thought experiment but a reality. With approximately one billion active daily users on Facebook, three hundred million on twitter and one hundred million on Instagram, it is not far-fetched to say that our *telepresence in cyberspace* by way of social networks has become an integral part of people's everyday lives.

This phenomenon raises numerous questions about the effects this has on people's day-to-day lives. Namely, how has self-understanding been affected by social networks? How does the self relate to its virtual online counterpart? Following Dreyfus, Kierkegaard, and Heidegger I hope to shed some light on these questions.

For Kierkegaard, the self is a relation that relates itself to itself. In other words, my understanding of who I am is directly dependent upon the stand I take on being that self. This stand however, is not a reflective, detached, or rational interpretation of who I am, but rather an active stance on the factical part of my self. I am, who I am, not because of what I think but because of what I do. I define who I am by acting upon it. In other words, I understand who I am by being a writer, a scientist, a mother, or by taking part in a cause that matters to me. For Kierkegaard our self-understanding depends on how we relate to our past through present everyday actions that meaningfully disclose our future.[2]

1   Hubert Dreyfus, *On the Internet*, Routledge, 2001a, p. 52.
2   Hubert Dreyfus, "Heidegger on the Connection between Nihilism, Art, Technology and Politics", 2001b, p. 1.

Kierkegaard considered that this active stance required for self-understanding was being undermined in the West by the detached philosophical reflection encouraged by the Enlightenment. In his prophetic book *The Present Age*,[3] written in 1846, he described his age as a time characterized by an unintentional reflection that leveled all concrete differences of value, authority, and meaning. Nothing was worth dying for because nothing mattered more than anything else. Idle curiosity and critical detachment had overshadowed involved commitment. Nietzsche later coined this modern condition, Nihilism. In his book, *On the Internet*, Dreyfus equates Kierkegaard's nihilistic descriptions of self-understanding in *The Present Age* to the self's relationship to the virtual landscapes of the Internet in 2001. The insightful parallels Dreyfus draws following Kierkegaard begin to eerily sketch out and define what an online self looks like in today's social-network-driven world. In order to flesh out what this online-virtual-self looks like, we must first understand why Kierkegaard described his age as nihilistic.

According to Dreyfus, Kierkegaard blames the nihilism of his age, the leveling in difference of value, authority and meaning, on a "monstrous abstraction, an all – encompassing something that is nothing, a mirage," a phantom he called "the Public." However, for him the Public itself is not solely to blame for this leveling, but rather the threat and force behind it, the Press. For Kierkegaard, writing in 1846, the public and the press were a cultural and religious threat that was overtaking Europe.

His specific focus of concern on the public, rather than on the proliferation of democracy or the birth of new technologies, is a direct result of what Jürgen Habermas calls the public sphere. Habermas pinpoints the rise of the public sphere during the middle of the eighteen-century. In this period the local press and coffee houses became host to a radically new modern form of political discourse. The public sphere engaged in political discussions that lay outside of the political circles of power, and thus allowed for the public to engage in rational and detached forms of political discourse. Rather than seeing this lack of political power as something negative, the Enlightenment intellectuals encouraged this modern form of discourse and celebrated it as a modern pillar of a free society. They saw the rational detached reflections of the social sphere as free spirited intellectual exercises that lead to new ideas and concepts that could one day help guide government and everyday life.

---

3   Soren Kierkegaard, *The Present Age*, Alexander Dru, trans., Harper & Row, 1962.

Over the next century, however, as a result of the vast expansion of the daily press, the public sphere became so excessively democratized that it became a serious concern for many intellectuals of that time. Thinkers like Mill and Tocqueville saw that the reign of democratized public opinion lead to a conformist leveling to the lowest common denominator instigated by the opinions of an ill-educated majority. For Kierkegaard the main threat of the Public Sphere ✳ was not, as most intellectuals claimed, the conformism promoted by the "the tyranny of the masses." In his eyes the real danger posed by the Public and the Press was that it instigated "risk-free anonymity and idle curiosity" that undermined responsibility and commitment. That, "in turn, leveled all qualitative distinctions and led to nihilism."

The rise of Nihilism, during Kierkegaard's age, was the consequence of different things. The emergence of the massive distribution of cheap newspapers filled with foreign desituated information that was immediately available to anyone set the ground for the birth of a detached reader or spectator. According to Kierkegaard, the rise of the press encouraged the public to have opinions about everything, and comment on all local or foreign matters without any sense of expertise on any matter whatsoever, but more importantly, without assuming any real responsibility or personally engaging with the issues being discussed. In other words the democratization of the press led to the ubiquity of anonymous talking heads that did not practice what they preached. Thus, creating a Public Sphere where principles spoke louder than committed actions. A Public Sphere where local issues that required real action were relegated to detached reflective discussions and endless abstract reflection that lead to nihilistic leveling:

> The abstraction of the press (for a newspaper, a journal, is no political concretion and only an individual in an abstract sense), combined with the passionlessness and reflectiveness of the age, gives birth to that abstraction's phantom, the public, which is the real leveler.[5]

In his book, *On the Internet*, Dreyfus draws an insightful and significant parallel between Kierkegaard's depiction of the social sphere in *The Present Age* and the rise of the Internet during his own age. According to Dreyfus, "Kierkegaard would surely have seen in the Internet, with its Websites full of anonymous information from all over the world and its interest groups that anyone in the world can join without qualifications and where one can discuss any topic endlessly without

---

4   Hubert Dreyfus, "Kierkegaard on the Internet: Anonymity vs Commitment in the Present Age", *Kierkegaard Studies Yearbook*, 1999.

5   Soren Kierkegaard, *The Present Age*, p. 64.

consequences, the hi-tech synthesis of the worst features of the newspaper and the coffeehouse."[6] In 2001, when Dreyfus wrote *On the Internet*, the Internet was becoming host to diverse news groups where anonymous commentators could post an opinion about anything, and equally respond to others in a detached manner from wherever, in both cases, never having to actually take a stand on the issues being discussed. For Dreyfus this foreshadowed the nihilistic leveling Kierkegaard had earlier described:

> Relevance and significance have, indeed disappeared. And this is an important part of the attraction of the Web. Nothing is too trivial to be included. Nothing is so important that it demands a special place…On the Web, the attraction and the danger are that everyone can take this godlike point of view. One can view a coffee pot in Cambridge, or the latest super-nova, study the Kyoto Protocol, find out what fellowships are available to a person with one's profile, or direct a robot to plant and water a seed in Austria, not to mention plough through thousands of ads, all with equal ease and equal lack of any sense of what is highly important. The highly significant and the absolutely trivial are laid out together on the information highway in just the way Abraham's sacrifice of Isaac, red, white and blue shoes strings, a thousand telephones that don't ring, and the next world war are laid out in Dylan's nihilistic "Highway 61."[7]

Dreyfus's description of the Internet prophetically depicts the leveled world of social networking years before the creation of Facebook, Twitter, Instagram or any other mayor social network. Today Dreyfus's Dylan inspired nihilistic image of the information highway, just sounds like an average stroll through one's Facebook news updates. Today, our Facebook profile is constantly bombarded with videos of cute kittens alongside horrific images of bombings in Syria, passionate political stands on gay rights next to equally passionate comments on the latest *Star Wars* film, followed by Facebook birthday alerts of estranged friends whose wall we are virtually obliged to post on, and requests by someone we barely know urging us to LIKE their "I Love Curly Fries page." In our Facebook news updates nothing matters more than anything else, be it that day's death toll in Syria or number of birthday alerts on our wall, yet we can show our seemly invested and momentary opinion about this or that, by commenting, posting, sharing, liking, or emojing anything at all, without having to act, take a stand on, or actual engage with anything we posted beyond that brief virtual encounter.

On February 4, 2004, with the launch of Facebook, our relationship with the Internet would change forever. Though other social networking sites such as MySpace already existed at the conception of Facebook, none would ever reach

---

6   Hubert Dreyfus, *On the Internet*, p. 78.
7   Ibid., p. 79.

its level of massification. What Facebook introduced into the world was the possibility to easily construct an *online self* via a Facebook Profile. What is so innovative and distinctive about this is that everyday people were now empowered to portray themselves whichever way they liked online; in other words, they were encouraged to create a flexible online identity of their choosing. On September 26, 2006, Facebook, previously exclusive for university students, became available to everyone older than thirteen with an email address, from that moment on to the present day a new relationship emerged between the situated self and the online self, a complex relationship that has ever since been constantly changing, warping, shifting, and redefining itself. Though Dreyfus never draws a clear distinction between the situated self and the online self, following Kierkegaard he sketches out some of the existential consequences and characteristics of having an online self.

According to Dreyfus, Kierkegaard would have denounced the Internet, just like he did the Press, for promoting two spheres of existence, the aesthetic and the ethical sphere. Because each one of these spheres of existence embodies a way of trying to escape the nihilistic leveling of the press and the web by "making some way of life absolute."[8]

In the aesthetic sphere, leveling is escaped by living in a world that revolves around enjoyment, a commitment to constantly seek new interesting things in order to avoid boredom. Such an aesthetic way of being is representative of a Facebook user that is constantly posting on their wall information they find interesting and frequently engages in liking, commenting, tagging, and sharing information that draws their attention. This aesthetic social networker avoids nihilistic leveling by making qualitative distinctions between what they find interesting and what they regard as boring, thus in the process creating a shifting online identity or online self whose identity is built upon what they post on their online profile. This way of life according to Dreyfus "consists in fighting of boredom by being a spectator at everything interesting in the universe and in communicating with everyone else so inclined. Such a life produces what we would now call a postmodern self – a self that has no defining content or continuity but is open to all possibilities and to constantly taking new roles."[9]

Kierkegaard felt that the reason why people were so enthralled with the press, and nowadays we can say with social networks, was because the spectator, or the online self, takes no risks. The aesthetic online self does not have a rigid self that

---

8   Ibid., p. 81.
9   Ibid, p. 81.

unlike a committed self with an active stance on who they are is always at risk
of humiliation, loss or even inexistence. The posts an online self in the aesthetic
sphere makes seem to be risk free because unlike real commitments they have
no apparent consequences. Liking a friend's comment supporting gay rights,
sharing the trailer of the new *Star Wars*, or commenting on the horrors of the
war in Syria, is in no way an active or committed stance on who I am, rather it is
a fleeting interest that avoids boredom. The likes, posts, tags, and comments an
online self makes are what Dreyfus refers to as "virtual commitments," or online
commitments that take no stand on the situated self and have no apparent real-
world consequences. As such the aesthetic online self is made up of the collection
of virtual commitments accumulated over time on his or her Facebook timeline,
Twitter feed, or Instagram page that results in a flexible and constantly changing
online identity that belongs to an equally shifting and active online community.

A further characteristic of the aesthetic online self is that it can be shaped in
whichever way its situated self wants to shape it; from creating a slightly idealized
version of the situated self to creating an all-together different self from the one
they actually are. As such, the resulting online self can be so potentially different
from the way of being of the actual self that it becomes completely immune or
threaten by any form of disappointment, humiliation or loss whatsoever. One's
online self can potentially be funnier, cooler, or smarter than the actual self; it
can be of a different age, social background or even gender.

The phenomenology of the selfie embodies this tendency to embellish or
slightly idealize the life of someone caught in the aesthetic sphere. Selfies, the
omnipresent pictures of ourselves, became commonplace after 2003 when Sony
Ericsson Z1010 launched the first cellphone equipped with a front facing camera
that allowed you to take selfies. Selfies became popular in mainstream culture after social media celebrities such as Kim Kardashian began to use selfies
as a way to portray their lives online as exciting, fun, and luxurious. The trend
quickly caught on. As of 2015, people between the ages of sixteen and twenty-
five spend an average of five hours a week setting up, photographing, and editing
their selfies in order to upload them to be seen on a major social network.[10]

Selfies encourage living in the aesthetic sphere by creating an idealized identity via an online self. The phenomenology of the selfie reveals the deep urge
to escape leveling by constantly creating and uploading idealized self-portraits.
When a selfie is taken, it is a quick and easy self-portrait that unlike a traditional
self-portrait by someone like Rembrandt, is composed, shot, and finalized within

---

10 Feelunique survey from Selfie culture among generations from techinforgrafics.com.

a "proof"; second-order experiencing

minutes. Selfies frame people not just as people, but as people in a given place at given time in a given mood. A selfie is not just a portrait that captures a moment in my life; it captures the fact that I am in that moment in my life. Thus, the act of capturing the moment takes precedence over being in the moment. The process of idealizing the self is furthered once the editing process begins: selfies are retouched, digitally enhanced, and sometimes all together altered in order to get the most idealized representation of the self. The retouched selfie is uploaded to a social network community, as another "interesting moment" that nourishes the ongoing process of building the online self on a timeline eager for likes, comments, or shares. This digital social practice allows the aesthetic self to fight off boredom and escape nihilism, but consequently widens the gap between who the situated self is and who the selfie portrays to be.

The interpretive speculative dimension of experience.

An interesting example of this is the case of the social media star and teen model Essena O'Neill, famous for her Instagram account with more then six hundred thousand followers. For years she posted daily selfies in everyday situations that championed a Zen-vegan lifestyle as the ultimate way to pursue happiness. At the height of her fame however, O'Neill created a media storm when she announced said she would quit social media because, in her words "social media is not real life," that is to say, she felt her online self was a misrepresentation of who she really was: "I was lost, with serious problems so beautifully hidden … If anything my social media addiction, perfectionist personality and low self esteem made my career," she said. "Over-sexualisation, perfect food photos, perfect travel vlogs – it is textbook how I got famous. Sex sells, people listen to pretty blondes, I just happened to talk about veganism, a trending thing on YouTube." Instead of deleting her Instagram, she deleted around two thousand selfies and edited the captions beside the selfies she left, exposing what she was actually feeling, going through, or hiding at the time. Besides a bathing suit selfie in which she appears relaxed and carefree she wrote, "and yet another photo taken purely to promote my 16-year-old body. This was my whole identity. That was so limiting. Made me incredibly insecure. You have no idea." Beneath another selfie where she seems happy and looks effortlessly beautiful she wrote, "I had acne here, this is a lot of makeup. I was smiling because I thought I looked good. Happiness based on aesthetics will suffocate your potential here on earth."

Social networks provided a virtual landscape where Essena O'Neill felt unshackled by the mundane consequences of commitment and was at no risk to create an idealized online self that lead a perfect and balanced life. This is surely what excites most people who choose to live in the aesthetic sphere via their online selves, a chance to experience a perfected version of themselves open to all possibilities of being. But according to Kierkegaard: "As a result of

This attachment is also in the service of her aesthetic online self.

knowing and being everything possible, one is in contradiction with one self."[11]
The contradiction that emerges is that since the aesthetic online self has no way
of distinguishing the meaningful from the meaningless, the relevant from the
irrelevant, everything becomes leveled, and thus leads the self to the realization
that it is back to very place it was trying to escape: the nihilistic indifference of
the present age. Such a realization Kierkegaard calls, despair. The contradictions
between O'Neill's self and online self, between what she virtually portrayed
to be and actually felt or thought was what ultimately brought her "to be lost
with problems so beautifully hidden." Coping with two identities made it difficult for her to distinguish what was actually meaningful or relevant about either
identity; an unsustainable contradiction that ultimately lead her to despair. In
Kierkegaard's view, "every aesthetic view of life is in despair, and everyone who
lives aesthetically is in despair whether he knows it or not. But when one knows
it a higher form of existence is an imperative requirement."[12]

Kierkegaard calls this higher form of existence, *the ethical sphere*. In it the
self takes up a stable identity and an active stance on the issues or concerns that
constitute his or her identity. As Dreyfus further explains, in the ethical sphere:

> Information is not played with, but sought and used for serious purposes. As long as
> information gathering is not an end in itself, whatever reliable information there is on
> the Web can be a valuable resource serving serious concerns. Such concerns require that
> people have life plans and take up serious tasks. They then have goals that determine
> what needs to be done and what information is relevant for doing it.[13]

In this view, an ethical online self would consistently make virtual commitments
that resulted in involved actions and would therefore use social networks as
tools to further his or her goals. Here we can think of someone who uses their
Facebook profile as way to speak about things that really matter to them by
posting videos about global warming, eye opening articles about local political
corruption scandals, and pictures of their committed relationship. In the ethical
sphere, however posting on your wall does not suffice, actual supported action
on each virtual commitment is required.

Kierkegaard however would hold that the multiplicity of virtual commitments
and the ease of making them by a simply posting on your wall, would eventually lead to the breakdown of the ethical sphere. Namely, because the online self
would be overwhelmed by so many virtual commitments and become paralyzed

---

11 Soren Kierkegaard, *The Present Age*, p. 68.
12 Soren Kierkegaard, *Either/Or*, Princeton University Press, 1959, vol. II, pp. 16, 17.
13 Hubert Dreyfus, *On the Internet*, p. 84.

or would fall prey of arbitrary choice as to which virtual commitments to seriously follow through. [According to Kierkegaard, a way in which the self can avoid arbitrary choice is by committing to something within the range of possibilities of one's life situation, namely by taking up relevant commitments constrained by, for instance, the self's talents, social roles, or personal relationships. In this view, as a way to avoid nihilistic leveling, an ethical social networker can devote their situated self and online self to something that truly matters to them based on a commitment constrained by some condition of their life situation.]

Essena O'Neill's story helps shed light on the implications of this view in the age of the selfie. During O'Neill's breakdown she became aware of her despair, of being trapped in a contradiction, and virtually sought a "higher form of existence." Her virtually committed answer was not only to expose her despair on her Instagram page and simultaneously leave Instagram, YouTube and Tumbler. She also launched a new website, called *Let's Be Game Changers*, a website with the sole virtual commitment to educate people about the destructive nature of seeking online approval, or in Kierkegaard's view of living life online in the aesthetic sphere. [O'Neill's personal situation pushed her to take up a new online self-devoted to something that really mattered to her: exposing that social media was not real life. On her website she posted a declaration of principles that she was committed to live by as a way to lead an authentic life: veganism, mental, fiscal, and spiritual health, and the preservation of the planet were amongst some of the principles. But above all things O'Neill seemed to be committed to lead a transparent life where the virtual commitments her online self made were actively acted upon by her situated self. By doing so, she sought to eliminate the gap between the online self she portrayed to be and the situated self she actually was.] Unfortunately, after repeated backlash by former online friends she took the website down and wrote a lengthy email questioning the negative response to her ethical online commitment:

> I was just shocked and honestly just confused… the way it all turned so negative just numbed me…As if I was making it all up? For what? Money? Fame? I had that before so that makes sense? That I was a genius manipulator and knew this would make world news? I was a hypocrite because I used social media to explain my story to the half a million people that once idolized me? That I was a fraud, a hoax, a brilliant actor just because I was smiling in the pictures and said those smiles weren't real? Seeing people I knew making videos as if my personal life, tears and obvious vulnerability… as if it was some kind of joke to them? I couldn't believe people couldn't just call me first, but wanted to make such a public spectrum.

Dreyfus and Kierkegaard would surely say that what O'Neill lacked was moral maturity, in other words, the moral ability to act lucidly and freely. Thus the goal of the person leading their life in the ethical sphere, online or situated, is not to fall prey of the accidental commitments imposed by one's life situation but rather to freely choose as an autonomous agent what is meaningful in their life and therefore truly worth pursuing. It is a free choice rather than a lucky accident.

But for Kierkegaard leading a life in the ethical sphere based on freedom of choice is ultimately unsustainable. Namely because according to Dreyfus "if everything were up for choice, including the standards on the basis of which one chooses, there would be no reason for choosing one set of standards rather than another."[14] That is to say, absolute freedom of choice in the ethical sphere, situated or online, results in taking up commitments that one can always freely choose to change or revoke. What this means for someone living in the ethical sphere via their online self is that social networks or personal blogs allow the situated self to constantly keep track and monitor the virtual commitments they make. However the flexibility of social networking and the constant flow of new information would offer them the possibility to freely make and unmake previous virtual commitments and thus ultimately lead them to despair.

The possibility of choice that the Internet provides is what ultimately led O'Neill to shut down her ethically committed website *Let's be Game Changers* and take up a third new online self: www.essenaoneill.com, an entirely different and new website devoted to speaking out about the effects of social media in one's life. Though the personal website takes up similar virtual commitments as the ones in her previous website, here the online self is newly branded and the information is presented in a less committed manner. In fact the personal website resembles more a Facebook account than an ethically committed personal blog. Divided into six sections mainly devoted to the negative effects of social media (TED Talks, documentaries, books, interesting short clips, books, veganism and music), it seems like the possibility of choice led her online self to a place somewhere between the ethical and aesthetic sphere where she gathers interesting information that helps inform others about her multiple virtual commitments. O'Neill recently announced that she is in the process of writing a satirical book called *How to be Social Media Famous*. A sense of ongoing despair resonates in her words: "It got to the point where I just wanted to write, the satire/memoir that I'm currently working on but more so fiction. Sci-fi novels have been my dream since I was 12," she said. "The next time I speak, the next time you hear from me, I'll be standing stronger than I could have ever stood before." After living a media storm that destroyed her former online self, and completely transformed

---

14   Ibid., p. 85.

her new online self twice, Essena O'Neill situated self, apart from the obvious despair she unknowingly or knowingly is trapped in, seems unscarred from the life-alerting incident. On her site under "Me?," she quotes: "It's okay. Even when it's not okay. You took the long road. You took a few wrong turns. But it's okay, you're on your way home."

Dreyfus, following Kierkegaard, shows us how social networking can lead the situated self to despair as a consequence of the flexibility of the virtual commitments an online self can freely make and unmake. In this view virtual commitments are flexible because they are 1) risk free and thus have no real-world consequences on the life of the situated self. The ease and plasticity of social networks allow the situated self to 2) easily make and unmake virtual commitments that constitute or infringe upon the identity of the online self.

This view of virtual commitments seems to apply to most of our day-to-day social networking engagements, and is thoroughly insightful on how the virtual self related to the situated self in the early days of the Internet. Over the past few years however, something has radically changed in the virtual landscape of social networking that I believe challenges the anonymity, flexibility, and risk-free nature of virtual commitments on the Internet. A shift so significant in how social networks work and are used that it has significantly altered the way the online self relates to the situated self.

Only until recently have there emerged academic studies by computer privacy experts and statisticians that ask questions concerning the implications of openly sharing personal data on social networks. In the study the *Private traits and attributes are predictable from digital records of human behavior*, researchers show how Facebook Likes, "can be used to accurately predict a range of highly sensitive personal attributes including: sexual orientation, ethnicity, religious, and political views, personality traits, intelligence, happiness, use of addictive substances, parental separation, age, and gender".[15]

What is so insightful about this study is that via mathematical models the researchers manage to predict with a high degree of accuracy very sensitive personal traits with Facebook likes, that though in certain cases the Likes relate more directly to the predicted attribute, such as the case of liking No H8 Campaign and homosexuality, in other instances *the Likes have no obvious connection to the predicted attribute.* For example, the best predictors of high intelligence include

---

15 *Private traits and attributes are predictable from digital records of human behavior* by
     Michal Kosinski, David Stillwell, and Thore Graepel. Proceedings of the National
     Academy of Sciences of the United States.

liking *Thunderstorms*, and *Curly Fries*, whereas indicators of low intelligence result from liking *I Love Being A Mom* and *Lady Antebellum*.

In a recent Tedtalk computer privacy expert Jennifer Goldberg explains the conundrum between liking curly fries and having a high IQ:

> Curly fries are delicious, but liking them does not necessarily mean that you're smarter than the average person. So how is it that one of the strongest indicators of your intelligence is liking this page when the content is totally irrelevant to the attribute that's being predicted? And it turns out we have to look at a whole bunch of underlying theories to see why we're able to do this. One of them is a sociological theory called homophily, which basically says people are friends with people like them. So if you're smart, you tend to be friends with smart people, and if you're young, you tend to be friends with young people, and this is well established for hundreds of years.[16]

What is so revealing about this study is that it shows that the phenomenology of making and unmaking virtual commitments has significantly changed in the past few years. Namely, in the present day we are revealing information about ourselves we did not know to be revealing in our most mundane social network engagements. In this new virtual landscape the online self is constantly making virtual commitments that reveal significant information about the situated self, without ever knowing it. In other words the seemingly anonymous and risk-free task of Liking on Facebook by the online self results in regularly making *Unintentional Virtual Commitments*. In this view, an *Unintentional Virtual Commitment* differs from a *Virtual Commitment* in so far as, when an online self makes the virtual commitment of LIKING Curly fries on Facebook they are just committing to fact that they LIKE curly fries and nothing more. The fact that such a LIKE or virtual commitment can potentially reveal further information about the situated self who made the LIKE, such as their sexual orientation or IQ, makes it a *Unintentional statement*, i.e. a claim about the situated self the online self was not committed to sharing with the Public.

How do unintentional virtual commitments affect the situated and online self's relationship in the virtual landscape of social networking? In order to answer this question we must first understand how information provided by unintentional virtual commitments is used, or can be potentially used. All the data we provide on social networking sites such as Facebook, e.g. likes, shares, pictures, videos, and personal information, is partially owned by the social networking site as soon as we share it with the public. The most common way

---

16 Tedtalk: *Jennifer Golbeck: The curly fry conundrum: Why social media "likes" say more than you might think.*

social networking companies use personal data is in revenue models that rely on sharing or exploiting it in some way or other. As Jennifer Goldberg points out "it's sometimes said of Facebook that the users aren't the customer, they're the product."[17]

Using customer data to increase or create profit, however, is not something new, it's been done for quite a while now. For decades companies like Target have regularly collected customer data of every person who has a purchasing history at their stores. Loyal customers are assigned a unique code, internally know as a Guest ID number, which records every single thing they ever purchase. Alongside the purchasing history, every Guest ID has demographic information about the customer: their age, marriage status, number of kids, estimated salary, how far they live from the nearest store and even what websites they visit. In the *New York Times* article "How Companies Learn Your Secrets," Charles Duhigg alludes to this very point:

> Target can buy data about your ethnicity, job history, the magazines you read, if you've ever declared bankruptcy or got divorced, the year you bought (or lost) your house, where you went to college, what kinds of topics you talk about online, whether you prefer certain brands of coffee, paper towels, cereal or applesauce, your political leanings, reading habits, charitable giving and the number of cars you own... For companies like Target, the exhaustive rendering of our conscious and unconscious patterns into data sets and algorithms has revolutionized what they know about us and, therefore, how precisely they can sell.[18]

In order to increase sales via precise marketing tools, statisticians working for Target create algorithms and mathematical models that allow them to predict very personal information about shoppers. With astounding accuracy for instance, they can predict when a customer has become pregnant, as well as their baby's due date. The upside of pregnancy prediction models is that Target can precisely market their baby products to customers who actually need them and create brand loyalties from early on. Ever since Target implemented prediction models as a marketing tool, their yearly revenue has significantly increased. At first hand this marketing tool seems like a win-win situation: customers are marketed what they actually need and companies increase their sells with more precise marketing strategies. However an anecdote Duhigg retells hints at the eerie implications these prediction models can have:

---

17 Tedtalk: *Jennifer Golbeck: The curly fry conundrum: Why social media "likes" say more than you might think.*

18 "How Companies Learn Your Secrets" by Charles Duhigg Feb. 16, 2012 *New York Times.*

...A man walked into a Target outside Minneapolis and demanded to see the manager. He was clutching coupons that had been sent to his daughter, and he was angry,
according to an employee who participated in the conversation. "My daughter got this
in the mail!" he said. "She's still in high school, and you're sending her coupons for baby
clothes and cribs? Are you trying to encourage her to get pregnant?" The manager didn't
have any idea what the man was talking about. He looked at the mailer. Sure enough,
it was addressed to the man's daughter and contained advertisements for maternity
clothing, nursery furniture and pictures of smiling infants. The manager apologized and
then called a few days later to apologize again. On the phone, though, the father was
somewhat abashed. "I had a talk with my daughter," he said. "It turns out there's been
some activities in my house I haven't been completely aware of. She's due in August.
I owe you an apology."

This anecdote reveals how unintentional virtual commitments could potentially
be used for invasive marketing schemes. It is no secret that in our social network
engagements we are targeted with ad campaigns as a result of our age, gender,
tastes, and geographical location. However, as Jennifer Goldberg aptly points
out, there is a potential use of unintentional virtual commitments as personal
data sets for identity attribute prediction models that has a significant implication beyond the consumer market. Namely, in using identity attribute prediction
models as tools for real-world situations such as prescreening people before job
interviews or supervising personnel at the companies they work for. Since identity prediction models can predict with great accuracy attributes like drug or
alcohol use, it is not farfetched to think that companies could implement these
models as a way to screen their current or potential employees. If this scenario
sounds too much like a remote Big Brother thought experiment, consider the
fact that in the early days of Facebook a large number of people lost their jobs
just for posting images that their employers deemed inappropriate. Regardless
of whether the consumer market or companies are implementing unintentional
virtual commitments as tools to predict personal attributes or not, what this
implies is that in the era of the selfie the virtual commitments the online self
makes on social networks are no longer anonymous and risk free, and therefore
can have real-world consequences for the situated self.

A foretelling example of this is what happened to Justine Sacco for writing
a tweet that came out badly. In his book, *So You've Been Publicly Shamed*, Jon
Ronson vividly narrates her story:

It was December 20, 2013. For the previous two days she'd (Justine Sacco) been tweeting
little acerbic jokes to her 170 followers about her holiday travels. She was like a social
media Sally Bowles, decadent and flighty and unaware that serious politics were looming.
There was her joke about the German man on the plane from New York: "*Weird German
Dude: You're in first class. It's 2014. Get some deodorant—Inner monolog as I inhale*

BO. Thank god for pharmaceuticals." Then the layover at Heathrow: *"Chili-cucumber sandwiches-bad teeth. Back in London!"* Then the final leg: *"Going to Africa. Hope I don't get AIDS. Just kidding. I'm white!"*
She chuckled to herself, pressed send and wandered around the airport for half an hour, sporadically checking Twitter. "I got nothing" she told me. "No replies."
She boarded the plane. It was an eleven-hour flight. She slept. When the plane landed, she turned on her phone. Straightway there was a text from someone she hadn't spoken to since high school: "I'm sorry to see what's happening." She looked at it, baffled. "And then, my phone started to explode," she said.[19]

What follows, Justine Sacco refers to as "a mass online destruction." During her flight, Sacco's tweet *"Going to Africa. Hope I don't get AIDS. Just kidding. I'm white!"* became the number one worldwide trending topic. The trend immediately spawned what Ronson calls an "online shaming" deeming her a racist. Her comment spread so quickly that paparazzi awaited her at Cape Town airport and her relatives only greeted her with: "This is not what our family stands for. And now, by association, you've tarnished the family." In the following month, upon returning to New York City, her name had been goggled 1,220,000 times, and the bad tweet had resulted in her not only being fired but in becoming socially ostracized.

Yet there is a far more revealing and deeper consequence that we can learn from Sacco's "mass online destruction" as evidenced in her own words:

> "I can't fully grasp the misconception that's happening around the world...They've taken my name and my picture, and have created this Justine Sacco that's not me and have labeled this person a racist. I have this fear that if I were in a car accident tomorrow and lost my memory and came back and googled myself, that would be my new reality....I'm thirty years old. I had a great career. If I don't have a plan, if I don't start making steps to reclaim my identity and remind myself who I am on a daily basis, then I might lose myself."[20]

What is so revealing about Sacco's words is that she is clearly aware that an online self "that's not her" replaced her situated self, and put her in a position where she struggles daily to "reclaim her identity." Sacco's online self's carefree social networking rants, which she clearly thought to be risk free and, if not anonymous, at least private in so far as her tweets were only meant to be read by her 170 followers, resulted in the *real-world* breakdown of her situated self. A breakdown that to this day Sacco has not been able to recover from as result of the inerasable online self that trails her like a specter wherever she goes.

---

19 Jon Ronson, *So you've been Publicly Shamed*, Riverhead Books, 2015, p. 68.
20 Jon Ronson, *So you've been Publicly Shamed*, Riverhead books, 2015, pp. 74, 80.

For Heidegger, what Justine Sacco went through is what he calls *world collapse*. World collapse is a form of existential or ontological death that Heidegger distinguishes from what he calls *demise*, i.e. death as a terminal biological or ontic phenomenon. For Heidegger terminal death is something distinctively impending, an event that will one day overtake each of us. But ontological death as Heidegger understands it is a way to be.[21] It is a way of living that takes account of our constant vulnerability to the collapse of our way of life.

Online death without demise is a sort of phenomena that can befall individual beings in cases of world collapse such as identity failure, e.g. as in the case of Justine Sacco, or the loss of an unconditional commitment, amongst other forms of ontological death. Unlike demise existential breakdown is lived through, for one can only experience world collapse if the collapse that is undergone is not a terminal one. In other words the individual that undergoes the experience must continue to exist for such a death to occur. In cases of complete existential ontological breakdown an individual's world fully collapses; the light that shed meaning on his or her life suddenly becomes dim and meaninglessness lurks in its place. Such a collapse of an individual's world occurs when a person can no longer cope with things in the way one would normally cope with them. Heidegger equates this sort of breakdown with an anxiety attack in which human beings lose their ability to act at all.

Justine Sacco is a clear example of someone who experienced *world collapse* a result of online identity failure. Her tweets (virtual commitments) were intended to be understood as jokes, as oppose to statements of what she actually believed. The fact that it was NOT her intention to sound racist with her remarks makes her tweets unintentional virtual commitments, that unlike Facebook Likes that *have no obvious connection to a predicted personal attribute*, her tweet could easily and quickly be misinterpreted as the predicted personal attribute she was associated with online, namely, that she was a racist. What we can gain from this insight is that virtual commitments such as 1) Facebook Likes as the ones previously described, i.e. unintentional virtual commitments that *have no obvious connection to a predicted personal attribute* are case of WEAK UNINTENTIONAL VIRTUAL COMMITMENTS and 2) virtual commitments such as Justine Sacco's tweet, i.e. unintentional virtual commitments that *have a clear connection to a predicted personal attribute*, *are cases* of STRONG UNINTENTIONAL VIRTUAL COMMITMENTS. Why I consider this to be

---

21 Martin Heidegger, *Being and Time*, trans. J. Macquarrie and E. Robinson (New York: Harper and Row, 1962), p. 294.

an important distinction is that these sorts of distinctions begin to draw a very different virtual landscape from the one of the early days of the Internet, where all virtual commitments had no risk whatsoever. In this new virtual landscape, the relationship between risk, anonymity and virtual commitments has varying degrees and potentially different outcomes.] *

A further distinction we can point out is when someone makes a committed online statement, i.e. an INTENTIONAL VIRTUAL COMMITMENT, and as a result suffers a *world collapse*. Say for instance when someone makes an online political, environmental, or personal claim on a social network about something that is truly meaningful to him or her. In the early days of the Internet, and in most present day social network engagements, such claims have no real-world consequences on the situated self whatsoever. A number of present day examples however, hint at how virtual commitments of this sort are also changing, and as consequence are altering the current day virtual landscape of social networking.

In 2012 a series of documents surfaced that showed that the fast-food chain Chick-Fil-A and its president Dan Cathy, financially backed anti-gay Christian organizations. Mayors from all across the United States voiced their opinions, and some like Boston Mayor Tom Menino, even vowed to sanction the fast-food conglomerate from opening up new restaurants in his city. Despite the public uproar Chick-Fil-A proudly stood by its anti-gay stance, inspiring supporters like former Arkansas governor Mike Huckabee to call for a *Chick-Fil-A Appreciation Day* as a way to take a stand against same sex marriage. On August 1, 2012, thousands flocked to Chick-Fil-A restaurants to show their appreciation and support, however a man by the name of Adam Smith decided to protest the event in his own way. Smith made a YouTube video of himself ordering free water at a Chick-Fil-A drive-through while mocking and criticizing a female employee for the company's anti-gay beliefs. The video quickly went viral, as a result Smith was subsequently fired from his job as the CFO of Vante, Inc., a medical device manufacturer. Smith recalls the consequences of the incident, "In one day, with one two-and-one-half minute YouTube video protest, my salary and equity vanished. The security I believed would keep me safe from chance, bad luck, bad people, Satan, and fire forever had been taken. More than one million dollars of value was gone in an instant. That free cup of water ironically cost me a million dollars."[22]

In the aftermath of the scandal, Smith and his family relocated to Portland, Oregon where he was hired as the CFO of another company. Two weeks later however, he was removed from the position when his new boss realized who he

---

22 YouTube video https://www.youtube.com/watch?v=rgwX2d810Oo.

was. A story that would repeat itself again and again, as Smith recalls, "over the next two years I received many offers for employment that were immediately rescinded after employers Googled my name." Since then he has continued to struggle to find a lasting job in the financial sector and has been living off food stamps in an RV with his family. In March 2015, he published a memoir titled *Million Dollar Cup of Water: Discovering the Wealth in Authenticity,* in which he reflects on his identity crisis. On his website, he describes the book as a search for authenticity in the face of darkest time in his life:

> With repeated rejections, an inability to provide for my young family, and the belief that my online reputation now defined me, I fell into an identity crisis that pushed me into the darkest time in my life. Through an authentic soul search and the healing presence of family and friends, I faced a reality that had always seemed too frightening and humiliating to accept.

Adam Smith, as in the case of Justin Sacco, suffered a *world collapse* as result of identity failure. What distinguishes Smith's case from Sacco's is that he openly believed, and still believes, what he said and posted online. In other words, he was COMMITTED to his virtual commitment of supporting a same-sex lifestyle. Since the episode however, Smith has continually tried to dissociate himself from the behavior of his online self by apologizing for *how* he voiced his beliefs on gay rights, but never for his *stance*, "I don't regret the stand that I took," he says in an ABC interview, "but I regret the way that I talked to her."

To this day Sacco's and Smith's online-self is identified with their virtual collapse. If you goggle either one of their names their scandal trails them for several pages and will most likely do so throughout their entire lives. The identity of their situated self will for the most part of their existence be linked and determined by an online self they no longer have any sort of control over. In other words, unlike the risk-free and flexible virtual commitments such as the ones made by Essena O'Neil in an attempt to escape leveling, intentional and unintentional virtual commitments are irrevocable and risky, and remain part of an individual's Internet search history, i.e. they become life long determining attributes of the online self. The phenomena of world collapse, the very tangible possibility of dying online without demise, is a foretelling example of one of many ways the *situated self can lose itself in the online self* while navigating the worlds of the social networking.

So far, following Dreyfus and Kierkegaard, we have learned that 1) finding meaning through risk-free and flexible virtual commitments on the Internet as way to escape nihilism leads to despair, and have shown 2) how in the virtual landscapes of social networking risky and irrevocable virtual commitments (intentional and unintentional) can lead to world collapse as a result of identity failure. This paints a very dim and hopeless picture of the Internet and social networking in the age of the selfie. So if we are to live in a world where the situated self is virtually coupled by an online self that proves to be pivotal in his or her self-understanding, how then can we embrace the Internet and social networks in a way that does not lead to despair or world collapse? This is an extremely difficult question, and one we will be attempting to answer for many years as the Internet continues to change and evolve.

Kierkegaard thought that only the way to escape the leveling of nihilism is by embracing an individual identity that discloses an individual world. This is achieved by committing yourself fully to a *calling* or *vocation* that becomes the center of your entire sense of being, in other words, it becomes the focus of what gives meaning to your life. These sorts of commitments are experienced as taking grasp of our lives. Political activism, religious devotion, falling in love, being a devoted mother, or having an artistic or academic vocation can take grasp of our lives in this precise manner. When we respond to these callings with what Kierkegaard calls *infinite passion*; when we embrace our calling as an *unconditional commitment*, our commitment discloses what will be the ultimate concern of our lives. Such unconditional commitments therefore elude leveling and *despair* by determining what will show up as significant and insignificant, important and irrelevant, serious and lighthearted, on the basis of that which most matters to us in our life. Living one's life by fully embracing an irrevocable unconditional commitment, according to Kierkegaard, is to live in the Christian/religious sphere of existence.

The unconditional commitments one lives by in the religious sphere differ from aesthetic and ethical commitments in so far as they are not flexible or risk free; rather they are irrevocable and thus *make one's individual identity vulnerable to failure.* According to Dreyfus, for Kierkegaard this vulnerability implies that:

> One's cause may fail. One's lover may leave. The detached reflection of the present age, the hyperflexibility of the aesthetic sphere, and the unbound freedom of the ethical sphere are always avoiding one's vulnerability, but it turns out, Kierkegaard claims, that, for that very reason they level all qualitative distinctions, and end in the despair of meaninglessness. Only a risky unconditional commitment and the strong identity it produces can give an individual a world organized by that individuals unique qualitative distinctions.[23]

---

23 Hubert Dreyfus, *On the Internet*, p. 87.

So, if according to Kierkegaard, the only way to escape the leveling of nihilism and the despair of the meaningless is by embracing an unconditional commitment in one's life, is it possible to pursue such a commitment on the Internet and on social networks? In other words, can there be such a thing as virtual unconditional commitments? For Dreyfus, hyperflexible and unbound virtual commitments, would lead Kierkegaard to argue that:

> While the Internet, like the public sphere and the press, does not *prohibit* unconditional commitments, in the end it *undermines* them. Like a simulator, The Net manages to captures everything but the risk.[24] ✳ *This is the authenticity lias.*

For Dreyfus, the sorts of commitments the Internet can encourage are imaginary or simulated commitments that have no real-world consequences and are restrained to a limited virtual domain.

> But the risks (of computer games and the Internet) are only imaginary and have *no long-term consequences*. The temptation is to live in a world of stimulating images and simulated commitments and thus lead a simulated life. As Kierkegaard says in the present age, it transforms the task itself into an unreal feat of artifice, and reality into a theatre.'[25]

This view clearly holds for cases such as the simulated life of Essena O'Neill as well as for many other Instagram celebrities. But as we have seen in the cases of Sacco and Smith, the *risk* of making intentional and unintentional virtual commitments on social networks is real and can have long-term consequences. Does this imply that social networks could potentially encourage and support unconditional commitments? Both Sacco and Smith suffered from world collapse as a result of identity failure, not as a consequence of losing an unconditional commitment. For Sacco and Smith, telling jokes and fighting for gay rights, was not a *calling* or *vocation* that disclosed the ultimate concern of their lives. Their virtual commitments made them vulnerable, but not *authentic*, as Heidegger would say, since neither embraced these commitments unconditionally with irrevocable passion. Pursuing such virtual commitments as risky unconditional commitments would entail embracing them as the focus of an individual's ultimate concern, i.e. as the focus of what is most meaningful in their lives. In other words, such unconditional virtual commitments would need to sustain and encourage an individual identity who's entire vulnerable and individual world, consisted in fighting for gay rights or telling jokes. In the case of the former, we can think of LGBT activists who put at risk their individual worlds by

---

24 Hubert Dreyfus, *On the Internet*, p. 88.
25 Hubert Dreyfus, *On the Internet*, p. 88.

embracing irrevocable unconditional commitments on social networks, such as the feminist protest punk band Pussy Riot.

In February 2012, the all-girl punk band stormed the Cathedral of Christ the Savior in Moscow wearing brightly colored masks, and performed in front of the golden Holy Doors a "punk prayer" for a camera and a handful of worshippers. Security guards quickly stopped them and stripped away their guitars, but the music video was completed and uploaded on YouTube. The music video, titled "Punk Prayer: Mother of God Drive Putin Away" is a direct attack at Putin's anti-feminist and anti-LGBT policies. The uploaded video of the strategically planned political protest was clearly an intentional virtual commitment on behalf of the members of Pussy Riot protesting Putin's anti-feminist and anti-LGBT political agenda. The video quickly caught online traction and consequently was brought to the attention of Russian authorities. In the aftermath of the virtual political protest, three members of the band Maria Alekhina, Nadezhda Tolokonnikova and Yekaterina Samutsevich were arrested for "hooliganism motivated by religious hatred," while the remaining two members fled the country. After a high-profile trial that caught the world's attention the trio was sentenced to two years in a penal colony.[26]

What distinguishes their intentional virtual commitment from Smith's is that they have consistently remained unapologetic and firm about their performance and its political significance, i.e. unlike Smith they fully embrace their virtual commitment and its implications. Although at the opening of the trial the women apologized for offending the Orthodox Church, they did so only to emphasize that their music video was meant as a political statement against Mr. Putin and against the church patriarch. After international pressure from world leaders and celebrities such as Madonna and Sting, the band members were subsequently released from prison two months before completing their two-year sentence. Since then they have passionately continued in their plight for LGBT and woman rights in Russia by posting more political music videos and furthering their cause on other social networks such as Facebook and Twitter.[27] Given that Pussy Riot's intentional virtual commitment sustains and encourages their vocation as LGBT and Feminist political activists, and thus discloses the ultimate concern of their lives, can we say that their virtual commitments are unconditional virtual commitments?

---

26 "Anti-Putin Stunt Earns Punk Band Two Years in Jail" by David M. Herszenhorn Aug. 17, 2012 *New York Times*.
27 "Pussy Riot Tells All" by Joel Nocera Feb 7, 2014 *New York Times*.

In sharing their music video on a major social network, the members of the band were aware of the high risk and possible consequences of their political activism. In other words given the anti-free speech political climate they were in, unlike Smith, they were aware that their intentional virtual commitment would have real-world consequences and perhaps even long-term repercussions. "Punk Prayer" is thus an act of civil disobedience akin to Mather Luther King's marches, Rosa parks refusal to sit at the back of the bus, and Gandhi's hunger strikes. Given that the members of Pussy Riot were gripped with such passion to take a stand against Putin's political machine, and were aware of the potential criminal charges they might face, i.e. aware of the possibility of world collapse, their intentional virtual commitments are clear examples of unconditional virtual commitments. What this shows is that in the current virtual landscape of social networks, the Internet has opened up the possibility to sustain and encourage unconditional commitments that can escape the leveling of nihilism and the meaninglessness of despair by embracing individual identities that disclose individual worlds.

Following Kierkegaard we saw how pursuing unintentional and intentional virtual commitments on social networks promotes nihilistic leveling and leads to the despair of the meaningless. And how, by way of unconditional virtual commitments, individuals can overcome nihilistic leveling and pursue meaningful lives. What this entails is that for Kierkegaard the leveling of the Internet and social networks menace individuals' identities and worlds. For Heidegger however, the danger of the leveling of technology, i.e. the nihilistic leveling of the Internet and social networks, menaces our very *understanding of being*. With the rise of social networks our *telepresence in cyberspace* has not only become an integral part of our everyday life but also of our understanding of being. This new technological understanding of being, as Heidegger refers to it, is now deeply ingrained in how we see and think about ourselves, how we relate to one another, and thus how we cope with the world.

Decades before the invention of the Internet, in his essay *The Question Concerning Technology*, Heidegger foresaw the deep cultural implications of social networks. For him, the essence of modern technology is to yield maximum organization, efficiency and flexibility in all human endeavors: "expediting is always itself directed from the beginning ... towards driving on to the maximum yield at the minimum expense."[28] In other words, the goal of modern

---

28 Martin Heidegger, "The Question Concerning Technology," *The Question Concerning Technology and Other Essays*, trans. William Lovitt (New York: Harper & Row, 1977) p. 23.

technologies, like social networks, is to order everything in the most efficient and cost effective manner. What this implies according to Heidegger is:

> Everywhere everything is ordered to stand by, to be immediately at hand, indeed to stand there just so that it may be on call for a further ordering. Whatever is ordered about in this way has its own standing. We call it standing-reserve.[29]

In our cultural paradigm of the technological understanding of being everything is treated as standing-reserve, in other words all things, including our virtual self-understanding, can be treated as resources to be used for further ordering. A good example that illustrates how this relates to social networks is identity attribute prediction models. The user data we share on our Facebook profile for instance is used to create a series of attribute predictions about who we are and what we like, and are thus stored and ordered to be used as a resource for what ever task a Facebook user (e.g. learning who we are), ourselves (e.g. networking) or Facebook (e.g. selling it for profit) may want to do with it.

As so, Heidegger concludes: "whatever stands by in the sense of standing-reserve no longer stands over against us as object."[30] Thus in this new ontical relationship "both subject and object are sucked up as standing reserve"[31] When both subject and object become resource, modern technologies like jet planes or social networks are only understood in their technological essence. They no longer show up as tools we can use for coping in a given task, but as flexible and efficient "gears" in the great machine of postmodernity. In this view, we no longer use transportation systems and social networks, but rather social networks and transportation systems use us. As Jennifer Gollbeck pointed out earlier, "it's sometimes said of Facebook that the users aren't the customer, they're the product."[32] In this technological paradigm, as Dreyfus following Heidegger aptly points out, "ultimate goals like serving God, society, our fellow men, or even ourselves no longer make sense. Human beings, on this view, become a resource to be used – but more importantly, to be enhanced – like any other."[33]

---

29 Ibid., p. 24.

30 Ibid, p. 24.

31 Ibid., p. 31.

32 Gollbeck, J. "The Curly Fry Conundrum: Why Social Media "Likes" Say More than You might Think". Ted Talk. October 2013. Last accessed: 10 Dec. 2017. Accessible from: https://www.ted.com/talks/jennifer_golbeck_the_curly_fry_conundrum_why_ social_media_likes_say_more_than_you_might_think.

33 Hubert Dreyfus, "Heidegger on the Connection between Nihilism, Art, Technology and Politics", 2001b, p. 30.

The "greatest danger" as Heidegger calls it, is that we become so captivated by this technological understanding of being, so entranced by constantly seeking maximum order and efficiency *for its own sake*, that as a result we ourselves are reduced to mere *resources* to be used and further enhanced. In other words, the current technological paradigm of the era of the selfie seeks "flexibility and efficiency, not for the sake of some further end, but just for the sake of flexibility and efficiency themselves."[34]

(handwritten margin note: ✳ OR: for the sake of material wellbeing, and thereby Psychological wellbeing.)

The technological understanding of being reaches it's full potential and expansion in the virtual landscape of social networks: *Facebook* allows us to efficiently organize and keep track of our "friends," *Tinder* provides an expedient platform to constantly meet new potential sexual partners, *Twitter* encourages our thoughts and ideas to be short and proficient, and apps such as *Whatsapp* makes communication so effective that we are expected to always be available no matter where in the world we finds ourselves. In the era of the selfie, we are constantly awestruck with apps, devices, or social networks that promise to make our lives better, more productive, healthier, smarter, stronger, happier, and so on. The ultimate drive of our current technological paradigm holds up for us that in order to lead a good life, we must be as efficient and productive as possible at the most minimum expense, *for its own sake*. "We thus become part of a system" says Dreyfus, "which no one directs but which moves towards the total mobilization and enhancement of all beings, even us. This is why Heidegger thinks the perfectly ordered society dedicated to the welfare of all is not the solution of our problems but the culmination of the technological understanding of being."

The most poignant present day example that illustrates Heidegger's "greatest danger" is the research being done at the *Quantified Self Labs*, a research facility in California that describes itself as "a global collaboration among users and makers of self-tracking tools exploring *self-knowledge through numbers*."[35] For its co-founder, Gary Wolf, the laboratory's sole objective is to achieve a deeper sense of self-understanding via digital tracking tools that amass quantitative measurements and self-tracking data. For this reason, Wolf regularly tracks his day-to-day movements:

> I got up this morning at 6:10 a.m. after going to sleep at 12:45 a.m. I was awakened once during the night. My heart rate was 61 beats per minute, my blood pressure, 127 over 74. I had zero minutes of exercise yesterday, so my maximum heart rate during exercise

---

34 Ibid., p. 21.
35 Gary Wolf website www.antephase.com.

wasn't calculated. I had about 600 milligrams of caffeine, zero of alcohol. And my score on the Narcissism Personality Index, or the NPI-16, is a reassuring 0.31.[36]

Wolf embarked on his data driven lifestyle when he and his partner, Kevin Kelly, noticed "that people were subjecting themselves to regimes of quantitative measurement and self-tracking that went far beyond the ordinary, familiar habits such as stepping on a scale every day. People were tracking their food via Twitter, their kids' diapers on their iPhone. They were making detailed journals of their spending, their mood, their symptoms, their treatments." Their basic assumption was, since "we use numbers when we want to tune up a car, analyze a chemical reaction, predict the outcome of an election. We use numbers to optimize an assembly line. Why not use numbers on ourselves?"[37]

Their discovery that *trackers*, as they refer to people who regularly subject themselves to self-tracking measurements, "instead of interrogating their inner worlds through talking and writing…are using numbers"[38] led them to the idea of exploring the possibility of a *quantified self*. As such, Wolf and Kelly's research focuses on finding ways to use these tracking tools not merely for marketing research, biometric security, or personal health reasons but in "using them to get some systematic improvement" and accomplish how "they can be useful for self-improvement, for self-discovery, self-awareness, self-knowledge."[39]

In their pursuit for self-improvement, the data sets trackers accrue on a daily basis are commonly shared on social networks in order to compare and contrast progress with other online trackers. As Kelly puts it, "personal data are ideally suited to a social life of sharing. You might not always have something to say, but you always have a number to report."[40] In this view, the *quantified self* serves as direct a bridge between the embodied self and the online self, in so far as it provides an objective portrayal of the day to day on goings of the embodied self to it's online community. What Wolf and Kelly's have hit upon is that these "new tools are changing our sense of self in the world." Yet unlike Heidegger and Dreyfus, they see the pervasiveness of people being captivated by the technological understanding of being as a turn for the better and as an opportunity for achieving a deeper understanding of being:

36 Wolf, G. (2010b) "The Quantified Self". Ted Talk. June 2010. Last accessed: 10 Dec. 2017. Accessible from: https://www.ted.com/talks/gary_wolf_the_quantified_self#t-31422.

37 "The Date Driven Life" by Gary Wolf April 28, 2010 *New York Times.*

38 "The Date Driven Life" by Gary Wolf April 28, 2010 *New York Times.*

39 Wolf, G. (2010b) "The Quantified Self". Ted Talk. June 2010. Last accessed: 10 Dec. 2017. Accessible from: https://www.ted.com/talks/gary_wolf_the_quantified_self#t-31422.

40 "The Date Driven Life" by Gary Wolf April 28, 2010 *New York Times.*

When we quantify ourselves, there isn't the imperative to see through our daily existence into a truth buried at a deeper level. Instead, the self of our most trivial thoughts and actions, the self that, without technical help, we might barely notice or recall, is understood as the self we ought to get to know. Behind the allure of the quantified self is a guess that many of our problems come from simply lacking the instruments to understand who we are. Our memories are poor; we are subject to a range of biases; we can focus our attention on only one or two things at a time. We don't have a pedometer in our feet, or a breathalyzer in our lungs, or a glucose monitor installed into our veins. We lack both the physical and the mental apparatus to take stock of ourselves. We need help from machines.[41]

For them "the self is just our operation center, our consciousness, our moral compass. So, if we want to act more effectively in the world, we have to get to know ourselves better." In other words, Wolf and Kelly are taken with the idea that the main focus of self-understanding is to constantly achieve maximum order and efficiency in our lives, that is, *for its own sake*. In Heidegger's view, what the notion of the quantified self does, is reduce human experience and thus people to mere *resources*, or data sets, to be used and further enhanced for no other reason than enhancement itself. In this bleak view, our technological understanding of being turns us into flexible and efficient cogs in a vast and ever-expanding network that no one is directing.

In order to resist the leveling of modern nihilism Heidegger urges us to rethink the essence of technology, and rather than resist modern technologies, such as social networks and digital tracking tools, embrace them in a positive new manner. For as Heidegger rightly points out, "it would be foolish to attack technology blindly. It would be shortsighted to condemn it as the work of the devil. We depend on technical devices; they even challenge us to ever greater advances."[42] Heidegger's goal is to find a way of living with technology that does not "wrap, confuse, and lay waste or nature"[43] and assures us that, "when we once open ourselves expressly to the essence of technology, we find ourselves unexpectedly taken into a freeing claim."[44] In other words, once we achieve a deeper understanding of the essence of technology we will gain a free relation to it.

41 "The Date Driven Life" by Gary Wolf April 28, 2010 *New York Times*.
42 Martin Heidegger, *Discourse on Thinking*, trans. John M. Anderson and E. Hans Freund, New York: Harper & Row, 1966, p. 53.
43 Martin Heidegger, "The Question Concerning Technology," *The Question Concerning Technology and Other Essays*, trans. William Lovitt (New York: Harper & Row, 1977) p. 24.
44 Martin Heidegger, "The Question Concerning Technology," *The Question Concerning Technology and Other Essays*, trans. William Lovitt (New York: Harper & Row, 1977), pp. 25–26.

For Heidegger, the way to gain a free relationship to technology is to open up to our technological understanding of being, and embrace it as our modern day human cultural paradigm. Once we see our technological understanding of being as our current way of being, as our cultural paradigm, and thus the cause of our anxiety; we realize that the world shows up to us as a network of resources because it is the way the world is made intelligible in this given moment in time. The fact that the world shows up to us as a collection of resources does not imply however, that we must engage and cope with everything, including ourselves, solely as mere resources. In other words, as Dreyfus tells us, once we comprehend "in our practices, of course, not just as matter of reflection – that we receive our technological understanding of being, we have stepped out of the technological understanding of being, for we then see that what is most important in our lives is not subject to efficient enhancement – indeed, the drive to control everything is precisely what we do not control."[45]

When we acknowledge the technological understanding of being as a historical understanding, we gain a free relation to technology and the world opens up in a way where we neither need to solely embrace the efficiency and flexibility of technology nor always resist it. As Heidegger puts it:

> We let technical devices enter our daily life, and at the same time leave them outside,
> ... as things which are nothing absolute but remain dependent upon something higher.
> I would call this comportment toward technology which expresses "yes" and at the same
> time "no", by an old word, releasement towards things.[46]

Releasement towards things, allows us to engage with modern day technology, such as social networks, with a comportment that acknowledges the *danger* of such engagements, namely of the nihilistic leveling of our modern day technological understanding of being. By doing so we realize that efficiency for its own sake is not the sole driver of being, but how things are made intelligible in the current cultural paradigm. Heidegger tells us that once we grasp the danger of our technological understanding of being as a danger itself, it becomes that which saves us from ourselves: "The selfsame danger is, when it is as the danger, the saving power."[47]

---

45 Hubert Dreyfus, "Heidegger on the Connection between Nihilism, Art, Technology and Politics," 2001b, p. 32.

46 Martin Heidegger, *Discourse on Thinking*, trans. John M. Anderson and E. Hans Freund, New York: Harper & Row, 1966, p. 54.

47 Martin Heidegger, "The Question Concerning Technology," *The Question Concerning Technology and Other Essays*, trans. William Lovitt (New York: Harper & Row, 1977), p. 39.

Free Relation; embracing the unfamiliar; the uncontrolled.

Releasement, however, is not sufficient to overcoming cultural leveling. It merely sets the ground for us to be receptive to what will ultimately allow us to have a free relation to modern technology and social networks. Thus, in order to counter the nihilistic leveling of our current cultural technological paradigm we most engage in social practices that resist efficiency and flexibility. For Daniele Quercia, a computer scientist and engineer whose work primarily focused on efficiency, a personal experience led him to this realization, namely that some of the most important things in our lives cannot be not subject to efficient enhancement:

> A few years ago, after finishing my Ph.D. in London, I moved to Boston. I lived in Boston and worked in Cambridge. I bought a racing bicycle that summer, and I bicycled every day to work. To find my way, I used my phone. It sent me over Massachusetts Avenue, the shortest route from Boston to Cambridge. But after a month that I was cycling every day on the car-packed Mass. Ave., I took a different route one day. I'm not entirely sure why I took a different route that day, a detour. I just remember a feeling of surprise; surprise at finding a street with no cars, as opposed to the nearby Mass. Ave. full of cars; surprise at finding a street draped by leaves and surrounded by trees. But after the feeling of surprise, I felt shame. How could I have been so blind? For an entire month, I was so trapped in my mobile app that a journey to work became one thing only: the shortest path. In this single journey, there was no thought of enjoying the road, no pleasure in connecting with nature, no possibility of looking people in the eyes. And why? Because I was saving a minute out of my commute.[48]

This experience led Quercia to question the role of efficiency in his everyday life as well as in his research. Now, rather than seeing efficiency as the primary goal of his work, he saw it as a "cult" that was blinding us from a "far richer reality." He shifted his research from traditional data-mining and began to think of how to create a digital navigation platform that focused on how we could potentially *experience* the city as oppose to how *fast* we could get through it.[49] The result of this is "the creation of new maps, maps where you don't only find the shortest path…but also the most enjoyable path." Via a crowdsourcing platform where thousands of people were asked to weigh in on what urban scenes they considered most beautiful, quiet, or happy he and his team devised a new map of London, "a cartography weighted for human emotions":

---

48 Quercia, D. (2014) "Happy Maps". Ted Talk. November 2014. Last accessed: 10 Dec. 2017. Accessible from: https://www.ted.com/talks/daniele_quercia_happy_maps
49 Daniel Quercia, Rossano Schifanella, and Luca Maria Aiello, "The Shortest Path to Happiness: Recommending Beautiful, Quiet, and Happy Routes in the City", 2014.

On this cartography, you're not only able to see and connect from point A to point B the shortest segments, but you're also able to see the happy segment, the beautiful path, the quiet path. In tests, participants found the happy, the beautiful, the quiet path far more enjoyable than the shortest one, and that just by adding a few minutes to travel time.[50]

What is so insightful about Quercia's research is that it embraces modern technology in a way that resists the technological understanding of being and attempts to free us of Heidegger's "greatest danger." Mapping tools that take experience in to account resist the temptation of navigating the world via the most efficient path, and as such, open up the world to us in a way that has been covered up by our technological cultural paradigm. As Quercia puts it, *Happy Maps* allow us to escape "a world fabricated for efficiency,"[51] and thus, in Heidegger's view, allows for a *releasement toward things*.

Quercia's *Happy Maps* illustrate well what Heidegger means by learning to value and embrace the saving power of insignificant things. For Albert Borgmann[52] there is an even more significant manner way in which to do this, namely by engaging with what he calls *focal practices*. Focal practices are social practices such as friendship, attending a live musical concert or an art exhibit, rituals such as marriages, and social gatherings such as political protests. These local gatherings disclose local ways of being that resist efficiency in of themselves. In other words, we do not seek to be efficient when we go out with friends to have a good time, nor when we attend a political protest or a concert, rather in these focal practices we seek to engage in a way in which we lose ourselves in them, and give our own most self to what the gathering solicits. Dreyfus, following Heidegger, further elaborates on focal practices:

> Local worlds occur around some everyday thing that temporarily brings into their own both the thing itself and those involved in the typical activity concerning the use of the thing. Heidegger calls this event a *thing thinging* and the tendency in the practices to bring things and people into their own, appropriation.

Heidegger thinks of bridges at different historical cultural paradigms in time, as an example of *technological thing* that gathers people around focal practices.

---

50 Quercia, D. (2014) "Happy Maps". Ted Talk. November 2014. Last accessed: 10 Dec. 2017. Accessible from: https://www.ted.com/talks/daniele_quercia_happy_maps

51 Quercia, D. (2014) "Happy Maps". Ted Talk. November 2014. Last accessed: 10 Dec. 2017. Accessible from: https://www.ted.com/talks/daniele_quercia_happy_maps

52 Albert Borgmann, *Technology and the Character of Contemporary Life* (Chicago: University of Chicago Press, 1984) pp. 196–210.

The bridge connects shores to shores, castles with cathedral squares, harvesting fields with villages, and highway bridges to highways. In other words, it connects worlds with other worlds: it connects the world of the harvest to the world of the village, and the world of the highway to the world of the city. As Heidegger tells us, "the bridge gathers, as a passage that crosses, before the divinities." The bridge as a *technological thing* gathers different worlds and thus allows *mortals* to access the focal practices that these worlds solicit. This notion of a technological thing that *gathers different worlds*, I believe to be the clue to how social networks can sustain and enable focal practices without converting them into flexible and efficient practices.

If we think of the Internet and social networks as *the information highway*, we can think of them as technological things that gather different worlds, just like any of Heidegger's bridges. In fact we can even think of social networks as the bridges of our current cultural paradigm, as the technological things that allows us to gather *online worlds* with *embodied worlds*. So how can social networks gather focal practices if they themselves cannot resist the flexibility and efficiency of the technological understanding of being?

The idea of creating a social network that creates online connections that result in meaningful face-to-face offline meetings was Scott Heifferman's main drive when he co-founded *Meetup*. For Heifferman a "Meetup is about the simple idea of using the Internet to get people off the Internet."[53] What is so significant about *Meetup* is that unlike other social networking sites that promote online to offline connections, such as Tinder or Facebook, is that it focuses on fomenting and enabling focal practices. *Meetups* are geared at building and strengthening the local practices of communities that allow for people to share and practice with one another what gives their lives meaning. As Heifferman explains, "people feel a need to commiserate or get together and talk about what's important to them. Our biggest categories are moms, small business, health support and fitness." Heifferman came up with the idea for *Meetup* during the aftermath of 9/11 when to his surprise he found comfort in the least excepted of places, in the communal mourning with strangers. Commiserating with his unknown next-door neighbors, attending a ceremony for the deceased in Union Square and volunteering with the Red Cross at Ground Zero led him to ask deep questions about the role of community in our everyday lives:

---

53 "The Pursuit of Community" by Scott Heiferman Sept. 5, 2009 *New York Times*.

"I never thought I was interested in community…but that experience led me to the basic questions of 'What brings people together? What gets them to talk to each other? How do people form powerful groups that can do good things?' "[54]

Heifferman's social networking site, which enables online users to create face-to-face offline group meetings centered around a common interest currently has over 25 million members who are part of 250,000 different groups in at least 100 countries around the world.[55] On its website, *Meetup* invites you to join a movement, to learn to cook, train for a marathon, hike a mountain or practice a language, within local community groups. In Heidegger's and Borgmann's view, *Meetup* discloses and enables focal practices that embrace the saving power of the insignificant by resisting efficiency and flexibility, without denying the role of the ordering power of our technological understanding of being. *Meetup* is an example that says "yes" and at the same time "no" to the technological understanding of being by denying what is most dangerous and celebrating what is most meaningful in our current cultural paradigm.

The menace of individual and cultural nihilistic leveling as result of the flexibility and ordering of social networks is ingrained in our current technological paradigm, and as a result in our self-understanding. The self of the age of the selfie is no longer made intelligible to us as a self, but rather as an embodied self in an ever-changing relationship with an online self that shows up as flexible, dynamic and highly ordered. Denying this is akin to denying our present way of being. Rather than resisting social networks we must, as Heidegger says, engage with them in a way that they "enter our daily life, and at the same time leave them outside." Our releasement towards social networks, towards our online self, enables us to understand the ordering power of social networks as the way the current world is made intelligible to us, rather than the way the worlds actually is, and thus allows us to embrace their essence to order everything in our lives but at the same time resist such ordering power. In other words, we must continue to find ways in which social networks enable and sustain our focal practices and unconditional commitments by harboring the power they have to *gather*: to connect us with others and ourselves. We must as well continue to learn to engage with our current virtual landscape in a way that allows for social networks to sustain and encourage unconditional commitments and enable focal practices that resist

---

54 "How 9/11 Inspired One of the First Social Networks" by John Bonazzo Aug. 7, 2016 The Observer.

55 "How 9/11 Inspired One of the First Social Networks" by John Bonazzo Aug. 7, 2016 The Observer.

the efficiency of our technological cultural paradigm, and thus allow us to gain a free relation with social networks and at the same time escape the leveling of modern nihilism. If we begin to view social networks as bridges, we can learn to regard them as divergent but interconnecting technological paths that if navigated in the appropriate manner, enable our embodied self to connect with our online self in a manner that encourages us to take up risky unconditional virtual commitments that open up the world to our upmost potentiality of being, to our authentic self, and thus disclose the vast array of meaningful focal practices that tacitly surround us with the power of the insignificant, and hide within what Dreyfus deems, the *sacredness* of our secular world.

Bibliography

Bonazzo, J. (2016) "How 9/11 Inspired One of the First Social Networks" , *The Observer*. August 7, 2016. Last accessed: 10 Dec. 2017. Accessible from: http://observer.com/2016/09/how-911-inspired-one-of-the-internets-first-social-networks/.

Borgmann, A. (1984) *Technology and the Character of Contemporary Life*. Chicago, IL: University of Chicago Press.

Dreyfus, H. (1999) "Kierkegaard on the Internet: Anonymity vs Commitment in the Present Age," in Schulz, H., J. Stewart, and K. Verstrynge (eds.). Kierkegaard Studies Yearbook. Berlin and New York: De Gruyter, pp. 96–109.

Dreyfus, H. (2001a) *On the Internet*. Abingdon, Oxon: Routledge.

Dreyfus, H. (2001b) "Heidegger on the Connection between Nihilism, Art, Technology and Politics." Last accessed: 10 Dec. 2017. Accessible from: https://eclass.uoa.gr/modules/document/file.php/PPP566/HdgerOnArtTechPoli.pdf.

Duhigg, C. (2012) "How Companies Learn Your Secrets" in *The New York Times*. February 16, 2012. Last accessed: 10 Dec. 2017. Accessible from: http://www.nytimes.com/2012/02/19/magazine/shopping-habits.html.

Gollbeck, J. "The Curly Fry Conundrum: Why Social Media "Likes" Say More than You might Think". Ted Talk. October 2013. Last accessed: 10 Dec. 2017. Accessible from: https://www.ted.com/talks/jennifer_golbeck_the_curly_fry_conundrum_why_social_media_likes_say_more_than_you_might_think.

Heidegger, M. (1962) *Being and Time*. New York, NY: Harper and Row.

Heidegger, M (1966) *Discourse on Thinking*. New York, NY: Harper & Row.

Heidegger, M. (1977) "The Question Concerning Technology," in *The Question Concerning Technology and Other Essays*. New York, NY: Harper & Row, pp. 3-35.

Heiferman, S. (2009) "The Pursuit of Community" in *The New York Times*. September 5, 2009. Accessible from: http://www.nytimes.com/2009/09/06/jobs/06boss.html.

Herszenhorn, D. (2012) "Anti-Putin Stunt Earns Punk Band Two Years in Jail" in *The New York Times*. August 17, 2012. Last accessed: 10 Dec. 2017. Accessible from: http://www.nytimes.com/2012/08/18/world/europe/suspense-ahead-of-verdict-for-jailed-russian-punk-band.html.

Kierkegaard, S. (1959) *Either/Or*. Princeton, NJ: Princeton University Press.

Kierkegaard, S. (1962) *The Present Age*. New York, NY Harper & Row.

Nocera, J. (2014) "Pussy Riot Tells All" in *The New York Times*. February 7, 2014. Last accessed: 10 Dec. 2017. Accessible from: https://www.nytimes.com/2014/02/08/opinion/nocera-pussy-riot-tells-all.html.

Quercia, D. (2014) "Happy Maps". Ted Talk. November 2014. Last accessed: 10 Dec. 2017. Accessible from: https://www.ted.com/talks/daniele_quercia_happy_maps

Quercia, D., R. Schifanella, and L. Maria Aiello, (2014) "The Shortest Path to Happiness: Recommending Beautiful, Quiet, and Happy Routes in the City." Online. Cornell University Library. Last accessed: 10 Dec. 2017. Accessible from: https://arxiv.org/pdf/1407.1031.pdf.

Ronson, J. (2015) *So You've been Publicly Shamed*. New York, NY: Riverhead Books.

Man Bullies Chick fil A Drive Thru Employee on 'Appreciation Day' Fox News Insider. YouTube Video. 2:20. August 7, 2012. Last accessed: 10 Dec. 2017. Accessible from: https://www.youtube.com/watch?v=rgwX2d810Oo.

Wolf, G. (2010a) "The Data Driven Life" in *The New York Times*. 28 April, 2010. Last accessed: 10 Dec. 2017. Accessible from: http://www.nytimes.com/2010/05/02/magazine/02self-measurement-t.html.

Wolf, G. (2010b) "The Quantified Self". Ted Talk. June 2010. Last accessed: 10 Dec. 2017. Accessible from: https://www.ted.com/talks/gary_wolf_the_quantified_self#t-31422.

Heidi Herzogenrath-Amelung

Speaking the Unspeakable: Heidegger and Social Media's 'Mouseclick Solidarity'

1 Introduction. The philosophical slug: philosophy doesn't tweet well

There is a meme that I like to show my first-year students: it shows the philosopher Plato as in Raphael's famous "School of Athens" painting in the Vatican in Rome, pointing skywards, one assumes to some higher truth. Only the meme shows Twitter's little blue bird hovering above the philosopher's trigger finger: it has taken the place of the higher truth Plato is pointing to. We can read this meme in two ways: on the one hand it points to the general reverence for social media dominating the public, as well as the academic imagination. Even the most mundane of businesses are asking their customers to "like" them on Facebook, politicians tweet passionately (if not always honestly)[1], and since the Arab Spring there has been a flurry of research into just how much exactly social media have aided protest movements around the world (a point we will return to). But it is the other reading that I am interested in, for now: the juxtaposition of philosophy and social media discourse. To my mind, philosophy doesn't tweet well.

Plato himself is the perfect example. None of Plato's philosophical arguments, painstakingly pursued in lengthy dialogues between Socrates and one or more of his students, could have taken place within the confines of a social media app. Twitter, for one, only offers its users 140 characters per Tweet[2], but Facebook and its contender sites are similarly designed to favour brevity. The first piece of advice Facebook gives its users for 'effective' posts is "keep it short" (Facebook 2016) – advice that was alien to the philosophers of old: what counted was to get to the bottom of things. Thus in one of his most famous quandaries, Socrates probes his student Thaetetus about the nature of knowledge. Thaetetus does what my own students would do, he gives examples – geometry and astronomy in his case (he is a very ambitious student). Socrates however responds that giving an example of a

---

1   I am playing on the title of important research published by Alice Marwick and Dana Boyd as "I Tweet Honestly, I Tweet Passionately: Twitter Users, Context Collapse, and the Imagined Audience" (2011).
2   Since the writing of this chapter Twitter has doubled the number of available characters to 280.

thing does not amount to a definition of the thing. A picture of a cat, for instance, does not yet convey essential 'catness'. Thaetetus suggests knowledge might be the confirmation of a statement as fact – I might tell you that a painting on a wall is hanging askew, and you might find that this is indeed the case. But Socrates counters that a true judgement may be purely accidental, and hence does not yet constitute knowledge. Similarly, human experience does not prove very reliable – I might say that I find it very hot in this room, but you may not agree. You get the idea. The conversation continues along these lines and we find ourselves in an even greater state of confusion than before (this state is so common an outcome of Socratic conversations it has its own name – *aporia*). What we have learnt, however, is the true *complexity* of what seemed at first a simple question.

It is on the matter of complexity that I wish to focus, as it seems that it is this, or rather the lack of it, which opens up the chasm between philosophical thought and social media discourse. Langdon Winner's apologetic musings about the "armchair-bound" image of philosophy (Winner 1993, 364) are rooted in fact: philosophy has always been about thought, about shining a light on a thing from all possible angles and exploring all its complexities – a pursuit that takes time and, as Adorno requested, is all the more important not to be interrupted in times of crisis (Adorno 2001 [1991], 200). And crisis is precisely what we are now facing as we move closer towards the centenary of the vast political and military, but above all ideological crisis that was the second World War and that occupied the first generation of Critical Theorists. The wave of uprisings referred to as the Arab Spring has destabilized political regimes across the MENA (Middle East and North Africa) region, and the world today is facing a multitude of threats: from Islamic fundamentalism, a war in Syria that, according to the European Commission, has caused "the world's largest humanitarian crisis since World War II" (European Commission 2016, 1) and the emergence and fortification of far-right sentiments and groupings in countries across Europe. Capitalism itself, a system seemingly without alternative (Fisher 2009), is said to be in crisis. Untangling the connections between these phenomena far exceeds the scope of this chapter; it is, again, a matter of complexity. Yet what is common to all these crises is that in these times so many have placed their hopes in social media: in their immediacy, their fast-paced nature and precisely their lack of complexity. Finally, as mainstream media commentators and academics around the world proclaimed, everyday people had been given a voice. Facebook, Twitter & co. were doing away with the institutional boundaries of mainstream media and the barriers of entry regulating public discourse (Benkler 2006; Castells 2012). They were proving themselves to be the first truly "social" media.

Philosophy has been largely absent from these debates, but is this surprising? After all, how should philosophy, this most sluggish of intellectual disciplines, grounding itself in the thought of people who have been dead for more than 2000 years, even begin to grasp the pace and scale of these developments? Karl Marx famously complained in his Theses on Feuerbach that philosophy only ever interprets the world, where the point is to change things (1998, 571). So far, we might say, it hasn't even offered us an interpretation of what's been happening. My argument, however, is that that we need the slow, meticulous questioning of philosophical thought now more than ever. We need it as an antidote to the mind-boggling pace at which issues rise and fall on social media, and because of the dangerous feeding ground it is nurturing for the expression of sentiment that is thoughtless at best, and malicious agitation or propaganda at worst. One of my favourite insights into the media comes from Marshall McLuhan: "whoever discovered water, certainly wasn't a fish" (cited in Taylor 2010, 9). His point, that it is impossible to see something for what it is when we are immersed in it, seems to ring truer than ever in the face of the omnipresence of social media chatter. Philosophy can help us slam on the brakes to take a closer look at what is happening – not with the aim of pronouncing judgment, as the shout-outs about a 'social media revolution' invite us to do, but, as Heidegger emphasized in his famous lecture "The Question Concerning Technology", as a "questioning that builds a way" (1977, 3).

2 Mindless chatter on social media: speaking the unspeakable

Elsewhere (Herzogenrath-Amelung 2016) I have remarked on the emergence of what appears to be a new 'culture of instantaneity', arguing that Twitter seems to be encouraging action before there is time for thought. Here I wish to expand on this, looking at the impact of social media on the debates around the most recent crisis to date, and explain why Heidegger can help us make sense of what is happening.

March 2016 saw the latest in a series of terrorist attacks across Europe with large numbers of civilian casualties, for which the militant group Islamic state (ISIS) has claimed responsibility. On the morning of the 22nd of March, three coordinated bombings took place in the Belgian capital of Brussels, two at Brussels Airport in Zaventem, and one more at Maalbeek metro station. 31 people died in the bombings as well as three suicide bombers, and more than 300 people were injured. Europe went into a state of shock over the attacks that recalled the atrocities in Paris in November 2015 and the Charlie Hebdo shootings earlier that year. Days of mourning followed as citizens and political leaders attempted to come to grips with what had happened. One image in particular seemed to capture the world's imagination (Khomami 2016): that of the Indian crew worker Nidhi Chaphekar, who survived the blast at the airport. The photograph, showing her "in shock" and "speechless", was retweeted and republished innumerable times as the most poignant representation of our initial response to the attacks: stunned silence.

Shock is often said to render 'speechless', and for psychologists, getting people to talk about traumatic experiences is a difficult and lengthy process. Trauma, it seems, is rooted in the domain of the unspeakable. Not being able to put something into words is an acknowledgement of the magnitude of what one is faced with. It is no coincidence that one of the strongest evocations of horror is Edvard Munch's painting *The Scream* – it fully realizes terror because it does not have to speak it. We can also remind ourselves of the French psychoanalytical theorist Jacques Lacan's argument (1977) that there is an eternal void between ourselves and the Real that was opened up by our entry into language. Language occupies the realm of the symbolic: it can only ever be an *approximation* to the Real, it is never identical with it. In fact, Lacan goes as far as to argue that language does violence to the Real – in the case of the Brussels attacks we might ask what words indeed would be powerful enough to grasp the horror of what happened. This is the reason why the image of Nidhi Chaphekar, blood trickling down her face and her flight attendant's uniform ripped to shreds exposing her belly, has become to define the attacks of Brussels, rather than anything we might have said about them.

Much of Heidegger's work is concerned with language, and though these ideas are not my central concern in this chapter, it is worth reminding ourselves that he refers to language as 'the house of Being'. Language, for Heidegger, is part of what "discloses" the world to us, and is intimately related with truth, though by truth of course he does not mean the mere correspondence of one thing with another (note the similarity with Socrates' argument about knowledge not simply being true judgment). Rather, language is related to truth in the sense that it has the power to "reveal" things to us as they really are. Our everyday use of language however ignores these powers, precisely because we "use" it – we could also say we rely on it as a tool for communication. This is what Heidegger refers to as our 'instrumental' or 'anthropological' view of language, grounded in the everydayness of its use:

> Man speaks. We speak when we are awake and we speak in our dreams. We are always speaking, even when we do not utter a single word aloud, but merely listen or read, and even when we are not particularly listening or speaking but are attending to some work or taking a rest. We are continually speaking in one way or another. (Heidegger 1971, 187)

Of course, to an extent we are forced to reduce language to an instrument in order to communicate – if we were to constantly contemplate it as the 'house of our Being', or even, as Lacan does, reflect on the eternal void between the words we use and what we are using them for, we would never be able to speak. Heidegger was aware of this, and nevertheless asks us to contemplate these powers now and then. He is deeply concerned that at worst, our everyday speech has declined to what he calls "idle talk" [Gerede] (Heidegger 2008 [1962], 211f) – one of the most acute examples of which we can find in posttraumatic-event social media discourse: thus, in the hours and days that followed the Brussels attacks millions took to Twitter using hashtags like #prayfornidhi, demonstrating just how much social media foster a reduction of language to what Heidegger calls "idle talk", insisting on speaking what is unspeakable.

It is ironic how amidst the brain fog brought on by something that was beyond comprehension, social media became the site for sense-making: #Brussels was the first hashtag to "trend" on Twitter, allowing users to spread news of the attacks, express their disbelief and their solidarity with the victims, relatives of victims, and Belgium as a nation. More specific hashtags quickly followed: #brusselsattacks, #jesuisbrussels (echoing the slogan "Je Suis Charlie" which topped the Twitter charts following the January 2015 attacks on the Charlie Hebdo magazine in Paris), #prayforbrussels, #istandwithbrussels and #unitedwithbrussels (BBC Trending 2016). Users tweeted quotes from Mother Teresa ("If we have no peace, it is because we have forgotten that we belong to each other") and Leonard Bernstein ("This will be our reply to violence: to make music more intensely, more beautifully, more devotedly than ever before"), messages of defiance featuring Brussels' well-known mascot the Manneken Pis, and images of vigils, tributes and solidarity gatherings around the world. Following a tweet from the Mayor of Paris that the Eiffel Tower would be illuminated in the colors of the Belgian Flag, some of the most popular images tweeted were of other public buildings that came to be lit up in the tricolor (the Brandenburg Gate in Berlin, London's National Gallery, London Bridge and Wembley Stadium). One of the most popular memes to spread was of a crying Tintin character (Henn 2016).

This flurry of social media activity did not take long to break into the silence of the immediate aftermath of the blasts. The speed with which social media cut into this void, however, demonstrated what Heidegger called the "enframing" qualities of modern technology: extreme instrumentalisation to the point that even human being-in-the-world is in danger of becoming a mere means to an end. Though not the first or only example of such instrumentalisation, I argue that social media pose an example of the most acute kind, precisely because of their emphasis on the "social". This makes them appear as a fitting channel for the messages of solidarity that followed the recent atrocities of Brussels: in a domain where everything is about 'sharing', why should grief not be shared also. However, in insisting on speaking the unspeakable, social media demonstrate the inherently instrumentalising and dehumanising features of digital technologies. What characterizes human being-in-the world, we will see, is its complexity and irreducibility to technological form; the 'mouseclick solidarity' that emerged in the wake of Paris, Brussels, etc. can thus be seen as an example of the extent to which human being-in-the-world is enframed, rather than liberated by, digital technologies.

3 The essence of technology is nothing technological: the enframing qualities of social media

Many disagree with Heidegger's overall assessment of technology, but few challenge the fact that he placed the age-old question concerning technology on a new footing. Rather than a neutral means to an end outside itself, or what Heidegger refers to as the "instrumental" understanding of technology (Heidegger 1977), he insisted that technology is in fact a way of "being-in-the-world". Thus his famous essay *The Question Concerning Technology*, is in fact part of his much bigger project pursued in *Being and Time* – an inquiry into the meaning of Being itself. His magnum opus begins with the very criticism that is at the heart of his critique of modern technology: that humanity is suffering from what he calls a "forgottenness" of Being. This sounds like precisely the kind of abstract, far-from-reality claim we like to accuse philosophers of, but for Heidegger it is the root of the hyper-rational, instrumental logic of technological modernity which, although these parallels are often downplayed, are also the subject of Max Weber's critique of the rationalisation of society and of Adorno and Horkheimer's critique of instrumental reason. In the compression of the horrors of Paris, Brussels, etc., into the mouseclick solidarity of social media we see precisely this forgottenness at work – and in exploring such a technologized reduction of the complexity of Being we are countering it with the power of thought.

Heidegger is not the first philosopher to have examined the question of Being, which is essentially the foundation of all ontology – the study of what there is. The question occupied the Ancients, and was dealt with by both Plato and Aristotle extensively. For Plato, all beings were imperfect approximations of ideal beings – every circular object was thus an imperfect "copy" of that perfect circle that existed in the world of ideas. Aristotle on the other hand took a far more practical approach and argued that being was best explained in terms of matter and form, the physical qualities of things. Nevertheless, Heidegger insists, despite more than 2000 years of philosophical thought and scientific progress, we still lack an understanding of Being. What for many is the "most universal and emptiest of concepts"[3] for Heidegger, remains "the darkest of all" (Heidegger 2008 [1962], 2–3): What does it mean for something to "be"? We don't know whether the act of "being"

> has the same character in *every* being ... or whether individual ways of being are mutually distinct. Which are the basic ways of being? Is there a multiplicity? How is the variety of ways-of-being possible and how is it at all intelligible? (Heidegger 1988 [1975], 18)

Not knowing, however, is not the problem for Heidegger. The problem is that we have stopped to ask. We have stuck our philosophical head in the sand and thus our Western ontological system does not differentiate between the way I *am*, you *are*, or the way a hippopotamus *is*. Once again, we have reduced what Heidegger views as a matter of infinite complexity to the simple fact of "presence".

There is a famous quotation from Adorno that says "there is no universal history [that] leads from savagery to humanitarianism, but there is one leading from the slingshot to the megaton bomb" (Adorno 2001 [1991], 4). For Heidegger, we can say a universal history runs from the reduction of all Being to simple presence to the instrumental logic of modern technology. Heidegger sees human Being as so fundamentally different from all other kinds of Being (us being the only beings that have an understanding of our own being) that it merits its own name: Dasein (meaning *being there*). And what matters is that this 'being there' is never a simple *being present* amongst other beings but a being-*with*: we encounter the world not as piles of things with physical properties, rather we *experience* it and everything in it as full of meaning. Human relationships are not interactions between physical matter, but deeply complex encounters that are irreducible to technological form. This is why the photo of the flight attendant was such a powerful image of the horrors of Brussels – it did not attempt to compress the horrors of what had happened into 140 characters. Because it did not rely on the complexity-reducing features of social media, it gave infinite space to human suffering. For Heidegger, the key moment that inscribed the levelling of Being into Western ontology was the decision of the French philosopher René Descartes that human consciousness preceded everything else. The temporal priority granted to human consciousness for Heidegger established

---

3   We must admit that it is practically impossible to even formulate the question "what is being?" without already invoking the concept we are questioning, without already moving within some kind of understanding of it.

human Being as ultimately a *being-over and against* other beings. This ontological priorisation gave rise to a world of the human subject for whom everything
else is an object, available to be acted upon and instrumentalized. At this stage,
Heidegger warns, we are encountering the gravest danger: the rationalisaton
and instrumentalisation of human beings themselves: their turning into what
Heidegger calls "standing reserve" (Heidegger 1977).

What role does technology play in all this? Technology, and this is a key point
for Heidegger, is not the driving force behind this rationalisation – it merely
manifests it (which is why to accuse Heidegger of Luddism is to perfectly misun-
derstand him). Every technology, Heidegger argues, "reveals" part of the world
to us in some way. As such it is deeply related to the Ancient Greek concept
of *poiēsis* or 'bringing-forth'. But where simple, hand-craft technologies like
hammers and chisels brought forth from the earth what it was ready to give –
what was, in a sense, already "slumbering" within it (think Michelangelo's David
as merely having been 'revealed' from within the marble), modern technologies
approach the world as a resource to be exploited. Modern technologies do not
reveal, they 'set upon' with the purpose of extracting value.

Let us take the simple example of how agriculture has changed. Early ways
of ploughing a field involved a farmer doing a hard day's toil, leading a horse
dragging a plough. Modern agricultural machines have made this a lot easier –
the yield is much greater with far less energy expenditure on the side of the
farmer. The crucial point for Heidegger, however, is that this machinery has
driven a wedge between human Being and all that *is* with him in the world. It
articulates a very different relationship between humans and the world than did
the hand-plough of old. Modern machines 'set upon' the earth to reveal itself in
terms of energy to be further processed for profit:

> The revealing that rules throughout modern technology has the character of a setting-
> upon, in the sense of a challenging-forth. That challenging happens in that the energy
> concealed in nature is unlocked, what is unlocked is transformed, what is transformed
> is stored up, what is stored up, in turn, distributed, and what is distributed is switched
> about ever anew. (Heidegger, 1977, 16)

This logic of minimum input and maximum yield is what Heidegger refers to
as the essence of modern technology: the 'Gestell'[4], or enframement. This is the

---

4   The English translation as 'enframing' misses the fact that the term Ge*stell* shares ety-
    mological roots with 'be*stellen*' ("to cultivate", in the agricultural sense) and '*stellen*'
    ("to place"). This etymological connection is crucial, as it highlights that the Gestell
    and 'bestellen' are both modes of *revealing* – Heidegger's point is that the *nature* in
    which this revealing unfolds is different.

meaning of his famously confusing claim that "the essence of technology is by no means anything technological" (1977, 4). By "essence", Heidegger is referring to the way of interaction with the world that technology represents, and which in modern technology manifests as an exploitative, instrumentalising form of "revealing".

Heidegger has often been criticized for his lack of specificity and relevant examples, and probably never more so than in his insistence on an "essence" of technology underlying its material manifestations that far surpasses them in importance. For Michael Heim the 'Gestell' is an "ominous and threatening" speculation, an "abstraction looming like a metaphysical sphinx, terrorizing thought with a puzzling lack of specificity" (Heim 1993, 57). When it comes to digital media, however, a system that is in itself based on abstraction from specific conditions (what else is binary code?), this lack of specificity emerges as a strength, not a weakness. Heidegger's concept of enframement allows us to identify the *unifying* features of modern technologies and their instrumentalising tendencies: social media are part of the overall myth of the "digital sublime" (Mosco 2004), the promise of a global transformation of society through the liberating and democratizing features of digital technology. In the next section of this chapter we will look at why they are its most powerful perpetuators: they continue to feed on the euphoria that arose during the Arab Spring, where the uprisings across the MENA region inspired claims that these countries were being transformed through a 'social media revolution'. The wave of solidarity following the attacks in Paris and Brussels was tweeted into the echoes of this promise, that social media have the power to build a better society by circumventing the access barriers and hierarchies shaping traditional media and political institutions. Heidegger's concept of enframement however allows us to see the passionate Tweets, Facebook profile picture filters and other signals of solidarity in a very different light: as signs that what, according to Heidegger, uniquely characterizes human being-in-the-world has been reduced to a technologized parody. Ultimately, human suffering and compassion both become instrumentalized for profit as social media corporations continue to exploit the myth of the digital sublime for financial gain.

4 Mouseclick-solidarity and the digital sublime

The concept of the digital sublime was introduced by Vincent Mosco to describe the overall mythology surrounding digital innovations. This essentially consists of:

"variatations on the theme that society and culture are in the process of a great transformation brought about by the introduction of computers and communication technology" (Mosco 2004, 18)

The promise that the digital era would transform society (a promise which, it
is worth remembering, also accompanied earlier waves of innovation like film
and radio) was initially driven by the rise of the New Economy, Silicon Valley
start-ups and favourable policy-making. The burst of the dotcom bubble did no
long-term damage to the myth – but it lacked a driving force until the emergence of Web 2.0 and social media, which promised to 'change everything'. The
mainstream media scurried to catch up, and media studies, amidst "celebratory
claims of rupture and transformation" (Andrejevic 2009, 36) prepared to throw
all established ways of sense-making out of the window.

As we assess the state of the world in the wake of the global uprisings and protest movements that put social media on research agendas everywhere question
marks have replaced the claim that "the revolution will be twittered" (Sullivan
2009). The Snowden revelations regarding the global surveillance programme
run by the US and their allies, which draws heavily on data from social media,
have cast another shadow over the myth of the digital sublime. The debunking
of a myth is always good news from a critical, scholarly perspective, but we need
to keep an eye on those who arguably stand to lose the most from its dissolution: the new media giants themselves. For here it lives on, and not without a
purpose. In a recent speech Mark Zuckerberg introduced his "10 year roadmap"
(Zuckerberg 2016) to resolve the issues of the world, arguing that he "care[s]
deeply about connecting the world and bringing people together". It is no coincidence that his "world view about connecting all people" will also greatly benefit
his business interests: as the amount of information Facebook users share grows,
the amount of data that can be sold to advertisers grows also. Here Heidegger's
concept of enframement shows its full critical potential, for it allows us to
see the various instrumentalising tendencies of social media underlying their
surface-level claims of connectivity and solidarity. Facebook's color filter and
'safety check', for which the magazine *Wired* coined the suitable term "tragedy
features" (Mchugh, 2015), are two particularly poignant examples: here grief,
sympathy and solidarity, experiences that from a Heideggerian perspective are
unique to human being-in-the-world, have become instrumentalized in the
sense that they serve to sustain the myth of the digital sublime, and its underlying business model.

Announcing the launch of the Facebook Safety Check feature on the site,
Mark Zuckerberg announced in 2010:

> Over the last few years there have been many disasters and crises where people have turned to the Internet for help. Each time, we see people use Facebook to check on their loved ones and see if they're safe. Connecting with people is always valuable, but these are the moments when it matters most. (Zuckerberg, 2014)

The purpose of the safety check tool is to allow people to easily tell their friends that they are safe in the wake of a disaster. If Facebook guesses that a user might be in an affected area, then they can mark themselves safe and have that message appear for their friends. Thus following the attacks in Brussels, the message displayed for anyone that the site assumed to be in Brussels, as well as connections of the people who had marked themselves safe. The message displayed reads: "Quickly find and connect with friends in the area. Mark them safe if you know they're OK" (Griffin 2016b).

What is at stake here is not the utility of the feature – there is no doubt that it set many minds at rest. What we need to question though is the degree of control this feature allows Facebook as a corporation to exercise over human feelings of fear and relief – sentiments that are essential aspects of human relationships and of what Heidegger calls being-in-the-world. Thus it is important to note that the feature is not permanently active, but is switched on centrally following a humanitarian or environmental disaster. The crucial point here is precisely this selectivity: the feature was not activated for people in Beirut, where 43 people were killed in a double suicide bombing in November 2015. Nor was it activated in Ankara, Turkey, when 102 died in attacks on the 10th of October 2015 – nor in Nigeria (bombs killed 145 at a market and a mosque) or after al-Shabab militants killed 147 people at a university in Kenya earlier that same year.

Why, critics became quick to ask, was Facebook selective about which disasters merited the activation of the feature? In the case of Ankara, Facebook gave in and activated the feature, although it did not give users the option of applying a Turkish flag filter to their profile pictures. As soon as Facebook had taken this step, new critics emerged: why had Facebook not activated the feature for those caught up in the attacks in Grand Bassam on the Ivory Coast that happened only hours before? As one user put it:

> "I wish to know if my friends and family are safe no matter where in the world something's happening, not just when Western lives are likely to be impacted". (Griffin, 2016a)

What emerges from these cases of selectivity is the extent to which Facebook's Safety Check-in feature constitutes a technologically "enframed" version of the *care* that, for Heidegger, fundamentally characterizes human being-in-the world (Heidegger 2008 [1962], 225f). Beneath the surface-level claims of sociality and solidarity we can see some of the deeply instrumentalizing tendencies of social media beginning to surface, of which the Facebook color filter is perhaps an even more acute example.

Following the attacks in Belgium in March Facebook, as it had done in the wake of the Charlie Hebdo attacks, offered its users the option of overlaying their profile pictures with the colors of the Belgian flag. Hundreds of thousands of users took advantage of this opportunity, inspired by friends or even by newspapers advertising the feature and giving instructions on how to implement it (Griffin 2016c). The British broadsheet *The Independent*, for instance, directed readers to the website rainbowfilter.io for a fast way to add the color filter to their profile picture. Current visitors to this site will read the following message:

> "Instantly add Belgium Filter to any of your profile pictures, photos, or logos. Show love for the people of Belgium with our Belgium filter! Add the Belgium flag to your profile picture to support Belgium and the Belgian people. Fly the Belgian flag with pride! Click the button!" (Rainbowfilter, 2016)

The emphasis, both by the coverage of *The Independent* and on the rainbowfilter. io website is clearly on convenience: it takes mere seconds to demonstrate solidarity with the victims of the attacks in a language that is universal – that of the image. The appeal of the filter is precisely its simplicity: it requires no prior knowledge of the history of the attacks, nor of the extremely complex political situation in which they occurred. It is conveniently carried out from the sofa, from the bus, from within a meeting. It costs the user nothing, while with every click adding to the value of Facebook.

However, what gets instrumentalized through the convenience of this form of mouseclick solidarity is ultimately the cause itself – as it becomes replaceable with the same level of convenience. *The Independent* article cleverly directed users to the Belgian flag on rainbowfilter.io as the currently most requested one, so I tried replacing 'belgium' in the URL with 'france'. It was a success – I was told I could "instantly add France Filter" to my profile picture to "show solidarity with Paris and the French people". Below the text of the appeal, separate buttons advertised an "Autism & Autism Awareness Filter!" as well as an "American Flag & USA Filter" – one assumes these are added with a similarly immediate effect. When I entered 'Turkey' into the search bar and clicked 'search filters', however, what I got was a list of Google ads relating to Turkey, the first being a Thomas Cook holiday ad. Replacing 'france' in the URL bar finally seemed to give me the option of a Turkey filter – however, Facebook was criticized for not offering the option of a Turkish filter following the attacks in Ankara.

Once a user has overlaid his profile picture with their filter of choice, it remains there until the user takes the decision to remove it. Following the attacks on a number of public venues (cafes, restaurants and a music hall) in Paris in November 2015 Mark Zuckerberg used the French filter for the duration of a weekend before removing it on the following Monday (Mchugh 2015) The question that emerges from the preceding analysis however is how Zuckerberg, or anyone else for that matter, decides what length of time constitutes an appropriate or sufficient period of mourning? What are the internal or external processes that trigger the decision to remove the filter? The Facebook profile picture filter allows its users to 'switch' their display of solidarity on and off – all it takes is a few clicks. The question then is to what extent this switching already corresponds to an internal process of switching solidarity on and off.

Heidegger's concept of enframement allows us to see common instrumentalising tendencies of social media in otherwise different contexts. During the Kony 2012 campaign to raise awareness concerning the Ugandan war criminal Joseph Kony, social media users were made to feel like activists by the simple act of clicking on the YouTube video made by the campaign originators *Invisible Children* and by sharing the video through their social media channels. Celebrities like Justin Bieber and Rihanna led the way in retweeting the video and the message to "make Joseph Kony famous". The retweeting of the "Make Kony famous" campaign, the Facebook color filter and the tweeted expressions of solidarity following the attacks in France and Brussels epitomize Heidegger's essence of modern technology: they occurred at minimum cost to the user while adding maximum value to the social media corporations, both in symbolic and actual terms. They reinforce the ideology surrounding these companies as truly "social" media (allowing the users to contribute to social causes) and add to the mass of user data (likes and affiliations) that is of value for marketing purposes. It is in this sense that Heidegger's concept of enframement cuts across apparent dissimilarities amongst digital media technologies to allow us to see the instrumentalising features that unite them.

5 Conclusion: the solidarity toolbox

This chapter has examined a variety of social media responses to the recent terrorist attacks in Belgium in March 2016, such as the mass outpourings of sympathy and solidarity on Twitter using hashtags such as #jesuisbrussels and #istandwithbrussels. The format of the hashtag #jesuisbrussels in particular recalled the events in Paris in the previous year, where attacks were launched on the French satirical magazine Charlie Hebdo, and later that year on a variety of public spaces like restaurants and music venues. The social networking site Facebook responded to the attacks in Brussels with the activation of its Safety

Check-in feature, as well as giving its users the opportunity to make a statement of solidarity by overlaying their profile pictures with the colors of the Belgian tricolor. In both these cases Facebook activated features that it had previously activated for other humanitarian or environmental crises – such as the attacks in France the previous year, or the earthquake that shook Nepal in the same year. The uptake of these 'tragedy features' was immense, with the leaders of the social media corporations as well as celebrities and heads of state leading the way in these mediated expressions of solidarity.

Writing in the British newspaper *The Independent*, the journalist Yasmin Ahmed reflected critically on this flurry of activity:

> On social media we have Facebook safety check-ins, Twitter hashtags and sharable [sic] cartoons. In real life the Belgian flag will be hoist or projected over the national monuments of neighbouring European countries. The responses have taken on the morbid ritual of a funeral.

Yet she noted that:

> arguably, they [the responses] are important to help us process the inexplicable horror and to give us some tools with which to communicate defiance in the face of terror. (Ahmed, 2016)

This chapter has taken a rather more critical approach, contrasting these passionate statements of solidarity with the silent and dignified stance of the flight attendant Nidhi Chaphekar, whose face was voiceless testimony to the horrors of what she had witnessed. Her stunned silence gave full expression to the impact of the attacks upon its victims their loved ones precisely because it did not seek to put it into words. Next to this silent testimony, the publicly mediated displays of solidarity on Twitter and Facebook appear as a deafening clamour, because they insisted on speaking what is, in essence, unspeakable.

What Ahmed has rightly hit upon, however, is the emergence of a 'toolbox' of social media actions that we can conveniently apply in the event of a terrorist attack, earthquake or other humanitarian disaster. A tweet only takes 140 characters, and Facebook's safety check and color filters are both mechanisms that are conveniently carried out with a few mouseclicks. In the shadow of the events that have made this toolbox popular, however, we can trace a series of events that, it was decided by social media corporations, did not merit such attention. This selectivity further underlines what the 'toolbox' nature of these quick and convenient expressions of solidarity on social media already suggest: that what we are facing is a technologized parody of the sympathy that characterizes authentic being-in-the-world as a being-with-others. Here Heidegger's critique of the "enframing" nature of modern technologies enables us to connect what is characteristic of modern technological rationality with the more fundamental fault of Western ontology: a forgottenness of Being. Only if we cease to forget and truly start to remember, will "social media" have a chance to become truly social.

Bibliography

Adorno, T. W., 2001 [1991]. *The Culture Industry: Selected Essays on Mass Culture.* London and New York: Routledge.

Ahmed, Y., 2016. Downing Street Raises the Belgian Flag and We Tweet for Brussels – But Where was This Sympathy After Ankara? *The Independent.* [Online]. Available at: http://www.independent.co.uk/voices/downing-street-raises-the-belgian-flag-and-we-tweet-for-brussels-but-where-was-this-sympathy-after-a6946271.html. Accessed 25 April 2016.

Andrejevic, M., 2009. Critical Media Studies 2.0 – An Interactive Upgrade. *Interactions: Studies in Communication and Culture,* 1(1), 28–40.

BBC Trending, 2016. 'Pray for Brussels': What People were Saying Online After Attacks. *BBC.* [Online]. Available at: http://www.bbc.co.uk/news/blogs-trending-35872170. Accessed 20 April 2016.

Benkler, Y., 2006. *The Wealth of Networks. How Social Production Transforms Markets and Freedom.* New Haven, CT: Yale University Press.

Castells, M., 2012. *Networks of Outrage and Hope: Social Movements in the Internet Age.* Cambridge, UK and Malden, MA: Polity.

European Commission, 2016. Syria Crisis: Echo Factsheet. European Commission. [Online]. Available at: http://ec.europa.eu/echo/files/aid/countries/factsheets/syria_en.pdf. Accessed 27 April 2016.

Facebook, 2016. Make Posts More Effective. *Facebook* [online]. Available at: https://www.facebook.com/business/learn/facebook-page-effective-posts. Accessed 27 April 2016.

Fisher, M., 2009. *Capitalist Realism: Is There No Alternative?* Ropley: O Books.

Griffin, A., 2016a. Ankara Bombing: Facebook Turns on Safety Check Feature as it did for Paris Shootings, but will not Add Option to Change Profile Picture. *The Independent.* [Online]. Available at: http://www.independent.co.uk/life-style/gadgets-and-tech/news/ankara-bombing-facebook-turns-on-safety-check-feature-as-it-did-for-paris-shootings-but-will-not-add-a6930761.html. Accessed 17 April 2016.

Griffin, A., 2016b. Brussels Attacks: Facebook Safety Check Activated Following Deadly Explosions at Airport and Metro Station. *The Independent.* [Online]. Available at: http://www.independent.co.uk/life-style/gadgets-and-tech/

news/brussels-attacks-facebook-safety-check-activated-belgium-zaventem-airport-maalbeek-metro-station-a6945636.html. Accessed 15 April 2016.

Griffin, A., 2016c. How to Change Your Facebook Profile Photo to Support the Brussels Attack Victims. *The Independent.* [Online]. Available at: http://www.independent.co.uk/life-style/gadgets-and-tech/news/brussels-belgian-flag-facebook-profile-photo-picture-black-yellow-red-a6947371.html. Accessed 25 April 2016.

Heidegger, M., 1971. Language. In: *Poetry, Language, Thought.* New York: Harper Collins, 185–208.

Heidegger, M., 1977. *The Question Concerning Technology and Other Essays.* New York, London, Toronto and Sydney: Harper & Row.

Heidegger, M., 1988 [1975]. *Basic Problems of Phenomenology.* 2nd ed. Bloomington, IN: Indiana University Press.

Heidegger, M., 2008 [1962]. *Being and Time.* Malden, MA, Oxford and Victoria: Blackwell.

Heim, M., 1993. *The Metaphyscis of Virtual Reality.* Oxford: Oxford University Press.

Herzogenrath-Amelung, H., 2016. The New Instantaneity: How Social Media are Helping us Privilege the (Politically) Correct over the True. *Media, Culture & Society.*

Henn, P., 2016. Britain Pays Tribute to Brussels: Iconic Landmarks Lit up in the Colours of Belgium Flag. *The Express.* [Online]. Available at: http://www.express.co.uk/news/uk/655143/Belgian-flag-Britain-UK-London. Accessed 19 April 2016.

Khomami, N., 2016. The Photograph that has Come to Define the Horrors of the Brussels Attacks. *The Guardian.* [Online]. Available at: http://www.theguardian.com/world/2016/mar/23/the-photograph-that-has-come-to-define-horrors-of-brussels-attacks. Accessed 23 April 2016.

Lacan, J., 1977. *Ecrits: A Selection.* London: Tavistock/Routledge.

Marwick, A. and D. Boyd, 2011. I Tweet Honestly, I Tweet Passionately: Twitter Users, Context Collapse, and the Imagined Audience. *New Media & Society* 13 (1), 114–133.

Marx, K., 1998. *The German Ideology: Including Theses on Feuerbach and Introduction to the Critique of Political Economy.* Amherst, NY: Prometheus Books.

Mchugh, M., 2015. Facebook's Tragedy Features and the Outrage They Inspired. *Wired.* [Online]. Available at: http://www.wired.com/2015/11/facebook-safety-check-french-flag-filter-tragedy-features-and-the-outrage-they-inspired/. Accessed 22 April 2016.

Mosco, V., 2004. *The Digital Sublime: Myth, Power, and Cyberspace*. Cambridge, MA and London: The MIT Press.

Rainbowfilter, 2016. Belgium Filter! *Rainbowfilter.io* [Online]. Available at: http://rainbowfilter.io/belgium. Accessed 25 April 2016.

Sullivan, A., 2009. The Revolution will be Twittered. *The Daily Dish*. [Online] Available at: http://www.theatlantic.com/daily-dish/archive/2009/06/the-revolution-will-be-twittered/200478/. Accessed 29 May 2014.

Taylor, P., 2010. *Zizek and the Media*. Cambridge: Polity.

Winner, L., 1993. Upon Opening the Black Box and finding it Empty: Social Constructivism and the Philosophy of Technology. *Science, Technology & Human Values* 18 (3), 362–378.

Zuckerberg, M., 2014. Post on the 16 October 2014. *Facebook*. [Online]. Available at: https://www.facebook.com/zuck/posts/10101699265809491. Accessed 17 April 2016.

Zuckerberg, M., 2016. Post on the 12 April 2016. *Facebook*. [Online]. Available at: https://www.facebook.com/zuck/posts/10102776390418141. Accessed 17 April 2016.

Dimitra V. Pavlakou

Thinking Architecture through Heidegger's Views

Over the years, philosophy and architecture have engaged in a continuous and open dialogue in order to achieve a better understanding and interpretation of architectural language. This chapter discusses the way that the philosophical discourse of the German philosopher Martin Heidegger intersects the field of architectural theory and praxis.

This discussion emerges as a research tool in seeking answers to questions generated during the architectural synthesis which, as a creative praxis, constitutes a quite complex process; architects are thinking by hand, while they draw a line recalling experiences, images and anamneses they set the frame for a new world to be constructed, for a new narration to be unfolded. The questions raised most often concern the nature of architecture and also the broader context in which it is placed.

Architecture contributes to the continuously deploying of culture, being at the same time in a dialogue with arts, such as painting, sculpture, and cinema. It has always appeared to be strictly related to humans as it refers to primordial aspects of our existence and to the human need for shelter. The enlightenment of the contemplations and discussions around the issue of architectural intervention in human existence and living is sought through philosophy.

Philosophy contributes to the investigation of the extreme boundaries of human thought, of deep questions concerning the human being and the place of *human beings* in the world; thus, reaching primordial situations that bound our lives such as birth and death. Regarding the fact that architecture builds for life in the face of death as one of its greatest challenges, it is necessary that the architectural praxis be redefined.

Architecture not only performs the role of a building enclosure but also refers to latent dimensions of the world. It is not reduced to the materialistic issues of 'building', it is not trapped in the form but goes beyond it. Heidegger introduces the term *Dasein,* developing his thought around the way that *we are,* the way we exist in the world. (Dasein: *Da* meaning 'there' and *sein* meaning 'to be'). The quest for *Dasein* approached in his lecture entitled *Building Dwelling Thinking* (Heidegger, 2001, p. 141) as being in the world, in the sense of emplacement, brings to light critical issues of architecture: the issues of place (*topos*[1]) and dwelling. It raises questions such as what is a place? How is a place perceived? What does it really mean to dwell and how is building related to dwelling? In the statement "man dwells in that he builds," Heidegger "has given the idea of dwelling its proper sense. Man does not dwell in that he merely establishes his stay on the earth beneath the sky, but by cultivating the land and simultaneously raising buildings" (Heidegger, 2001, p. 225). Moreover, the term *Dasein* not only addresses the idea of being in a place which expresses the bounded and lived spatiality over time, but also contains an interpretation of the truth of being. In this context, the issues addressed concern the real meaning of dwelling as a central research object in phenomenology of architecture, focusing on the concept of truth as it is approached by Heidegger.

The essence of architecture might then be conceived through a series of revelations if we consider Heidegger's perspective that "art is the becoming and happening of truth" (Heidegger, 2001, p. 69) and that the truth of being lies in the concept of unconcealment (*aletheia*).[2] Consequently, the place between art and architecture becomes a field of exploration. Michelangelo, in his work of art *Prisoners or Slaves*, shapes the invisible, architects build around the unseen as a re-telling of a human condition while Andrei Tarkovsky, in his film *Nostalghia*, is sculpting in time to reveal life worlds. These distinctive aspects of dwelling will meet as different embodiments of Heidegger's scheme of 'the fourfold.' The main references for unfolding the above discussion is the concept of boundary as a prerequisite of place and the concept of time seen through the prism of memory.

The following paragraphs brings to light how Heidegger's philosophy provides links between architecture, sculpture, and cinema considering the creative praxis as a tool for a person to conceive her/his place in the world, to define her/his relationship with her/his surroundings, and thus to understand her/his true nature.

---

1 Architectural term originating from Greek meaning 'place'.
2 The Greek word for 'truth'. The term Unconcealment (*Unverborgenheit*) is introduced in Martin Heidegger's early philosophical discourse as a translation for the Greek word *alêtheia* (truth). Heidegger approached the term following the literal translation: a-*letheia which means* "not concealed." Truth appears as an uncovering and a happening to someone, to a human being, a being-there (Dasein), thus revealing the hidden ontological aspect of the word truth as disclosure. This notion of truth penetrates Heidegger's entire work.

1 Heidegger for architecture

Architecture not only addresses what is directly perceived through human eye but also challenges our emotions which are triggered through real-life experience. Such a notion may raise questions such as 'what is architecture? ' and 'how does man dwell? ' The answers to such concerns should be sought in architecture's substance and its relation to philosophical contemplations on human being.

Martin Heidegger's lecture entitled *Building Dwelling Thinking* (*Bauen Wohnen Denken*) in 1951, given in an architectural symposium under the general topic of 'Man and Space', has been influential on the deployment of architectural theory and praxis, opening up new horizons in the quest concerning one of the most crucial issues of architecture: the issue of *dwelling*.

The issue of *dwelling* addresses the investigation into the essence of human being as *Dasein*. The quest of *being* penetrates Heidegger's entire thought in different ways over time in his work. In his early and most famous work, *Being and Time* (1927), the term *Dasein* appears as the idea of *being in the world*. Later, there will be a shift in his thought known as 'the turn' (*die Kehre*) (1930–1940), a turn not in his own thinking but a turn in his philosophy of being. In the period from the mid-1940s onward, *Dasein* will be associated with the notion of place (*topos*) and a sense of belonging.

Although Heidegger's work starts with the investigation of space and more precisely the relationship between man and space, the notion of place (*topos*) becomes central in the deployment of his philosophical discourse and subsequently to architectural theory and praxis. In this context, Jeff Malpas, in *Heidegger and the Thinking of Place: Explorations in the Topology of Being*, notes that "Heidegger's own work cannot adequately be conceived except as topological in character, and so as centrally concerned with place" (2012, p. 43). In fact, Heidegger himself in 1969, accentuated the topological features of his thinking using the expression the 'topology[3] of being' (Heidegger, 2001:12). The meaning of this topological approach derives from the sense of finding ourselves 'there', situated in 'place', as *Dasein* implies.

In this framework, it is meaningful to mention that "man dwells by spanning the *on the earth* and the *beneath the sky*" (Heidegger, 2001:221). But what is the origin of dwelling? What does it mean that human beings as mortals are able to dwell upon earth? To dwell means to understand ourselves in relation to our surroundings, to be located somewhere by identifying our position in relation to

---

3   Topology is connected etymologically with the discourse about place (It derives from
     the Greek words *topos* meaning place and *logos* meaning discourse).

the horizon, addressing at the same time human's need of belonging, stability, and feeling of protection. Dwelling deals also with the concept of boundary in contrast with nature (*physis*) which exists without borders. Consequently, *Dasein's* dimension of place reflects the bounded and lived spatiality that designates 'being-in-the-world' and in this way it expresses the concept of landscape (*topio*) in architecture.

Dwelling is not necessarily related to a materialistic construction. Human presence can be a sufficient condition for dwelling. The latter is also concerned with a wider spectrum of human activities. Thus, *building* manifests itself as an expression of the possibility of man being able to dwell.

Considering language as the highest and one of the most important means of representation, able to address the essence of things, Heidegger starts the deployment of his philosophical discourse on the basis of the etymological analysis of both words dwelling (*wohnen*) and building (*bauen*). In this way particularly, language serves as the ground for argumentation in his theory. Analyzing the German term *bauen* (building), Heidegger emphasizes on the following three conditions:

1. Building is really dwelling.
2. Dwelling is the manner in which mortals are on the earth.
3. Building as dwelling unfolds into the building that cultivates growing things and the building that erects buildings (Heidegger, 2001:146).

It becomes apparent here that the word 'building' in the German language is included in the act of dwelling; the latter, as previously mentioned, is defined as the way for human beings to exist upon earth as mortals. In this context of etymological analysis, the notion of building refers to the protection and cultivation of the land but it also includes the human activity of raising a structure/ building. It is evident that dwelling and building work together as a unity. Both these terms are an integral part of one another and both serve as tools for understanding our being in the world.

Human presence, being strictly associated with dwelling, turns nature (*physis*) into place (*topos*), into a bounded spatiality, which provides us with the ability of taking measure. Taking measure, apart from defining distance, recognizing what is far away or what is close in relation to the boundaries, gives substance to a sense of belonging; "we do not dwell because we have built, but we build and have built because we dwell, that is, because we are *dwellers*" (Heidegger, 2001:146).

In terms of architecture, *dwellers* should definitely go beyond the issue of designing an enclosure in a continuous pursuit of the essence of dwelling.

They need to be under a continuous interrogation about the real meaning of dwelling. In this way, architecture should be more concentrated on the intellectual dimension of a problem than on finding a specific solution. Following this existential line of thought, which puts emphasis on the human being and its true nature, Heidegger looks back into history. Through his rethinking of the past a rethinking of architecture can emerge. His point of view is very often debated and he has been accused of perpetuating a conservative approach, especially when he appears to recall ethical values of the past which contradict recent modes of thinking based on aesthetics. Heidegger seems to criticize such aesthetic assertions in detecting a failure of contemporary architectural theory; a failure, the start of which he positions at the beginning of the Renaissance when there was a shift in the world, as evidenced from Descartes' shift from to a world of exclusively comprised of subjects and objects.

His lecture *Building Dwelling Thinking* may be read as an indirect criticism against architectural praxis in the framework of modernity, post modernity and deconstructivism. He argues that the development of technology appeared to be responsible for the detachment of a building structure from its surroundings, restricting the role of architecture to the field of aesthetics. Crucially then, the form of a building is the center of interest rather than its architectural meaning. The bridge in Heidelberg was used by the philosopher in his lecture as the paradigm that frames the importance of place (*topos*) in this whole discussion about dwelling. Based on Heidegger's assertion that, "only if we are capable of dwelling, only then can we build" (Heidegger, 2001:158), we attempt to define the notion of place (*topos*), that arises from dwelling, through the bridge paradigm (seen as an architectural intervention). The bridge is seen here as a human intervention that does not just connect the two shores, allowing people to cross the river, but it also unites its surroundings. The bridge is not a self-referential structure that enables our activity but it is a 'thing' (Heidegger, 2001, p. 161). The bridge's presence refers to a reconstruction of a 'world', a new narration. There emerges a new topography that reveals something that already existed. It is the tool that interprets the landscape by opening up a dialogue with what is around us (earth, sky, mountains, river, shores, and so on). This interpretation delimits a new way of seeing, allowing the existing topography to appear. Such an intervention is revealing of the way that a human being perceives, 'reads' the place that he/she belongs to. The example of the bridge as a place bounded by the horizon line, "*gathers*" to itself in "*its own way*", earth and sky, divinities and mortals, embodying Heidegger's idea of the fourfold. The fourfold is defined as the four elements-earth and sky, divinities and mortals. These four elements belong together in a unity, none of those can be conceived without the other three (Heidegger, 2001, p. 171). Heidegger's fourfold finds its expression in the example of the bridge as it concentrates everything around it in a whole, in a unity: place. Therefore, the fourfold in architectural terms gives the definition of the place.

2 Revealing the existent (the concept of *aletheia*)

A plethora of questions arise when defining place through the schema of the fourfold. Here I would like to focus on two of these questions: (1) How is the mystery of places (*topos*) approached with regard to the invisible aspects of their phenomena? (2) Which is the real space, the one that we see and experience every day or the one that emerges in our consciousness forming its own shape and geometry?

The mystery of places and the meaning of architecture as a creative praxis lie beyond the form, in the concept of unconcealment *(Unverborgenheit), aletheia* as it is defined by Heidegger. The idea of unconcealment derives from the Greek term *aletheia* which is translated as 'truth' *(Wahrheit)*. The etymological analysis of the word *aletheia* addresses its real essence through its primary fundamentals, *aletheia*: a – lethe which means something that is not concealed, to bring to light, to reveal something that already exists but it is hidden.[4] Unconcealment is an aspect/state of human being and belongs to the idea of *Dasein* as a factor which uncovers things. Recalling Heidegger's assertion that "art is the becoming and happening of truth" (Heidegger, 2001:69), we can thus turn to sculpture in order to approach the idea of the revealing truth through unconcealment. The essence of all art is concentrated in the effort it makes in order to unconceal what is: the truth of being and the truth of being in the world. Sculpture is a particularly good example because of the pronounced way in which unconcealment seems to happen; namely, through sculpting figures from existing (raw) materials— shaped but not sculpted. Heidegger himself recognized sculpture as a tool

---

4   This idea, while often attributed to Aristotle, has its origins in the work of ancient Greek philosopher Heraclitus, and also in the pre-Socratic philosopher Parmenides' poem entitled *On Nature*. Heraclitus perceived the world as a whole dominated by a hidden harmony. When this harmony is revealed to somebody, then she/he has reached *aletheia* while Parmenides in the part of his poem entitled "the way of truth" perceives the world as an unchanging 'One Being'. He exposes the duality of appearance and reality while he states that there are two ways of research *that it is* and *that it is not*. (truth–untruth). Heidegger delivered a lecture in 1942–1943 entitled *Parmenides* focusing on the question of truth and the primordial understanding of it.

to develop his ideas concerning space in terms of the human body and used sculpture's paradigm in his work extensively.

In this frame of reference, the researcher might find an interesting connection between Heidegger and the Italian sculptor of Renaissance Michelangelo di Lodovico Buonarroti Simoni. Michelangelo says that in every block of marble he can see a statue as plain as though it stood before him, shaped and perfect in attitude and action. He has only to hew away the rough walls that imprison the lovely apparition to reveal it to the other eyes as his eyes see it.

> The marble not yet carved
> can hold the form
> Of every thought the greatest artist has,
> And no conception can yet come to pass
> Unless the hand obeys the intellect (Buonarroti & Jennings, 1969).

According to Michelangelo, the artist doesn't need to give form to the world, the form already exists, it is there but it is not visible to all of us. The only thing humans have to do is to find a way to liberate it from the excess stone.

The artist asserts that the sculpture is already complete within the marble block before he starts his work. It is already there, he just has to chisel away the superfluous material. In this context, his series of four sculptures entitled *Prisoners or Slaves* (1531–1532), constitutes one of his most representative approaches in terms of bringing something to light, unveiling it. Each of those incomplete figures is emerging from a block of marble. They look like being imprisoned/entrapped in the stone and they are struggling to get out of the material. As a metaphor, it reflects man's struggle to free the spirit from matter. Specific parts of the bodies are revealed, heads and faces are the least developed, the grooves of the chisel are visible, while other parts, like legs and shoulders, are complete in detail. The way the Slaves stand, with most of their weight on one foot and their shoulders and arms in a twist off-axis, triggers the spectator's emotions and senses. Specifically, *The Atlas or Bound*, is a reference to the primordial Titan holding on his shoulders the entire world; being the less complete sculpture, it exposes creative praxis as a revealing process of primary structures. It deals with the concept of boundary as an important aspect of dwelling in a place, representing at the same time the eternal exertion of human being to transcend matter. The idea of creating an unfinished sculpture refers to the destruction of its prison, to the redefinition of the boundary between the body and what surrounds it. The figure and the unsculpted marble are under a dialectic relationship. Sculptures are the embodiment of a place (*topos*) while a human being is an integral part of *topos* (*Dasein*: 'being there'). Therefore, the prisoner reflects the cosmic harmony which is hidden in the world. The work of art does not need to be complete. The unfinished artwork underlines the dynamic aspect of the relationship between human being and place and also praises the simplicity of the essential. What is hidden, allusive, implied and incomplete refers to the essential, to the poetic dimension of the substance, challenging our mind to conceive the whole, to give shape to the world that is projected onto our senses and our unconscious.

Reading Heidegger's work, it may be construed that through the work of art, a world is unfolded, opening up a space for *Dasein,* for the human being to exist not independently but as part of a whole. In order to investigate the relationship between body and space, Heidegger focuses on the art of sculpture where this idea of relationality is more evident. In Heidegger's thought, the incorporation of space in the sculptural body arises as a prominent theme. However, as he explains 'art as sculpture: no occupying seizure of space. Sculpture would not be a confrontation with space' (Heidegger in Mitchell, 2010, p. 68). For him, then, sculpture is the embodiment of places.

When a sculptor reveals a body he/she does not create a representation of the physical body but instead addresses the 'bodying' (*Leiben*)[5] (Elden, 2001, p. 55) of the 'being-in-the-world'; the latter is not visible but existent. Heidegger claims that: "the artist brings the essentially invisible into figure and, when he [or she] corresponds to the essence of art, each time allows something to be caught sight of which hitherto had never been seen" (Heidegger in Mitchell, 2010:48). Sculpture can shape the invisible. To make an analogy between sculpture and architecture, the latter reaches the essence, unconceals the hidden, and unveils *aletheia* not by imitating nature (*physis*) but through the mimesis of situations exemplary of the human condition like, for example, birth and death (*Architecture and Continuity,* 1982:12).

3 Sculpting in time: from Michelangelo to Tarkovsky

Aletheia, as it is defined by Heidegger, comes out of a series of revelations in which, as mentioned above, sculpture reveals the unseen and architecture builds around the unseen. Architecture may, then, derive as a re-telling of the human condition. This may also be said about the art of cinema.

---

5   Heidegger explains that: "We do not 'have' a body in the way we carry a knife in a sheath. Neither is the body [*Leib*] a body [*Körper*] that merely accompanies us and which we can establish, expressly or not, as also present-at-hand. We do not 'have' a body [*Leib*]; rather, we 'are' bodily [*leiblich*]" (Elden, 2001:54).

The example of Andrei Tarkovsky's poetic film is pertinent here. Tarkovsky's cinematic frame not only represents human life (stories), but also constitutes another expression of truth as unconcealment. Like an architect, the director sets a frame around the subtle intricacies of his heroes and their dwelling. Furthermore, in the same way the sculptor chisels a block of marble to bring forth the hidden figures, Andrei Tarkovsky is sculpting in time to reveal lifeworlds. Tarkovsky writes about the centrality of time in the art of cinema: "I think that what a person normally goes to the cinema for is time. For time lost or spent or not yet had. He goes there for living experience" (Tarkovsky, 1989, p. 63). For the Russian filmmaker, the essence of his own work lies in the notion of time. The act of 're-telling' happens here not through 'editing' fragments of activity together but simply through allowing time to reveal itself: "time in the form of fact: again I come back to it. I see chronicle as the ultimate cinema; for me it is not a way of filming but a way of reconstructing, of recreating life" (Tarkovsky, 1989, pp. 64–65). Tarkovsky perceives time as a lump of unsculpted marble ready for milling/sculpting. What he has to do is just to remove all unnecessary elements, keeping only what touches the essential meaning of life.

> What is the essence of the director's work? We could define it as sculpting in time. Just as a sculptor takes a lump of marble, and, inwardly conscious of the features of his finished piece, removes everything that is not part of it—so the film-maker, from a 'lump of time' made up of an enormous, solid cluster of living facts, cuts off and discards whatever he does not need, leaving only what is to be an element of the finished film, what will prove to be integral to the cinematic image (Tarkovsky, 1989, pp. 63–64)

The cinematic image is dominated by an inner power, an internal rhythm which forms the basis of his filming. Tarkovsky rejected editing techniques that impose a sequence of different shots progressing in time. His own technique considers the shot as a self-organizing structure allowing a kind of spontaneous unification which means bringing together separate scenes according to their own pattern of relationships and articulations. Therefore, Tarkovsky's idea, proposes cinema as the representation of distinctive currents of time, conveyed in the shot by its internal rhythm reaching in this way the core of what he calls *poetic film*.

At this point, it is necessary to clarify the meaning of the terms rhythm and *poiēsis* in this context. Rhythm refers to the pressure of time that runs through the shots and not to the duration of it. This is the condition for the authenticity of the image, the fact that time lives within it. The term poetic cinema goes beyond the concrete idea of depicting aspects of real life under the rules that montage imposes (linear sequentiality), but it deals with rhythm, allegories, and symbols without losing its structural wholeness - unity. The Heideggerian truth (*aletheia*) of film image lies on this poetic dimension of cinema. Although *poiēsis* is a quite broad term, for Tarkovsky it is the awareness of the world and also this particular way of relating to reality (Tarkovsky, 1989, p. 21). He writes: "I find poetic links, the logic of poetry in cinema, extraordinarily pleasing. They seem to me perfectly appropriate to the potential of cinema as the most truthful and poetic of art forms" (Tarkovsky, 1989, p. 18). According to Heidegger all art is poetry in an Aristotelian sense of interpreting *poiēsis as an act of* making and revealing something, bringing what is latent from concealment to light. In this way poetry is associated with truth.

The poetic aspect of dwelling appears in Heidegger's reading of Friedrich Hölderlin's poem "In Lovely Blueness" (*In lieblicher Blaue*).[6] Heidegger's reading of the poem brings forth the idea of taking measure. This measure refers to the essence of the human being conceiving himself/herself as a mortal in relation to the earth and the sky as a wholeness: "man measures himself against the divinities. The divinities is the *measure* with which man measures out his dwelling, his stay on the earth beneath the sky. Only insofar as man takes the measure of his dwelling in this way is he able to be commensurately with his nature" (Heidegger, 2001, pp. 218–219). In other words, this poetic dimension lies in the concealed presence of the divine element in everything that surrounds human beings.

4 Dwelling in the cinematic frame

The existential structure of Heidegger's fourfold [Earth–Sky–Mortals–Divinities] seen as an architectural schema in terms of defining place (*topos*), takes shape in the cinematic frame of Tarkovsky. More precisely, it finds its embodiment in the longest take – the scene where the protagonist repeatedly walks across an empty pool with a candle in his hands – of his film *Nostalghia* (1983). This long shot becomes a place where the poetic dimension of dwelling is distinctly expressed.

In the nine-minute uninterrupted take, a man is carrying a candle across St. Catherine's drained pool in memory of his dead friend Domenico. The act that occurs in a holy place along with its prolonged duration and the painful effort to keep the flame alive, reflects the circle of human life, reaching its very essence. As soon as he approaches the opposite site of the emptied pool the character collapses from a heart attack. In this scene of *Nostalghia*, Tarkovsky aspired to "display an entire human life in one shot, without any editing, from beginning to

---

6   '... Poetically Man Dwells....' is the verse that Heidegger takes for the title of his lecture delivered on 6th of October 1951. It is contained in Friedrich Hölderlin's poem "In lovely blueness" (*In lieblicher Blaue*).

end, from birth to the very moment of death" (Bird, 2008, p. 192). The boundaries of the cinematic frame unfold a world, revealing the essence of the human being, a man in front of the possibility of dying performs a ritual walking upon the earth and beneath the sky. He is consciously aware of the emotional and at the same time symbolic meaning of his act. The flame is a metaphor for the core essence of human experience.[7]

Tarkovsky gives shape to what Heidegger calls poetic dwelling. In the candle scene, a man is tracing for himself, emplaced 'between' (Heidegger, 2001, p. 218); between the earth and the sky and between birth and death. As a mortal, he exists in a sense of 'being-towards-death' (Heidegger, 1962, p. 236). Through the remembering of death and the instability of our existence, we come in touch with our primordial nature. The long take of *Nostalghia* establishes Tarkovsky's time-rhythm (the pressure of time) theory of cinema which finds its full expression in his chapter 'Imprinted Time' (Tarkovsky, 1989, p. 57). The importance of the shot can be conceived through his own words. Before commencing with the filming of *Nostalghia*, Tarkovsky met the actor Yankovsky and challenged him by saying:

> If you can do that, if it really happens and you carry the candle to the end–in one shot, straight, without cinematic conjuring tricks and cut-in editing—then maybe this act will be the true meaning of my life. It will certainly be the finest shot I ever took—if you can do it, if you can endure to the end. (Bird, 2008, p. 192)

It is compelling for the writer to search for connections between Tarkovsky's cinematic articulations of 'being in the world' (through his method of 'sculpting in time') and architecture's intension to frame the unseen, to create spaces in which 'being in the world' happens. If the essence of architecture can be (however loosely) read in Tarkovsky's empty pool, then Heidegger's lack of homeland finds its place in Tarkovsky's *Nostalghia*. Heidegger's thinking is projected onto architecture as contemporary man's longing for a lost motherland. The human being is always under a continuous pursuit of his true nature (substance) toward *Dasein*. The pursuit of a man's homeland is, then, the only way to reach the real meaning of dwelling. Therefore, the film may be read as a speculation for what it really means to dwell in a place. In *Nostalghia* the cinematic image turns into a symbol of the lost motherland and also of the lost childhood, youth, and lost time.

---

7   In the words of French poet and philosopher Gaston Bachelard "the flame is an image of life" (Bachelard, 1988).

5 Architecture practicing nostalgia

Nostalgia is known as a sentimental condition implying very often a senti-
mentality for the past, it is also considered as a medical condition with various
symptoms, sometimes leading to death. In the eighteenth century it was also
considered as a form of melancholia. What is important here is that nostalgia
refers to the deep desire of belonging somewhere. The etymological analysis of
the term shows that it derives from the Greek root *nostos* (Homeric word) which
means 'return home' and *algos* which means 'longing' and also, interestingly,
'pain'. *Nostos* is the reminiscing of a home that no longer exists or has never
existed. Projecting the notion of nostalgia on the creative praxis of architecture we deal with the particular moment that the present meets with the past
and the dream imprinted in the unconscious mind intersects with reality (the
material becomes one with the immaterial). The real space and the space of the
myth acquire common boundaries, and also the time past coexists with the time
present.[8]

According to Boyom (2001, pp. 41–57), nostalgia manifests itself in two
ways: 'restorative nostalgia' a wish to return to the past, and 'reflective nostalgia'
which is expressed as collective memory. In the context of architecture, the distinction between 'restorative nostalgia' and 'reflective nostalgia' is about the
way in which we deal with the "reality" of architecture in relation to memory.
Architecture does not have to reproduce the exact image of the past as an ideal
condition (or to imitate the past) but instead needs to function as creative praxis
that unfolds a 'new world', a new narration, recomposing the latent elements of
the past in a new schema. Looking back to the history of architecture's origins,
not in a restorative way but with a reflective view, means that we do not go
back just for the sake of it but because we aspire to recall in our memory all the
forgotten meanings of critical situations such as death and birth. At this point
it is significant to underline that 'reflective nostalgia' as memory, activates the
anamnesis serving as the driving force that challenges the desire for creation.
On the contrary, 'restorative nostalgia' is more of a passive condition, a type
of melancholia strictly associated with the nostalgic contemplation of a past
forever lost.

Nostalgia is triggered by human senses and external factors such as smell,
sound, light and shadows that may bring to the forth memories and situations

---

8   One might think of T.S. Elliot's verse: 'Time present and time past Are both perhaps
    present in time future, And time future contained in time past. If all time is eternally
    present All time is unredeemable' (Eliot, 1968).

of the past. All these stimuli demonstrate the phenomenological approach of architecture: light, shadow, and sound contain space within them. Their presence designates a space that is not restricted to the built environment but goes beyond it, in the invisible side of their phenomena. Their changing shapes can mirror our feelings, revealing each time a never before seen aspect of a space. Architect Peter Zumthor, recalling how he once asked his students to design a house without form, notes: "it's about creating emotional space." Architects have to consider the dialectic between the human body moving through space and the physical presence of a building. We need to invent a new emotional language. Instead of just focusing on the material aspect of the design of a building we also have to design an experience, to evoke an atmosphere.

The architectural atmosphere could be interpreted as an aspect of the phenomenon 'spirit of place' (Frampton et al., 1989) or "genius loci" (Norberg-Schulz, 1991) which refers to the ambience of each place and its unique character. This is what the Greek Architect Dimitris Pikionis demonstrated in his essay entitled "Sentimental Topography" (Frampton et al., 1989). The spirit or the essence of a place in his essay is described as something immaterial but latent in any given place. The spirit of a place is emitted from the ground (earth) and its substance depends on the ground's texture (ibid).

Human beings perceive places and experience them through senses that activate memory which in turn provokes emotions. The language of feelings has the ability to reshape the place, creating a different scale, an emotional *metron* (taking measure) (Heidegger, 2001, p. 219), revealing the real dimensions of the *topos*. For instance, fear can make any distance feel bigger than it is in reality. The 'real topography', Pikionis argues, is revealed when the existent topography opens up a dialogue with history and myth. Considering that the history of places is inextricably linked with the human being (*Dasein*), Pikionis is trying to conceive the moment when inhabitants had not yet lost their touch with myth. He implies that the relationship between man and place remains unalterable. In other words, 'sentimental topography' is associated to memory as 'reflective nostalgia.' The result is the redefinition of the boundaries of dwelling. The boundaries of myth merge with the boundaries of present, real time.

In this context, the architectural intervention unfolds a 'new world' conceived through human experience. History, myth, and any reference of the past emerge through memory. They are conveyed in time and converted (transformed) into something new (a new world), completing the image of the place.

The architectural intervention being an intermediate between man and nature is called to re-establish their dialectic, to redefine their relationship. Each architectural intervention is not a way to cover our needs but reveals our relationship with the place and with the world. It reveals the horizon. The architectural elements exceed their functional role and are transformed into symbols, compressing time and space into one gesture, just as Tarkovsky does in the long take in his film *Nostalghia*. The power of symbolic representation allows us to move from one situation to the other recognizing the similarities and analogies: the poetic of their metamorphosis (*Architecture and Continuity*, 1982, p. 11). The poetic of metamorphosis constitutes the key to the process towards the essence of architecture:

> May I take you to the shores of a mountain lake? The sky is blue, the water green and everywhere is profound tranquillity. The clouds and mountains are mirrored in the lake, the houses, farms, and chapels as well. They do not look as if they were fashioned by man, it is as if they came straight from God's workshop, like the mountains and trees, the clouds and the blue sky. And everything exudes an air of beauty and peace...
> But what is this? A discordant note in the tranquillity. Like an unnecessary screech. Among the locals' houses, that were not built by them, but by God, stands a villa. The creation of an architect. Whether a good or bad architect, I don't know. All I know is that the tranquillity, peace and beauty have vanished. [...]
> Architecture arouses moods in people, so the task of the architect is to give these moods concrete expression.[...] If we were to come across a mound in the woods, six foot long by three foot wide, with the soil piled up in a pyramid, a somber mood would come over us and a voice inside us would say, 'There is someone buried here'. That is architecture (Loos, 1987, p. 73).

6 Conclusion

The true nature of architectural praxis, its own truth (*aletheia*), does not lie on the material aspect of buildings but on Dasein's dwelling as a preservation of Heidegger's schema of the fourfold. Just as Tarkovsky chooses the long shot to sculpt the true essence of time in his films and just as Michelangelo unveils his sculptures as latent figures waiting to be found within un-sculpted marble, the architect strives to intervene by redefining the boundaries of a place based on the dialectic between the existence of the place through time and its future perspectives.

Bibliography

Vesely, D., Mostafavi, M., 1982, *Architecture and Continuity, Kentish Tower Projects/Diploma Unit 1*, Architectural Association, London.

Bachelard, G., 1971, *The Poetics of Reverie, Childhood, Language, and the Cosmos*, Beacon Press, Boston, MA.

Bachelard, G., 1988, *The Flame of a Candle*, Dallas Institute Publications, Dallas, TX.

Bachelard, G., 1994, *The Poetics of Space*, trans. Maria Jolas, Beacon Press, Boston, MA.

Bird, R., 2008, *Andrei Tarkovsky: Elements of Cinema*, Reaktion Books, London.

Boyom, S., 2001, *The Future of Nostalgia*, Basic Books, New York.

Bowie, A., 2003, *Aesthetics and Subjectivity: From Kant to Nietzsche*, Manchester University Press, Manchester and New York.

Buonarroti, M. & Jennings, El., 1969, *The Sonnets of Michelangelo*, trans. Eliza bethJennings, with a selection of Michelangelo drawings, Allison & Busby, London.

Descartes, R., 1999, *Discourse on Method* and *Meditations on First Philosophy*, trans. Donald A. Cress, 4th ed. Hackett Publishing Company, Indianapolis, IN and Cambridge (Originally published in 1637).

Elden, St., 2001, *Mapping the Present: Heidegger, Foucault and the Project of a Spatial History*, Continuum, New York.

Eliot, T.S., 1968, *Four Quartets*, Mariner Books, New York.

Frampton, K., Antonakakis, D., Argyropoulos, Th., Condaratos, S., Pikionis, D., Pikionis, A., Smithson, A. & Smithson P., 1989, *Dimitris Pikionis, Architect, 1887-1968: A Sentimental Topography*, Architectural Association, London.

Heidegger, M., 1962, *Being and Time*, trans. John Macquarrie & Edward Robinson, Blackwell Publishers Ltd., Oxford.

Heidegger, M., 2001, *Poetry, Language, Thought*, trans. Albert Hofstadter, Harper Perennial Modern Classics, New York.

Loos, A., 1987, *Spoken into the Void: Collected Essays by Adolf Loos, 1897–1900*, trans. Jane O. Newman, John H. Smith, MIT Press, Cambridge, MA.

Malpas, J., 2008, *Heidegger's Topology: Being, Place, World*, A Bradford Book | The MIT Press, Cambridge, MA.

Malpas, J., 2012, *Heidegger and the Thinking of Place: Explorations in the Topology of Being*, The MIT Press, Cambridge, MA.

Mitchell, A., 2010, *Heidegger Among the Sculptors: Body, Space, and the Art of Dwelling*, Stanford University Press, Stanford, CA.

Norberg-Schulz, Ch., 1991, *Genius Loci: Towards a Phenomenology of Architecture*, Rizzoli, New York.

Paden, R., 2007, *Mysticism and Architecture: Wittgenstein and the Meaning of the Palais Stonborough*, Lexington Books, Lanham, MD.

Tarkovsky, A., 1989, *Sculpting in Time: Reflections on the Cinema*, trans. Kitty Hunter-Blair, University of Texas Press, Austin, TX.

Vesely, D., 2004, *Architecture in the Age of Divided Representation, The Question of Creativity in the Shadow of Production*, The MIT Press, Cambridge, MA.

Zumthor, P., 2006, *Atmospheres*, Birkhäuser, Basel.

Zumthor, P., 2010, *Thinking Architecture*, Birkhäuser, Basel.

Tony Richards

Take a Wander in My Shoes: Of Zombeing, T*w*ombs, and Equipmentality

1 Equip-*mentality*/equipment-*ality*

This chapter considers the continued critical import of Heidegger's notion of equipmentality in grappling with contemporary currents and problems within the mediatory or, as I prefer to term it, the *im*mediatory sphere. Within Heidegger's thought "equipmentality" marks out an exhilarating conception that equipment is never something that exists objectively "out there" (*Vorhanden*) but which instead inheres so deeply within our each and every comportment (*Verhalten*) that we rarely get to see it in operation. For when such equipment is ready-to-hand (*Zuhanden*) and is operating effectively, and when it is really there working for us, we do not really recognize, in any removed sense, *that* we are there using it. Equipmentality thus bypasses classical notions of a detached "mentality" and so we must never, according to Heidegger, equate equipmentality in any cognate way with calculative cognition. This is the first sense in which we can think equipmentality as "equip-*mentality*," in that it marinates the entirety of who we are and is thus never in any way at all some sheer "thing" that we would pick up and apply. Such is the "space" of equipment, in that it is never distanced or decidedly set apart from us. Secondly, it is in the very character of equipment that it has the quality, the "equipment-*ality*," of structural holism. As a consequence of this holism, equipment is *never* engaged with in the singular, and so one can never isolate any single "part" of it outside of the ongoing whole, without losing this equipment-*ality* that provides its resolve. This is the "time" of equipment, in that each and every part is *deferred* and is thus always lying in wait for other component parts within which it will find its meaning and significance (*Bedeutung*). Equipmentality then is something that inheres within really everything *that* we are. In so inhering, within everything that we are, it is never some mere mental "side" (*res cogitans*) placed in opposition to some physical "side" (*res extensa*). In thus never taking sides, equipmentality always already coheres into its coherent qualitative whole. It is such coherence that we find so lacking in the zombie.

2 His head's gone

For the zombie, just as "the animal" was famously for Heidegger, is "poor in world."[1] Humans, or Dasein,[2] are the only entity under the sun, according to Heidegger, who exist "with" being and are thus bestowed with the art or comportment of Da-sein or, as I will translate it here, being-t/here.[3] What happens however when the human being goes rogue or goes ape, when its mentality and its attendant ability to deal or to cope with equipment, and thus to "have" Zeughaftigkeit or equipmentality, disappears? S/he devolves into an "it," loses their name, and becomes simply a zombie.

Zombies, as some surviving scientists will typically point out within the genre, lose their cerebral cortex and thus, in losing a head that is able to orient and to figure things out, become aimless eating machines, flesh machines. In losing then this "figuring head" they may just so happen to carry guns and cigarettes upon their "person" but cannot any longer comport themselves toward these items as such, and so such items, articles, pragmata or paraphernalia are then erased for them and consequently recede into a thick disinhibiting fog. With the zombie

---

1   Martin Heidegger, *Fundamental Concepts of Metaphysics: World, Finitude, Solitude.* Bloomington, IN: Indiana University Press, 1995.

2   Heidegger clarifies that Dasein is not exchangeable or restricted within the ambit of the human. This signature, and somewhat polemical, stroke on Heidegger's part, distances or separates the concept of Dasein from the traditional Latinate metaphysical concept of *humanitas*. He states elsewhere (Martin Heidegger, "Letter on Humanism" in *Pathmarks*, edited and translated by William McNeil. Cambridge: Cambridge University Press, 1998) that *humanitas* does not actually value the human highly enough. There is then an oppositional separatism, on a higher level, of the human from all other (ontic) entities, whether animal, vegetable or mineral, who cannot ever hope to heed the call of being as they are not *of* or ever called upon *by* being.

3   I ask, in translating Dasein into English, that we avoid the commonly utilized "being-there," or the less often utilized "being-here," but instead split such singular spacing into "being-t/here." By adding a slash, and thus doubling the "Da" (for in German Da can mean both here *and* there), we recognize the folding and the intimately ecstatic nature of this spatio-temporal mode of being that is Dasein. Thus, whilst we often leave this key Heideggerean term to dwell within its original German setting, we also often inevitably do (i.e. internally) translate this. When hearing Dasein, I therefore request that the reader hear also a strong note of "continuity," a being t/here, that deeply entwines and which is thus not restricted tidily within any one location but transcends and enwraps both. We are "being here/there." In choosing only here *or* there, there remains the clear and present remnant of a duality that could certainly bear some further thought.

now inhabiting such a thick disinhibiting fog or ring[4] they also strictly lack in possibilities of comporting themselves toward one another and instead swarm the planet as contagious hominid insect machines making the equipmental totalities that they once, as Dasein, occupied, fall apart. Such is the bare or mere half-life of Zombeing without country and without polis.

For the zombie, caught within this mere and aimless taking up of or swarming down upon space, is no longer faced with the option of inhabiting such space *as* "place," that is as a space structured or bestowed with meaningful arrangements, and so loses any gathering or congregating toward futurial projects and horizons. The zombie, as we will soon see, is lacking entirely in what Heidegger calls "as structure" (*als struktur*). As a fallen human then, as the walking or wandering dead, the zombie is now no longer equipped to deal and to make any pact or agreement with space in any way so as to turn or to "bring it about"[5] as place.

---

4   For it is *within*, as it were, this image of the disinhibiting ring that Heidegger will join forces, or better, clasp hands, with Jakob Von Uexküll in severing, separating and cordoning off the impoverished category of the animal from the upright house-inhabiting human. Heidegger spends some time strolling with Uexküll and values him highly as that rare form of biologist who avoids falling prey to either the mechanistic worldview of a Darwin or the entelechial idealism of a Hans Driesch. Within Uexküll's diagrams in the humanizing or self-popularizing of his theories, there are the qualitatively differing *Umwelten* of flies and dogs sharing a "space" with each other and with the human but of never having the possibility of partaking of the institution of a room, within which only the human can comport or reside. For *in* this room are books, but the dog, disinhibitedly trapped within its ring, can only "see" things to ingest and things to sit on whilst the fly sees only things to ingest. "The" animal then, within *all* its plural unity, according to Heidegger, is held fast within captivation (*Benommenheit*) and, in having no possibility of deploying a copula, also cannot copulate, as it were, with the real via a little and yet very giant "is" or "as." The human has an "as structural" (*als strucktur*) apprehension of the space, *as* we will see. For Uexküll's argument, in its popularized form, see Jakob von Uexküll, *A Foray into the Worlds of Animals and Humans*. Minneapolis, MN: University of Minnesota Press, 2010). For Heidegger's appreciative engagement with Uexküll, see Martin Heidegger, *Fundamental Concepts of Metaphysics: World, Finitude, Solitude*, Bloomington, IN: Indiana University Press, 1995.

5   For equipment is a vehicle, and this vehicle is also simultaneously the power (*Macht*) that alters economies of course. Transitions in equipment co-directionally accompany changes in investments. As any social investment or formation changes, so, almost tautologically, will its equipment. I have termed this elsewhere "*equipower*," to denote the intimate or immanent intertwining of equipment, power, economy and mentality. See Tony Richards, "Of Excrementality: Ecanomie, Signification and Autoimmunity," *Canadian Journal of Communication*, Vol. 38 (2013), pp. 477–496. We envisage some useful comparisons here with the Foucault's biopolitical concept of governmentality.

The zombie may have overrun or overtaken this space that it disinhibitively-inhabits but it cannot, for all that, make any declaration of independence for this space to equip or maintain[6] itself within place, domicile or abode, and thus to concomitantly exist within-a-world. It is not equipped with what Heidegger calls being-in-the-world (*in-der-welt-sein*). We move then toward introducing our main concern with equipmentality and that sense of place, time and world that it stages, presents and ultimately affords.

Before landing squarely upon the question concerning this dearth or deficiency in equipmentality that Zombeing entails, and thus of a problem also concerning a blurring of the ontico-ontological difference, of that supposed cardinal difference between b*eing* and b*eings* that makes up an emergent mode that I will call Zombeing, let me open up here a sort of brief parenthesis to trailer a space that we will return to more fully in our concluding and more programmatic final stage of the argument. Simply stated, equipmentality and Zombeing will not be about any fictional being known under the rubric of "the zombie," but will instead be about that marking out of a programmatic or pragmatic path that beckons us to follow, or better a ground to absorb and to learn to wander upon. For where "it" wanders, we wander after and also. We are, as it were, deputized to wander about within their deposited zombie tracks. We will come to see then how such zombie wandering co-contaminates us and how the contemporary zombie genre *itself*, functions for us as a performative item or marker placed within a vastly connected economic equipmental contexture, and thus as a non-allegorical lever or equipmental driver, or even key educator, within our comportments. This sense of a non-allegorical equipmental function of the genre, of a genre set within a larger equipmental contexture, will be a key plank in finding a use or exchange value for Heidegger's concept of equipmentality, that marries with a recent performative turn within media and media theory.[7]

---

6   And here we could explore the conventional matrix of equipment, maintenance, hand (*main*) and equip*mentality*. Zombies may still be able to stand on their own two feet and yet they cannot ever take a stand with their hand. For a masterful discussion of Heidegger in relation to this conceptual handful or nexus, see Jacques Derrida, "Heidegger's Hand (Geschlecht II)," *Psyche, Inventions of the Other, volume II*. Stanford: Stanford University Press, 2008, pp. 27–62.

7   Indeed the sharpness of this turn might call for a rethinking of this domain's very title as the word "media" irrevocably calls upon images of separation and mediation, where a better word might be "*im*mediation" given this thorough lack of distance between so-called media and what they would supposedly mediate, or meditate, upon. If, media were ever media, they are less so now. Hence, also, the key related term of performativity that does things. For the key text on this immersive "doing"

As a corollary of this then we can conceive texts such as *The Walking Dead* as equipmental items that we "handle," or better, which handle us, and which thus drive us toward, what I am calling here, the very *un*fictionalized, and thus very economically practical space or housing, of "Zombeing." The equipmentality of Zombeing is, as I will argue, *the* par excellence contemporary economic shaping.

Such television programming then is never some mere representation *of* zombies, from which we would be safely or sovereignly separated off by some barrier or "screen," for we ourselves *are* this "Zombeing" and are thus, in our very economic[8] element, headless or acephalic wanderers. The difference here between Dasein's much praised and thus raised "be*ing*" and those lower "be*ings*" that it comports itself toward or encounters, becomes here a more general space of Zombeing where no such separations can ever any longer be maintained. Such will be the drive of our conclusion. It should be noted from the outset that this is not intended as a somewhat melodramatic or moral charge, as a sort of accusation or a deploring of a direction that television has recently taken, as I measure my meaning here very carefully in sketching out this marked channel turn[9] toward Zombeing or zombie media. For it will all finally hinge or pivot upon what exactly we mean by "zombie media" or "Zombeing" and also whether partaking of or even *being* this decapitated Zombeing would be such a negative

---

see John L. Austin, *How to do Things with Words*. Oxford: Oxford University Press, 1975. For a productive complication of this, and a necessary stage on any journey in understanding the, for Austin underthought, inherent complications of this as a non-representational repository that complicates concepts of symbolic "communication," see Jacques Derrida, *Limited Inc*. Evanston: Northwestern University Press, 1988. From here onwards Derrida will come to operate his own renewed or mutated notion of performativity that shares some interesting resonances with equipmentality and that complicates traditional use cases of some top-down meditative intentionality.

8   We should here recognize the etymology of economy as arising from Oikos, which is Greek for household. Just as equipmentality is something that substantially contains us, so the Oikos is that homely space which measures and constrains, and allows us to make sense of our movements. We are thus nothing without equipment and its attendant "housing."

9   For it really is about an equipmental restructuring and a turning and retuning (*umstimmen*) of the channels or the televisual tide, as we will see, away from the upstanding centralized networked ("humanist") channels of the networks (NBC, ABC, BBC, etc.) toward the availability of less immunally protective and more "long tail" economic cable spaces such as AMC, HBO, Cinemax, etc. Whilst the networks deal in high handed economically protective heroics, these newer spaces are dealing in what we might call fallen or "damaged goods."

eventuality to find ourselves dwelling within. For "being" a zombie, or simply Zombeing, might finally involve something of an ethical turn, even if it is not any longer one that involves the rule or the figure of an ethically distanced and governmentally charged "head." Such will be the rather active or revisionary use I will be making of Heidegger's notion of equipmentality as the argument unfolds.

To keep this introductory section open for a while longer let me briefly outline the stakes of *The Walking Dead* as an equipmentality made to measure out a revised relation to the head. In contradistinction to many classical televisual works of upright cephalic handling and restoration, in *The Walking Dead*, a figure of organized authority or of fatherly law,[10] a police sheriff's deputy, is knocked somewhat off-course, and will come in time to cede his organization and his authority to the newly disorganized and aporetic zombie *de*governmental space that he will, in all senses, "turn" or "awaken to" and come to wander within and occupy, no longer equipped to restore or to reverse this disorder through the deployment of well-maintained or terminated in-order-to's (*Um-zu*). Such equipping of himself, within this newly emerging disordered environment, will be found no longer then to operate as transparently ready-to-hand (*Zuhanden*) and thus, will no longer be arranged within some logical order and in train toward some grand central terminus point for the very sake of which (*Worum-willen*), and in the very first place, he is able to find and to measure his existence. Simply stated, there is no grounding plan available. *Zombeing opens toward the interminable.*

And so here, within the equipmental region of *The Walking Dead*, and as some strange form of absent or absconded evidence, we will find and we will seek no stabilizing transcendental American flags[11] of union either replanted or even nostalgically encountered, and so the pragmata or paraphernalia of past policing will come to simply deform itself into just so much unconnected entropic waste,

---

10 This "law of the father" and the classical figure of the phallus, and its relation to masculine stiff ce-phalic ordering might provide some useful orientation here?
11 Here we would need to rework and rethink the classical Barthesian notion of the pregnant absence of exnomination. Here, in short, is a flag, an absent flag, involved in a process of ex-nomi-Nation. Such reworking is not any repressed absented marginalization and is simply not a part of the emergent equipmentality of Zombeing. It is too terminal a sign for that. The flag is *simply* unimportantly absent. Unlike in post-apocalyptic shows such as *The Last Ship*, where lost flags are continually hankered after, *The Walking Dead* never concerns itself with regaining the solid grounding of the nation state.

unfit any longer for the new existence for which such equipment and comportment would be impracticable for purpose. Here, as with most amulets of order, the protective figure of the sheriff deputy's hat, will still be handed down from father Rick to son Carl, but not any longer as *aide-memoire* or as aiding the further establishment of order, but really as a somewhat ironic, present-at-hand (*Vorhanden*), non-equipmental period piece to help to keep the brute and direct heat of the sun at bay. This sheriff deputy's hat is not held in stock then as an item of equipment, and placed upon some larger contextual aims-oriented horizon. In terms of classical equipmental being we think of Heidegger's famous maxim: "taken strictly, there *is* no such thing as 'an' equipment."[12] In terms of the dismantled equipmentality of Zombeing, we would work toward a revision of this key Heideggerian explanatory algorithm: there *is* now however "an" hat, but shorn of any superior context and disconnected from a terminal temporal purpose or goal. *Zombeing does not exist along the horizon or comportments of a for-the-sake-of-which* (*Worum-willen*).

The Walking Dead thus helps us to plot or to cope (Sorge) with a course that it enacts within its space and which it sees as exemplary of a contemporary existence and will mark a transition or a step change away from previously goal oriented ends-aimed equipmental narratives.

In the forthcoming argument we will come to see that *The Walking Dead* operates "itself" as a sort of simultaneous "tomb" and "womb," of what we will thus coin a "t*w*omb," that is, an equipmental topography practically performing the closing down of one space (a tomb) and the simultaneously housed or synchronized opening up of another (a womb). And so, rather than seeking to reverse, revitalize or resuscitate that space, it provides instead a sort of performative t*w*omb from which emerges a new form of equipmental coping that does not take the well-formed shape that more network-oriented shows seek to reproduce or resuscitate. With Zombeing we are dealing with some form of half-life mutation. As some form of mutation, then, we will come to see that *The Walking Dead* is nothing but the embodiment of a performative "t*w*omb" that gives birth and gives berth to that living dead equipmentality of Zombeing. To investigate this retuning toward Zombeing we will now turn, as it were, to look at this specific t*w*ombic "hinging" of *The Walking Dead* in much more detail, employing a number of key Heideggerian terms, the original German terms of which, will then be each time placed within brackets to draw attention to their place within

---

12 Martin Heidegger, *Being and Time*. Oxford: Blackwell Publishing, 2005, p. 97.

the Heideggerian arguments regarding equipmentality that the reader can then follow up in more detail.

3 *The Walking Dead* and its equipmental turning toward Zombeing

In terms of the story, and in a sort of *in media res*, in the first minutes of the opening episode of *The Walking Dead*, Deputy Rick Grimes, a much respected law enforcement officer within the King's County Georgia Sherriff's Department, will be fired upon whilst "projecting" (*Entwurfen*) and "throwing" (*Geworfen*) himself into the line or the "calling" (*Ruf*) of duty. As so thrown, as Heidegger would say, Rick Grimes does not ever live to get see behind himself, as it were, to sovereignly reflect upon this role that he has come to occupy so well, but simply finds himself performing it and awaits the result.[13] This is not to say that he is never conscious of whom he is, but that this consciousness will always be aimed finally toward being the policeman that he is and so he can never once be found naked "outside" (*ausser*) of that equipmental character that he is. Everything about him is already given (*gegeben* or *gibt*) or bestowed and *who* he is will always be built or predicated upon *what* and *how* he is. Into this world then he is always-already (*immer schon*) thrown and immersed and he is thus never the puppet master to his own sense of being who exactly he is, finitely placed into those structures as he always-already has been or ever will be.

Who then knows at what exact point one Rick Grimes really decided or fell into being this officer and upholder of the law and, performatively holding up his right hand and swearing, without partiality or prejudice, to uphold and maintain the constitution that he serves, but we do, much more often than we would care or like to think, simply find ourselves falling (*Verfallen*) into things. And, even when we *think* that we do take these on as "conscious" decisions, those pictures and places that we come to occupy are always so much larger than we could ever hope to control or comprehend, no matter how much we might fantasize about redirecting or rebooting the given machine we are working within. Such is the one and only way we can become equipped to write out our signature and take our place. The machinery or the equipmental structures into which we are

---

13 For an excellent discussion of the concept of "awaiting" and self-understanding and the intertwining of the structurality of equipment and of a relative and, one might even say, essential, passivity in the very performing of duties that we are implying here, see William Blattner, *Heidegger's Temporal Idealism*. Cambridge: Cambridge University Press, 1999, pp. 129–163.

thrown then are really all that "matters" in the end. Our very ability to hold onto the space of an identity is always already, and irrevocably, predicated upon our falling into line or else we are simply written out.

Almost tautologically, it must be said, we have always to be equipped to deal with the equipment we are faced with and that equipment is always out of our hands at the same exact moment that it is so heavily at our disposal, all the way down to the very bottom of our being, the essence of which will always follow upon existence, in reversal of the classical Cartesian ordering. Within such a total purview of equipment, it can never really be our very own power that we are experiencing and, in truth, this equipment is everything that we have and all that we have to give. It is not ours for the taking. For, *in order to* in any way even to "be" ourselves, we must borrow the tools *in-order-to* even begin "signifying" (*Bedeutung*) and to have or to feel our way along the "significance" that we have at our disposal, yet never within our control. Heidegger would see this equipmentality and this comportment (*Verhalten*) as a constant, no matter in which culture one happens to be raised. It is culture itself, essentially. This, for Heidegger, is what separates the well-equipped singular human from all the various animals that we referred to near the opening: animals "behave," whilst humans comport. For the individual human *to* comport, all signature maneuvers must supervene upon the availability of context. In being "thrown," quite ahead ourselves, we "fall" into equipmentalities which are here so well exemplified by the well-trodden line that we find Rick walking upon toward the opening of an opening or inaugural episode that will augur or bring such a change to his life and to all that connected equipment with which he sought to understand this life and to maintain and find his accommodation with it. And, for the moment, he certainly continues to follow this "call" (*Ruf*) which houses and which furnishes and which builds and maintains his being in this matter and this matrix.

To interrupt this "call" and consequently his place within this larger equipmental structure, Deputy Rick Grimes is fired upon then, this day, whilst attempting, along with his partner Deputy Shane Walsh, to apprehend a fugitive who had been speeding dangerously across the county lines that they share with Linden County. The dispatch officer advises, across their well-connected police radio (*Zeug*), that a Linden County officer has been wounded in pursuit on their side of the border. Luckily these two sides of a border communicate well in the pursuit of one larger cross-state cause within which they are subsumed and so happily united. In preparation and "in-order-to" (*Um-zu*) ready himself for engaging the fugitives "for-the-sake-of" (*Worum-willen*) helping to maintain state and civil order, Deputy Walsh quickly and semi-automatically (*Zuhanden*) dons both gloves and a sniper hat (items of *Zeug*) whilst Deputy Grimes drives

speedily with siren shrieking and signing (*Zeigen*) its warnings along the publically regulated highway. Such a sign, "thrown" out by the police vehicle "*is an
item which is ready-to-hand for the driver in his concern with driving, and not
for him alone.*"[14] And so such a use of their equipment-for-warning-the-other,
equipment that is not *or ever* for themselves alone, will forewarn and allow the
civilians "*by virtue of this reliability [of the police equipment] she is sure of her
world*"[15] to know to move aside, but also to know, more importantly, that this
is an "in-order-to" that both ensures and insures that order is maintained and
restored and so to live consistently upon some sense of solid truth, reason or
ground (*Grundes*). Equipment (here, the shrieking siren) is always testamen-
tary of a solidly built "with-world" (*Mit-welt*) as equipment is, by its definition,
always publically readable and available. Such is the very principle of a shared
and well-maintained ground that constitutes the "truths" that we live and stand
on guard by.

   Without however having to step back and "thematically" (*thematisch*) consider this larger terrain that they co-occupy, and thus help to shepherd and maintain, and having then stopped and placed a TDD or "tire deflation device" in
the oncoming criminal car's path, "*in-order-to*" (*Um-zu*) force it off the road,
the oncoming speeding car that shelters its fugitives unexpectedly tosses over
multiple times upon hitting the TDD and lands, upturned upon its roof, in a
field adjacent to the road. The law enforcement officers were now being fired

---

14 Martin Heidegger, *Being and Time*. Oxford: Blackwell Publishing, 2005, p. 109. Here
    Heidegger speaks of the position of an arrow (easily exchangeable for a tail light) that
    allows the driver to signal their intention to those travelling in similar vehicles behind.
    The world of traffic regulations is here under discussion, as well as the "being structure"
    of equipment, but this is always but one archaeological component or relic of a larger
    related equipmental terminally organized totality. It cannot be bitten off to stand alone.
15 Martin Heidegger, "The Origin of the Work of Art," in: *Poetry, Language, Thought*.
    New York: Harper Collins, 1974, p. 33-34. Van Gough's "depicted" peasant shoes,
    surrounded or mired in much controversy, in terms of a conveyance of world, might
    resonate and resound into our own argument regarding Rick's own transformed mode
    of transport and of journeying. In any event, Heidegger, in discussing the "peasant
    woman" that he believes Van Gough to be carrying over the concerns of within the
    shoes depicted within his painting, continues "World and earth exist for her, and for
    those who are with her in her mode of being, and only thus – in the equipment…for the
    equipment first gives [es Gibst] to the simple world its security…" (Martin Heidegger,
    The Origin of the Work of Art, p. 34). It is a total *loss* of security and sure footing that
    the wanderer Rick will come to grapple with and come to appreciate, in terms of its
    purchase on his growing sense of Zombeing.

upon from behind this upturned immobilized vehicle, the outlaw's own now broken, somewhat "unready-to-hand," (*Unzuhanden*) item of equipment. In then believing that they had restrained the two fugitives through their return fire, and after Deputy Grimes had been squarely hit by a bullet to his protective police vest, a third, previously unseen, fugitive climbs out from the upturned car and shoots Deputy Grimes in the shoulder, now bypassing the protection of that vest.

As Deputy Grimes falls to the ground and begins sinking into unconsciousness, Deputy Walsh calls out to his fellow deputies to secure an ambulance and, looking into his partner's eyes in an us-including point-of-view, implores Deputy Rick Grimes to "stay with me." Here, one element of maintaining law must now give way to the well-regulated "comportments" (*Verhalten*) of another. Such a well-regulated interconnectedness of equipmental institutional spaces will be what safely separates and clearly cordons off the comportment of humans from the mere bare disinhibited behavior of the animal. Here police and hospitals are intimately connected within one larger world (*welt*) and no animal, no matter how ambitious it may be, will ever proceed "up" to such a space, station or calling.

Whilst Deputy Walsh, adhering to convention, calls "*police officer down*" over the state's radio apparatus, a call that evidences an interconnected and well-regulated force (*Macht*) of law and biopolitics, Deputy Grimes himself sinks into unconsciousness. This unconsciousness then persists apart from a strobed and blurry, also us-including, point-of-view shot of a hospital visit from Deputy Walsh bringing flowers from the department, and saying that "*we're still hanging in.*" Looking through a indistinct Deputy Grimes' eyes, it seems that he has visited the hospital's recovery ward often and yet something *else* seems also have transpired, as indicated by this peculiar deployment of the "we're still…," as if some sickness were being precariously contained, somewhat paradoxically, outside of this space. This, it seems and portends, is not some troubled hospital visitor speaking sensitively to their comatose close one. Then, all the activity of nearby bleeps and far-off tannoys, heard within the background of his friend and colleague's somewhat resigned reporting, all suddenly disappears in a, now sharp, reverse angle of Rick's awakened sweat-covered unshaven face. All around now is soundless and uncannily clear. Everything seems to have, unmarkedly, changed since the last camera shot and yet, giving a uncanny sense of elapsed time, Rick replies that the vase containing the flowers "*is something special…*" as he seeks return repartee from the now absented visitor.

…Let us take a brief parenthetical pause in the proceeding and the progress of this beautifully maintained narrative arc. For here we have reached something of a "hinge" and a "turn," and a "change-over" (*Umschlag*) and a "passage" (*gelenkt*) within the narrative of Rick's journey as agency of the letter of the law. Within this masked and elided cut, deputy sheriff Rick Grimes will, not unlike a Dorothy who will never find her feet to be able to make the return journey home, fall asleep within a world of solid geometry, where equipment lines itself up to terminate in delivering something *for-the-very-sake-of-which* (*Worum-willen*) it is there, to then wake up in an uncanny (*unheimlich*) space where the tracks of equipment cannot any longer be followed toward any terminal aims and endpoints. The solidity of the prior equipmental tracks have now dissolved out and no yellow brick road will make itself available to plot a return course home toward that previously solid equipmental structure that had formerly been taken so much for granted and been so ready-to-hand (*Zuhanden*), even in its failings.

In situating Rick's awakening, we might think of the *Wizard of Oz's* tornado-tossed house[16] that, once transplanted into the strange land of Oz, always-already structured Dorothy's disembarkation around a terminal *for-the-sake-of* to be assured of an eventual return, just as the larger housing of the manufacturing "equipment" of classical Hollywood film always promised and promoted the very real "equipmentalities" and "copings" of which they were such an intimate and heartfelt part. For these bygone Dorothean cinematic spectators were not simply doing their spectating across a stage divided proscenium arch or vast Cartesian chasm but were equiprimordially (*gleichursprünglich*) coping (*Sorge*) in a world that they were being-in and being-amongst. Our own contemporary Rick, then, exactly like a somewhat mutated Dorothy, will soon emerge from his displaced and empty hospital housing, a hospital housing whose intricately cocooned contours were so well-shaped to institutionally offer out their works of recuperative hospitality, into a world where that housing is now disconnected from any larger equipmental totality. Like Dorothy's house, then, Rick's own hospital housing will seem to have lost its previous way and so all that remains of *The Walking Dead* narrative saga, from this first part of the first episode onward, will really all be about pushing thorough a lack of terminations and terminuses. In interminably lacking such terminable paths or for-the-sake-of-whiches, there will, concomitantly, never ever be any shoes that can click made available to Rick to aid his purchase within-the-world, to be able to find his return journey home[17] and we will thus now realize that Rick is no longer, and never will be again, the

---

16　And again, we should recall the etymology and remember that a house is coterminous with economy and institutional dwelling and thus is never that simple and symbolic sign pointing homeward, as in some place of ultimate sovereign interiority. There is no home ownership.

17　Again, we are talking about the home as oikos and economy here.

police deputy that he was. In losing the demand for such shoes, to make return journeys home, Zombeing is all around and about becoming equipped to wander. Let us think a little on the function of this hospital as t*w*omb, and just why Rick must wait for a while, and be put on hold, outside of this equipmental conversion.

This highly punctuated point in time within the narrative, and this primal equipmental space from which Rick is awakening or emerging, is not then unlike some simultaneous tomb and womb (a t*w*omb, as we're neologistically coining it), a life-death double helix. This white hospital bed, this uncanny mise-en-scene of both tomb *and* womb, connected up so intimately to the attentive matrix-apparatus of the hospital, which itself connects up to all the other institutions (including home) does indeed have strong echoes of a womb from which he will soon emerge. Unable, for example, to feed or to take a stand on his own individual being, he must draw all of his sustenance from a space that he, in his comatose slumber, has been so thoroughly unaware of occupying. To all intents and purposes, and so dead to the world, and thus so blissfully unaware of the world that awaits him "on the out," he will soon climb out of this womb-turned-coffin *or* this coffin-turned-womb. As umbilically connected he *and* we will soon disconnect and be forced to make his *and* our own way and to quickly play catch up with those characters who are already in a position to know, out there in a story which has moved on without us for a time, outside of the restrictions and the tale tellings of the plot.

For, in speaking of the separation and of the briefly severed connections of story and of plot, and with Rick and ourselves (i.e. Rick as our issued avatar) having been bed ridden and restricted to our t*w*ombic plot, a plot or allotment whose story has most assuredly moved onward and upwards and which we must now emerge and catch up with, a strange form of duality then makes its way into this space as *beyond* the tombic and the wombic duality of this broken hospital bed from which both he *and* we will dually awaken. Like he, we *also* then interconnectedly participate in his utter ignorance and inexperience of this new world disorder and so he, and we, together, will all soon surface to make our first simultaneous baby steps once the plot, again, catches up to and converges upon the locale of the story. Perhaps, in viewing this uncanny mise-en-scene of *both* tomb *and* womb, which forms into this topographic t*w*omb, this topography might hatch and resonate with all manner of disciplinarily displaced Dorothy mournfully surveying and digesting Rick's responses to a departed Deputy Walsh and to all the other cephalic agencies of the law having also "cleared the building" only to make their return as "turned" or retuned headless *a*cephalics?[18]

---

18 We might find some interesting cross-pollinations here with Bataille's acéphale and this new headless form of equipmental coping.

We return from this parenthetical pause to Rick's return, from his death bed, into the land of the living as he moves to unplug himself from this matrix of dead equipment[19] and makes his way through the t*w*ombic death-birth canal into this new world disorder of Zombeing…

…Rick now then finds himself occupying an empty room[20] with, rather uncannily, no sound at all bleeding in from the vast corridors that one would habitually expect to carry the flow of much movement and of organized noise. In Rick's waking haze, the dead or broken flowers that he looks around to see, grasp and touch (conveying thus, concretely, to him that his friend has long since cleared this scene), is soon joined by other faulty "unready-to-hand" (*Unzuhanden*) or "broken equipment" (*Zeughaften*) itemized by his gaze as a stopped clock, an empty intravenous drip from which he must now umblically disconnect and an utter *utter* grave silence (for institutional windows block out birdsong) that speaks of a larger equipmental absence that will conspicuously obtrude upon his previous sense of regime. But this list-itemizing-gaze of Rick's, which includes the lack of an expected return-gaze from the non-hailable nurse,[21] is then quickly paused or thrust aside by an exceeding blinding thirst.

After guzzling water from his restroom's still-operating (*Zuhanden*) faucet and suddenly seeing the weeks of previously concealed transformation reflected in the restroom's mirror he, tumbling over a seemingly out of place gurney that was bolt up against the outside of his door, moves out of this room, and soon

---

19 Again, this is certainly, and ontically, "hospital equipment" but it also certainly, and metonymically, stands in for all the further equipment that granted Rick his previous life before making his transition toward Zombeing. Again, we analytically bite off this local piece of equipment, but the matrix spreads much further out and so much more is rippling through, and being reborn, within this umbilical disconnection, than we are able to maintain with this restricted image.

20 In reference to equipmentality and community and of equipment shorn of purpose, termination and community there is some interesting discussion in Jeff Malpas, *Heidegger's Topology: Being, Place, World*. Cambridge, MA: MIT Press, 2006, pp. 94–95.

21 For absence (*Nicht*) is *itself* a form of presence that assails our relation to equipment and which always, when and *qua* absent, bespeaks a certain urgent drive for equipmental readjustment. These productive powers and procuring pressures of equipmental absences, perhaps, could fruitfully be explored much further from a Heideggerian point of view? Absence, as quasi-transcendence, is perhaps something a Heideggerian framework can supply in reading difficult inscriptions. Such absent presences, as absent representations, could perhaps be called "repres*s*entations" and "repres*s*ences"?

finds that the larger hospital is abandoned and with the few lights still in operation, flickering more off than on.

This is certainly not a clean hospital that we are finding ourselves wandering within, feeling somewhat at sea, and nothing is in its place. Entropy springs to mind, with all manner of matter dispersed and out of place. Where are the people who help to organize this matter that has now drifted so thoroughly and thoughtlessly out of place and who help to dispose us toward this matter made into order? Where are those who themselves, like the now "departed" sheriff's deputy Rick Grimes, "fall" (*verfallen*) daily into their own interconnected duties, occupations and equipmentalities.

Nothing, including phone lines to the outside world, seems to be working, and all that Rick approaches to try and take hold of, seems now so thoroughly "unready-to-hand" (*Unzuhanden*) and nobody at all is around to call out to, to help us figure out its now conspicuous (*auffällig*), obstinate (*hartnäckig*) and obtrusive (*aufdringlich*) operations. So much really seems *not* to be working, that the catalogue is almost too long even to begin to undertake. It is hard to follow any logic, along this corridor, as fragment jars into fragment with no flows of connections any longer taking place. It really is amazing, we cannot help but think, that in its intricate spatial weave and in its intricate weaving through time, just how much one is asked to take as *granted* within this equipment that we use and through which we tacitly, safely and inconspicuously experience our only available being-in-the-world (*in-der-Welt-sein*).

This "grantedness," in the sense of the everyday gifts that are continually bestowed upon our movements, has now however been voided, withdrawn and rescinded. Much has indeed transformed then, it seems, in those long weeks of coma and, as Rick wanders along corridors, each more disheveled and lacking in the logic/logos of layout than the last, it seems like some descent toward the very heart of an empty darkness, consummating, as it were, on the figure of a ravaged corpse seen through a ward's corridor divider windowpane. In cutting then somewhat brutally to the strangest change of all, we very quickly find a hospital occupied largely by zombies, "who" are clearly quite unlike Dorothy's own beloved Munchkins, and *nothing* of the old world's way of working holds sway any longer. Rick is presently making his way through this birth-death canal.

On walking down some darkened stairs, in-order-to (*Um-zu*) attempt to reach the periphery of this misshapen metamorphosed space, he reaches an exit sign that is uncovered or made visible only very dimly by a match that he had struck and held out very tentatively in front of him, not knowing at all what this light would reflect and present to him in return. Here, upon emerging from the exit, on the periphery of this failed and fallen institution, the very heart of this darkness is now finally reached within an unaccustomed blinding light that discloses or uncovers (Heidegger calls this *Aletheia*) the appearance of an utterly failed biopolitical state, evidenced for him in a sprawl of army helicopters and of endless undisturbed fly-soaked corpses.

The institutions that usually come calling so automagically in emergencies, hailing us in methods and in ways that are so much more than soft powered Althusserian interpellations, appear here to have totally closed down and to have totally given up the ghost. Something is rogue and unhomely. The habitual "*Hey You There!*" modes-of-address that marinate and secure us in everything we make contact with can only fall now on the deafest of ears, given the total abandonment and withdrawal of what once helped to keep it all moving along within its constant and constrained biopolitical blood supply and flow. What has happened to the larger encompassing, positively constraining, (American) "way," that for-the-sake-of-which (*Worum-willen*), this all ultimately and terminally connected up to and which it, in turn, connectedly helped to guard and maintain?

Rick is "thrown" (*Geworfen*) then into midst and the mists of an entirely new world of "being-t/here" (*Da-Sein*), and this new world environment (*Umwelt*), that he finds himself thrust into, is an environment and an environing changed out of any and all recognition. That time before, for Rick, before this criminally induced coma, is a time that seems really to have only taken the blink of an eye to complete.

We might begin to see that this deeply unsettling "narrative," of the first episode of *The Walking Dead*, here rhetorically recounted within an attempt to mimic its equip*mental* movements, might turn out, itself, to be about laying down the groundwork (*Grundriss*) for a time-space entirely lacking in termination. In lacking in such settling classical narrative motivation, in lacking an anchoring for-the-sake-of-which (*Worum-willen*), it would thus also be all about the lack of any ultimate return address for this agency of the letter of the law of the show in and of itself. For the show, in and of itself, forms into equipment not formed at all for terminal destinations but for permanently errant wandering or, what Derrida called, in a purposefully misshapen echo of Heidegger's more purposive schema, "destinerrance", or a destiny, as it were, permanently in errance.

From this tracking of the narrative, we will now move onto the more substantive analytical stage before finally returning to this world of zombies, occupied by all manner of agencies now destin-errantly lacking for-the-sake-of-whiches that have really gone somewhat "rogue." The next section then is concerned with enabling us to look at this show "itself" as an item of equipment or component of a larger equip*mentality*, a larger structuring whole, that helps develop and maintain a certain grip or purchase upon our contemporary lived scene.

4 Zombeing and time

We have just looked in some detail at a pivotal section of the opening episode of *The Walking Dead* for the purpose of underlining a certain equipmental "transition" that the episode attempts to grapple with concerning Rick's "turn" in coping within a period of transition from a solid architectural structure geared around strong termination points (*for-the-sake-of-which*) toward an errantly un-toward world inhabited by zombies that forces or managerially marinates, in soaking him to the bone, into a much less terminal mode of coping (*Sorge*) geared around fluid mutating toward-whiches (*Um-zu*) that lack in those terminal temporalized for-the-sake-of-whiches.

I stressed before, to help situate it within a larger equipmental field, that *The Walking Dead*, forgetting or bracketing Rick, was really about a transition in our *own* modes of equipmental coping that I then termed "Zombeing." This is not then a mere symbolic or allegorical narrative around and about Zombies, as fictional beings, but about moving or settling into the newly emerging condition or abode of Zombeing as a mode or process of equipmental coping (*Sorge*) within which we are deeply marinated or intricately enthreaded. It must be pointed out that, contra classical Heidegger, such a temporal mode of Zombeing questions the traditional Heideggerian view of the Dasein as that singular creature, that special "quality," safely ensconced on the ontological side of the ontico-ontological difference or divide (between be*ing* and be*ings*) and so here a certain collapse, as it were, *exhumates* the traditional human animal endowed *with* being into, what we might see as a creature of the intricately entwined ontico-ontological *différance*. Différance is Derrida's term to denote the sense in which nothing terminates in the transcendental signified (in brief, an arrival of meaning where the play of difference is safely halted in say "God" or in "being") and so everything is different and deferred (spatial and temporally) into every other term in the chain of différance or the trace. Without final destinations, Rick forms, within the topography of the t*w*omb, into the perfect reborn and rebooted avatar of this, now *ex*human being, this reformed temporalized de-ontologized "being" that we call, Zombeing.

"Texts," in an age of neoliberal intervention into the bodily space,[22] reflect this breaking down of the protective ontological shell or firewall as the sovereign difference of the "ontological" (be*ing*) and the "ontical" (be*ings*) becomes

---

22 And the recent growth in editorially reflexive bioengineering and synthetic biology might give Heidegger further pause along another train of the question concerning (bio)technology.

*in*humed and *ex*humed so that the "human" entity, endowed with some special gift (handling equipment within the compass or purview of some magisterial magnetic transcendental belief, signified, or aim), cedes to an entity that can be broken into or generally hacked as with any other entity. Recent advances within genome technology, synthetic biology, bioengineering and biodiscovery patenting are the mere local ontic reproductive regions of this larger neoliberalized fracturing of the world picture of the walking upright hominid transformed into something more infinitely deferred, wandering or meanderthal.[23] The death of equipmentalities that would terminate within points of "transcendental guarding," a death performatively embodied in the transformative t_wombic topography outlined above, is clearly exemplified here by a form of beingness deferred along a chain of endless "toward-whiches." *The Walking Dead* (along with a number of other performatively constructed neoliberal equipmental spaces such as *Breaking Bad, The Shield, Westworld, Godless,* etc.) cohere around a veritable incurable incoherence and thus performs a work of *ex*humation upon the humanist model of terminally organized being. The topography of Rick's t_womb is the pivotal site of this *ex*humation.

In view of this, we will come to see quickly, in *The Walking Dead*, that any curative restorative reversal is simply not a part of its equipmental space or operative floorplan. Those traditional staple televisual stabilizing avatars, or seemingly essential high points, of policemen, teachers, doctors, judges, pathologists, etc. metamorphose from such key guiding figures into errant *dis*figures, or damaged goods, who will find passage into new neoliberal equipmental practices that they now will solidly give into rather than ever hoping to heroically assuage or overcome. This is not about any outward or upward navigation, within narratives of overcoming, but about simply joining in. This particular space of *The Walking Dead* is, to be sure, considerably encrypted, and yet, clearly the, what we might call, "tugging" of this series is toward a certain synchronization with the neoliberal equipmentalities that are being introduced into the general economic space, a time and space which the zombie helps to foster and prepare us for: a fully occupied mode of "Zombeing."

---

23 I coin this term, somewhat poetically, to give some sense of a new being that, a little like the popularized image of the Neanderthal, has no solid sense of goal-oriented tool being. This new being, the "Meanderthal," is confidently misplaced within the emergent equipmentality of meandering and so does not obey the classical Heideggerian/ Aristotelian model being who resides under the tutelary and tributary direction or dictum of the for-the-sake-of-which. *Zombeing meanders itinerantly from in-order-to (Um-Zu) to in-order-to.*

As signs of "giving way" along this path, often series such as *The Walking Dead* involve figures of authority, figures once devoted and denoted as safely or ontologically immune to neoliberalisation becoming the very cutting edge of this process of transforming ontology into general ontics. We might then call these "decentral" rather than central characters or even portmanteau them as "*antago*protagonists," *if* the concept of antagonist were not itself simply outdated as the very opposite of trustworthy authority or equipment. For similar reasons the concept of the anti-hero seems also a little ill-suited to such neoliberal or liquidic equipmental spaces, such as *The Walking Dead*, that lack so totally in any distinction of the classical humanist hero from rogue (animal) antagonist. This, then, is the new temporality or timekeeping of Zombeing, involving a departure from the ontologized figuring head and thus necessitating that pivotal period of t*w*ombic topographic gestation that Rick/we have undergone and, as a reminder, such a temporo-topography does not fit the classical Heideggerian well-Daseined picture.

In our wanderings, we have deployed a number of Heideggerian concepts that fuse together into the larger concept of equipmentality, but we should pause for a moment to look at the resources of this word. We think of equipment as something, as some stretched out "thing" or object, albeit joined intimately together with others, that we "use" as gathered unto some purpose. A commonsense Cartesian view would see a separation between a safely ensconced and separable mindful agency that *uses* and a series of interconnected things that are then *used* to achieve this intended purpose. Equip-mentality, though, underlines the intimate interconnections of equipment *and* mentality that is so much more than being merely "connected," but which instead is formed into one general or continuous whole that moves *as* one, as an enfolding t/here.

Now the classical movement toward transcendental signifieds and "for-the-sake-of-whiches" (a terminality that formed such an, as it were, terminal element within Heidegger's framework) is clearly lacking in *The Walking Dead* and so the zombification process is all about learning to cope (*Sorge*) with this journeying into Zombeing. As such, it is conterminously centered upon the de-tethering of a previous anchoring or terminating environment (again, I would remind of the strangely unmarked and unmissed "absence" of the American flag in the show). The Zombie is the perfect embodiment then of this deworlded lack of the terminal for-the-sake-of-which, which we are adjusting here in recognition of this very real move toward Zombeing.[24] To be clear, this chapter proposes a revision of Heidegger's classical handling of equipmentality and our concomitant need to

---

24 Indeed we might even call such a rewired or suitably hacked version, *Zombeing and Time*, in some obvious perverse mutated homage to Heidegger's major tome.

recalibrate it for the contemporary mise-en-scene taking place, and *using* space, on both "sides" of the screen or "camera."

5 Heidegger's mishandling of zombies

So, whilst the deworlded (*Entweltlichung*) "species" of the zombie holds some considerable interest to many of us as a member of a larger en-compassing post-apocalyptic genus, Heidegger's own concerns would turn more toward the obsti-nate equip*mental* breakdowns that seem to have taken place in the intervening weeks whilst Deputy Rick Grimes was enclosed within his comatose state. We need not remind ourselves that we, like Deputy Rick Grimes himself, did not ourselves ever bear direct witness to this transition, but instead must retrospec-tively exhume and excavate it from its various traces, residues and remainders that we also have, as it were, woken up to within that elided t*w*ombic transi-tion and plot. Rick, as we ourselves then, must reconstitute the story and begin to catch up to this wandering that has already been established. Much of the opening episode, after falling asleep in some solid geometry and then waking up in the abandoned liquefied hospital, is in accommodating himself, and thus also by extension *ourselves*, to this "turning" and thus retuning of the world, in terms of the evident failures of equipment and the consequent transition toward new ways of coping and caring (*Sorge*). This *shared* work of a *shared* excavation, between a mutated Rick and ourselves, is not then insignificant or a mere bit part player.

For this shared absence of a live experiencing of the transition, decisively, works to solidify the connection and the close kinship relation, giving our-selves a very strong *share*, that is thus not an option, in existentially being and becoming Rick. In outlining the plot of the opening of episode one, much of this equipment was initially found clearly working and ready-to-hand (*Zuhanden*) before our sinking into the t*w*ombic coma and then as clearly and initially grasped as unready-to-hand (*Unzuhanden*), and even somewhat present-to-hand (*Vorhanden*[25]), in our waking up from it and fully grasping that lack of a terminal home note and thus of any grounding for-the-sake-of-which.

This is exactly where Heidegger would fail to grasp or appreciate both the Zombie and our own journey or way (*Weg*) into this new interminable Zombeing, given the trimming out of its *and our* ontological security, and of its *and our* reduction toward a series of mutable and wandering toward-whiches. The

---

25 As properties no longer grasped as deficient but simply thematically analyzed.

transition or the turn into new equipmental "conducts" and copings, that quickly took place upon emerging from the topographic t*w*omb, quickly sweeps aside all that terminally-oriented ontologically "bossy" equipment that he once worked so ably to co-operate with. We witness now that there is no power for him really to resist, to side or slide back into this old terminal equipmentality, and here and everywhere we *ourselves* are resonantly finding, and thus not at all coincidentally, *our own* new t*w*ombic topographies or equipment (equipment that, *we must never forget*, also includes this show) *also* forming pathmarks into temporary toward-whiches that never gather themselves up into the rooted promise or promotion of the for-the-sake-of-which. Such is the mutation within equipmentality that Zombeing "shrinks" itself into and helps to liquidically maintain.

The solid equip*mental* totality (*Zeugganzes*), organized along the horizon of a terminal for-the-sake-of-which, toward which Rick always previously marched in assured and easy steps, and that *we ourselves* are very familiar with marching within, would certainly hold much more interest for Heidegger, rather than the worldless zombies, as we said above. Heidegger would steadfastly *not* appreciate this time or temporeality of the zombie. He could never handle the zombie or the zombie's timekeeping.

In such clear and antagonistic opposition to the zombie then and its attendant de-ontologized Zombeing, Heidegger would seek to secure, and maintain, both a clear difference and a clear deference of the ontological (human) over and sovereignly above the ontic (the animal-machine). These zombies however, just as Heidegger saw for the ontic "animal" in that lecture series[26] given just two short years after the publication of *Being and Time*, represent for him an utter poverty of world and thus of a mere programmed or, indeed, "zombie" behavior in opposition to the serene gravity and that grave orientation of human comportment. The animal and the zombie do not mindfully gravitate-toward, and are thus both equidistantly and equally lacking in gravity, and so cannot walk upon the earth or be buried within it, cannot bear witness to it, cannot swear upon it. For, according to Heidegger, whilst the human is world forming (*Weltbilden*) and the stone is worldless (*Weltlos*), the animal is programmatically poor in world (*Weltarm*) and so cannot possibly grasp equipment or its structure (*als strukur*). This poverty of the animal (no matter of what species within its "kingdom") is continually worked over and wrestled with by Heidegger and always works to safely operate and maintain a cleared chasm and a protected and protracted distance from the world forming human, so handily maintained.

26 Published as Martin Heidegger, *Fundamental Concepts of Metaphysics: World, Finitude, Solitude*. Bloomington, IN: Indiana University Press, 1995.

An abyss of being then apparently opens up, as the human can, as it were, grasp the hammer *in-order-to* strike nails into a piece of wood and thence into further pieces of sculpted wood organized in-*order-to build* a house, *for-the-sake-of* securing a family, if that is where things end, and yet for the animal this self-same "object" (i.e. not a hammer, which only ever "hammers" in relation to *its* nails, *its* wood and *its* goal or *its* plan) would be something infinitely more immediate and "brute." This thing would not *thing* for the animal: the being of the object would fold out into no "da."

Now sadly for the sovereign empire of the human, the presumed zombie virus in *The Walking Dead* has performed a sort of act or outbreak of *de*volution and has taken the zombie back down below even the animal. As totemic of this lack of clear passage, the zombie is forever eating and never seems to process or digest any of the matter at hand. "Do zombies pass faeces?" may seem a frivolous question to ask, a question that might seem to land us in some theoretical cul-de-sac or backed-up shithouse, but these heedless heads, that no longer lead or head toward such a classical digestion of matter, are not the only zombies in the story. This zombie, as we know, is strangely forever insatiably eating, and always passing on through, and we discover at the end of season one of *The Walking Dead* that the zombie's "bite" is now irrevocably always already passed on to all the human characters who co-occupy its land, without them ever needing to actually ever be bitten by them. They are always-already contaminated and just waiting for that final push. Rick's journey is a journey into the hearth and the heartland of Zombeing, where everything is always indigestibly, or continually-digestibly, "passing-through" and hand-to-mouth, without ultimate equipmental purpose. We will call this excre-mentality to signal that strange new topographic bond between the orifices, now the head no longer has the upper hand, and is no longer in charge and eating well with due diligence and care. Such a "*decapitation*" and "*decapitalisation*" and active devolution is obviously *the* key marker of the show and in thus sweeping up the non-zombie characters into a stream, liquefied and thus themselves shorn of any for-the-sake-of-whiches, *we* ourselves are also touched and bitten by such transitional "transmission." Such contagious Zombeing now then stretches across three generations (zombies, characters *and* ourselves) in this story of downright devolution.

In terms of the opposing, and previously more common, story of uplifting upright evolution, we think easily of the opening sequence of Kubrick's *2001: A Space Odyssey* and of the great gravity of gift of equipment bestowed unto the animal in forming that sudden leap from the privated paw into the cradling hand of humanity. For only a hand can come to grasp equipment and thus main-tain itself within a steady equipmental state. Here, the impoverished brute being of the paws of the primate, through some bestowal by the Obelisk's "it gives" (*Es Gibt*), is transformed into something that opens up the epic story of a gap or, as Heidegger would say, an abyss between "the animal" and this emergent and specially aimed being of a Dasein, a Dasein given unto terminal aims with its eyes now fixed steadfastly upon horizons and with its hands consequently now able and available to, as it were, *see* that it gets to exactly where it is going.[27] After touching then, or being touched by, the Obelisk, it is a sudden "very big step" as this brute bone trans-forms, through this sudden bestowal or gift, into equipment and thus into equipmentality. In the film then cutting transparently, and brutally,[28] to the graphically matched boned-shaped space station orbiting the earth many many (many) years later, it is also, conterminously, a very small step from the sudden equipmentalized bone to this bone-shaped space station. *Time* is compressed, famously, here, just as also is the *space* between the hammering bone and the hammer-shaped ship. The animal is equally distant from both. We now return from this brief excursion into evolution to the less uplifting "devolving" odyssey toward Zombeing.

From then this evolutionary horizon, promised and classically promoted[29] by Kubrick's *2001* (for there is a second promised visitation, in this film, that takes man into the second giant leap onto the platform or plateau of the *Ubermensch* or Superhuman), we move here, within *The Walking Dead*, to a markedly devolved touch and a transmission of "Zombeing," and thus into a de-terminalized space where all links in the chain of equipment, which would once be joined together and

27 A similar story, more closely, or overtly, aligned under the shadow of Heidegger's story of equipment is told within Malick's *The Tree of Life*. Here, again, Dasein's entry upon a mise-en-scene of tool and for-the-time being is preceded in the film by a long introductory stretch of timeless time that, for aeons, contains no ontologically-charged being, only unknowing blind ontics. *The Tree of Life*, 2013 (film), Directed by Terence Malick, USA: Fox Searchlight Pictures. It is well known that before becoming a film director Malick was a Heidegger scholar and, in 1969, had provided a translation of *Vom Wesen Des Grundes*. In many ways *The Tree of Life* is a meditation upon both worlding of the world and upon equipmentality and the grounding that it gives (Es Gibt) and of finding, through equipment, one's place and time within-the-world.

28 Analogous, it must be said, to that equally transparent, and yet colossal, cut that transported Rick, without him, as a newborn, as yet knowing it, across the threshold into the tool being of Zombeing, hence the use of our comparison to Kubrick's more classical exposition of odyssey and progress and "*getting* there."

29 Itself presaging and promoting the moon landings, if withdrawing from their sizable locally stepped rhetoric of "man-sized" steps of this specific single step that would wish to diminish its proximity to the original bone>tool "step."

temporally organized toward some great projective horizon, have here been severed. Nothing, in *The Walking Dead* (and in many other equipmentally related spaces) any longer then, will join up to form a chain to cross a river or to stem a rogue criminal tide. Whilst objects will certainly still form into equipment, it will also, as we are observing, begin to reduce the horizonal or temporalized sense of termination or for-the-sake-of-which (Worum-willen). The zombies then will support us, and guide us, to help *imm*ediate us toward this character of the equip*mental*.

We have seen then that the zombies *in and of* "*themselves*" are not of a great deal of concern nor, also, the equipmental breakdowns that *The Walking Dead* and *Fear the Walking Dead* (and numerous other post-apocalyptic meditational spaces), would seem to imagine for themselves. We have been much more interested in Rick's t*w*ombic equipmental turn and of *The Walking Dead* itself which is helping us, *as* we "watch," to concurrently equip ourselves for our own domain of wandering, of ourselves then *as* having to learn to cope with a marked t*w*ombic equip*mental* turn into neoliberal mutable geometric spaces (for "places" would speak too much of flagged stability) that lack then in those forms of stabilized transcendental signifieds or for-the-sake-of-whiches, whatever any given unique empirical content. We *are* being bitten, within this withdrawal from the for-the-sake-of-which, by the equip*mental* working of a show that itself (as metonymic bonded agency of larger patterns) works us over as a key equip*mental* adjuster. For, as for Rick himself, who just after arising from his t*w*omb, is himself *forced* to quickly retune his instru*mentality* and move along, under threat of simply getting off a world that he cannot hope to stop "turning," and must, in turn, then "turn" himself toward these new modes of liquidic equip*mental* coping, in his changing landscape of nothing-but-ever-new emerging and submerging terminalless equipment. Numerous scenes in both *The Walking Dead* and *Fear the Walking Dead* play out this turning over, or *ex*huming, of a stabilized humanist being into mutable Zombeing.

In terms of *The Waking Dead's* sister series *Fear the Walking Dead*, a character, Victor Strand, shares what he sees as an emerging truth as he sees the old solid world, of which he was never much a part, burning down and being liquefied: "*The only way to survive in a mad world is to embrace the madness.*" *Fear the Walking Dead*, much more than *The Walking Dead*, *is* about exhibiting the live t*w*ombic transitioning that has been lost on Rick, asleep and yet to emerge from his own mutated gestating t*w*omb. Rick is thus placed further downstream than Strand, to hear and thus heed this call. In *Fear the Walking Dead* we see people in their periods of transitioning and having to *begin* breaking loose from the older stabilized equipmentalities, as those older stabilized institutions such as families and schools break apart and deform instead into wandering itinerant factions and where madness and errancy become the general livable survivable norm.

In *Fear the Walking Dead*, we see happening then what has already happened in *The Walking Dead*. As in many post-apocalyptic spaces we will see characters within both who were *already* living fluidly, before the outbreak, and who are thus already equipped and easily available to be marinated or soaked further within this emergent fluidity of equipment and so such characters, who previously lacked in use-value within the solid for-the-sake-of-which regimen now emerge as fully equipped and are thus resonantly able to mouth a line, in answer to that other character and say "*I feel like the rest of the world is catching up with me.*" Nick, unlike sheriff's deputy Rick Grimes, was previously a drug addict and will thus very easily, handily, come to don the dress of Zombeing and will cover himself with the blood of zombies and come to handle and main-tain himself in that spirit so as to endure and to sustain himself in that fluidity and to thus become attuned (*Stimmung*) to the wandering shape that the world has taken on and is pressing him to help service. Whilst Rick might be a fellow traveller, even a sort of non-native migrating Moses, on the journey into Zombeing, Nick is simply a readily equipped Zombeing native who is there to help guide those previously hardwired late starters, like his own mother Madison, formerly a school guidance counselor, in-order-to play catch-up.

In journeying with them both, as they both "literally" coat themselves in the blood of the zombie, there is an attunement that we ourselves are undertaking and so where they wander, we wander too and Heidegger's highly tuned and tightly strung story of equipmentality, organized around the temporal zone or punctum of the for-the-sake-of-which here shrinks into the shorter fluid toward-which of Zombeing. Such *im*mediatory shows are simply the congealing corpuscular elements of that equipmental coping that forms itself into something much more performative than mere projections or constative representations.

As such, we are never just "sat here," simply observing fictional zombies and survivors wandering by, but are *doing* and thus performing within our own attuned form of *de*capitated acephalic Zombeing. This is clearly not, any longer, the equipmentality of Heidegger's very well Daseined hand. Zombeing's time has come, and it is a time whose existence is continually without measure. This is the time of Zombeing.

Bibliography

Jacques Derrida, *Limited Inc*. Evanston: Northwestern University Press, 1988.

Jacques Derrida, *Psyche, Inventions of the Other*, volume II. Stanford: Stanford University Press, 2008.

Jakob von Uexküll, *A Foray into the Worlds of Animals and Humans*. Minneapolis, MN: University of Minnesota Press, 2010.

Jeff Malpas, *Heidegger's Topology: Being, Place, World*. Cambridge, MA: MIT Press. 2006.

John L. Austin, *How To Do Things With Words*. Oxford: Oxford University Press, 1975.

Martin Heidegger, "The Origin of the Work of Art," in: *Poetry, Language, Thought*. Edited and translated by Albert Hofstadter, New York: Harper Collins, 1974.

Martin Heidegger, *Fundamental Concepts of Metaphysics: World, Finitude, Solitude* Bloomington, IN: Indiana University Press, 1995.

Martin Heidegger, "Letter on Humanism," in: *Pathmarks*. Edited and translated by William McNeil, Cambridge: Cambridge University Press, 1998.

Martin Heidegger, *Being and Time*. Oxford: Blackwell Publishing, 2005.

Tony Richards, "Of Excrementality: Ec*a*nomie, Signification and Autoimmunity," *Canadian Journal of Communication*, Vol. 38 (2013), pp. 477–496.

William Blattner, *Heidegger's Temporal Idealism*. Cambridge: Cambridge University Press, 1999.

Sascha Rashof

Heidegger's Topology in the World/s of Ubiquitous Computing

Even though Martin Heidegger has, directly or indirectly, influenced many media theorists, few have substantially engaged with his work. Two exceptions are Bernard Stiegler and Peter Sloterdijk. Stiegler's indebtedness to Heidegger is evident in nearly all of his writings, however first and foremost in his *Technics and Time* [*La Technique et le Temps*] series,[1] where he developed the groundwork for a technical ontology, primarily through the question of time. Also Sloterdijk uses Heidegger pervasively in almost all of his writings, most importantly in his main media-theoretical work *Spheres* [*Sphären*],[2] where he conceives Heidegger's thought, and further develops it, through a spatial framework. However, apart from the short "Excursus" on "Heidegger's Lesson of Existential Place",[3] where he "unconceals" the notion of Being-in as foundation of (human) *Dasein's* spatiality,[4] explicated in the first division of *Sein und Zeit* [*Being and Time*], Sloterdijk largely implicitly reads Heidegger in his "spherology". In contrast to Stiegler and partly with Sloterdijk, this essay aims to reveal Heidegger's ontology of medial place [*topos*] across (a selection of) his works. As Sloterdijk writes himself, *Spheres* has to be read as "Being and Space".[5] Thus, although he recognizes the importance of place in Heidegger's work, he does not really distinguish between space and place, and ultimately subordinates the latter under the former. The intent of the following pages is not to conceive place merely as a subcategory of the more universalising conceptions of space and time, i.e. as simply a point *in*, portion or modification *of* these, like most modern philosophy in "the West" has

1   Bernard Stiegler, *Technics and Time 1: The Fault of Epimetheus*, trans. Richard Beardsworth and George Collins (Stanford: Stanford University Press, 1998); Bernard Stiegler, *Technics and Time 2: Disorientation*, trans. Stephen Barker (Stanford: Stanford University Press, 2008); Bernard Stiegler, *Technics and Time 3: Cinematic Time and the Question of Malaise*, trans. Stephen Barker (Stanford: Stanford University Press, 2011).
2   Peter Sloterdijk, *Sphären I: Blasen* (Frankfurt am Main: Suhrkamp, 1998); Peter Sloterdijk, *Sphären II: Globen* (Frankfurt am Main: Suhrkamp, 1999); Peter Sloterdijk, *Sphären III: Schäume* (Frankfurt am Main: Suhrkamp, 2004).
3   Sloterdijk, *Sphären I*, pp. 336–345.
4   Against the primarily temporal readings of Heidegger's work (in philosophical circles).
5   Sloterdijk, *Sphären I*, p. 345; cf. Sloterdijk, *Sphären II*, p. 59.

done.[6] Place will not be understood as deriving *from* time *or* space, but indeed *as* time *and* space – place as the *in-between* of time and space: a singular – not particular – space-time.

The importance of place is significant in an epoch where computation has become pervasive to the point of ubiquity.[7] It seems apparent to understand "the world" as techno-logical monosphere, in Heidegger's words as "*Ge-Stell*", which "enframes" or "sets" the beings in it according to instrumental rationales. Its only limit is itself, or so it appears to be. In order to develop a *differentiated* theory of the globalizing-globalized "world" at the beginning of the 21st century however, a change of its formation [*Bildung*] needs to *take place*. "The world" should not be conceived as universal, but as a singular place, produced through pluralities of singular places, where immanence and transcendence converge in multi-dimensional forms.

Even though notions of place appeared in Heidegger's writings and lectures from the very beginning, only little attention has been paid to them in philosophical circles, including by (especially the early) Heidegger himself.[8] As a critique of the "Western" tradition of metaphysics, *Sein und Zeit* attempted to develop a *processual* notion of *Being* – mainly via (human) *Dasein*, which is most "proximate" to it – in order to de-struct the "present-at-hand" [*vor-handene*] understandings of *beings*, especially in their Aristotelian, Cartesian and Kantian versions. Platiality (and even spatiality) were thus "secondary" to temporality.

---

6   See philosopher of place Edward S. Casey on this point: *Getting Back into Place – Toward a New Understanding of the Place-World* (Bloomington: Indiana University Press, 2009); *The Fate of Place – A Philosophical History* (Berkeley, London and Los Angeles: University of California Press, 1997).

7   I am aware of the (sometimes difficult-to-delineate) differences between ubiquitous- and pervasive- as well as other forms of contemporary computing. For the sake of the argument however, ubiquitous computing shall serve as an umbrella term and I am thus arguing that most people *already* live in ubiquitous computing environments, some to higher degrees than others.

8   Exceptions include Casey's "Proceeding to Place by Indirection – Heidegger", in: *The Fate of Place* (pp. 243–284); Jeff Malpas' *Heidegger's Topology: Being, Place, World* (Cambridge, MA and London: MIT Press, 2006), *Heidegger and the Thinking of Place – Explorations in the Topology of Being* (Cambridge, MA and London: MIT Press, 2012) and Miguel de Beistegui's "The Place of Architecture", in: *Thinking with Heidegger – Displacements* (Bloomington: Indiana University Press, 2003, pp. 139–168). These explorations however largely take place outside of media-theoretical contexts and are moreover unclear at times about the difference between space/s and place/s.

In his later works after "the turn", Heidegger then put more emphasis on the *places* of Being, in order to close the phenomenological circle. As he wrote in 1949, "This turn is not a change of standpoint from 'Being and Time', rather in it, the attempted thinking firstly arrives at the place [*Ortschaft*] of the dimension out of which 'Being and Time' is experienced and indeed experienced out of the fundamental experience of the oblivion of Being".[9] Later, in the *Seminar in Le Thor 1969*, Heidegger revealed the three stages of his thinking throughout life: Meaning – Truth – Place (*topos*).[10]

Since Heidegger's conceptions of and around (medial) place, as well as their importance, have been inconsistent across his works and since this *topical* reading tries to think through and with as much as beyond and against Heidegger,[11] this chapter will "proceed to place by indirection", in Casey's words. The following pages will not so much attempt to *determine* notions of place in Heidegger, but take a more constructive approach by explicating his most important conceptions (within the limitations of this book chapter) of the *places around* it. These conceptions include: "Being-in(-the-World)", "Being-with", "Thingliness",[12] "*Ge-Stell*" and "Dwelling". After close readings of selected texts (chosen according to how they can develop the above notions throughout the following pages), this essay will conclude by pointing out the limitations of Heidegger's topo-logical conceptions in the contemporary world/s of ubiquitous computing, via Sloterdijk and Stiegler.[13]

1 Being-in(-the-world)

In *Sein und Zeit* (*SZ*) from 1927, Heidegger started his explication of platiality (however largely described as spatiality, or "roomliness" [*Räumlichkeit*]) through

---

9   Martin Heidegger, *Über den Humanismus* (Frankfurt am Main: Vittorio Klostermann, 1968), p. 17 [author's translation].

10 Martin Heidegger, "Seminar in Le Thor 1969," in: "Seminare," in: *Gesamtausgabe* (Frankfurt am Main: Vittorio Klostermann, 1986), p. 344 [author's translation].

11 The topicality of this reading also includes my own topical translations of Heidegger's work.

12 This section includes a number of Heidegger's writings and lectures, which have been worked through in a historically linear way in order to show the evolution of his thought.

13 I do not deem it useful here to go into a discussion about potential links between Heidegger's notions of place and his temporary involvement with Nazism – Jeff Malpas gives an overview of these debates in the "Introduction" to *Heidegger's Topology* (pp. 17–27).

the notion of being-in-the-world, the kind [*Art*] of Being which is most proximate to (human) *Da-sein* [being-there]. Being-in-the-world always has to be
seen as a structurally unitary phenomenon and is grounded in, or oriented
through, the primary dimensionality of Being-in:

> What is meant by *Being-in*? We define this expression firstly as Being-in "in the world"
> and are inclined to understand this Being-in as "Being in …". This terminus designates
> the kind of Being of being which is "in" something else, such as water "in" the glass,
> the dress "in" the wardrobe. By the "in" we mean the relation of Being of two beings
> extended "in" space towards each other in relation to their place [*Ort*] in this space.
> Water and glass, dress and wardrobe are both in the same way "in" space and "at" a place.
> This relation of Being can be expanded, e.g.: The bench in the lecture theatre, the lecture
> theatre in the university, the university in the city and so on, up to: The bench in "space"
> [*Weltraum*]. These beings whose being-"in"-each-other can be defined in this way all
> have the same kind of Being of being-present-at-hand as things which are there "within"
> the world. […] Being-in on the other hand means a condition of Being [*Seinsverfassung*]
> of *Dasein* and is an *existentiale*. With this, one cannot then think of the being-present-
> at-hand of a corporeal thing (human corps) "in" a being that is present-at-hand. […]
> "In" is derived from innan-, dwelling [*wohnen*], habitare, to be located [*sich aufhalten*];
> "at" means, I am accustomed to [*gewohnt*], familiar with, I care for something; it has
> the meaning of colo in the sense of habito and diligo. […] Being as infinitive of "I am",
> i.e. understood as *existentiale*, means dwelling by [*wohnen bei*]… being familiar with…
> *Being-in is thus the formal existential expression for the Being of Dasein, which has the
> essential condition of being-in-the-world.*[14]

Being-in as condition [*Verfassung*] of *Dasein* thus must not be understood as a
relation between beings in a place *contained* in space, but as existential openness.
Hence, *Da-sein*, which locates itself [*sich auf-hält*][15] there [*da*], has a relation *with*
the world *in* which it dwells.

Dasein is in the world through different ways of *Besorgen* [con-cerning],[16]
by having to do with something, producing something, using something etc.
The most proximate world for *Dasein* is its *Um-welt* [environment][17] *in* which
intra-worldly beings encounter. The *process* through which *Dasein deals* with
intra-environmental beings Heidegger called the *Um-gang*.[18] Via the *besorgende
Umgang, Dasein handles* and *uses* beings that are ready-to-hand [*zu-handen*] and
not yet "theoretically looks" at ob-jects [*Gegen-stände*][19] that are present-at-hand.

---

14 Martin Heidegger, *Sein und Zeit* (Tübingen: Max Niemeyer, 2006), pp. 53/4.
15 Literally: "holds itself open".
16 Also meaning "obtaining" or "getting"; "*Sorge*" can be translated with "care" or "anxiety".
17 Literally translated as "around-world" or "surrounding world".
18 Difficult to translate – maybe "going-around", "dealing" or "intercourse".
19 Literally: "against-standings".

In this way, *Dasein* under-stands [*ver-steht*] the world *constantly*. Only through the *besorgende Umgang* in the world, which is grounded in Being-in, ob-jects *can* act-ually be grasped *in the first place*. *Dasein* is thus not a "subject" separate from the world, i.e. simply reflecting on it from the outside, but is ek-sistentially *in* and engaged *with* it.

Encountering intra-worldly beings is only possible due to the primary dimensionality of Being-in for the sake of where [*wo-rumwillen*][20] *Dasein* is. In its dimensionality, *Da-sein* is never firstly "here", but "yonder" – through the "yonder" it comes back to its "here" and hence situates itself [*befindet sich*][21] in the openness of the "there" [*da*]: "In Dasein, there lies an essential tendency toward proximity"[22] – i.e. by being *by* [*bei*], in the sense of being "close to", beings in the world, *Dasein* can *be*. In this proximity to beings, *Dasein* is platial through de-distance [*Ent-fernung*] and directionality [*Aus-richtung*], to be understood in an active and transitive sense, i.e. as existential categories. *Dasein* is ek-sistentially de-distancing and lets other beings encounter into proximity through ways of *Besorgen* [concerning]. De-distancing is proximately circum-spective [*um-sichtige*] approximation, i.e. bringing close in the sense of obtaining, pre-positioning, having to hand. Through de-distance and directionality, the "solid" directions of left and right spring forth, which *Dasein* always takes *with* it in the sense that it is with*in* them, and thus orients itself in the world.[23]

2 Being-with

Although Heidegger, overall, did not say very much about being-with-others (i.e. other humans) across his works, in *Sein und Zeit* he explicated *Dasein* as co-existential with being-with [*Mitsein*]. In its everydayness, *Dasein* is proximately and mostly "not itself" by "holding" oneself in the one [*Man*] of "the others" – the averageness into which *Dasein* is thrown. This inauthenticity

20 Generally translated as "for the sake of which".
21 Also in the sense of *Dasein*'s affectivity and "state of mind".
22 Heidegger, *Sein und Zeit*, p. 105.
23 In the second division of *SZ*, Heidegger's explication of *Dasein*'s (being-in-the-) world becomes more complex due to historialisation, however now being essentially grounded in (more horizontal) temporality and not in (more dimensional) Being-in anymore, which grounds all phenomena in the first division – or rather: the latter becomes subordinated to the former. It is hence difficult to do a close reading of the second division of *SZ* through the conception of place, especially within the constraints of this book chapter.

[*Un-eigen-tlichkeit*],²⁴ or "vulgarity", Heidegger refers to as a "falling" [*Ver-fallen*]²⁵ – a kind [*Art*] of Being through which *Dasein* flees itself into untruth, while however still staying in the *realm* of truth. The being-with-each-other in the one is a being-with-*any*-other. "These others are thereby not *specific* others. On the contrary, any other can substitute them. Decisive is only the inconspic-uous sovereignty of the others, which has already unawares taken over Dasein as being-with. One belongs to the others oneself and solidifies their power".²⁶ Being "one"-self is really being "no one" [*Niemand*] – the neutrum. This does not mean that being "no one" is being nothing. The *Niemand* is simply a modality of *Dasein* – a difference that is qualitative or structural, rather than quantitative – i.e. it is positive in any way. Falling *Dasein* is simply in the *way* of a "groundless floating" in which it is everywhere and nowhere – it is without location [*auf-ent-halts-los*]²⁷: "one" does not dwell; it is "unhomely" [*unheimlich*].²⁸ By proximately and mostly being "scattered" in the publicness [*Öffen-tlichkeit*]²⁹ of the one – for example through "chitchat" or "hack writing", i.e. the kinds [*Arten*] of Being of being-with-each-other – *Dasein* has a tendency toward levelling its possibilities-for-Being. The sovereignty of public "laid-out-ness" [*Aus-gelegtheit*]³⁰ decides the possibilities of *Dasein*'s attunement [*Gestimmtheit*] – i.e. "one" fore-sketches [*vor-zeichnet*] *Dasein*'s situatedness [*Befindlichkeit*] in the world; "one" determines what and how "one" perceives, how "one" under-stands. *Dasein* which "holds" itself in the one is cut off from authentic [*eigen-tliche*] relations of Being toward the world. It is in constant temptation to fall into business [*Betrieb*] – out of itself into itself; into the groundlessness of inauthentic everydayness; into alienation. The one constantly tears away *Dasein* from designing [*ent-werfen*]³¹ authentic possibilities, i.e. it prevents *Dasein* from being "at home" and thus from devel-oping its own place.

---

24 "Non-singularity" is also possible; "-*eigen*-" means "(one's) own".
25 Also in the sense of 'falling *for*' as well as 'decay'.
26 Heidegger, *Sein und Zeit*, p. 126.
27 "-*haltslos*" meaning "without hold".
28 I.e. "uncanny".
29 Includes "*offen*", i.e. "open".
30 I.e. "interpretation".
31 *Ent-werfen* is literally translated as "de-throwing", but can also mean "modelling", "experimenting", "projecting", "planning", "drafting", "outlining", "laying out", "con-ceiving" and "proposing".

3 Thingliness

By aiming to de-struct the metaphysical tradition of (present-at-hand) ob-jects and things, Heidegger broadly distinguished between three kinds [*Arten*] of being throughout his works, which are characterized by different degrees of ek-splicitness [*Aus-drücklichlichkeit*] and become ever more platial: equipment [*Zeug*],[32] work [*Werk*] and thing [*Ding*]. In *Sein und Zeit*, Heidegger focused on ready-to-hand equipment and work. Through the *besorgende Umgang* ["concerning dealings"], sewing-, working-, transportation-, measuring equipment etc. (such as needles, hammers, cars and thermometers, for instance, today also mobile phones and laptops) can be encountered in the world. However, equipment is never just equipment "in itself", but is always part of an equipment unity. Equipment is always *in* the world, lying *in* a region [*Gegend*], which is *in* the circum-ference [*Um-kreis*] of so and so. Equipment is always "some'thing' in-order-to …". In this structure of "in-order-to" [*Um-zu*], there is a reference [*Ver-weisung*][33] of some"thing" to some"thing". Equipment "is" always out of the belonging to other equipment. The different *ways* of the *Um-zu*, such as serviceability, conduciveness, usefulness and handleability, create the equipment unity. By referring to some"thing", *as* a relating [*Be-ziehen*],[34] equipment is discovered [*ent-deckt*], in the sense that it has a *Bewenden* ["involving"][35] *with* it and *by* it. The where-by [*Wo-bei*] equipment has its *Bewenden* is the toward-where [*Wo-zu*][36] of serviceability, the where-for [*Wo-für*] of usefulness. The involvement [*Bewandtnis*] unity, i.e. the character of Being of the ready-to-hand, is always *earlier* than an item of equipment and is grounded in a primary toward-where that is the for-the-sake-of-where [*Wo-rum-willen*] of *Dasein*, i.e. Being-in. The *Je-schon-haben-bewenden-lassen* ["always-being-involved-already"] is the *a priori* perfect tense that characterizes *Dasein* – it is the *way* through which *Dasein* continuously under-stands Being, which is its possibility.

Through the *besorgende Umgang* with equipment in the world, *Dasein* does not grasp the "thing" yet, neither thematically/theoretically nor in its equipment structure since equipment lacks self-sufficiency. The less equipment is simply

---

32 "Stuff" or "tools" are also possible.
33 Can also be translated with "assignment"; broadly speaking even as "relevance" or "meaning".
34 "-*ziehen*" meaning "(to) drag" or "(to) pull".
35 Impossible to translate – can be understood in the sense of "being interested in", "caring about" or "referring to".
36 Generally translated as "towards-which".

being looked at, but act-ually and immediately used and handled, the more original the relation is to it and the more revealing is *its* truth, i.e. the equipment's specific handleability. The Being of equipment is readiness-to-hand [*Zuhandenheit*],
i.e. the ontologico-categorical determination of being as it is "in itself". The ready-
to-hand *essentially* withdraws itself in order to "be" ready-to-hand. However,
readiness-to-hand (the Being of being *proximately* encountered) always relates
to the presence-at-hand [*Vorhandenheit*] (the Being *of* being). Only *through* the
ready-to-hand, the present-at-hand can be determined: "With the discovered
'environment', 'nature' discovered in this way is encountered."[37]

Equipment as the everyday ready-to-hand is the being which *Dasein*
encounters proximately – it is "close by". This proximity is not determined by
measured distances, but comes about through the circum-spection [*Um-sicht*] of
Besorgen in the world, which "fixates" the item of equipment directionally. Every
item of equipment either has its place [*Platz*] or it "lies around", which is different
to having a position [*Stelle*] somewhere in three-dimensional space. The place of
an item of equipment is always determined as "the place of this equipment to…"
out of a unity (one could say a system or network) of places of equipment that
are directed toward each other. The place is not to be understood as a "where"
of a present-at-hand of a thing, but as a specific yonder [*Dort*] and there [*Da*] of
the belonging-to of an item of equipment. The possibility of a placeable item of
equipment that belongs somewhere is the (slightly more encompassing) region,
the where-to [*Wo-hin*], which it is oriented toward. Regions are not firstly
formed through things that are present-at-hand, but are always *already* ready-
to-hand *in* places. The places themselves either get assigned to the ready-to-
hand in the circumspection of *Besorgen* [concerning] or they are found as such.
Each "where" is thereby dis-covered by *Dasein* through the everyday (technical)
Umgang [dealings] in the world and circum-spectly laid out, not solidly installed
"in space".

Ready-to-hand equipment is generally "inconspicuously familiar" and only
becomes visible through deficient modes of *Besorgen*. Equipment can be unusable – for example it can be broken or unsuitable for a particular use. This is
dis-covered through circumspection. The equipment thus stands out [*fällt auf*].
This standing-out makes the equipment somehow un-ready-to-hand, i.e. more
present-at-hand. However, the equipment as ready-to-hand that in its being
unusable becomes more present-at-hand immediately withdraws itself again
into readiness-to-hand. If the equipment needed is lacking, i.e. simply is not at

---

37 Heidegger, *Sein und Zeit*, p. 70.

hand, it is in the mode of ob-trusiveness [*Auf-dringlichkeit*]. The more ek-sigently the lacking equipment is needed, the more it encounters in its un-readiness-to-hand, so that it seems to lose its readiness-to-hand and thus shows itself as presence-at-hand. The equipment can also show itself in the mode of ob-stinacy [*Auf-sässigkeit*], if it just "lies in the way", i.e. when it is not lacking and is not unusable. These three modes – *Auffälligkeit*, *Aufdringlichkeit* and *Aufsässigkeit* – all have the function of showing the *character* of the present-at-hand of the ready-to-hand. By disturbing the reference within the equipment unity (i.e. the *Um-zu* [in-order-to] is not referring to a *Da-zu* [toward-there]), the reference merely becomes ek-splicit – not yet as ontological structure, but ontically. In this way, the world announces itself. However, for the ready-to-hand to *not* stand out and therefore "be" ready-to-hand "in itself", the world needs to *not* announce itself, which is the (positive) condition for readiness-to-hand.

The everyday *Umgang* proximately locates itself not really by equipment though, but by the "work" [*Werk*] that is be-ing set forth [*her-ge-stellt*],[38] i.e. pro-duced, through equipment – it is the toward-where of equipment, the equipment's usefulness. The work, such as a shoe be-ing produced (to be worn), is also of the kind of Being [*Seinsart*] of equipment and carries the reference unity *in* which equipment encounters. The work, which situates itself through its working [*sich in Arbeit befindene*], is essentially usefulness and at the same time lets the toward-where of *its* usefulness encounter with it as well. The work to be set forth is not just useful for ..., but is itself a using *of* some"thing" for some"thing" and thus refers to a "where-out" [*Wo-r-aus*], i.e. "materials" used. The work can hence not at all be understood as a present-at-hand. The work furthermore refers to the product user who *is* already part of the labour process, for example in the sense of later wearing a shoe or a watch that is *specifically* made for her or him (even in mass production). Therefore *with* the work, not just the ready-to-hand encounters, but also the user and thus "the world".

In his lecture *The Origin of the Work of Art* (*Der Ursprung des Kunstwerkes*) from 1935, Heidegger continued his critique of thingliness by explicating the work as specifically a work of art, and thus *places* his ontology a bit more. The work is here however quite different from the work of *Sein und Zeit* – it is not just a ready-to-hand *process* anymore, but some"thing" more self-sufficient, i.e. singular. He also introduces the notion of *techné* as a revealing [*ent-bergen*] (of truth) in this lecture, which will become even more important later in his

---

38 Note the importance of "*stellen*", i.e. "(to) set", and its relation to "*Stelle*", i.e. "position"/"location"/"site".

thinking on (the essence of) technology. Since the work is a thing in some ways, Heidegger started his explication of the work of art by criticising three habitual [ge-wöhnliche] notions of thingliness in "Western" thought: 1) the thing as substance and bearer of certain properties, 2) the thing as mental unity perceptible through sensations and 3) the thing as formed matter. Since the work of art is not a "mere thing" (such as a stone or a piece of wood), but is brought forth through the human hand, it has more of a relation to a "thing" of use. When considering a "thing" of use that is made by the human, the former two conceptions are not very suitable, Heidegger argued, and one also cannot talk about form being the effect of a distribution of matter. On the contrary, form always *determines* the arrangement of matter, and even influences the kind [*Artung*] and choice of it. Form and matter are thus interwoven. This interweaving is however *before-hand* determined by the serviceability toward where the "thing" is to be serviceable. Such serviceability is neither assigned nor added to the "thing" later on nor is it the end or effect of it. Serviceability is rather the fundamental tendency [*Grund-zug*] through which the "thing" of use *is*. I.e. both the formative act and the choice of material are grounded in serviceability and as such also the form/matter structure. The useful "thing" is always the product [*Er-zeug-nis*] of a production [*An-fertigung*][39] – it is equipment [*Zeug*] – hence form and matter are "at home" in the essence of equipment, which Heidegger here did not call readiness-to-hand anymore, as the in-order-to [*Um-zu*] referential structure in *SZ*, but reliability [*Ver-läß-lichkeit*].[40]

The work is however also not mere equipment since it is more self-sufficient and thus has more of a relation with the "self-growthness" [*Eigen-wüchsigen*] of the thing in certain ways. In order to better work out the thingly character of the work of art, Heidegger thought the thingly character of the work out of the workly character of the work (not vice versa) since the work is not *just* a thing. He thus considered a work of art in its essential "space" [*Wesensraum*] (better: essential place), rather than seeing it as an ob-ject of the art business: a van Gogh painting which re-presents [*dar-stellt*][41] some equipment, i.e. a pair of peasant shoes. Although we can only look at the peasant shoes and not actually wear them, the picture nevertheless speaks to us by *immediately* revealing the truth about the shoes as equipment, i.e. their reliability; it tells us what they *are*. In the work of art, truth [*alétheia*] has set itself into the work, in the sense of

---

39 Includes "-fertig-" meaning "finished"; "anfertigen" thus could loosely be translated as "towards-finishing".
40 Includes "-lassen", meaning "(to) let".
41 Literally: "sets there".

bringing itself to a stand. For Heidegger, what is decisive in the work of art is thus not beauty or aesthetics, but the revealing of truth – the opening-up, i.e. clearing [*Lichten*], of the Being of being.

Heidegger furthermore considered a built work – a Greek temple – in order to better grasp the working [*Wirken*][42] of truth in the work of art. The temple encloses the figure [*Gestalt*] of God and lets it, in this concealing, stand forth into the holy domain [*Bezirk*], i.e. through the temple, God essences [*west*] in the temple. The temple-work gathers and joins the unity of relations (or systems/networks) around itself, which is the "world" of the historical people. The temple at the same time rests on solid rock, with-stands the storm and shines through the sun, all of which it brings into appearance *in the first place*. This coming-forth and arising in itself and in the whole is what the Greeks used to call *physis*, which Heidegger terms "earth" – not to be understood as a present-at-hand however: "The earth is that toward where the arising brings back all that arises and indeed as such. In the arising, earth essences as the concealing [*das Bergende*]."[43] Earth is the ground – the essentially self-closing. Upon the earth and in it, the historical human being grounds its dwelling in the world. The earthly character is a thingly character. Earth can only come forth through a "world" which opens up. The world "worlds" and *is more* [*ist seiender*] than the graspable and conceivable [*Ver-nehm-bare*].[44] The temple-work sets up a world and at the same time sets it back unto the earth so that the world is held in its essential remains. In contrast to equipment, which takes matter into its service that hence disappears in serviceability, the work lets matter come forth and into the openness of the world of the work. By setting up a world, the work sets forth the earth into which it sets back. Setting-up and setting-forth are two essential tendencies [*Wesens-züge*] in the work-being of the work, however belong together as a unity through which the work stands in itself, in the sense of a resting. The relation between world and earth Heidegger called "strife" [*Streit*],[45] or "room to play" [*Spielraum*],[46] in which each tries to carry the other beyond itself. This strife as room to play is the *happening* of truth (i.e. Being-in in *SZ*) that the work carries

---

42 Related to "*Wirklichkeit*", i.e. "reality"; "*wirken*" also means "(to) be effective" or "(to) take effect".

43 Martin Heidegger, *Der Ursprung des Kunstwerkes* (Stuttgart: Philipp Reclam jun., 1970), p. 42.

44 Includes "*nehmen*", i.e. "(to) take" or "(to) grasp".

45 Can also be translated with "dispute", "argument", "conflict", "fight" or "counterplay".

46 Literally "playroom" or "playspace". "Leeway", "space to move" or "scope" are also possible translations.

and preserves [be-wahrt].[47] It is the motion that is gathered and thus rests in the work. Truth, i.e. un-concealedness, which *happens* in the work, is thus ambiguous as the against-each-other of the strife. It is hence "un-truth" in its essence. By standing *in* being, truth, as the open middle, appears in the world, however always in an*other* way than it "is" since it *is more* than being.

After having thought through the *workly* character of the work, Heidegger could thus further explicate the *thingly* and *equipmental* characters of the work, which is self-sufficient as well as created through the human artist. The creating of a work is a bringing-forth, which is also how equipment is produced. As Heidegger writes, the Greeks had the same name for craft and art – *techné* – which is a *way* of knowledge [*Wissen*]. The essence of knowledge is *alétheia*, i.e. revealing, thus *techné* is the bringing-forth of the concealed into the unconcealed, and not the (artist's) activity of a making. The becoming-work of the work is an opening up, i.e. (the happening of) truth. Truth happens by installing itself [*sich einrichten*][48] through the room to play. One way in which truth installs itself is setting-itself-into-the-work (other ways are, for Heidegger, the state-founding act or the essential questioning of the thinker). By installing the truth (through the truth), the work includes the essential tendencies of the strife of world and earth, which can then be decided on by the historical people at strife. Truth *as* strife/room to play that is solidly set into the work is the figure, which is the being-created [*Geschaffensein*] of the work. Heidegger here also called truth the "creating Design" [*der schaffende Ent-wurf*],[49] which brings the strife into the open [*das Offene*] through the work. In contrast to the creating of a work, the pro-duction of equipment is never immediately the happening of truth. The being-finished of equipment merely means that it is let to "arise" beyond itself in serviceability. The being-finished of equipment and the being-created of the work are both brought forth, however the being-created of the work is authentically [*eigens*] created *into* the created, so that it pro-trudes from it. The work, in which its being-created happens, is the non-habitual through which the work works [*wirkt*]. In its uniqueness, it lets truth originate [*ent-springen*],[50] which is a thrust into history, a beginning – which transforms the habitual relations of the historical people toward the world and earth. Truth setting-itself-into-the-work is Poetry for Heidegger – the clearing Design. In

---

47 Related to "*Wahrheit*", i.e. "truth".
48 "(To) furnish" also possible. "*Einrichten*" is furthermore related to "*Richtung*", i.e. "direction".
49 See above.
50 "*Springen*" meaning "(to) spring" or "(to) jump".

this way, truth in the work is thrown toward the historical people and opens up that into which *Dasein* is always already thrown.

In his later lecture *Das Ding* from 1949, Heidegger focused on the even more platial thing, while formulating a theory of (the essence of) proximity that goes beyond present-at-hand ob-jectivity: "Proximate to us are what we care to call things. [...] The human has so far given no more thought to the thing as a thing than to proximity".[51] Heidegger argued that contemporary uniform and "unhomely" non-distance [*Abstandlose*] – he also called it the "de-setting" [*Ent-setzende*][52] – does not bring proximity, "for proximity does not consist in the small measure of distance. What stands in the smallest distance to us route-wise, through the image in film, through the sound in radio, can remain remote to us. What is unsurveyably far route-wise can be proximate to us. Short distance is not yet proximity. Great distance is not yet remoteness".[53]

In order to think the essence of proximity, Heidegger gave the example of a jug, i.e. a thing that is proximate to us. A jug is a vessel, which stands in itself – it is "self-standing", i.e. independent. A thing is different to an ob-ject, however can become an object if we set it *before* ourselves. Object and thing cannot be determined in the same way, as the jug remains a vessel, whether we set it before ourselves or not. However, the vessel's standing-in-itself alone does not determine it as a thing. The jug has come to a stand due to a process of setting-forth. Thereby, the potter uses earth, which is specifically chosen and prepared for the jug through a "toward-sight" [*Hin-sicht*] to the thing's standing-in-itself. Earth is however through which the jug *consists* [*be-steht*], thus standing-in-itself is not just that which setting-forth *aims* at, but that which *persists* [*be-steht*] throughout. The jug is not a vessel because it was set forth, but it had to be set forth because it *is* this vessel which stands in itself. The authenticity [*das Eigene*] of the essence of the jug as thing is thus also not produced by setting-forth. Released from its production, the self-supporting jug gathers, or appropriates in the sense of happening [*er-eignet*], "earth", "sky", "mortals" and "divinities",[54] in its *own* way into a onefold. The thing gathers the while [*Weile*] of the fourfold into *this* thing

51 Martin Heidegger, "Das Ding", in: *Vorträge und Aufsätze* (Pfullingen: Günther Neske, 1954), p. 164.

52 From "*Entsetzen*", i.e. "horror".

53 Heidegger, "Das Ding", in: *Vorträge und Aufsätze*, p. 163.

54 It is difficult to know what Heidegger exactly meant by this "fourfold" [*Geviert*], a concept he derived from the poet Friedrich Hölderlin. It can be read as a de-struction of "the world" – i.e. the "one" that in his later work becomes more differentiated into the "four" through which the thing places itself.

that "whiles". The fourfold gathered by the thing is a mirror-play, in which each of the four is set free toward the others, but also essentially bound with them. This mirror-play that is *happening* in the thing Heidegger here also calls "the world". For mortals, which are part of this mirror-play of the world, the thing is a contested matter, which is why the thing [*res*] publicly [*öffen-tlich*] approaches [*an-geht*] them. The thing that "things" in this way thus approximates the world.

The unity of the fourfold Heidegger here calls the "fouring", which essences as the mirror-play and is the "worlding" of world (i.e. what he used to call Being-in in *SZ*). The fouring Heidegger also calls the ring [*Gering*], which "rings" by playing *as* mirroring. This ring is the authentic [*eigentliche*] dimension of the mirror-play of the world – it is approximating proximity, i.e. the essence of proximity. In order to think the thing as thing among the sovereignty of non-distance, Heidegger wants us to take a step *back*, from the thought that simply *sets before* to the thought that thinks *toward* [*an-denkt*].[55]

4 Ge-Stell[56]

In *Die Frage nach der Technik* [*The Question Concerning Technology*] (1954), first given as the lecture *Das Ge-Stell* (1949), Heidegger further explicated *techné* as a revealing, as he had already done to some extent in *UdK*. Technicity is here not just *in* the world anymore, through *Dasein*'s use of ready-to-hand beings in *SZ*, but becomes "world" itself. In order to work out the essence of (modern) technology, Heidegger aimed to go beyond the anthropological and instrumental conceptions that had used to explain technology as a human activity and a means for an end since the Greeks. Since the "correct" (ontic) is not yet the "true" (ontological), he revisited Aristotle's four causes: *causa materialis, causa formalis, causa finalis* and *causa efficiens*. Although these four causes are different from each other, they nevertheless work together. Thus, Heidegger asked: Why are there *four* causes? What *unites* them *a priori* and *how* can they work together? Traditionally, the *causa efficiens* – the human agent, i.e. the craftsperson or the artist – had been conceived as the most important since s/he is that which effects, that which brings something about. S/he is the *that* and the *how* of coming into appearance. This coming into appearance is a *Ver-an-lassen* [occasioning][57] in

---

55 "*Andenken*" also in the sense of "remembering" (Being/-in).
56 *Ge-Stell* is widely translated as "enframing", however this translation neglects the importance of "*stellen*" [(to) set] and also of "*Stelle*" [position/site/location], hence it will here be translated as "set". Cf. *das Ent-setzende* [de-setting] in *Das Ding*.
57 "*-lassen*" meaning "(to) let", see above.

the sense of a bringing-forth – *poiésis*. For the ancient Greeks, the word *poiésis* was not just used with regard to handicraft manufacture or artistic and poetic bringing into appearance and concrete imagery. *Physis* was also a bringing-forth – indeed in the highest sense since *physis* has the arising out of itself, belonging to bringing-forth, *in itself*. In contrast, what is brought forth by the artist or craftsperson does *not* have *poiésis* in itself, but rather needs a human agent. Bringing-forth, i.e. causality as occasioning, brings the concealed into the unconcealed and is grounded in a revealing, i.e. *alétheia* [truth].

"Technology" stems from the Greek word "*technikon*", meaning that which belongs to *techné*. It was the name for the skills and activities of the crafts-person *as well as* for the arts of the mind and the fine arts. *Techné* thus belongs to bringing-forth, i.e. to *poiésis*. Until the beginnings of "Western" metaphysics, *techné* was linked with *epistémé* – both terms for knowing [*Erkennen*] in the widest sense. They mean a being-acquainted with [*Sich-aus-kennen in*] some-thing and a being-skilled, and enable an opening-up [*Auf-schluss*].[58] Aristotle in his *Nicomachean Ethics* then distinguished between the two: *Techné* is a mode of *alétheuein* ("getting to the truth") – it reveals whatever does *not* reveal itself through itself. *Techné* is a kind [*Art*] of revealing through the four ways of occasioning. These ways of occasioning (variable) always have their objective in the (invariable) *telos* – the end determines the means. *Techné* is thus grounded in *epistémé* – a disposition for making something by way of "true knowledge". For Heidegger, on the other hand, what is decisive in *techné* is *not* making and handling, *not* the using of means, but the aforementioned revealing as *poiésis*. Revealing is the essence of technology – *alétheia*. *Techné* hence does not *have* a *telos*, but rather "*is*" the *telos* – it is a granting that endures. It is thus both a means and end in itself and hence does not need a human agent.

The essence of *modern* technology (grounded in the "exact" modern sciences) for Heidegger however does *not* reveal as a granting in the sense of *poiésis*, i.e. bringing-forth, but rather as a challenging-forth in the sense of setting [*stellen*]. Challenging-forth sets Nature in the way that it furthers by un-locking and setting out [*her-aus-stellen*] through regulating and securing. Modern technology is not limited by Nature anymore, instead Nature has become a fundamental stand-by part [*Grund-be-stand-stück*][59] of challenging-forth. Challenging-forth is a furthering that is always, "secretly and in advance", directed toward

---

58 "-*schluss*" meaning "end" or "closing".

59 "*Bestand*" is mostly translated as "standing reserve", however "stand-by" is the most literal translation as well as points out the continuous readiness, and restlessness, of *Bestand*.

furthering something else. Revealing never comes to an end – it is a continuous un-concealment. This continuous un-concealment of the stand-by [Be-stand] is a circular motion of ordering [Be-stellen].[60] The way of revealing the "real" as stand-by is the Ge-Stell [set] – in and as which ordering circulates. This is the essence of modern technology. The set gathers the setting that sets the human (and other beings). Revealing in terms of poiésis and revealing in terms of Ge-Stell are both ways of alétheia since they both set forth [her-stellen] and re-present [dar-stellen], however in fundamentally different ways. In the Ge-Stell, what is set-forth is not in the domain of what approaches the human anymore. The set sets the single whole [das Eine Ganze] of what is present into stand-by. In the Ge-Stell, the thing does not "thing" anymore. At most, the Ge-Stell brings forth the ob-ject, although even that eventually decays into the Same, which is always "on the spot" [auf der Stelle zur Stelle],[61] without difference.

The essence of technology sends the human upon a way of revealing. This sending that gathers (historically) is a destining [Ge-schick][62] – which is always the danger – if it reigns as the Ge-Stell, it is the supreme danger. In the age of modern technology, this danger appears in two ways: On the one hand, in this total objectlessness the human becomes merely the orderer [Be-steller] of the stand-by and thus is in danger of becoming stand-by as well. At the same time, the human is in danger of seeing itself as "master of the earth" and in this way can think that it only encounters itself. But in truth, said Heidegger, nowhere does the human encounter only itself, i.e. its essence, anymore. The human stands so decisively in the follow of the challenging-forth of the Ge-Stell that it does not grasp it as a claim anymore – which thus leads to a loss of ek-sistence, i.e. "homelessness". The Ge-Stell conceals revealing as poiésis – it is no bringing-forth of truth. "But where danger is, grows/the saving power also".[63] Technology is not "bad", but its essence is "mysterious". In order to experience revealing as a granting in the sense of poiésis, Heidegger wants us to question the essence of technology in the sense of grappling [sich aus-ein-ander-setzen][64] with it. He wants us to ask how the instrumental is essentially a way of causality. Since the essence of technology

---

60 Literally: "by-setting".
61 Literally "on the position/site towards the position/site", but can also be understood as "immediately ready".
62 "Schicken" meaning "(to) send".
63 Martin Heidegger, "Die Frage nach der Technik," in: Vorträge und Aufsätze (Pfullingen: Günther Neske, 1954), p. 36.
64 Literally: "(to) set oneself out with one another".

is nothing technological, this grappling has to happen in the realm of art (not "mere" aesthetics) through which the poetic essences.

5 Dwelling

In *Bauen Wohnen Denken* [*Building Dwelling Thinking*] (*BWD*) from 1951, Heidegger further developed the "saving power" in the essence of technology. In this lecture, he thought the relation between technicity and singular place/s through dwelling as the fundamental tendency (i.e. Being/-in in *SZ*). Things here explicitly *are* places, not just *have* or are *in* places, like equipment in *SZ*.[65] By trying to overcome the "Western" metaphysical tradition, which had explained dwelling simply as the aim of building, Heidegger in this text criticized the lack of dwelling/s in the industrialized world: "Bridge and hangar, stadium and power station are buildings, but not dwellings; [...] The truck driver is at home on the motorway, but he does not have his lodgings there".[66] The human inhabits buildings, but does not dwell in them – we work "here", but dwell "yonder". Even though buildings are in the realm of dwelling, dwelling in modernity is not *experienced* as the Being of the human anymore; it is not thought as the fundamental tendency and thus has fallen into oblivion. The modern human is "homeless".

Out of Language – the "mistress of the human" – Heidegger explicated "building" in three ways: a) Building is authentically [*eigen-tlich*] dwelling b) dwelling is the way in which mortals are on earth and c) building as dwelling un-folds itself into a building that cultivates growth and into the kind of building that erects buildings. Building, from the Old High German "*buan*", i.e. dwelling, is understood in the sense of a remaining and a locating-oneself [*Sich-auf-halten*]. This is a conserving [*Schonen*] in the sense of leaving something in, as well as freeing something into, its essence. This dwelling-conserving as fundamental tendency is the play of the fourfold,[67] which is essentially a locating-oneself *with* things. Dwelling as conserving safeguards the fourfold in things. Things however reveal the fourfold only when they themselves *as* things are left in their essence.

Regarding the question "What is a built thing?", Heidegger considered a bridge. Rather than the bridge connecting banks that are already present-at-hand, the banks only emerge as banks in the crossover of the bridge. The bridge

---

65 Whereby the difference between places and spaces is not entirely clear, other than the latter being a bit more encompassing.

66 Martin Heidegger, "Bauen Wohnen Denken", in: *Vorträge und Aufsätze* (Pfullingen: Günther Neske, 1954), p. 145.

67 See above.

lets the banks lie across from each other. It brings stream, banks and land into a reciprocal neighbourhood, which are each in turn also part of different neighbourhoods. Thus, the bridge as thing gathers, in its own (singular) way, the fourfold (of "earth", "sky", "divinities" and "mortals"), in the sense that it allows a site [*ver-stattet eine Stätte*] for it. But only something that is a place [*Ort*] itself can make room for [*ein-räumen*] a site. The place was thus not present-at-hand before the bridge, but *from the bridge itself* a place comes to a stand [*ent-steht*]. Through the thing that allows a site for the fourfold, places and paths are determined through which space is then made room for. Things that as places allow a site are called 'buildings' as they are brought forth through building. The relation [*Be-zug*] of place toward the human who locates itself [*sich auf-hält*] 'by' it lies in the essence of these things as places. This essence is dwelling.

Things as places *in the first place* allow sites for "spaces". A space is always released into a boundary. A boundary is not that at which something ends, but from where its essence begins – it is an origin, not a terminus. That which is made room for is gathered through a place, i.e. a thing. Hence, "spaces receive their essence from places and not from 'space'".[68] Space is thus not something that faces the human – it is neither an external ob-ject nor an internal experience. Spaces are made room for in the location [*Auf-ent-halt*] of mortals. By going *through* spaces, mortals stand in them. We always go through spaces in such a way that we are already sustaining them by locating ourselves *by* things as places that are near as well as remote. Someone "far away" can be closer to a thing than somebody who stands right "next to" it. A place makes room for the fourfold in two senses: it admits the fourfold and installs it. Making-room-for as admitting and making-room-for as installing belong together. A place, as two-fold making-room-for, is a "house". Things of this kind [*Art*] of place shelter the location of the human. Building, in the sense of *techné* as bringing-forth and letting-appear (of places), is thus closer to the essence of space than geometry and mathematics.

Thinking, as building, belongs to dwelling. According to Heidegger, if the relation between building and dwelling is considered by thought, and thus the homelessness of the industrialized world becomes *the* question, dwelling will be brought into the fullness of its essence. As he had already said in *Über den Humanismus* [*On Humanism*] a few years before: "Language is the House of Being. In its dwelling, the human dwells. Those that think and poeticize are the guardians of this dwelling […]. Thinking does not become action only when an

---

68 Heidegger, "Bauen Wohnen Denken," in: *Vorträge und Aufsätze*, p. 155.

effect emanates from it or when it is applied. Thinking acts insofar as it thinks. This thinking is presumably the simplest and highest because it approaches the relation of Being toward the human."[69]

6 Conclusion: Toward a techno-social ontology of place/s

This essay has unconcealed Heidegger's (germinal) ontology of medial place [*topos*] across a selection of his texts. In the world/s of ubiquitous computing at the beginning of the 21st century however, one must also think about how to develop it further. Two questions should be opened up here: the one of the technical and the one of the social. In Heidegger's epoch, technical evolution was at a very different stage than today, leading him to think mostly in terms of simple tools/equipment in *Sein und Zeit*, rather than entire technological systems, which operate in and organize (the) world/s pervasively, often latently and to an extent autonomously, while increasingly complexifying social relations. Even though his later work, especially *Die Frage nach der Technik*, did start to think these new conditions, Heidegger did not go quite far enough, and (relatively) opposed the "natural" (i.e. poetic/authentic [*eigentliche*]) condition to the industrial (i.e. exactifying/inauthentic [*uneigentliche*]) one. In the world/s of ubiquitous computing, "the poetic" and "the exact" must be thought as essentially *converging* in complex social (sub-)systems, not simply in ways where the latter compromises the former, in just *one Ge-Stell*.

   An attempt at taking Heidegger into the techno-social condition has been made by Peter Sloterdijk in his *Spheres* trilogy, i.e. "Being and Space". Going far beyond Heidegger's thought itself, *Spheres* "substantializes" (one might say "onticizes") the existential analytic and develops it in more (post-)anthropological constructivist, pluralistic, medially complex and social forms. Instead of understanding Being(-in) as rather disembodied universal, Sloterdijk, at its most fundamental, *situates* it *in* a "bubble" – i.e. the mother's womb, where the human comes *toward* "the world" through (pre-)technical social relations (for example via the umbilical cord and the mother's voice). *Dasein*, for Sloterdijk, is not already "thrown" into the world as relatively individual, authentic [*eigentlich*] only if it cuts itself off from the "vulgarity" of the one [*Man*] and the domain of the *Ge-Stell*, but is *originarily* a (pre-)technical being-with (with humans and other beings). *Dasein*, for Sloterdijk, is essentially in/authentic. *Spheres* moves from *Bubbles* [*Blasen*] ("micro spherology"), i.e. the anthropogenesis, over to *Globes* [*Globen*] ("macro

---

69 Heidegger, *Über den Humanismus*, p. 5.

spherology"), i.e. the metaphysical age, where the *subject* sets "the world" before
[*vor-stellt*] as present-at-hand, over to *Foams* [*Schäume*] ("plural spherology"),
i.e. the technological epoch, where humans de-construct (the) world/s through
multiplicities of hybrid systems, or "*Ge-Stelle*". In the epoch of foams, one cannot
conceive dwelling as a rather passive *conserving* anymore, but as an active and
ek-splicit *pro-ducing* of world/s. For Sloterdijk, *the* "House of Being" is not
Language ultimately, but, indeed, *a* house. Being-in-the-world means being-in-
houses. As much as Sloterdijk takes Heidegger's ontology into the techno-social
epoch however, he explicates it largely, and ultimately, through the conception of
space, and not of place.[70] Furthermore, like Heidegger, Sloterdijk does not grant
sufficient importance to the singular dynamics, or place/s, of technical objects
themselves – i.e. what Heidegger called the ready-to-hand (and even the more
"reductive" present-at-hand), the work, thing and even *Ge-Stell* (when understood as technical ensemble, such as a power plant or smart home infrastructure, for example) – which is Stiegler's argument in *Technics and Time*. Sloterdijk,
like Heidegger, does not sufficiently think about how technical objects themselves mediate (power) relations between humans (and other Being/s). In order
to develop a differentiated theory in the world/s of ubiquitous computing, one
needs to de- as well as further construct Heidegger's ontology through the formation [*Bildung*] of *technical place/s*.

Bibliography

de Beistegui, Miguel. *Thinking with Heidegger – Displacements*.
    Bloomington: Indiana University Press, 2003.

Casey, Edward S. *The Fate of Place – A Philosophical History*. Berkeley, London
    and Los Angeles: University of California Press, 1997.

Casey, Edward S. *Getting Back into Place – Toward a New Understanding of the
    Place-World*. Bloomington: Indiana University Press, 2009.

Heidegger, Martin. *Vorträge und Aufsätze*. Pfullingen: Günther Neske, 1954.

Heidegger, Martin. *Über den Humanismus*. Frankfurt am Main: Vittorio
    Klostermann, 1968.

Heidegger, Martin. *Der Ursprung des Kunstwerkes*. Stuttgart: Philipp Reclam
    jun., 1970.

---

70 As mentioned above, I understand place as the in-between of (the tendencies/idealities)
    time and space.

Heidegger, Martin. "Logik – Die Frage nach der Wahrheit." In: *Gesamtausgabe*. Frankfurt am Main: Vittorio Klostermann, 1976.

Heidegger, Martin. "Seminar in Le Thor 1969." In: "Seminare." In: *Gesamtausgabe*. Frankfurt am Main: Vittorio Klostermann, 1986, pp. 326–371.

Heidegger, Martin. "Bremer und Freiburger Vorträge." In: *Gesamtausgabe*. Frankfurt am Main: Vittorio Klostermann, 1994.

Heidegger, Martin. *Sein und Zeit*. Tübingen: Max Niemeyer, 2006.

Heidegger, Martin. "Zeit und Sein." In: "*Zur Sache des Denkens*." In: *Gesamtausgabe*. Frankfurt am Main: Vittorio Klostermann, 2007, pp. 3–30.

Malpas, Jeff E. *Heidegger's Topology: Being, Place, World*. Cambridge, MA and London: MIT Press, 2006.

Malpas, Jeff E. *Heidegger and the Thinking of Place – Explorations in the Topology of Being*. Cambridge, MA and London: MIT Press, 2012.

Sloterdijk, Peter. *Sphären I: Blasen*. Frankfurt am Main: Suhrkamp, 1998.

Sloterdijk, Peter. *Sphären II: Globen*. Frankfurt am Main: Suhrkamp, 1999.

Sloterdijk, Peter. *Sphären III: Schäume*. Frankfurt am Main: Suhrkamp, 2004.

Stiegler, Bernard. *Technics and Time 1: The Fault of Epimetheus*. Trans. Richard Beardsworth and George Collins. Stanford: Stanford University Press, 1998.

Stiegler, Bernard. *Technics and Time 2: Disorientation*. Trans. Stephen Barker. Stanford: Stanford University Press, 2008.

Stiegler, Bernard. *Technics and Time 3: Cinematic Time and the Question of Malaise*. Trans. Stephen Barker. Stanford: Stanford University Press, 2011.

Philippe Theophanidis

A Decisive Mediation: Heidegger, Media Studies, and Ethics*

When it comes to the ways in which media studies intersects with Heidegger's philosophical work, two crucial problems cannot be overlooked: the definition of media and Heidegger himself. The former is a notoriously fuzzy concept, while the latter was infamously involved with Nazism and anti-Semitism. This chapter opens a path to addressing those problems. This path exposes not a solution, but instead highlights the issue of how we are for one another, and the care that is consequently required from and for us.

In the first part of this chapter, I expand on the two problems initially identified—media and Heidegger—and provide them with contextual background. I cast the problem of defining "media" and "media studies" as an epistemological one. In doing so, I show how one common way to borrow from Heidegger in media studies is to reference modern communication technologies. Since this is a relatively recent and rather specialized extension of the idea of medium, I argue Heidegger's influence in the nascent field of media studies is neither straightforward nor clearly established. Turning more specifically to Heidegger's own prejudices, I outline the well-documented and more complicated problem of his involvement with Nazism and anti-Semitism. I cast this problem as a political one. While some have argued that Heidegger's distorted political views contaminated all his work, I suggest that this is no reason for media studies to steer away from it. Going back to the emergence of the fields of communication and media studies, I show how the epistemological always was and still remains entangled with the political. While banning Heidegger is ultimately an ineffective way to deal with the nature of the problematic views he presented (and getting rid of him does not spare us from the issues of prejudice anyway), merely sidestepping his involvement in the Nazi party is clearly not responsible either. I suggest instead that both the epistemological and political require ethical engagement. I outline how such an ethical engagement is of special concern for media studies, since

* A version of this chapter was presented in October 2017 at the international conference Heidegger: Dwelling, Thinking, and the Ethical Life held at King's University College, London, Ontario. I am grateful both to the organizers and to the participants for their generous comments.

it can be cast as a process of mediation. This approach offers alternative routes through the epistemological and political issues identified in Heidegger's works.

1 An epistemological problem: media

To rigorously assess the role played by the Heideggerian corpus in media studies, let alone to propose new developments in and beyond his work, it is important to clearly establish what exactly scholars study in this field. One possibility for a simple answer can be identified in the common object shared by all those participating in this plurality of studies: media. A quick examination, however, requires any inquiring mind to acknowledge that "media" is as common and popular a term as it is equivocal in what exactly it refers to: very familiar in the various ways it is used, yet elusive in its meaning. As a German media theorist observed, the fact that the "concept of media" is an issue is "raised by every wiseacre."[1] How is that so?

It is still possible to find straightforward answers to the question, "what is a medium/media?" For example, in Hartley's *Communication, Cultural, and Media Studies: The Key Concepts*, the entry "Medium/media" opens with this rather confident assertion: "A medium (plural, media) is simply any material through which something else may be transmitted. [...] Media of communication are therefore any means by which messages may be transmitted."[2] Alternatively, the *Oxford English Dictionary* lists 29 different meanings for the word "medium,"[3] excluding special meanings, some dating back to classical Latin. The recent conflation of the term "medium" with "media"[4] in the narrow sense as a "main means of mass communication" still strongly informs the common usage. In this perspective, media are understood as material things—technological artifacts[5]—or a system of things

---

1 Bernhard Siegert, "Cacography or Communication? Cultural Techniques in German Media Studies," Grey Room, Vol. 29 (2007), p. 28.

2 John Hartley, ed., *Communication, Cultural and Media Studies: The Key Concepts* (London: Routledge, 2011), pp. 142–143. This entry explicitly restricts the definition to processes involving "human semiosis" and implicitly restricts "communication" to a process of transmission. For a divergent take on the meaning of the word "communication," see Derrida (Limited Inc., pp. 1–12).

3 "medium, n. and adj.," OED Online, June 2017, Oxford University Press, Oct. 27, 2017, http://www.oed.com/view/Entry/115772

4 "media, n.2," OED Online, http://www.oed.com/view/Entry/115635

5 Artifacts or instruments, equipment, apparatus: here, the important distinctions that can be made between all these terms are left aside.

fulfilling a function (transmission) for a given end (communication).[6] Indeed, in a recent article examining new historical perspectives in communication studies, the authors observe that the "history of media is foremost the history of technical objects" (Thibault and Trudel, 2015, 12; my translation).

At first glance, this technological understanding of what media are helps to identify one of the common meeting points between specific aspects of Heidegger's work and media studies.[7] Heidegger's discussions about the hammer as *das Zeug* ("equipment") in section 15 of *Being and Time*,[8] the typewriter in his lecture on Parmenides,[9] or technology as "positionality" (or "enframing") in the oft-quoted *The Question Concerning Technology*,[10] all seem to offer logical applications in the field of media studies. This is not to suggest that such applications fell prey to technological reductionism nor a technologically determinist understanding of media. Many scholars working with a technical understanding of media do engage critically both with technological determinism and, when it applies, with Heidegger's elaborate treatment of technology (a treatment that, since its formulation, has not itself remained exempt of critical and rigorous examination).[11]

For example, Gunkel and Taylor introduced their recent book *Heidegger and the Media* by arguing that themes of "language, truth, telepresence and technological determinism constitute the four key related aspects of what makes Heidegger's purportedly abstract and esoteric work so useful for revealing very practical and radical insights into the media's role as a structuring element of our everyday lives" (2014, p. 8). Further examples of the diversity applications of Heidegger's ideas

6   Media as material means or a system of material means for communication in a transmission process: see Marcel Danesi, *Dictionary of Media and Communications* (Armonk: M.E. Sharpe, 2009), p. 192. The way "system" is understood here is distinct from the system theory developed by Luhmann regarding media (see Jesper Tække and Michael Paulsen, "Luhmann and the Media," *MedieKultur: Journal of Media and Communication Research* Vol. 26, No. 49 (2010): 1–10).

7   Don Ihde briefly comments Heidegger's familiarity with "the beginnings of late modern communication technologies" in his book, *Heidegger's Technologies: Postphenomenological Perspectives* (Fordham University Press, 2010, pp. 4, 128–139).

8   Martin Heidegger, *Being and Time*, trans. John Macquarrie and Edward Robinson (Oxford: Blackwell, 1962), pp. 95–102.

9   Heidegger, *Parmenides*, trans. André Schuwer and Richard Rojcewicz (Bloomington: Indiana University Press, 1998), pp. 85–87.

10 Heidegger, *The Question Concerning Technology, and Other Essays*, trans. William Lovitt (New York: Garland Publishing, Inc.), 1977.

11 See, for example, Stiegler (*Technics and Time*, 1998), Babich ("The Essence of Questioning," 1999), and Ihde (*Heidegger's Technologies*, 2010), to name a few.

regarding a technological understanding of media include, but are not limited to, postmodernism (Vattimo, *The Transparent Society*, 1992), television (Fry, ed., *RUA/ TV? Heidegger and the Televisual*, 1993; Scannell, *Television and the Meaning of Live*, 2014) and radio (Scannell, *Radio, Television and Modern Life*, 1996; Babich, "Constellating Technology: Heidegger's *Die Gefahr/The Danger*," 2014), media consumption (Wilson, *Media Consumption in Malaysia: A Hermeneutics of Human Behaviour*, 2015), media users theory (Wilson, *Understanding Media Users: From Theory to Practice*, 2009), cybernetics in the media age (Poster, "High-Tech Frankenstein, or Heidegger Meets Sterlac" 2002), technology and biology (Kember and Zylinska, *Life After New Media*, 2012), the sense of place (Malpas, "New Media, Cultural Heritage and the Sense of Place: Mapping the Conceptual Ground," 2008), the idea of communication (Peters, *Speaking into the Air*, 2000),[12] environment and nature (Peters, *The Marvelous Clouds*, 2015), emerging media and big data (Floyd and Katz, eds., 2015), entanglement and transhumanism (Babich, "O! Superman!" 2013; "Heidegger on Technology," 2017), online learning (Cressman and Hamilton, "The Experiential Dimension of Online Learning," 2010), and media as such (Bay and Rickert, "New Media," 2008), especially in the tradition of German media studies (Kittler, *Optical Media*, 2010; *The Truth*, 2014; Weber and Cholodenko, *Mass Mediauras*, 1996; Siegert, "Cultural Techniques," 2013; Winthrop-Young, "Krautrock, Heidegger, Bogeyman," 2011a; *Kittler and the Media*, 2011b).

This is by no means an exhaustive survey of the relevant literature, nor necessarily a representative sample of Heidegger's influence on media studies.[13] Based strictly on this set of references, it is possible to assert that Heidegger's work has been and still is influential, at least to some degree. The precise extent or the

---

12 Peters explains in the introduction of his book *Speaking into the Air: A History of the Idea of Communication* (Chicago: University of Chicago Press, 2000) that he uses "communication theory" in a "loose, ahistorical sense." This is what allows him to argue that "communication" was a central concept for philosophy in the 1920s. Among the "[m]ajor works probing the possibility and limits of communication," he lists *Being and Time* alongside Wittgenstein's *Tractatus Logico-philosophicus*, Freud's *Civilization and its Discontent*, Dewey's *Experience and Nature*, and others (2000, p. 10).

13 Furthermore, it is worth noting this survey is concerned specifically with technological from the perspective of media. The secondary literature pertaining to the broader issue of technology as such in Heidegger's philosophy is significant and keeps expanding. Although two decades old, Borgmann and Mitcham's "critical review of the literature" on the topic represents a good starting point ("Critical Review," 1987). At the time of writing yet another collection is forthcoming under the title *Heidegger on Technology*, which promises to offer "the first comprehensive and definitive account of Martin Heidegger's philosophy of technology" (Wendland, Merwin and Hadjioannou, 2018).

exact significance of this influence on the field of media studies has much to gain from a closer and more systematic investigation, which is currently lacking. This shortfall may have to do with the difficulty such a task entails. Two reasons can be briefly offered here to explain this difficulty.

First, it is worth noting that a large portion of communication and media studies—however those two fields relate, when they do—still simply manage without any direct reference to Heidegger. Numerous handbooks, readers, and encyclopaedias dealing specifically with communication and media make no mention of his work or include only passing allusions to it. In Littlejohn and Foss's *Encyclopedia of Communication Theory*, which contains about 400 entries, Heidegger is mentioned in relation to the traditions of phenomenology, herme-neutics, dialogue theories, rhetoric and existentialism, but not to "medium theory" or technological issues. In Donsbach's 12-volume *International Encyclopedia of Communication*, Heidegger is associated with the same topics, but is also men-tioned in entries about the history of communication and media studies, the his-tory of the idea of communication and virtual reality (2008).[14] Heidegger's name does not appear in the index of the second edition of *Reading Media Theory* (Mills, 2012), nor are any of his texts included in Larousse's *Sciences de l'information et de la communication* (published in the "Essential Texts" collection of the French pub-lisher Larousse; Bougnoux, 1993). There are merely two mentions in the 500-plus page *The Handbook of Communication History*, while four are found in the massive revised edition of *Media and Cultural Studies: KeyWorks* (Simonson, ed., 2013; Durham and Kellner, 2006).[15] The following works, which all take media studies as their main concern, do not make any reference to Heidegger, or scarcely mention him: *Oxford Handbook of Film and Media Studies* (Kolker, 2008), *Media Studies: An Introduction* (Kolker, 2009), *Media Studies: A Reader* (Thornham, Bassett, and Marris, 1996), *The Media Study Reader* (O'Sullivan and Jewkens, 1997), *Why Study The Media?* (Silverstone, 1999), *Home Territories: Media, Mobility and Identity* (Morley, 2002), *A Companion to Media Studies* (Valdivia, 2006, *Media Rituals: A Critical Approach* (Couldry, 2003), *The Media and Globalization* (Rantanen, 2004), and *Key Concepts in Media and Communications* (Jones and Holmes, 2011). This is again a rather modest sample,[16] but at the very least it suggests that Heidegger's work, although it exerts a certain influence with some authors, is far from being

---

14 Those latter three entries having been authored, in order, by Peter Simonson and John Durham Peters, John Durham Peters, and Sean Cubitt.

15 All four are found in an entry on "postmodernism" penned by Frederick Jameson.

16 A more rigorous study should comb a defined set of communication journals for Heidegger's name, based, for example, on the SCIMAGO Journal & Country Rankings.

central or pervasive in the field of communication and media studies.[17] As Gunkel
and Taylor themselves twice asserted in their book, *Heidegger and the Media*,
to this day Heidegger remains "largely ignored by Media and Communication
Studies" (2014, p. 170).

The second reason that can explain the difficulty of assessing more clearly
the influence of Heidegger on the specific field of media studies is related to
the problem raised at the start of this section: the uncertain identity of this
field. Despite the technological understanding I already discussed being largely
accepted, what the labels "media studies," "media," and "medium" encompass
are much more diverse. As one media and communication historian recently
commented, regarding the absence of a dominating journal in his disciplinary
field, "[i]f media and communication has no flagship, it is because there is no
coherent discipline in the first place" (Pooley, 2015, p. 1247). This observation is
not a new one. In 1974, Raymond Williams argued that the diversity of the field
of communication research should be welcomed instead of lamented, observing,
"[t]hat communication scientists cannot communicate with each other is by now
one of those old jokes that with repetition become melancholy" (1974, p. 18). In
his classic study on media and society, James W. Carey warned the reader, "[of]
all the areas or subareas within communications, that of the mass media has
proved to be the most fiercely resistant to adequate theoretical formulation—
indeed, even to systematic discussion" (1989, p. 69). Robert T. Craig, who in
1999 penned an influential proposition for a "meta-model" of communication,
observed fourteen years later in an interview that the nature of the field remained
fragmented, adding, "[c]oherence is an elusive goal" (Boromisza-Habashi, 2013,
pp. 421–422). John Durham Peters wrote more colorfully in the early 1990s of a
"fascinating communication theory galore" (1993, p. 134). When allowed to stand

---

In the *Journal of Communication*, the highest rank in the category for "communication,"
a search for Heidegger returned 35 results between the years 1973 and 2012. There
were 46 results in *Communication Theory* (fourth in rank) spread between 1991 and
2016, 29 results in *New Media and Society* (fifth) between 2003 and 2016, and none in
Communication Research (seventh) for the same time period. Those numbers would
certainly require further exploration to increase their relevance for the issue at hand.

17 The question of just how much an influence can be rigorously established presents its
own set of problems, the first having to do with search parameters: is explicitly mentioning the name of Martin Heidegger the only acceptable marker? Stanley Cavell,
for example, is an important figure in cinema and media studies who was strongly
influenced by Heidegger's work. The title of one of his most renowned books, *The
World Viewed: Reflections on the Ontology of Film*, was inspired by Heidegger, yet in it
Heidegger's name appears on only six pages (Cavell, 1971).

outside of its common technological confines, the concept of "medium" shows just how rich a semantic field it belongs to. Media scholars who propose to take a step back from this instrumental understanding find themselves struggling to do so. We currently lack a rigorous examination of just how mass media research, communication studies, media studies, media archeology and, more recently, *Medienphilosophie* relate and differ from one another. An interesting attempt at a broader historical and epistemological survey can be found in Thibault and Trudel (2015). Under renewed scrutiny, the terms "medium" and "media" appear to be "ambiguous," characterized by "a strange fuzziness" or "conceptual fuzziness" (Mitchell, 2010, p. 93; Tholen and Krapp, 2002, p. 661; Winthrop-Young and Wutz, 2003, p. 1). For some, the equivocal nature of media is worrying, as it carries the threat of "a boundless concept" (Mitchell, 2008, p. 12). The debate is described by these scholars as "confusing, multivocal and heterogeneous," and deeply characterized by the absence of consensus (Krämer, 2015, p. 27). Weighing in on this "heated debate," others have provocatively asserted "there are no media," hence broadening an earlier, similarly negating claim: "There are no mass media" (Horn, 2007, p. 7; Siegert, 1996; see also Siegert, 2015, p. 85).

From the fuzzy boundaries of the concept, we nonetheless see new understandings emerging about media phenomena, especially in relation to spatial meanings associated with the notion of "medium." It is opportunities for further developments in this direction that I will outline in the final section of this chapter, specifically as it offers grounds for ethical possibilities. To understand the relevance—if not the urgency—of such a development, we must turn to the second problem at hand: namely, the political issues associated with Heidegger and his work.

2 A political problem: Heidegger

Even though the exact extent of Heidegger's influence on media studies and the contours of the field are not easy to establish, all is not lost to fuzziness. American scholar Thomas Sheehan put it succinctly: "Two facts about Martin Heidegger (1889–1976) are as incontestable as they are complicated: first, that he remains one of the century's most influential philosophers and, second, that he was a Nazi." (1988). The statement was made some thirty years ago and, at the time, was hardly breaking news.[18] Nonetheless, those two facts have been further

---

18 Heidegger's involvement with Nazism was common knowledge during his lifetime and subject to scholarly criticism even then. Marcuse publicly attacked the political involvement of Heidegger's existentialism as early as 1934 (2009, pp. 1–30). In

complicated by the recent publication of Heidegger's *Black Notebooks* (2016).[19] This publication brought additional material, and publicity, to an already complex case.[20] In a recent essay situating the *Notebooks*, Jeff Malpas thus reiterates the problem: "That Heidegger was a Nazi and that he also held anti-Semitic views

---

1940, Vivian Jerauld McGill, founding editor of the Marxist journal *Science & Society*, examined Heidegger's "blindness" in a wider essay on the state of philosophy in Nazi Germany (1940). In 1946, a former student of Heidegger, Karl Löwith, published an essay titled "Les implications politiques de la philosophie de l'existence chez Heidegger" ("The Political Implications of Heidegger's Existentialism") in an issue of *Les temps modernes* (Wolin, 1991, pp. 167–185). In 1948, Günther Anders, former husband of Hannah Arendt, published a vehement charge against what he perceived as the "pseudo-concreteness of Heidegger's philosophy." Anders does not criticize Heidegger's involvement with Nazism explicitly. He takes a different angle, arguing that "moral or political participation or action [...] has become extinct in Heidegger's philosophy" (1948, p. 350). He further points to "the emptiness of [Heidegger's] moral rigorism" (1948, p. 361). A review published by Jürgen Habermas in 1953 bears an unequivocal title: "Thinking with Heidegger and Against Heidegger: On the Publication of Lectures Dating from 1935" (Wolin, 1991, pp. 186–197). Theodor W. Adorno's own well-known *Jargon der Eigentlichkeit: Zur deutschen Ideologie* was published in 1964 (1973).

19 At the time of writing, three volumes of the *Black Notebooks* have been published by Vittorio Klostermann. Those three volumes have been translated by Richard Rojcewicz and published in English by Indiana University Press under the titles *Ponderings II–VI: Black Notebooks 1931–1938* (2016), *Ponderings VII–XI: Black Notebooks 1938–1939* (2017a), and *Ponderings XII–XV: Black Notebooks 1939–1941* (2017b). The *Black Notebooks* are published as part of Heidegger's *Complete Works* (*Gesamtausgabe*) and correspond to volumes 94 to 96. For more information, see Escudero (2015).

20 For reviews of and discussion about *The Black Notebooks*, see Krell (2015, pp. 127–160), Trawny (2015), Farin and Malpas (2016), Nancy (2017), Mitchell and Trawny, eds. (2017). A series of unconnected conferences also brought together scholars around the issues raised by the newly published notebooks: on April 8, 2014, at the Goethe Institute in New York City, Peter Trawny (who edited the three volumes of the *Black Notebooks*) discussed the issue with Roger Berkowitz, Academic Director of the Hannah Arendt Center at Bard College; September 5–6, 2014, at Emory University, in Atlanta (Peter Trawny was keynote, while panelists included Bettina Bergo, Robert Bernasconi, Eduardo Mendieta, Richard Polt and Tom Rockmore); September 11–12, 2014, at CUNY, in New York (panelists included Richard Wolin, Emmanuel Faye, and Thomas Sheehan); January 22–25, 2014, at the Bibliothèque Nationale de France, in Paris (panelists included Alain Finkielkraut, Jean-Claude Milner, Peter Sloterdijk, François Fédier, Peter Trawny, Barbara Cassin, Donatella di Cesare, Babette Babich, and many others). Recordings of those public panel discussions are available online. Proceedings of the conference held in Paris were published in 2015.

are simple facts," he argued, before adding, "[a]s soon as one recognizes the need to clarify what is at issue in talk of Heidegger's Nazism and anti-Semitism, then the fact that Heidegger was indeed a Nazi and an anti-Semite starts to appear rather more complicated and much less straightforward" (quoted in Farin and Malpas, 2016, pp. 5–6). This case, which is not only about what Heidegger wrote and said but also about what he did not write and remained silent about, has been and still is being documented by important—if often controversial—efforts which cannot be examined in detail here.[21]

A general awareness of the issue at hand has made its way from the rather specialized corner of continental philosophy to the blinding spotlight of mainstream media.[22] It has come in a burst of shards, fragments, and controversial tidbits of information. Those are sometimes treated with care and intelligence. Other times, they seem to be conjured up only to fuel oversimplified judgments. For example, some authors may have a general awareness of Heidegger's involvement with the National Socialist German Workers' Party and his membership card, while others may have heard of his alleged fascination with Hitler's hand. A set of short excerpts from the *Black Notebooks* was translated and circulated online even before the publication of the three volumes in Germany, in 2014. Thus, we may have heard of Heidegger commenting about the "world Jewry"

---

21 Those contributions started during Heidegger's lifetime and continue to this day. While an exhaustive list is beyond the scope of this chapter, the following references can serve as indicators: Lacoue-Labarthe (2007), Farías (1989), Wolin (1990), Sluga (1993), Faye (2011), Janicaud (2015), and Nancy (2017). As stated, some of this work has been and still is subject to heated debate.

22 English and French venues which dealt with the publication of the Notebooks in the spring of 2014 include (but are not limited to) *The Guardian, The National Post, Slate, The New York Times, The Huffington Post, The Telegraph, Foreign Affairs, Le Monde,* and *Libération.* This relatively recent media coverage triggered by the publication of parts of the *Black Notebooks* could alone support research also titled "Heidegger and Media," although with a likely different outcome. In an earlier, online version of his examination of the Black Notebooks, Gregory Fried observed, "[p]eople delight in the tabloid spectacle of a once-famous figure made infamous by their own failings" ("The King Is Dead," 2014). Babette Babich commented more specifically on the "digitalization" of the controversy, noting, "today's Heidegger scandal transpires on Facebook, via video, via shared online articles and posts: instant announcement with instant commentary on no less than three dedicated Facebook Group pages" ("Heidegger's Black Night," 2016a, pp. 66–67). She remains one of the few observers who has refused to ignore the intimate relation between those modes of mediation and the core of the controversy: "What is the effect of the medium of dissemination and expression on reflection?" ("Heidegger's Black Night," 2016b, pp. 66–67).

(*Weltjudentum*).[23] We've read short quotes supporting his reputation as a major philosophical figure of the twentieth century, but also statements from well-known public figures denouncing his dishonesty and political beliefs. Hence, the controversy manifests itself as a difficult tension between being unwilling to deny the importance of his contribution to philosophy, while vehemently refusing to overlook or forgive what he did. This tension found an exemplary expression in a comment shared by French philosopher Emmanuel Lévinas: "Despite all the horror that eventually came to be associated with Heidegger's name—and which will never be dissipated—nothing has been able to destroy in my mind the conviction that the *Sein und Zeit* of 1927 cannot be annulled, no more than can the few other eternal books in the history of philosophy—however much they may disagree" (1998, p. 208). Those facts cannot be glossed over or ignored.

This alone should be enough to indicate just how much of a rigorous and serious effort is needed to adequately assess the full scope of the problem. To grasp what is at stake, one would need more than a minimal understanding of what historical Nazism, structural fascism, radical nationalism, cult-like Hitlerism, and anti-Semitism each entails, where they overlap and interlock, and how they nonetheless differ.[24] For example, the comments made since the publication of the *Black Notebooks* include remarks about "being-historical anti-Semitism," "cultural anti-Semitism," and "metaphysical anti-Semitism," all of them distinguishable from the typology once proposed by Adorno and Horkheimer in a different context (Trawny, 2016; Farin and Malpas, 2016, p. 6; Cesare, 2016; Adorno and Horkheimer, 1941). Understanding clearly how all of this intertwined with the "question of being" (*Seinsfrage*), Heidegger's main philosophical concern during most of his career, at least according to traditional

---

23 *Weltjudentum* is sometimes translated as "world Judaism." There are important discussions about the translation problems of this expression into French (Trawny, 2015, translator's foreword) and into English (Babich, "Heidegger's Black Night," 2016a, pp. 63–64).

24 Ernesto Laclau opens a chapter of *Politics and Ideology in Marxist Theory* dedicated to "Fascism and Ideology" by quoting from Ortega y Gasset: " 'Fascism has an enigmatic countenance because in it appears the most counterposed contents [....] Whichever way we approach fascism, we find that it is simultaneously one thing and the contrary, it is A and not-A [....]" (quoted in Laclau, 1977, pp. 81–82). The first line of Ian Kershaw's preface to the third edition of his study, *The Nazi Dictatorship: Problems and Perspectives of Interpretation* underlines another aspect of this problem: "[s]cholarly research on Nazism has produced a literature so immense that even experts cannot hope to master all of it" (1993, p. vii).

readings of his work,[25] may very well be just as important an issue. This last task requires knowledge not just of fragments and excerpts, or a selection of essays, but the bulk of the Heideggerian corpus.

Over the years, the constraints imposed by such a situation have informed various strategies to navigate both Heidegger's philosophy and his political commitment to Nazism and anti-Semitism. One of those strategies is total excommunication of both the thinker and the thought, the persona and the whole of his work. To implement this ban, scholars must not use his name or even one line of his work, unless it is for the specific and explicit purpose of adding to the blame.[26] Another strategy consists of bracketing or amputating the political and ideological contaminant while saving part of the philosophy. This treatment may rely on the ignorance or explicit recognition of Heidegger's involvement with Nazism and anti-Semitism, but in any case, it allows for some of his ideas—deemed unpolitical or at least uncompromised—to be put to use. While the first option is sacrificial in nature, the second is instrumental. Both operate on the assumption that a form of exclusion—total for the former, partial for the latter—represent an adequate solution to a complicated problem.

Like others, I do not think either of those solutions are adequate or satisfactory. On the one hand, I do not find myself in a position where I could competently and rigorously declare all of Heidegger's philosophy to be contaminated.[27]

---

25 What constitutes the core of Heidegger's inquiry—*die Sache selbst*, according to an expression used in *Being and Time* (34)—has been and is still being challenged, at least by the American reception of his work. This challenge takes the form of a call for a "paradigm shift" in Heideggerian studies (Sheehan, 2014).

26 This is the position held by Christian Fuchs, who concluded a recent journal article with those words: "It is now also the moment where scholars should consider stopping to eulogise and reference Heidegger when theorising and analysing the media, communication, culture, technology, digital media, and the Internet" (2015, p. 75). Fuchs references Heidegger's work, critically, in subsequent publications (2016, 2017).

27 "Contamination" is the issue raised—and the vocabulary used—by Peter Trawny in his book *Heidegger and The Myth of Jewish World Conspiracy* (2014). The metaphor of contamination carries its own set of problems, as it involves at its premise the idea of an uncontaminated thought or, for that matter, an uncontaminated life. The consequence of such a view should be carefully weighed: it operates based on the opposition between clean and dirty, pure and impure, which has been used by Nazi rhetoric and political discourse in general (Perry, 1983; Mutsaers, 2016). Trawny briefly acknowledged the issue without developing its consequences ("Heidegger and the Myth," 2014, pp. 12–13). This issue is more than tangentially related to the study of communication

On the other hand, I am unwilling to accept the idea that parts of it could be conveniently isolated and instrumentalized, while the contentious parts are circumvented. Short of sidestepping this issue, the remaining alternative seems to consist of a head-on confrontation. The difficulties that come with such a task are immense, more so from the perspective of a non-specialist. Considering what is at stake, is this complicated problem better left to the judgment of experts? Or, to phrase it differently, shouldn't media scholars simply avoid Heidegger's work altogether and find alternative ways through problems raised by research on media?

I argue to the contrary. There is both an epistemological and a political necessity to consider Heidegger, not despite his association with fascism and anti-Semitism, but because of it. To be clear, I am not arguing that from the point of view of communication and media studies Heidegger's only interest is found in the problematic aspects of his life, beliefs, and thinking. In another context, I could point out that since existence is foremost coexistence—or *Mitsein*, as Heidegger puts it in section 26 of *Being and Time*—then being together or "being-with" is the originary communicative condition of all things (although Heidegger restricts this condition to the human being alone, that is, to *Dasein*). As such, communication and media studies could and should be concerned with the work of Heidegger if only because they offer a privileged perspective on the question of being *qua* being-with. In all their equivocality, communication and media are indeed concerned with commonality, relationality, in-between-ness, and mediation. If such an argument is carefully developed, it underlines how media and communication studies relate to major aspects of Heidegger's philosophy, and most notably to the *Seinsfrage*. Such an argument would nonetheless need to address Heidegger's political leanings and anti-Semitism. In fact, this problem is, in more than one way, quite intimately related to the issue of "being-with" and community. Hence, it is this political problem that I address here, although briefly, if only to show how this controversy is not a reason to ignore Heidegger's work.

At least two complementary perspectives support the idea that Heidegger's work, political commitments are of legitimate concern for communication and media scholars. The first one is general, and does not depend on the specificities of an academic field or discipline. However, it is of special interest for communication and media studies, as it is concerned with the ways we live together,

---

(when understood as the process opposite to immunization) and media studies (as they were once associated with medical metaphors, such as the "hypodermic" metaphor, which I will address later).

relate with one another, and organize and share our lives in common. For this argument, this perspective can be viewed as broadly concerned with the political. As such, it is of relevance for everyone, including media and communication scholars. The other perspective is epistemological. It pertains to some of the specific aspects that have shaped and still are shaping the disciplinary fields of mass media research, communication studies, and media studies. I will further outline those two perspectives in order to highlight how ethics can be the site where media and Heidegger, the epistemological and the political, all converge.

First, fascism—of which Nazism can be considered a "permutation" or not (Griffin, 1991, p. 110; Passmore, 2014, p. 21)—is not a private matter, nor an uncommon problem. To the contrary, it is a common problem in both senses of the word: it is at once public (shared) and prevalent (ordinary). Fascism is common in the sense of being public because it concerns us all. More precisely, it is concerned with "us" and it belongs to "us." It concerns the very possibility of saying "we."[28] As Foucault once argued, fascism is "not only historical fascism, the fascism of Hitler and Mussolini—which was able to mobilize and use the desire of the masses so effectively—but also the fascism in us all, in our heads and in our everyday behavior, the fascism that causes us to love power, to desire the

---

28 The condition that allows for the production of a "we"—thus of political synthesis—has received renewed attention in recent years, both by English and French scholars (Geffroy, 1985; Vogel, 1994; Pagano, 2013; Garcia, 2016; Macé, 2017). In 2013, the issue was the central topic for the conference Discovering the "We": The Phenomenology of Sociality held in Dublin. Swiss writer Denis de Rougemont first pointed out the relationship between fascism and the utterance of a "we" (1936, pp. 236–241). Jean-Luc Nancy's main effort since the late 1970s has focused on this very problem through a re-examination of the notion of "community." In Being Singular Plural, a central contribution to this effort, he observes, "this is us, we who are supposed to say we as if we know what we are saying and who we are talking about" (2000, pp. xii–xiii). Recent events surrounding the election of President Donald Trump have shown just how accurate his diagnostic still is. While Richard B. Spencer—a known spokesperson for the far right in the United States—was addressing a conference in Washington in November 2016, a large screen featured the slogan for his presentation: "Become Who We Are" (Rappeport and Weiland, 2016). In his book On Tyranny written in December 2016 and published just weeks after the United States presidential inauguration, American historian Timothy Snyder, who wrote extensively on the issue of fascism, observed, "[w]e see ourselves as a city on the hill, a stronghold of democracy, looking out for threats that come from abroad. But [...] human nature is such that American democracy must be defended from Americans who would exploit its freedoms to bring about its end." (2017, p. 27).

very thing that dominates and exploits us" (2002, p. 108).[29] Fascism can thus be regarded as a common problem in the specific sense that it is a shared problem, a problem "we" *have* and "we" *are* in common, as it brings us together and tears us apart. As soon as one recognizes that he or she lives a life in common—that is, not exclusively a private life—one recognizes the utmost necessity not to ignore this issue: the issue that "we" are for one another.[30] This last observation must be understood not quite simply in the general sense that "we" represent an issue for one another, but in the specific sense that being together means sharing the conditions of this coexistence as a common issue. In an essay titled "The King is Dead: Martin Heidegger after the *Black Notebooks*," Gregory Fried concluded with similar concerns: "[w]e may rightly despise Heidegger for his anti-Semitism and Nazism, and his entire body of thought must be reconsidered in light of increasingly decisive evidence of how deeply he adhered to these convictions. But who we are, and who we are going to be as human beings in a newly global world, is very much the question, and we seem allergic even to asking it seriously. As a genuine adversary, Heidegger brings what is at issue into focus; if we don't raise the question at all and think it through, we will lurch blindly to our fate." (quoted in Farin and Malpas, 2016, p. 55). Others have similarly argued that Heidegger, even with his fascism and anti-Semitism, is still very much "our" problem, and that casting him away is not an adequate solution (Agamben, 2006, pp. 273–281; Nancy, 2014).

Fascism is also common in the sense that it is not confined to a one-time, exceptional occurrence in our recent history: a monstrous error that happened only once and from which we have been able to stay clear of since. As Mark Neocleous put it, borrowing from Klaus Theweleit, "fascism is in fact a problem of

---

29 Foucault's statement regarding "the fascism in us all" may sound provocative. It is reminiscent of another similar observation, shared this time by Roland Barthes at the occasion of the Inaugural Lecture he delivered at the Collège de France on January 7, 1977: "But language—the performance of a language system—is neither reactionary nor progressive; it is quite simply fascist; for fascism does not prevent speech, it compels speech" (1979, p. 5). Barthes's observation offers yet another angle from which fascism should appear especially interesting for communication and media scholars.

30 This is Werner Jaeger's well-known conception of the dual life in archaic Greece: "Now, every citizen belongs to two orders of existence; and there is a sharp distinction in his life between what is his own (ἴδιον) and what is communal (κοινόν). Man is not only 'idiotic,' he is also 'politic.' As well as his ability in his own profession or trade, he has his share of the universal ability of the citizen, πολιτικὴ ἀρετή, by which he is fitted to co-operate and sympathize with the rest of the citizens in the life of the polis." (1945, p. 111).

the 'normal' organization of our lived relations" (1997, p. x). Far from being confined to historical research in some specialized corner of academia, it manifests itself in all corners of our daily lives, informing the experience we have living with one another.[31] As such it does not concern the few, but the many: populations, crowds, masses, have all been and still are concerned with fascism (Jonsson, 2013).[32] It has been and still is intimately linked with some forms of society and community.[33] Today, it is associated with the rise of right-wing extremism, radical nationalism, xenophobia, and violence on most continents.[34] Researchers have long been studying how the Internet is being used to spread neo-Nazi and far-right ideologies (Back, Keith, and Solomos, 1996; Thiesmeyer, 1999; Burris, Smith, and Strahm, 2000; Copsey, 2003; Atton, 2006; Caiani and Parenti, 2009;

---

31 Sadly, I wrote this chapter during the events and aftermath of the Charlottesville, NC, Unite the Right rally, when various far-right groups clashed with counter-protesters, leaving one dead and many injured. While the U.S. President was calling for unity ("Lets come together as one!" [sic]), the far-right protestors were chanting "one people, one nation" (Wang, 2017; Scherer, 2017). At the time of writing, the normalization of fascism was not a matter of theoretical discussion: for many in the United States, it felt like an impending if not immediate threat.

32 The growth of cities that accompanied the industrial revolution raised concerns about the psychology of the crowd that led to well-known studies. Some of those studies became entangled in the development of fascism itself (Le Bon, 1896; Tarde, 1962), while others explicitly targeted it (Bataille, 1979; Reich, 1946).

33 It is worth remembering the bond that brings together community and fascism, especially as ideologies (Kitchen, 2008; Pine, 2017). Thomas Kühne has examined the relationship between the desire for a communal belonging (*Volksgemeinschaft*) and crime committed in the name of an ethno-national unity under Hitler (2013). Already in 1939, Svend Ranulf made the argument that founders of sociology—including Ferdinand Tönnies and Émile Durkheim—were the true precursors of fascism: "indulgence in glorifications of the *Gemeinschaft* and in deprecation of the *Gesellschaft* is equivalent to a piece of fascist propaganda unsupported by genuine science" (1939, p. 34). In France, the very efforts of the members of the Collège de Sociologie to save their community from fascism raised serious issues (Falasca-Zamponi, 2006). This may help explain why Walter Benjamin was openly critical of their activities and also why, despite Georges Bataille's explicit and active resistance to fascism, Benjamin once told him "At bottom, you're working for fascism!" (Agamben, 1998, p. 113; Lacoue-Labarthe, 2007, p. 66).

34 The relationship between fascism and nationalism cannot be that of a straightforward identification: there are clearly elements of fascism and nationalism that do not overlap. Nonetheless, there are active ultranationalist parties that have been widely and explicitly associated with fascism, such as Golden Dawn, a political party in Greece (registered in 1993, the party holds 17 seats in the Hellenic Parliament at the time of writing).

Eatwell,1996). During the 2016 election campaign in the United States, it was raised as an issue associated with white supremacy and social media under the euphemistic label "alt-right" (Rosenfeld, 2017; Malmgren, 2017; Lyons, 2017; Nagle, 2017). An incident in the early weeks of 2017 illustrates the way fascism, as an issue, pervades mainstream media outlets. At the time, a video of white supremacist Richard B. Spencer being punched became viral. In the days that followed, it spurred a (mostly) online debate about morality and Nazism, with *The New York Times* titling one of its pieces: "Attack on Alt-Right Leader Has Internet Asking: Is It O.K. to Punch a Nazi?" (Stack, 2017). Following the tragic incidents that took place in Charlottesville on August 11–12, 2017, the discussion about the ways the Internet enables right-wing extremists was once more reignited.

This brings us to the second perspective from where it appears relevant to examine the issue of Heidegger's involvement with Nazism and fascism. This perspective is epistemological, and more specifically concerned with communication and media studies as academic fields. As I have already suggested, Heidegger's views on technology represent an obvious point of access. However, there is an even more direct link between the growth of those fields and the history of fascism. This link is not only historical; instead it appears as a continuous issue that runs from the ways far-right ideologies spread on social media today to the role played by mass media in the context of the two world wars in the twentieth century.

Just how important the influence of war and fascism have been to the emergence of both the discipline of communication and the study of media is starting to be more clearly recognized by the development of new historical perspectives in the field (Buxton, 1996; Sproule, 1997; Gary, 1999; Glander, 1999; Wahl-Jorgensen, 2004; Pooley, 2008; Pooley and Park, 2013; Turner, 2013; Babe, 2015; Thibault and Trudel, 2015). Specifically, this new research shows that the study of communication did not emerge "out of nowhere during the 1930s and 1940s," but is intimately linked to collective "anxieties" regarding propaganda and the diffusion of new mass communication technologies between the two world wars (Buxton, 1996; Gary, 1996, 1999). This new historiography explicitly moves beyond both the Manichean history, centred around the mythical "hypodermic model" (Sproule, 1989; Lubken, 2008; Thibault, 2016), and the "founding fathers" narrative promoted by Wilbur Schramm and others (1963, p. 116; Rogers, 1994; for a critical assessment see Pooley, 2008; Babe, 2015, pp. 99–104). Instead, it relies on archival investigation to provide a more nuanced history concerning the impact of various wars (including the Cold War) and propaganda on the birth, shaping, and further development of mass communication research, especially in the United States.

The study of this impact goes beyond explaining how Paul Lazarsfeld—and indeed many European scholars, including some the principal figures of the Frankfurt School—fled Europe to escape the rise of fascism, causing what some have dubbed a "transnational flow of ideas" (Löblich and Averbeck-Lietz, 2015 pp. 25–45; see also Sills, 1979, pp. 411–427).[35] It also goes beyond the story of single historical figures, such as Guglielmo Marconi, who joined the Italian fascist party in 1923, before becoming a member of the Fascist Grand Council in 1930 (Raboy, 2016, pp. 549–576). Rather, this examination acknowledges how the birth of fascism, in between the two world wars, raised wide-ranging concerns about the use and effects of mass communication technologies in democratic societies, as "it caused people to take seriously the issues surrounding the growth of propaganda and mass communication" (Glander, 1999, p. 15). This anxiety stems from the intersection of the rise of mass society, developments of social sciences, and mutations in modes of government (Gary, 1992). As Fred Turner explains in *The Democratic Surround*, "[w]hen they gazed across the Atlantic to Hitler's Germany, and, to a lesser extent, Stalin's Soviet Union and Mussolini's Italy, American journalists and social scientists saw their long-standing anxieties about the power of mass media harden into a specific fear that newspapers, radio, and film were engines of fascist socialization" (2013, p. 16).

Hence, in his own effort to revisit the traditional historiography of communication and media studies, Brett Gary has underlined the ambivalent function for communication studies of this unique historical setting, at once perceived as an opportunity and a threat. "The contradictory imperatives of modern liberalism," he writes, "simultaneous commitment to and fear of the expansion of the modern state, with its information and opinion control apparatus—pervaded the debates of the first generation of communication researchers" (1996, p. 124). Indeed, many were concerned not only with how to prevent the enemies of democracy from using this power against Americans, but also with how to develop beneficial applications without falling prey to its dark power. As it is well known now, those concerns were serious enough to fuel new initiatives in research, sponsored and supported by government agencies and private foundations. Among those private foundations, the new historiography shows just how crucial a role the Rockefeller Foundation came to play, especially to the initial launch of mass

---

35 Everett Rogers put it the most bluntly: "Two of Hitler's direct contributions to American communication science were Kurt Lewin and Paul F. Lazarsfeld" (1986, p. 101).

communication research. It did so by funding the Communication Seminar (also known as the Communication Group). As Gary states, "the evolution of the emerging discipline's first research model was ineluctably tied to its historical moment. Its history cannot be separated—intellectually, institutionally, or epistemologically—from the impending crisis of World War II" (1999, p. 88).

To emphasize the good faith behind the effort to find useful applications to mass communication, Gary coins the expression "prophylaxis propaganda" (1999, pp. 89, 102, 125). However, as he also clearly shows, this concerted effort cannot obfuscate the fact that despite good faith, or because of it, moving this research effort "in the direction of national security" also represented a risk. As one of the Rockefeller Foundation officers wrote at the time, "[t]here is always a danger that if emergency mechanisms are not recognized as such, that they become permanent" (1999, p. 102). Other officers of the foundation were more explicit, arguing that those research efforts resembled "the methods by which democracy has been destroyed" (Gary, 1996, pp. 139–140). Commenting on a report produced by the foundation titled "Research in Mass Communications," some officers explicitly called on what they perceived as the "fascistic tendencies" embedded in it (1999, p. 104). Historian of communication and media studies Jefferson Pooley argues those risks were not entirely avoided as "emergency effort became routinized, through inertia and the subsequent cold war context, into the national security state" (2008, p. 63, n. 46).

Thus the legacy of fascism—as a threat to democracy and a shaping force—informs the fields of communication and media studies up to this day. As "big data" and surveillance studies are gaining more momentum, what Gary wrote more than twenty years ago has not lost any of its relevance: the difficult birth of the field "linked the emergence of mass communication research as a scholarly field with the growth of the surveillance apparatus of the modern national security state" (1996, p. 123). In other words, today's familiar debates about the impact of the Internet and social media on democracies inherit—without simply duplicating it—from a tortured past. In more than one way, Heidegger's work and political commitments belong to this long-standing issue because they are concerned with the emergence of new communication technologies (among other technological developments) and as they are, at least partially, entangled in the ideology of fascism. Although the argument cannot be fully developed here, they also belong to it as his philosophy can be viewed as centrally concerned—in a problematic way, as should be clear by now—with contemporary modes or ways of co-belonging or coexistence.

With this background, we can now turn to the final part of the argument. Here, I want to show how the epistemological and political issues we have examined so far expose the crucial importance for an ethical decision. This decision is not about Heidegger, and whether to read his work or not, or whether to engage with his ideas or not. To understand this, ethics must be distinguished from the sphere of morality. This distinction will serve two purposes. First, it will underline how this decision is not about settling on a position: it is not an end-point, but a process. This certainly is not to say that we should be hesitant about fascism and Nazism; quite the contrary. The risk is such that it should be constantly reassessed. We must be careful not to think we can come to a decision once and for all, and forget about it, or get used to it. We must continuously and relentlessly come to a decision, without falling prey to the temptation of believing that the case is closed. Such a decision allows us to maintain our engagement with the political issues identified above, and hence ourselves. This decision, as a process, opens ourselves to one another. What is thus being held is not so much a given set of values, but the opening itself, as the possibility for "us" to exist. Since the issues identified above concern "us," the very conditions of our co-belonging, such a decision should indeed be concerned with our ways of coexisting. Second, I will show how such an understanding of ethics relates to space: the opening where we "take place." In such a spatial configuration, the ethical decision names the conditions of a milieu of existence: it becomes a process of mediation. This idiosyncratic understanding of ethics brings it in line with the study of medium and media.

3 Ethics as mediation

When it comes to "ethics," the general meaning of the term has come in recent times to be conflated or confused with morals. This conflation has its reasons. Ethics refers to the Greek ἦθος (hereafter transliterated as *ēthos*), meaning character.[36] To some degree, it is thus equivalent to the Latin *mores* which gives us

---

36 In his *Nicomachean Ethics,* Aristotle explains how ἦθος "comes into being as a consequence of ἔθος, on account of which it even gets its name by a small inflection from ἔθος" (*Nic. Eth.* 1103a.14). For Aristotle, ἔθος—different from ἦθος only by the first accented letter—means "habit." Hence, *ēthos* and ethics derive from or constitute a modification of habit (Woerther, 2007, p. 144, n. 33). In his translation, H. Rackham similarly observed in a note, "It is probable that ἔθος, 'habit' and ἦθος, 'character' (whence 'ethical', moral) are kindred words" (in Aristotle, Nicomachean, 1934, p. 70). In a newer translation, Joe Sachs further remarked, "[h]ow the condition meant by character derives from habit is more complex" (in *Aristotle, Nicomachean*, 2002, p. 22). The details of the relationship between the two words—ἔθος and ἦθος—is being partly discussed by Aristotle in the subsequent section of his Ethics. In contemporary

"morals" (also *mœurs* in French).[37] Nonetheless, some twentieth-century authors have made a strong argument to distinguish between the two terms. In her striking introduction to *The Life of the Mind*, Hannah Arendt already distinguishes between rules of conduct and conduct, "the Latin word [*mores*] being associated with rules of behavior, whereas the Greek word [*ēthos*] is derived from habitat, like our 'habits'" (1978 p. 5). Michel Foucault develops a similar line of reasoning in the third part of his Introduction to *The Use of Pleasure*, the second volume of his inquiry, *The History of Sexuality*. He unfolds the many differences between moral codes and the "ethical subject," arguing that "a rule of conduct is one thing; the conduct that may be measured by this rule is another" (1990, p. 26).[38] Paul Ricœur similarly underlines the authoritative nature of "moral" while examining the relationship between "ethics and morality." He proposes his own differentiation, where he reserves "the term 'ethics' for the aim of an accomplished life and the term 'morality' for the articulation of this aim in norms characterized at once by the claim to universality and by an effect of constraint" (1992, p. 170). Jacques Rancière also makes a distinction between ethics and morality, using another point of differentiation: "[b]efore recalling law, morality or value, ethos indicates the abode [*séjour*]. Further, it indicates the way of being which corresponds to this abode, the way of feeling and thinking which belongs to whoever occupies any given place" (2006, p. 5). For the issues at hand, it is specifically this spatial aspect of ethics, also hinted at by Arendt, that we shall employ. A few brief observations will suffice, while keeping in mind they do not in any way exhaust the discussion about this richly complex topic.

What is most important to the present argument is the spatial qualities associated with earlier uses of ēthos (especially in its plural form, ἤθεα, or *ēthea*). Indeed, before it came to mean "character," *ēthos* first meant "an accustomed

times, this discussion has been reopened mainly by scholars interested in Aristotle's treatment of rhetoric. Further discussions about how the two orthographies could be related are found in Petit (1999), Frobish (2003), and Woerther (2005, 2007). For thorough discussions of the relationship between habituation, habit, and character, see Vergnières (1995) and Lockwood (2013). For a good overview of previous effort and examination of the relationship between the two Greek words and its implication for rhetoric, see Miller (1974).

37 See, for example, Sidgwick (1988, p. 11) and Dewey (1932, p. 3).

38 See also his 1984 interview, "The Ethics of the Concern for Self as a Practice of Freedom," where he further develops the concept of ēthos as it was understood in ancient Greece (1997, pp. 281–301).

seat: hence, in pl., haunts or abodes of animals" (Liddell and Scott, 1901, p. 644).[39] Heidegger points to this relation in his 1946 Letter on "Humanism": "ἦθος means abode, dwelling place" (1998a, p. 269).[40] In 1984, Charles Chamberlain offered one of the first detailed, although concise, overviews of the spatial meaning of *ēthos* in its plural forms. He observes that if *ēthos* can be understood to mean "character" for most writers after the fifth century (including Aristotle), such a translation hardly makes sense for earlier writers (1984, p. 97). In his argument, he insists on the spatial dimension of the plural *ēthea* in early sixth and fifth century BC writers, such as Homer, Hesiod, Theognis, Herodotus, Hippocrates, and Thucydides. He suggests the word *ēthea* named, for those earlier writers, "an arena or range in which the animal naturally belongs" and, as such, how it was then associated with "the places where animals are usually found" and "animal haunts" (1984, p. 97). Extending its use to humans, the term *ēthos* "refers to the range or arena where someone is most truly at home" as well as to "the arena in which people and animals move" (1984, p. 99; see also Woerther, 2007, p. 34). In a more recent and much more thorough examination of the meaning of ἦθος in Aristotle, Frédérique Woerther offers additional precision. Although she argues that the spatial meaning does not belong to the "semic core" of ἤθεα, she acknowledges it is an important "contextual seme" (2007, pp. 22–42, 300; my translation).

By themselves, these few observations do not stand as a demonstration, nor do they follow Aristotle's understanding of ethics.[41] They nonetheless reveal

---

39 Similar definitions are found in French etymological dictionaries as well (Bailly, 1935, p. 894; Chantraine, 1968, pp. 407–408). In Boisacq, the article for ἦθος references back to the article for ἔθος, where the spatial meaning is nonetheless listed among the meanings of the term (1916, p. 218). In a more recent account of the etymology of the words, the articulation of the slight difference between ἔθος and ἦθος is also addressed (Beekes, 2010, p. 511). At the time of writing, Woerther's remains the most thorough philological examination (2005, 2007).

40 He does so in a discussion about fragment DK B119 from Heraclitus: "ἦθος ἀνθρώπῳ δαίμων" ("human's ēthos is his daimon"). Although it cannot be discussed here, the passage is important for the issues at hand, as it is prompted by a remark shared by Jean Beaufret regarding the relationship between ontology and ethics. Heidegger's comments take the form of an answer to a question he remembers being asked: "When are you going to write an ethics?" (1998, p. 268).

41 Other paths allow us to relate the space-shaping process—mediation—to ethics. For example, keeping with Plato and Aristotle, it would be worth exploring the relationship between μέθεξις (participation) and μεταξύ (between, amongst, amid), especially given the proximity of *ēthos* and *hexis* (Gadamer, 2000; Nancy, 2007; Alloa, 2009). This is not exclusive to Western philosophy either, as shown in the work of Japanese philosopher

a perspective where ethics is cast as a constitutive horizon for media studies. Indeed, they allow us to sketch the outlines of a perception of ethical decisions as a process of mediation. Ethics can be understood as mediation if the spatial meaning of the word medium is reinstated. When it is, mediation names a process of conditioning and transformation: not only of character, but also of a milieu. In this first part of reconceptualization, mediation becomes the process through which a specific place is made familiar by habituation, and where characters are eventually shaped.

The spatial context associated with such an understanding of ethics does not refer to space in any abstract way. It points to places as they are constantly transformed, conditioned, and accustomed by habits. Conversely, those modes of existence are not random behavior, accidental action, or a matter of fixed repetition. Habits are at once plastic and resilient. If habits change, the accustomed place will not be the same; if the place changes, the habits will likewise transform. Such a perspective runs contrary to the idea that a given milieu has the power to determine unilaterally the character of individuals, societies, or populations dwelling there. This has important consequences for media studies, as it shows that mediation is incompatible both with the idea of media as mere containers or conduits, and with the idea that a container unilaterally conditions its content.[42]

Tetsuro Watsuji regarding ethics (1996; see especially his discussion of the etymology of *ningen*, the Japanese word for "human being").

42 In another context, this would require a discussion about Aristotle's hylomorphic scheme. Instead, it will suffice to point to the long-lasting idea that a milieu of existence determines a character. Such a conception can be found in a wide variety of authors from ancient Greece through the medieval period, all the way to early modernity: Herodotus, Hippocrates, Ibn Khaldun, Herder, and Taine all supported this view. For a general "outline of the history of the idea of milieu," see Koller (1918). Two further observations are worth noting. Mediation as ethics, as it is being discussed here, is thus incompatible with the idea that a specific character could be grounded in a specific place once and for all. Ideas that seek to assign an essential identity (often ethnical) to a geographical location are always at risk of devolving into dangerous ideologies. This was the case with Nazi ideology as it championed the slogan "*Blut und Boden.*" The exact implication of this slogan for Heidegger's philosophy is outside the scope of this chapter and has already received a significant amount of attention (see, for example, Harries, 1976; Malpas, 2006, pp. 17–27; Bernasconi, 2010). Finally, it should be clear that such a processual mediation does not coincide with Kittler's often-quoted idea that "media determine our situation" (1999, p. xxxix). This is not to say, however, that such an idea is incompatible with a treatment of technology; quite the contrary. It takes the issue of technics seriously as a condition—not an instrument—of existence, as Nancy once argued, "existing is technological through and through" (2003, p. 24).

Furthermore, it should be clear now that such ethics, conceived as a continuous process of mediation, of space conditioning, is not reducible to a given set of moral rules, values, or norms that would be external to contextualized and ever-changing ways of life. Moral codes can claim an abstracted nature indifferent to the contingencies of daily existence and the passing of time. Ethics, in the sense discussed here, cannot. Rather, such an understanding of ethics points to the fact that what is ultimately at stake are precisely those modes or ways of existence or, more aptly, coexistence. When both the ways of life and the milieu where they take place are related to the point of inextricability, ethics is not and cannot be the concern of a single individual. Ethics always names shared characters or dispositions, for there are no such things in isolation. At the very least, a character always marks a relation, a "between," a "with." It is never an endpoint, but always an ongoing process of exchange: hence, mediation. In this light, abstract ethics make no sense: they are always actualized or enacted in coexistence as a shared praxis (although by no means necessarily harmonious). They always manifest as a specific context, a given situation: indeed, a site in the making. Hence, mediation as ethics is also about the shaping and conditioning of the milieu we are in[43]: not just the space between us, but the milieu opens by the fact that "we" happen, "we" take place.

It is worth noting the development of digital technologies and the rise of environmental and ecological concerns—both linked to the intensification of globalization processes—have encouraged the exploration of a wider understanding of the notion of media, including ways that are concerned with the design of space. This exploration further extends, and sometimes questions, the traditional metaphors of media as technological instruments, means, or containers. Hence, for example, David Morley's recent plea for a "non-media-centric" understanding of media (2009). Morley urges researchers "to transcend

---

43 The difference between *milieu* as a centre and *milieu* as an intermediary field has been examined by Georges Canguilhem in his book *The Knowledge of Life*. In a chapter titled, "The Living and his Milieu," Canguilhem links the discovery of our medial condition to the process through which we were forced to abandon the idea that human beings occupy an exceptional position in the universe. The decentering, as he explains, comes with the realization that "[man] is no longer in the middle [*milieu*] of the world, but *he is a milieu*" (2008, p. 117; emphasis in the original). This discussion on *milieu* was picked up by Michel Serres in his major doctoral thesis on Leibniz (1968, pp. 673–683), and more recently by Pierre Macherey (2017). For more discussion on the history and evolution of the concept of "milieu," see Chien (2007), Gandolfo (2008), and Feuerhahn (2009).

their narrowly media-centric focus on the technologies for the transmission of information" and to embrace a broader frame of concern (2009, p. 116). This is hardly the first nor only effort by media scholars to claim back the rich conceptual pedigree associated with the notion of "medium." Others, unaffiliated or marginally affiliated with media studies have expressed an interest in the notion for more than a century.[44]

I have established how the ethical perspective I outlined above does not define "media" in the narrowly instrumental and technical sense it has acquired during the first half of the twentieth century. Instead, it relies on the spatial meaning of the word medium, perceiving it as a dynamic milieu. As such, it is concerned with the milieu we are becoming: the various, ever-changing spaces we share, and those which keep us apart. It is not an abstracted space, but each time provides the places of our common disposition and mutual customs. It is not the world we live in, as subjects in an objectified container, but the world we are. We are not this world once and for all, but instead continually decide to open ourselves toward one another. It is through this opening that "we" take place at once as parts and whole, singular and plural (Nancy, 2000).[45] What does it mean regarding the decision to engage Heidegger's work? In my conclusion, I suggest that such a decision is not only a matter of understanding the philosophical argument of Heidegger, but also an ethical commitment. The decision can be seen as ethical, since it concerns the conditioning, styling, and modification of the milieu we are to ourselves.

4 A Decisive mediation

We have seen how mass media of communication—along with mass media research itself—shares a history with the two world wars of the twentieth century, and with fascism. As we have also seen, some argue that this history is

---

44 Theoretical interest in the notion of medium encompasses a wide variety of approaches, including Fritz Heider's epistemology of "thing and medium" (1925), Robert E. Park's concept of the city (1925), the idea of "medium specificity" discussed by art theorists (Greenberg, 1993), the emergence of various media ecologies (Fuller, 2005), the city as medium in German theory (Kittler and Griffin, 1996), man as medium (Oosterling, 2000), intermediality, *médiologie* (Debray, 2000), *médiance* (Berque, 1990), the recent emergence of *Medienphilosophie* (Mersch, 2016; Krämer, 2015), medium as a concept of sociology (Tosini, 2006), media as living circumstances (Canguilhem, 2008; Sloterdijk, 2009), and medium as ambiance (Spitzer, 1942; Somaini, 2016).

45 Jean-Luc Nancy's essay "Being Singular Plural" is an explicit attempt to move beyond Heidegger's existential analytic, toward a co-existential analytic (2000).

ambiguous, at least to one extent. On the one hand, new technologies of mass communication were thought at the time to represent a threat to democracy. On the other hand, efforts were made to find ways to use them as a safeguard of democracy.

The argument for this ambiguity—at once both threat and opportunity—is qualitatively different from the oppositional perspective that works actively to resolve the ambiguity: threat or opportunity, one or the other. This oppositional perspective is an old and enduring trope, opposing worried concerns against enthusiastic discourses, pitting pessimist views against optimistic ones, with a regularity closely matching the endless cycle of technological innovations.[46] Today it is found in debates about what virtual reality might eventually do to social relations, or what the Internet is currently doing to our brain; just as not so long ago, it was fueled by what television was said to be doing to democracy. This argument, it is possible to demonstrate, goes back to Plato's criticism of writing in *Phaedrus*, as every student of communication and media studies is likely told.

The alternative to this never-ending feud takes the form of an argument that opens the false dichotomy to ambiguity as the defining trait of technology (see, for example, Esposito, 1995). In turn, this alternative suggests a concept of media that is neither one definition nor another, neither good nor bad, but fundamentally and decisively mediocre, vague, and inauthentic (Oosterling, 2007; Mersch, 2013; Siegert, 2015).[47] Mediation as a process of creating spaces, or openings, is inherently in-definite. The fuzziness I discussed in the first section can be treated not as a problem, but as a feature. It is does not get in the way when we try to understand media for what they really are: instead it is constitutive of them, defining how they are. This mediation adequately answers for the political ambiguity historically tied to technological media. At this point, in this opening, epistemology meets politics.

---

46 For an analysis of how this opposition played out within the Frankfurt School's assessment of mass media, see Negt and Adelson's rigorous overview (1978).

47 There is a lot more to say about this, from Charles S. Peirce's remarks about the vagueness of communication, to Heidegger's observation about the averageness (*Durchschnittlichkeit*) of language. Here, it will suffice, if only suggestively, to recall Wittgenstein's discussion about a question he asked himself in his *Philosophical Investigations*: "But is a blurred concept a concept at all?" (1963, p. 34). Given the opportunity, it would be possible to show how this structural and functional ambiguity is also at work in the concept of communication at least since the Pythagoreans' understanding of what "common" ("κοινόν") meant.

This way of presenting the problems with media and Heidegger blurs the traditional distinction between the object of knowledge and the knowing subject. We are, for ourselves, the issue we must address.[48] Media, Heidegger, fascism: those topics concern us to the extent that they concern the actual conditions of our various political associations and political dissociation. Given the current global situation, this issue is not merely of theoretical or historical interest. Instead it is of the utmost ethical importance for us, here and now. It certainly does not follow that communication and media scholars are somehow required to concern themselves with Heidegger's work. However, it does follow that Heidegger's work and his political commitments are constitutively concerned with and by an ethical decision.

Before being ethical, such a decision certainly is a matter of understanding the ideas themselves. It demands that we pay attention to the words he coined and the many concepts he developed. It likely requires a knowledge of the different ways in which his texts were edited and published. The transformations his arguments underwent during the span of his life should also be examined and weighed to identify consistencies and contradictions. This interpretative rigour is a necessary hermeneutical commitment; it is by itself an important and serious task. Attentiveness is just as crucial for non-specialists—among whom I must place myself—who do not carry Heidegger's work at the heart of their main research effort. Often, as a result, only a few essays are studied, if thoroughly, but as such they remain abstracted from a much larger body of work, and sometimes also from the larger historical context in which they were produced.

---

48 "We are": this is an ontological proposition, but from an ontology quite distinct from the "first philosophy" laid out by Aristotle, and more akin to Heidegger's treatment of the question of being. It is the case because its logic is one where the essential is found in the existentiell or, to put it in other words, where the essence of being is entirely in the modes of existence. It is akin to Heidegger, but also different. If it were developed, it would put an emphasis on mediality, whereas Heidegger's crucial observations on *Mitsein* in *Being and Time* were and remain in the shadow of his sustained examination of *Dasein*. This emphasis on mediality would further mean a distancing from anthropocentric views, and a renewed attention to space (as place, milieu, site, topos, etc.). For all those reasons, it must be noted that existing propositions to the effect "that media are our situation," that "we are media and of media," or that "[m]edia are our infrastructures of being" have yet to fully engage what this means in the long history pertaining to the question of being (Mitchell and Hansen, 2010, p. xxii; Parikka, 2010, p. xxvii; Peters, 2015, p. 15). Developments in that direction can be found in Peter Sloterdijk's treatment of media as it appears in various works, but most centrally in his "Spheres" trilogy (2011, 2014, 2016).

Additionally, when knowledge of German is missing, those texts are accessed through translations.[49] This, I infer, is likely the situation many media scholars find themselves in when they are working with, against, and beyond Heidegger's ideas. However, given the political problems I discussed above, the decision that is at stake here cannot be reduced or limited to hermeneutics alone. Instead, this decision is also, to a large extent, an ethical matter.

Another way to make the argument is to suggest that hermeneutics itself—the issue of understanding Heidegger's ideas—does not float above political concerns, nor does it take place outside of history, from some privileged position. Instead, the hermeneutical concern is at once an ethical one. Although they do not subscribe to the spatial understanding of ethics developed here, some authors have highlighted how it relates to hermeneutics. Pinning an ethics of interpretation against a Habermasian ethics of communication, Vattimo observed in *The Transparent Society* "that hermeneutics is distinctly inclined toward ethics" (1992, p. 105). More recently, Dennis J. Schmidt's understanding of "hermeneutics as original ethics" takes on ethical concerns in the work of Heidegger and finds crucial development in Hans-Georg Gadamer's work (2008, pp. 35–47). He argues that Gadamer's hermeneutics is fundamentally concerned with thinking through what Heidegger called "originary ethics." Indeed, while it remains a subject of debate, a significant number of commentators have called attention to Heidegger's discussion about ethics in his work, prior to and beyond the treatment given in his 1946 *Letter on Humanism*.[50]

This comes as a surprise when "ethics" is conflated with "moral," or when Heidegger's concern with the "question of being" is associated with an ethereal abstraction. Indeed, it would be hard to try to reconcile Heidegger's political commitments and personal outlook with moral guidance. Additionally, if

---

49 Elsewhere, it would be possible to argue that the knowledge of German is not sufficient by itself to guarantee a rigorous—certainly not a more authentic—access to the text. In other words, one can be fluent in German and yet still stumble amid Heidegger's unfamiliar ideas. This observation pertaining to the opacity of language is a point where some of Heidegger's ideas meet with issues of concern in communication and media studies.

50 For indicative purposes only, as a more exhaustive literature review would require its own analysis, see Caputo (1971), Bernstein (1992, pp. 79–141), Vogel (1994), Hodge (1995), Olafson (1998), Nancy (1999), Paley (2000), Lewis (2005), Brook (2009), Esposito (2010, pp. 86–111), Webb (2011), Gak (2015), Artemenko (2016), and Babich (2016a). For a more thorough bibliography of texts published between 1979 and 1999 that deal with the questions of ethics and co-existence in Heidegger, see Annalisa Caputo's exhaustive bibliography (2001, pp. 142–147).

ontology is understood as being strictly concerned with what is essential, then understandably it has nothing to do with contingencies of history or politics, let alone ethics. This is not, however, how Heidegger understood ontology. If the question of being (*Seinsfrage*) is considered from a practical perspective, then the considerations of ethics in Heidegger appear less surprising. In other words, the ethical dimension of Heidegger's work makes sense if "being" or, more to the point for the discussion at hand, "being-with" (*Mitsein*) is understood as the concrete issue that it is. Hence my proposition to understand ethics from a spatial perspective, as a process of mediation. An interpretation of Heidegger's work must not only put it in context, but also must acknowledge its situation: the specific ways in which the process of interpretation itself takes place, being opened by a shared concern and, in turn, opening the possibility for collective care. This decisive mediation concerns our modes of existence, how we are together in our daily existence, the way we live, our customs, and indeed our ethics. It is worth noting how this ethical perspective regarding coexistence—while not necessarily cast in a spatial perspective— is not restricted to Heidegger alone. It belongs to a twentieth-century tradition—often influenced by and critical of Heidegger's work, it is true—that has attempted to explore the relationship between ethics and "first philosophy" or ontology (Lévinas, 1989; Nancy, 1999; Desmond, 2001; Taylor, 2003; Esposito, 2010, pp. 86–111, Przylebski, 2017, pp. 43–62).

The ethical issue at hand in the interpretation of Heidegger's work is consequently not entirely foreign to an ethical issue that is also of concern for Heidegger. This relationship certainly is not one of identity, as "our" attitude toward fascism and anti-Semitism precisely does not, and must not, coincide with Heidegger's attitude. The relation might be described as a rupture, dissonance, or dislocation. It is nonetheless a fracture we share, one that is still constitutive to some extent of how we are toward one another. Hence the ethical decision to think with and beyond him,[51] using the knowledge of the texts we can access, and in ignorance of the material that remains to be published.[52] This decision must be constantly

---

51 Others have argued for the necessity to pit Heidegger against himself. This was Jürgen Habermas's proposition in the 1953 review I mentioned in note 18. This position is sustained in the foreword Habermas wrote for the German edition of Victor Farías's book, *Heidegger and Nazism* (1989). Jeff Malpas makes a similar proposition when he suggests his project be read "as setting Heidegger against Heidegger" (2016, p. 20, emphasis in the original).

52 As of 2017, of the 102 volumes of Heidegger's *Gesamtausgabe*, eleven volumes have not yet been published by Vittorio Klostermann (Frankfurt am Main). Some of the published volumes have yet to be translated into English.

reassessed and reopened. As such, it asks for a sustained and insistent attentiveness. The decision is endlessly transitive and must be maintained as a possibility, an opening against all definitive closure or bans.[53] The decision is a situation we create and shape for and through the ways we relate.

This, at least, is one way to conceive of engaging with the issues presented by Heidegger and his work. This engagement, while being concerned with technological artifacts and systems, is at once epistemological and political. In such a light, it casts ethics as a decisive mediation and is, for this reason, of the utmost relevance for the study of media.

Bibliography

Adorno, Theodor W., and Max Horkheimer. "Research Project on Anti-Semitism." *Studies in Philosophy and Social Science*, Vol. 9, No. 1 (1941), pp. 124–143.

Adorno, Theodor W. *The Jargon of Authenticity.* Trans. Knut Tarnowski and Frederic Will. Evanston: Northwestern University Press, 1973.

Agamben, Giorgio. *Homo Sacer: Sovereign Power and Bare Life.* Trans. Daniel Heller-Roazen. Stanford: Stanford University Press, 1998.

Agamben, Giorgio. *La puissance de la pensée essais et conférences.* Trans. Joël Gayraud and Martin Rueff. Paris: Payot & Rivages, 2006.

Alloa, Emmanuel. "*Metaxu.* Figures de la médialité chez Aristote." *Revue de métaphysique et de morale*, No. 62 (2009), pp. 247–262.

Anders, Guenther (Stern). "On the Pseudo-Concreteness of Heidegger's Philosophy." *Philosophy and Phenomenological Research*, Vol. 8, No. 3 (1948), pp. 337–371.

Arendt, Hannah. *The Life of the Mind.* New York: Harcourt, 1978.

Aristotle. *Nicomachean Ethics.* Trans. by H. Rackham. Cambridge: Harvard University Press, 1934.

Aristotle, *Aristotle's Nicomachean Ethics: Translation, Glossary, and Introductory Essay.* Trans. Joe Sachs. Newburyport: Focus Publishing/R. Pullins Company, 2002.

---

53 A similar argument is made by Tracy B. Strong in the Introduction to his *Politics without Vision* (2012, pp. 1–5). It is also raised by Peter E. Gordon in his review of Emmanuel Faye's *Heidegger: The Introduction of Nazism into Philosophy in Light of the Unpublished Seminars of 1933–1935* (2010). For an in-depth discussion about the conception of decision as "opening," specifically in the context of reading Heidegger, see Jean-Luc Nancy's essay "The Decision of Existence" (1993).

Artemenko, Natalia A. "The 'Ethical' Dimension of Heidegger's Philosophy: Consideration of Ethics in Its Original Source." *Russian Studies in Philosophy*, Vol. 54, No. 1 (2016), pp. 62–75.

Atton, Chris. "Far-Right Media on the Internet: Culture, Discourse and Power." *New Media & Society*, Vol. 8, No. 4 (August 1, 2006), pp. 573–587.

Babe, Robert E. *Wilbur Schramm and Noam Chomsky Meet Harold Innis: Media, Power, and Democracy*. Lanham: Lexington Books, 2015.

Babich, Babette. "The Essence of Questioning After Technology: Τεχνή as Constraint and the Saving Power." *Journal of the British Society for Phenomenology*, Vol. 30, No. 1 (1999), pp. 106–125.

Babich, Babette. "O, Superman! Or Being Towards Transhumanism: Martin Heidegger, Günther Anders, and Media Aesthetics." *Divinatio*, Vol. 36 (2013), pp. 41–99.

Babich, Babette. "Constellating Technology: Heidegger's *Die Gefahr/The Danger*." In: *The Multidimensionality of Hermeneutic Phenomenology*, eds. Babette Babich and Dimitri Ginev. New York: Springer, 2014, pp. 153–182.

Babich, Babette. "Heidegger's Black Night: The Nachlass and Its Wirkungsgeschichte." In: *Reading Heidegger's Black Notebooks 1931–1941*, eds. Ingo Farin and Jeff Malpas. Cambridge, MA: MIT Press, 2016a, pp. 45–57.

Babich, Babette. *Un politique brisé: le souci d'autrui, l'humanisme et les Juifs chez Heidegger*. Paris: Harmathèque, 2016b.

Babich, Babette. "Heidegger on Technology and Gelassenheit: Wabi-Sabi and the Art of Verfallenheit." *AI & Society*, Vol. 32, No. 2 (2017), pp. 157–166.

Back, Les, Michael Keith, and John Solomos. "Technology, Race and Neo-fascism in a Digital Age: The New Modalities of Racist Culture." *Patterns of Prejudice*, Vol. 30, No. 2 (1996), pp. 3–27.

Bailly, Anatole. *Dictionnaire grec-francais*. Paris: Hachette, 1935.

Bataille, Georges. "The Psychological Structure of Fascism." Trans. Carl R. Lovitt. *New German Critique*, No. 16 (1979), pp. 64–87.

Barthes, Roland. "Lecture in Inauguration of the Chair of Literary Semiology, Collège de France, January 7, 1977." Trans. Richard Howard. *October*, Vol. 8, 1979, pp. 3–16.

Bay, Jennifer, and Thomas Rickert. "New Media and the Fourfold." *JAC, A Journal of Rhetoric, Culture, & Politics*, Vol. 28, No. 1/2, 2008, pp. 209–244.

Beekes, Robert Stephen Paul. *Etymological Dictionary of Greek*. Leiden: Brill, 2010.

Bernasconi, Robert. "Race and Earth in Heidegger's Thinking during the Late 1930s." *The Southern Journal of Philosophy*, Vol. 48, No. 1 (2010), pp. 49–66.

Bernstein, Richard J. *The New Constellation: The Ethical-Political Horizons of Modernity/Postmodernity*. Cambridge: MIT Press, 1992.

Berque, Augustin. *Médiance: de milieux en paysages*. Paris: Belin/Reclus, 1990.

Boisacq, Émile. *Dictionnaire étymologique de la langue grecque, étudiée dans ses rapports avec les autres langues indo-européennes*. Paris: Klincksieck, 1916.

Borgmann, Albert, and Carl Mitcham. "The Question of Heidegger and Technology: A Critical Review of the Literature." *Philosophy Today*, Vol. 31, No. 2 (May 1, 1987), pp. 98–99.

Boromisza-Habashi, David. "Which Way Is Forward in Communication Theorizing? An Interview with Robert T. Craig." *Communication Theory*, Vol. 23, No. 4 (2013), pp. 417–432.

Bougnoux, Daniel. *Sciences de l'information et de la communication*. Paris: Larousse, 1993.

Brook, Angus. *The Early Heidegger and Ethics: The Notion of Ethos in Martin Heidegger's Early Career*. Saarbrücken: VDM Verlag, 2009.

Burris, Val, Emery Smith, and Ann Strahm. "White Supremacist Networks on the Internet." *Sociological Focus*, Vol. 33, No. 2 (2000), pp. 215–235.

Buxton, William. "The Emergence of Communications Study: Psychological Warfare or Scientific Thoroughfare?" *Canadian Journal of Communication*, Vol. 21, No. 4 (1996). http://www.cjc-online.ca/index.php/journal/article/view/961 (28 Oct. 2017).

Caiani, Manuela, and Linda Parenti. "The Dark Side of the Web: Italian Right-Wing Extremist Groups and the Internet." *South European Society and Politics*, Vol. 14, No. 3 (2009), pp. 273–294.

Canguilhem, Georges. "The Living and his Milieu." In: *Knowledge of Life*. Eds. Paola Marrati and Todd Meyers. Trans. Stefanos Geroulanos and Daniela Ginsburg. New York: Fordham University Press, 2008, pp. 98-120.

Caputo, John D. "Heidegger's Original Ethics." *New Scholasticism*, Vol. 45, No. 1, 1971, pp. 127–138.

Caputo, Annalisa. *Vent'anni di recezione heideggeriana: (1979–1999); una bibliografia*. Milano: Angeli, 2001.

Carey, James W. *Communication as Culture: Essays on Media and Society*. New York: Routledge, 1989.

Cavell, Stanley. *The World Viewed: Reflections on the Ontology of Film*. New York: Viking, 1971.

Cesare, Donatella Ester Di. *Utopia of Understanding: Between Babel and Auschwitz*. Trans. Niall Keane. Albany: State University of New York Press, 2012.

Cesare, Donatella Ester Di. "Heidegger's Metaphysical Anti-Semitism." In: *Reading Heidegger's Black Notebooks 1931–1941*. Eds. Ingo Farin and Jeff Malpas. Cambridge: MIT Press, 2016, pp. 181-194.

Chantraine, Pierre. *Dictionnaire étymologique de la langue grecque: histoire des mots*. Paris: Klincksieck, 1968.

Chamberlain, Charles. "From Haunts to Character: The Meaning of Ethos and Its Relation to Ethics." *Helios*, Vol. 11, No. 2 (1984), pp. 97–108.

Chien, Jui-Pi. "Umwelt, Milieu(x), and Environment: A Survey of Cross-Cultural Concept Mutations." *Semiotica*, Vol. 2007, No. 167 (2007), pp. 65–89.

Copsey, Nigel. "Extremism on the Net: The Extreme Right and the Value of the Internet." In: *Political Parties and the Internet: Net Gain?* Eds. Rachel K. Gibson, Paul Nixon, and Stephen Ward. New York: Routledge, 2003, pp. 218–233.

Couldry, Nick. *Media Rituals: A Critical Approach*. London: Routledge, 2003.

Cressman, Darryl, and Edward Hamilton. "The Experiential Dimension in Online Learning: Phenomenology, Technology and Breakdowns." In: *Phenomenology and Media: An Anthology of Essays from Glimpse, Publication of the Society for Phenomenology and Media, 1999-2008*, eds. Paul Majkut and Alberto J.L. Carillo Canán. Bucharest: Zeta Books, 2010, pp. 54–82.

Danesi, Marcel. *Dictionary of Media and Communications*. Armonk: M.E. Sharpe, 2009.

Debray, Régis. *Introduction à la médiologie*. Paris: Presses Universitaires de France, 2000.

Derrida, Jacques. *Limited Inc*. Trans. Samuel Weber and Jeffrey Mehlman, Evanston: Northwestern University Press, 1988.

Desmond, William. *Ethics and the Between*. New York: State University of New York Press, 2001.

Dewey, John. *Ethics*. Revised edition. New York: Henry Holt & Company, 1932.

Donsbach, Wolfgang. *The International Encyclopedia of Communication*. Malden: Blackwell, 2008.

Durham, Meenakshi Gigi, and Kellner, Douglas, eds. *Media and Cultural Studies: Keyworks*. Malden: Blackwell, 2006.

Eatwell, Roger. "Surfing the Great White Wave: The Internet, Extremism and the Problem of Control." *Patterns of Prejudice*, Vol. 30, No. 1 (1996), pp. 61–71.

Escudero, Jesús Adrián. "Heidegger's Black Notebooks and the Question of Anti-Semitism." *Gatherings: The Heidegger Circle Annual, Heidegger Circle*, Vol. 5 (2015), pp. 21–49.

Esposito, Roberto. "Donner La Technique." *Revue Du MAUSS*, Vol. 6, No. 2 (1995), pp. 190–206.

Esposito, Roberto. Communitas: The Origin and Destiny of Community. Trans. by Timothy Campbell. Stanford: Stanford University Press, 2010.

Falasca-Zamponi, Simonetta. "A Left Sacred or a Sacred Left? The College de Sociologie, Fascism, and Political Culture in Interwar France." *South Central Review*, Vol. 23, No. 1 (2006), pp. 40–54.

Farías, Víctor. *Heidegger and Nazism*. Eds. Joseph Margolis and Tom Rockmore. Philadelphia: Temple University Press, 1989.

Farin, Ingo, and Jeff Malpas, eds. *Reading Heidegger's Black Notebooks 1931–1941*. Cambridge: MIT Press, 2016.

Faye, Emmanuel. *Heidegger: The Introduction of Nazism into Philosophy in Light of the Unpublished Seminars of 1933–1935*. Trans. by Michael B. Smith. New Haven: Yale University Press, 2011.

Feuerhahn, Wolf. "Du milieu à l'Umwelt : enjeux d'un changement terminologique." *Revue philosophique de la France et de l'étranger* Vol. 134, No. 4 (2009), pp. 419–438.

Floyd, Juliet, and James E. Katz. *Philosophy of Emerging Media: Understanding, Appreciation, Application*. Oxford: Oxford University Press, 2015.

Foucault, Michel. The Use of Pleasure. Trans. by Robert Hurley. *The History of Sexuality*, Vol. 2. New York: Vintage Books, 1990.

Foucault, Michel. Ethics: Subjectivity and Truth. Ed. by Paul Rabinow. Trans. by Robert Hurley et al. *Essential Works of Foucault, 1954–1984*, Vol. 1. New York: New Press, 1997.

Foucault, Michel. *The Essential Works of Michel Foucault, 1954–1984*. Vol. 3, Power. Ed. by James D Faubion. Trans. by Robert Hurley. New York: Penguin Books, 2002.

Fried, Gregory. "The King Is Dead: Heidegger's 'Black Notebooks.'" *Los Angeles Review of Books*, September 13, 2014. Accessed Oct. 28, 2017. https://lareviewofbooks.org/article/king-dead-heideggers-black-notebooks/

Frobish, Todd S. "An Origin of a Theory: A Comparison of Ethos in the Homeric Iliad with that Found in Aristotle's Rhetoric." *Rhetoric Review* Vol. 22, No. 1 (2003), pp. 16–30.

Fry, Tony, ed. *RUA/TV?: Heidegger and the Televisual*. Sydney: Power Publications, 1993.

Fuchs, Christian. "Martin Heidegger's Anti-Semitism: Philosophy of Technology and the Media in the Light of the 'Black Notebooks'. Implications for the Reception of Heidegger in Media and Communication Studies." *tripleC: Communication, Capitalism & Critique. Open Access Journal for a Global Sustainable Information Society* Vol. 13, No. 1 (2015), pp. 55–78.

Fuchs, Christian. *Critical Theory of Communication: New Readings of Lukács, Adorno, Marcuse, Honneth and Habermas in the Age of the Internet*. London: University of Westminster Press, 2016.

Fuchs, Christian. "Günther Anders' Undiscovered Critical Theory of Technology in the Age of Big Data Capitalism." *tripleC: Communication, Capitalism & Critique. Open Access Journal for a Global Sustainable Information Society* Vol. 15, No. 2 (2017), pp. 582–611.

Fuller, Matthew. *Media Ecologies: Materialist Energies in Art and Technoculture*. Cambridge: MIT Press, 2005.

Gadamer, Hans George. "Plato as Portraitist." Trans. by Jamey Findling and Snezhina Gabova. *Continental Philosophy Review* Vol. 33, No. 3 (2000), pp. 245–74.

Gak, Martin. "Heidegger's Ethics and Levinas's Ontology: Phenomenology of Prereflective Normativity." *Levinas Studies* Vol. 9, No. 1 (March 20, 2015), pp. 145–81.

Gandolfo, Gabriel. "Le concept de milieu dans les sciences du vivant." *Noesis*, No. 14 (2008), pp. 237–47.

Garcia, Tristan. *Nous*. Paris: Bernard Grasset, 2016.

Gary, Brett. "*American Liberalism and the Problem of Propaganda: Scholars, Lawyers, and the War on Words, 1919–1945*." Ph.D. diss., University of Pennsylvania, 1992.

Gary, Brett. "Communication Research, the Rockefeller Foundation, and Mobilization for the War on Words, 1938–1944." *Journal of Communication* Vol. 46, No. 3 (1996), pp. 124–48.

Gary, Brett. *The Nervous Liberals: Propaganda Anxieties from World War I to the Cold War*. New York: Columbia University Press, 1999.

Geffroy, Annie, et al. "Le Nous Politique." *Mots* Vol. 10, No. 1 (1985). Accessed Oct. 28, 2017 http://www.persee.fr/issue/mots_0243-6450_1985_num_10_1

Glander, Timothy. *Origins of Mass Communications Research during the American Cold War: Educational Effects and Contemporary Implications*. New York: Routledge, 1999.

Gordon, Peter E. "Review of Heidegger: The Introduction of Nazism into Philosophy in Light of the Unpublished Seminars of 1933–1935, by Emmanuel Faye." *Notre Dame Philosophical Review*, March 12, 2010. Accessed Oct. 30, 2017. http://ndpr.nd.edu/news/heidegger-the-introduction-of-nazism-into-philosophy-in-light-of-the-unpublished-seminars-of-1933-1935/

Greenberg, Clement. "Modernist Painting." In: *The Collected Essays and Criticism; Volume 4: Modernism with a Vengeance, 1957–1969*. Ed. John O'Brian, Chicago: University of Chicago Press, 1993, pp. 85–93.

Griffin, Roger. *The Nature of Fascism*. London: Routledge, 1991.

Gunkel, David J., and Paul A. Taylor. *Heidegger and the Media*. Cambridge: Polity Press, 2014.

Harries, Karsten. "Heidegger as a Political Thinker." *The Review of Metaphysics* Vol. 29, No. 4 (1976), pp. 642–669.

Hartley, John, ed. *Communication, Cultural and Media Studies: The Key Concepts*. London: Routledge, 2011.

Heidegger, Martin. *Being and Time*. Trans. by John Macquarrie and Edward Robinson. Oxford: Blackwell, 1962.

Heidegger, Martin. *The Question Concerning Technology, and Other Essays*. Trans. by William Lovitt. New York: Garland Publichsing, Inc., 1977.

Heidegger, Martin. *Parmenides*. Trans. by André Schuwer and Richard Rojcewicz. Bloomington: Indiana University Press, 1998a.

Heidegger, Martin. *Pathmarks*. Ed. by William McNeill. Trans. by Frank A. Capuzzi. Cambridge: Cambridge University Press, 1998b.

Heidegger, Martin. *Ponderings II–VI: Black Notebooks 1931–1938*. Trans. by Richard Rojcewicz. Bloomington: Indiana University Press, 2016.

Heidegger, Martin. *Ponderings VII–XI: Black Notebooks 1938–1939*. Trans. by Richard Rojcewicz. Bloomington: Indiana University Press, 2017a.

Heidegger, Martin. *Ponderings XII–XV: Black Notebooks 1939–1941*. Trans. by Richard Rojcewicz. Bloomington: Indiana University Press, 2017b.

Heider, Fritz. "Ding Und Medium. [Thing and Medium.]." *Symposium* Vol. 1 (1925), pp. 109–58.

Hodge, Joanna. *Heidegger and Ethics*. New York: Routledge, 1995.

Horn, Eva. "There are no Media." *Grey Room* (2007), pp. 6–13.

Ihde, Don. *Heidegger's Technologies: Postphenomenological Perspectives*. New York: Fordham University Press, 2010.

Jaeger, Werner. *Paideia: The Ideals of Greek Culture*. Vol. 1. Archaic Greece: The Mind of Athens. Trans. by Gilbert Highet. Oxford: Oxford University Press, 1945.

Janicaud, Dominique. *Heidegger in France*. Trans. by François Raffoul and David Pettigrew. Bloomington: Indiana University Press, 2015.

Jones, Paul, and David Holmes. *Key Concepts in Media and Communications*. London: SAGE, 2011.

Jonsson, Stefan. *Crowds and Democracy: The Idea and Image of the Masses from Revolution to Fascism*. New York: Columbia University Press, 2013.

Kember, Sarah, and Joanna Zylinska. *Life after New Media: Mediation as a Vital Process*. Cambridge: MIT Press, 2012.

Kershaw, Ian. *The Nazi Dictatorship: Problems and Perspectives of Interpretation*. London: Edward Arnold, 1993.

Kitchen, Martin. *The Third Reich: Charisma and Community*. Harlow: Pearson Education, 2008.

Kittler, Friedrich A. *Gramophone, Film, Typewriter*. Trans. by Geoffrey Winthrop-Young and Michael Wutz. Stanford: Stanford University Press, 1999.

Kittler, Friedrich A. *Optical Media*. Cambridge: Polity Press, 2010.

Kittler, Friedrich A. *The Truth of the Technological World: Essays on the Genealogy of Presence*. Trans. by Erik Butler. Stanford: Stanford University Press, 2014.

Kittler, Friedrich A., and Matthew Griffin. "The City Is a Medium." *New Literary History* Vol. 27, No. 4 (1996), pp. 717–29.

Kolker, Robert Phillip, ed. *The Oxford Handbook of Film and Media Studies*. Oxford: Oxford University Press, 2008.

Koller, Armin Hajman. *The Theory of Environment*. Menasha: Banta, 1918.

Kolker, Robert. Media Studies: An Introduction. Malden: Blackwell, 2009.

Krämer, Sybille. Medium, Messenger, Transmission: An Approach to Media Philosophy. Trans. Anthony Enns. Amsterdam: Amsterdam University Press, 2015.

Krell, David Farrell. "Heidegger's 'Black Notebooks, 1931–1941.'" *Research in Phenomenology*, Vol. 45, No. 1 (2015), pp. 127–60.

Kühne, Thomas. *Belonging and Genocide: Hitler's Community, 1918–1945*. New Haven: Yale University Press, 2013.

Laclau, Ernesto. *Politics and Ideology in Marxist Theory: Capitalism, Fascism, Populism*. London: NLB, 1977.

Lacoue-Labarthe, Philippe. *Heidegger and the Politics of Poetry*. Trans. by Jeff Fort. Urbana: University of Illinois Press, 2007.

Le Bon, Gustave. *The Crowd: Study of the Popular Mind*. Trans. anonymous. New York: Macmillan Co., 1896.

Lévinas, Emmanuel. "Ethics as First Philosophy." In: *The Levinas Reader*, ed. by Seán Hand, trans. by Seán Hand and Michael Temple. Oxford: Basil Blackwell, 1989, pp. 75–87.

Lévinas, Emmanuel. *Entre Nous: On Thinking-of-the-Other*. Trans. by Michael B Smith and Barbara Harshav. London: Athlone Press, 1998.

Lewis, Michael. *Heidegger and the Place of Ethics*. London: Bloomsbury Academic, 2005.

Liddell, Henry George, and Robert Scott. *A Greek-English Lexicon*. Oxford: Clarendon Press, 1901.

Littlejohn, Stephen W., and Karen A. Foss, ed. *Encyclopedia of Communication Theory*. London: SAGE, 2009.

Löblich, Maria, and Stefanie Averbeck-Lietz. "The Transnational Flow of Ideas and Histoire Croisée with Attention to the Cases of France and Germany." In: *The International History of Communication Study*, ed. by Peter Simonson and David W. Park. New York: Routledge, 2015, pp. 25–46.

Lockwood, Thorton C. "Habituation, Habit, and Character in Aristotle's Nicomachean Ethics." In: *A History of Habit: From Aristotle to Bourdieu*, ed. by Tom Sparrow and Adam Hutchinson. New York: Lexington Books, 2013, pp. 19–36.

Lubken, Deborah. "Remembering the Straw Man: The Travels and Adventures of Hypodermic." In: *The History of Media and Communication Research: Contested Memories*, ed. by David Park and Jefferson Pooley. New York: Peter Lang, 2008, pp. 19–42.

Lyons, Matthew N. et al. *Ctrl-Alt-Delete: An Antifascist Report on the Alternative Right*. Montreal: Kersplebedeb, 2017.

Macé, Marielle, et al. "*Nous*" Critique, no. 841–842 (2017).

Macherey, Pierre. *S'orienter*. Paris: Kimé, 2017.

Malmgren, Evan. "Don't Feed the Trolls." *Dissent* Vol. 64, No. 2 (2017), pp. 9–12.

Malpas, Jeff. *Heidegger's Topology: Being, Place, World*. Cambridge: MIT Press, 2006.

Malpas, Jeff. "New Media, Cultural Heritage and the Sense of Place: Mapping the Conceptual Ground." *International Journal of Heritage Studies* Vol. 14, No. 3 (2008), pp. 197–209.

Malpas, Jeff. "On the Philosophical Reading of Heidegger: Situating the *Black Notebooks*." In: *Reading Heidegger's Black Notebooks 1931–1941*. Eds. Ingo Farin and Jeff Malpas. Cambridge: MIT Press, 2016, pp. 3-22.

Marcuse, Herbert. *Negations: Essays in Critical Theory*. Trans. by Jeremy J Shapiro. London: MayFlyBooks, 2009.

McGill, Vivian Jerauld. "Notes on Philosophy in Nazi Germany." *Science & Society* Vol. 4, No. 1 (1940), pp. 12–28.

Mersch, Dieter. "Tertium Datur: Introduction to a Negative Theory of Media." *MATRIZes* Vol. 7, No. 1 (2013), pp. 207–22.

Mersch, Dieter. "Meta/Dia: Two Approaches to the Medial." In: *Media Transatlantic: Developments in Media and Communication Studies between North American and German-Speaking Europe*, ed. by Norm Friesen. Switzerland: Springer International Publishing, 2016, pp. 153–180.

Miller, Arthur B. "Aristotle on habit (εθō) and character (ηθō): Implications for the rhetoric." *Speech Monographs* Vol. 41, No. 4 (1974), pp. 309–16.

Mills, Brett. *Reading Media Theory: Thinkers, Approaches and Contexts*. London: Routledge, 2012.

Mitchell, William John Thomas. "Addressing Media." *MediaTropes* Vol. 1, No. 1 (2008), pp. 1–18.

Mitchell, William John Thomas, and Mark B. N. Hansen. *Critical Terms for Media Studies*. Chicago: The University of Chicago Press, 2010.

Mitchell, Andrew J., and Peter Trawny, eds. *Heidegger's Black Notebooks: Responses to Anti-Semitism*. New York: Columbia University Press, 2017.

Morley, David. *Home Territories: Media, Mobility and Identity*. New York: Routledge, 2002.

Morley, David. "For a Materialist, Non-Media-Centric Media Studies." *Television & New Media* Vol. 10, No. 1 (2009), pp. 114–16.

Mutsaers, Inge. *Immunological Discourse in Political Philosophy: Immunisation and Its Discontents*. London: Routledge, 2016.

Nagle, Angela. *Kill All Normies: The Online Culture Wars from Tumblr and 4chan to the Alt-Right and Trump*. Washington: Zero Books, 2017.

Nancy, Jean-Luc. "The Decision of Existence." Trans. By Brian Holmes. In: *The Birth to Presence*. Stanford: Stanford University Press, 1993, pp. 82–109.

Nancy, Jean-Luc. "Heidegger's 'Originary Ethics.'" Trans. By Duncan Large. *Studies in Practical Philosophy* Vol. 1, No. 1 (1999), pp. 12–35.

Nancy, Jean-Luc. *Being Singular Plural*. Trans. by Robert D Richardson and Anne Elizabeth O'Byrne. Stanford: Stanford University Press, 2000.

Nancy, Jean-Luc. *A Finite Thinking*. Trans. by Simon Sparks. Stanford: Stanford University Press, 2003.

Nancy, Jean-Luc. "The Image: Mimesis and Methexis." *Theory @ Buffalo* Vol. 11 (2007), pp. 9–26.

Nancy, Jean-Luc. "Heidegger et Nous/Jean-Luc Nancy." *Strass de la philosophie (blog)*, June 1, 2014. Accessed Oct. 28, 2017. http://strassdelaphilosophie. blogspot.com/2014/06/heidegger-et-nous-jean-luc-nancy.html

Nancy, Jean-Luc. *The Banality of Heidegger*. Trans. by Jeff Fort. New York: Fordham University Press, 2017.

Negt, Oskar. "Mass Media: Tools of Domination or Instruments of Liberation? Aspects of the Frankfurt School's Communications Analysis." Trans. by Leslie Adelson. *New German Critique*, No. 14 (1978), pp. 61–80.

Neocleous, Mark. *Fascism*. Minneapolis: University of Minnesota Press, 1997.

OED Online. June 2017. Oxford University Press. Accessed Oct. 28, 2017. http://www.oed.com/view/Entry/115635, http://www.oed.com/view/ Entry/115772

O'Sullivan, Tim, and Yvonne Jewkens, eds. *The Media Studies Reader*. London: Arnold, 1997.

Olafson, Frederick A. *Heidegger and the Ground of Ethics: A Study of Mitsein*. Cambridge: Cambridge University Press, 1998.

Oosterling, Henk. "Interest and Excess of Modern MAn's Radical Mediocrity: Rescaling Sloterdijk's Grandiose Aesthetic Strategy." *Cultural Politics* Vol. 3, No. 3 (2007), pp. 357–80.

Oosterling, Henk. "Anaesthetics 0.1 Man as Medium of All Media" *Naples*, 2000. Accessed Oct. 30, 2017. http://www.academia.edu/5845445/ Anaesthetics_0.1_Man_as_medium_of_all_media_

Pagano, Emmanuelle. *Nouons-nous*. Paris: P.O.L., 2013.

Paley, John. "Heidegger and the Ethics of Care." *Nursing Philosophy* Vol. 1, No. 1 (2000), pp. 64–75.

Parikka, Jussi. *Insect Media: An Archaeology of Animals and Technology*. Minneapolis: University of Minnesota Press, 2010.

Park, Robert E. "The City: Suggestions for the Investigation of Human Behavior in the City Environment." *American Journal of Sociology* Vol. 20, No. 5 (1915), pp. 577–612.

Passmore, Kevin. *Fascism: A Very Short Introduction*. Oxford: Oxford University Press, 2014.

Perry, Steven. "Rhetorical Functions of the Infestation Metaphor in Hitler's Rhetoric." *Central States Speech Journal* Vol. 34, No. 4 (1983), pp. 229–35.

Peters, John Durham. "Genealogical Notes on 'The Field.'" *Journal of Communication* Vol. 43, No. 4 (1993), pp. 132–39.

Peters, John Durham. *Speaking into the Air: A History of the Idea of Communication.* Chicago: University of Chicago Press, 2000.

Peters, John Durham. *The Marvelous Clouds. Toward a Philosophy of Elemental Media.* Chicago: The University of Chicago Press, 2015.

Petit, Daniel. "Chronique d'étymologie grecque." *Revue de Philologie, de Littérature et d'Histoire Anciennes*; Paris Vol. 73, No. 1 (1999), pp. 87–88.

Pine, Lisa. *Hitler's "National Community": Society and Culture in Nazi Germany.* London: Bloomsbury Academic, 2017.

Pooley, Jefferson. "The New History of Communication Research." In: *The History of Media and Communication Research: Contested Memories*, ed. by David W. Park and Jefferson Pooley, New York: Peter Lang, 2008, pp. 43–70.

Pooley, Jefferson. "Sinking the Flagship: Why Communication Studies Is Better Off Without One." *International Journal of Communication* Vol. 9, (2015), pp. 1247–1255.

Pooley, Jefferson, and David W. Park. "Communication Research." In: *The Handbook of Communication History*, ed. by Peter Simonson. New York: Routledge, 2013, pp. 76–92.

Poster, Mark. "High-Tech Frankenstein, or Heidegger Meets Sterlac." In: *The Cyborg Experiments: The Extensions of the Body in the Media Age*, ed. by Joanna Zylinska. New York: Continuum, 2002, pp. 15–32.

Przylebski, Andrzej. *Ethics in the Light of Hermeneutical Philosophy: Morality Between (Self-)Reflection and Social Obligations.* Zurich: LIT Verlag Münster, 2017.

Raboy, Marc. *Marconi: The Man Who Networked the World.* Oxford: Oxford University Press, 2016.

Rancière, Jacques. "Thinking between Disciplines: An Aesthetics of Knowledge." Trans. by Jon Roffe. *Parrhesia*, no. 1 (2006): 1–12.

Rantanen, Terhi. *The Media and Globalization.* London: SAGE, 2004.

Ranulf, Svend. "Scholarly Forerunners of Fascism." *Ethics* Vol. 50, No. 1 (1939), pp. 16–34.

Rappeport, Alan, and Noah Weiland. "White Nationalists Celebrate 'an Awakening' After Donald Trump's Victory." *The New York Times*, November 19, 2016. Accessed Oct. 28, 2017. https://www.nytimes.com/2016/11/20/us/politics/white-nationalists-celebrate-an-awakening-after-donald-trumps-victory.html

Reich, Wilhelm. *The Mass Psychology of Fascism*. New York: Orgone Institute Press, 1946.

Ricœur, Paul. *Oneself as Another*. Trans. by Kathleen Blamey. Chicago, London: The University of Chicago Press, 1992.

Rogers, Everett M. *Communication Technology: The New Media in Society*. New York: Free Press, 1986.

Rogers, Everett M. *A History of Communication Study: A Biographical Approach*. New York: Free Press, 1994.

Rosenfeld, Jean E. "Fascism as Action through Time (Or How It Can Happen Here)." *Terrorism and Political Violence* Vol. 29, No. 3 (2017), pp. 394–410.

Rougemont, Denis de. *Penser avec les mains*. Paris: Albin Michel, 1936.

Scannell, Paddy. *Radio, Television, and Modern Life: A Phenomenological Approach*. Oxford: Blackwell, 1996.

Scannell, Paddy. *Television and the Meaning of Live: An Enquiry into the Human Situation*. Cambridge: Polity Press, 2014.

Scherer, Michael. "President Trump Struggles with Charlottesville Aftermath." *Time*, August 12, 2017. Accessed Oct. 28, 2017. http://time.com/4898422/charlottesville-white-nationalist-donald-trump/

Schmidt, Dennis J. "Hermeneutics as Original Ethics." In: *Difficulties of Ethical Life*, ed. by Shannon Sullivan and Dennis J Schmidt. New York: Fordham University Press, 2008, pp. 35–47.

Schramm, Wilbur. "Communication Research in the United States." In: *The Science of Human Communication. New Directions and New Findings in Communication Research*, ed. by Wilbur Schramm. New York: Basic Books, 1963, pp. 1–16.

Serres, Michel. *Le système de Leibniz et ses modèles mathématiques Etoiles-Shémas - Points*. Paris: Presse Universitaire de France, 1968.

Sheehan, Thomas. "Heidegger and the Nazis." *The New York Review of Books* Vol. 35, No. 10 (1988), pp. 38–47.

Sheehan, Thomas. *Making Sense of Heidegger: A Paradigm Shift*. Lanham: Rowman & Littlefield, 2014.

Sidgwick, Henry. *Outlines of the History of Ethics*. 5th edition. Indianapolis: Hackett Publishing Company, Inc., 1988.

Siegert, Bernhard. "There Are No Mass Media" (1996), In: *Mapping Benjamin: The Work of Art in the Digital Age*. ed. Hans Ulrich Gumbrecht and Michael Marrinan. Stanford: Stanford University Press, 2003, pp. 30–38.

Siegert, Bernhard. "Cacography or Communication? Cultural Techniques in German Media Studies." *Grey Room* No. 29 (2007), pp. 26–47.

Siegert, Bernhard. "Cultural Techniques: Or the End of the Intellectual Postwar Era in German Media Theory." *Theory, Culture & Society* Vol. 30, No. 6 (2013), pp. 48–65.

Siegert, Bernhard. "Media after Media." In: *Media after Kittler*, ed. by Eleni Ikoniadou and Scott Wilson. Blue Ridge Summit: Rowman & Littlefield, 2015, pp. 79–91.

Sills, David L., ed. "Paul Lazarsfeld." In: *International Encyclopedia of the Social Sciences*. New York: The Free Press, 1979, pp. 411–427.

Silverstone, Roger. *Why Study the Media?* London: SAGE, 1999.

Simonson, Peter. *The Handbook of Communication History*. London: Routledge, 2013.

Sloterdijk, Peter. *Terror from the Air*. Trans. by Amy Patton and Steve Corcoran. Los Angeles: Semiotext, 2009.

Sloterdijk, Peter. *Bubbles: Microspherology*. Trans. by Wieland Hoban. Spheres. Vol. 1. Los Angeles: Semiotext(e), 2011.

Sloterdijk, Peter. *Globes : Macrospherology*. Trans. by Wieland Hoban. Spheres. Vol. 2. Los Angeles: Semiotext(e), 2014.

Sloterdijk, Peter. *Spheres. Plural Spherology*. Trans. by Wieland Hoban. Spheres. Vol. 3. Los Angeles: Semiotext(e), 2016.

Sluga, Hans D. *Heidegger's Crisis: Philosophy and Politics in Nazi Germany*. Cambridge: Harvard University Press, 1995.

Snyder, Timothy. *On Tyranny: Twenty Lessons from the Twentieth Century*. New York: Tim Duggan Books, 2017.

Somaini, Antonio. "The 'Medium of Perception': Walter Benjamin's Media Theory and the Tradition of the Media Diaphana." In: *Theorizing Images*, ed. by Krešimir Purgar and Žarko Paić. Newcastle: Cambridge Scholar Publishing, 2016, pp. 84–110.

Spitzer, Leo. "Milieu and Ambiance: An Essay in Historical Semantics." *Philosophy and Phenomenological Research* Vol. 3, No. 2 (1942), pp. 169–218.

Sproule, J. Michael. "Progressive Propaganda Critics and the Magic Bullet Myth." *Critical Studies in Mass Communication* Vol. 6, No. 3 (1989), pp. 225–46.

Sproule, J. Michael. *Propaganda and Democracy: The American Experience of Media and Mass Persuasion*. Cambridge: Cambridge University Press, 1997.

Stack, Liam. "Attack on Alt-Right Leader Has Internet Asking: Is It O.K. to Punch a Nazi?" *The New York Times*, January 21, 2017, sec. Politics. Accessed Oct. 28, 2017. https://www.nytimes.com/2017/01/21/us/politics/richard-spencer-punched-attack.html

Stiegler, Bernard ed. *Technics and Time, 1: The Fault of Epimetheus.* Trans. by Richard Beardsworth and George Collins. Stanford: Stanford University Press, 1998.

Strong, Tracy B. *Politics without Vision: Thinking without a Banister in the Twentieth Century.* Chicago: University of Chicago Press, 2012.

Tække, Jesper, and Michael Paulsen. "Luhmann and the Media." *MedieKultur: Journal of Media and Communication Research* Vol. 26, No. 49 (2010): 1–10.

Tarde, Gabriel de. *The Laws of Imitation.* Trans. by Elsie Worthington Clews Parsons and Franklin Henry Giddings. Gloucester: P. Smith, 1962.

Taylor, Charles. "Ethics and Ontology." *The Journal of Philosophy* Vol. 100, No. 6 (2003), pp. 305–20.

Thibault, Ghislain, and Dominique Trudel. "Excaver, tracer, réécrire : sur les renouveaux historiques en communication." *Communiquer. Revue de communication sociale et publique,* No. 15 (2015), pp. 5–23.

Thibault, Ghislain. "Needles and Bullets: Media Theory, Medicine, and Propaganda, 1910–1940." In: *Endemic. Essays in Contagion Theory,* ed. by Kari Nixon and Lorenzo Servitje. London: Palgrave Macmillan, 2016, pp. 67–92.

Thiesmeyer, Lynn. "Racism on the Web: Its Rhetoric and Marketing." *Ethics and Information Technology* Vol. 1, No. 2 (June 1, 1999), pp. 117–25.

Tholen, Georg Christoph, and Peter Krapp. "Media Metaphorology: Irritations in the Epistemic Field of Media Studies." *The South Atlantic Quarterly* Vol. 101, No. 3 (2002): 659–72.

Thornham, Sue, Caroline Bassett, and Paul Marris, eds. *Media Studies: A Reader.* Edinburgh: Edinburgh University Press, 1996.

Tosini, Domenico. "Medium as a Basic Concept of Sociology: Contributions from Systems Theory." *Social Science Information* Vol. 45, No. 4 (2006), pp. 539–60.

Trawny, Peter. *Heidegger & the Myth of a Jewish World Conspiracy.* Trans. by Andrew J Mitchell. Chicago: The University of Chicago Press, 2016.

Turner, Fred. *The Democratic Surround: Multimedia & American Liberalism from World War II to the Psychedelic Sixties.* Chicago: The University of Chicago Press, 2013.

Valdivia, Angharad N., ed. *A Companion to Media Studies.* Malden: Blackwell, 2006.

Vattimo, Gianni. *The Transparent Society.* Trans. by David Webb. Baltimore: Johns Hopkins University Press, 1992.

Vergnières, Solange. *Éthique et politique chez Aristote: "physis", "éthos", "nomos"*. Paris: Presses Universitaires de France, 1995.

Vogel, Lawrence. *The Fragile "we": Ethical Implications of Heidegger's Being and Time*. Evanston: Northwestern University Press, 1994.

Wahl-Jorgensen, Karin. "How Not to Found a Field: New Evidence on the Origins of Mass Communication Research." *Journal of Communication* Vol. 54, No. 3 (2004), pp. 547–64.

Wang, Amy B. "Analysis | Trump Breaks Silence on Charlottesville: 'No Place for This Kind of Violence in America.'" *Washington Post*, August 12, 2017. Accessed Oct. 28, 2017. https://www.washingtonpost.com/news/the-fix/wp/2017/08/12/trump-responds-to-charlottesville-protests/

Watsuji, Tetsurō. *Watsuji Tetsuro's Rinrigaku: Ethics in Japan*. New York: State University of New York Press, 1996.

Webb, David. *Heidegger, Ethics and the Practice of Ontology*. London: Continuum, 2011.

Weber, Samuel, and Alan Cholodenko. *Mass Mediauras: Form, Technics, Media*. Stanford: Stanford University Press, 1996.

Wendland, Aaron James, Christopher D. Merwin, and Christos M. Hadjioannou, eds. *Heidegger on Technology*. New York: Routledge, 2018.

Williams, Raymond. "Communications as Cultural Science." *Journal of Communication* Vol. 24, no. 3 (1974), pp. 17–25.

Wilson, Tony. *Understanding Media Users: From Theory to Practice*. West Sussex: John Wiley & Sons, 2009.

Wilson, Tony. *Media Consumption in Malaysia: A Hermeneutics of Human Behaviour*. New York: Routledge, 2015.

Winthrop-Young, Geoffrey. "Krautrock, Heidegger, Bogeyman: Kittler in the Anglosphere." *Thesis Eleven* Vol. 107, No. 1 (2011a), pp. 6–20.

Winthrop-Young, Geoffrey. *Kittler and the Media*. Cambridge: Polity Press, 2011b.

Winthrop-Young, Geoffrey, and Michael Wutz. "Introduction: Media – Models, Memories, and Metaphors." *Configurations* Vol. 10, No. 1 (2003), pp. 1–10.

Wittgenstein, Ludwig. *Philosophical Investigations*. Trans. by G.E.M Anscombe. Oxford: Basil Blackwell, 1963.

Woerther, Frédérique. "Aux origines de la notion rhétorique d'èthos." *Revue des Études Grecques* Vol. 118, No. 1 (2005), pp. 79–116.

Woerther, Frédérique. *L'éthos aristotélicien: genèse d'une notion rhétorique*. Paris: Vrin, 2007.

Wolin, Richard. *The Politics of Beging: The Political Thought of Martin Heidegger.*
New York: Columbia University Press, 1990.

Wolin, Richard. *The Heidegger Controversy: A Critical Reader.*
New York: Columbia University Press, 1991.

Pieter Lemmens

From Ontology to Organology: Heidegger and Stiegler on the Danger and Ambiguity of Technology and Technical Media

Martin Heidegger is a constant reference in the work of Bernard Stiegler. As for Jacques Derrida, his principal teacher, Stiegler understands his philosophical project in the first place as enabled and inspired by the work of Heidegger. Already from the title of his still unfinished magnum opus *Technics and Time* one can gather that the thought of Stiegler is motivated by the questions that have been put forward for the first time by the author of *Being and Time*. Whereas Heidegger in this book tried to think being in terms of time, Stiegler aims to show in his ground-breaking treatise that this time, the temporality or the temporal happening of being that takes place in and through human being-there [*Dasein*], is constituted and conditioned by technology in an original manner. If it is true that the basic question of Heidegger's thought, the question of being, is addressed along the path of his thinking more and more emphatically as the question concerning technology or more precisely as the question concerning the *essence* of technology, and this essence was itself explicitly thought by him as being not techno-logical but indeed profoundly onto-logical in nature, i.e., of the order of being, then Stiegler shows to the contrary that this essence of technology *is* thoroughly technological (in an ontic sense) after all and that as a consequence we need to understand that which Heidegger tried to think as 'being' from the perspective of technology, and that is to say from the fundamental technicity of the human being. Of course it goes without saying that this completely contradicts the intuitions of the 'dark sphinx' of the Black Forest.

A detailed discussion of the place of Heidegger in the work of Stiegler, let alone an exposition of all the similarities and differences of their philosophical projects, would require an entire book and there is no space for that here. In this chapter, I only want to confront, in a quite explorative way, Heidegger's views of technology, especially as it emerges in his later work, with that of Stiegler, focusing on their respective understanding of technology – and for Stiegler also concrete technical media – as embodying both a threatening or dangerous and a liberating or salvatory 'force' with regard to the 'essence' of man, be it that they conceive of this ambiguity in a rather different way. I will thereby compare Heidegger's ontological or onto-historical understanding of technology and its ambiguity with Stiegler's pharmaco-organological view of it as an 'ontico-ontological' (as I will call it here) phenomenon, i.e., as initially ontico-accidental in nature yet with an ontological effectiveness or constitutivity.

Ultimately, this contribution is also an attempt to get a better grip on Heidegger's rather esoteric and practically hardly helpful notion of the ambiguity of technology as representing both the danger and the possible deliverance from that danger on the basis of Stiegler's understanding of technology, namely by interpreting this danger from a Stieglerian, pharmacological, and that is to say more ontical or indeed ontico-ontological conception of the 'nature' of technology; and this with the hope of being able to say somewhat more about what this means for how we should relate to technology and more specifically of how to respond in a more practical sense to Heidegger's most important question of how man could enter into a more free relationship to technology and technical media.

1 Heidegger on the essence of technology

Let me first recall Heidegger's famous analysis of the essence of technology, especially as developed in his famous 1950 essay 'The Question Concerning Technology' (henceforth referred to as the technology essay). The exclusive purpose of this meditation, as Heidegger states directly in the very first paragraph, is to search for and prepare a *free relationship* to technology in the sense of a freeing or opening ourselves to its essence, a liberation which, as in all of Heidegger's philosophical endeavours, amounts to a '*liberation of the Dasein in man*', as he puts it in a lecture course from 1930 (Heidegger 1995, 172).

This freeing of the being-there [*Dasein*] in man is sought here in a freeing of ourselves toward the essence of technology, where 'essence' [*Wesen*] is to be understood in a completely different sense than the traditional metaphysical one (derived from Plato and Aristotle). And it is precisely technology itself, as Heidegger submits near the end of his meditation, that puts us on the track, yes indeed compels us to think 'essence' in a totally different manner: not anymore in the classic, substantivist-static-timeless sense but in a verbal-dynamic-temporal sense as 'coming to presence' [*Wesung*] and more precisely as an 'enduring' [*Währen*] and 'preserving' [*Gewähren*] (terms that will be explained below) in which our own verbal-dynamic-temporal essence as being-there is involved in a very 'intimate' way. And is in the intimate involvement of our being-there with the coming to presence of technology's essence, which Heidegger understands as being totally independent of any relation to concrete technical media, that its 'liberating call' lies. But I'll return to this more extensively below. We will see that the relationship between technology and human freedom is also a central issue in Stiegler and that his thinking is also concerned with some kind of liberating of ourselves toward technology but from a different conception of the relation between the human, technology and being than is suggested by Heidegger.

As is well known, Heidegger stresses in the first place that the essence of technology is itself nothing technological, which means that it should not be sought at the level of concrete technologies or more generally at the ontic level of things or beings. On the contrary, the essence of technology is onto-*logical*. It fundamentally relates to our *understanding* of beings, that is to say of their *being*, of the manner in which they *appear* for us. Stiegler definitely also entertains a kind of ontological conception of technology, although in his case we may rather speak, employing a term from Peter Sloterdijk, of an onto-anthropological conception (Sloterdijk 2017). But for him the essence of technology is first of all decidedly ontic-technical in nature since he considers technology in a decidedly concrete sense as being constitutive for being-there's mode of being and understanding of being and thus also of the being of beings encountered by it. We might call Stiegler's conception of technology therefore ontico-ontological.

Transcending the ontical perspective, Heidegger rejects the traditional (= metaphysical) definition of technology as a sheer means or instrument used by man to achieve his goals. This anthropological-instrumental definition is not incorrect but nevertheless does not touch upon the essence of what technology is. The latter can only be sensed when we first ask what this means-goals relationship itself exactly comprises. Such a relationship is at play wherever goals are achieved and this always entails 'causality', or more precisely the bringing together of causes in order to realize, create or produce something, in the sense of bringing something forth or bringing it into the world. This is called *poiein* by the ancient Greeks and is also a fundamental feature of nature, of *physis* as *phyein*. However, while *physis* is a spontaneous, self-caused or auto-generative bringing or springing forth of beings, technology – in Greek: *techne* – is a bringing forth of beings which has its origin in something else, namely in man as a craftsman or artisan (Heidegger 1977, 11).

Now the ancient Greeks understand every producing or bringing forth of something in the most fundamental sense as a revealing, unconcealing or disclosing [*entbergen*], i.e., as bringing something from concealment into unconcealment [*Unverborgenheit*]. And precisely therein lies according to Heidegger the very essence of technology: it is a way of revealing, what the Greeks call *alétheuein* as a bringing forth of beings [Greek: *ta onta*] in unconcealedness, in ancient Greek: *alétheia*, what we translate as truth. The essence of technology according to this analysis is nothing technical, instrumental or anthropological but *ontological-aletheialogical*. Technology involves the *being* of beings and their understanding [*legein, logos*] and should be located as such in the domain of *truth*, i.e., truth in the (according to Heidegger) original sense as the domain of concealment and unconcealment (Heidegger 1977, 13). This unconcealment into which everything fabricated is brought to the fore is itself not a fabrication of man, Heidegger emphasizes, and therefore it is not something over which man disposes. Rather the opposite is the case: all technical activity of man is nothing but the response to a call that calls upon him from out of the unconcealment (Heidegger 1977, 19).

In other texts, Heidegger speaks about this truth as unconcealment explicitly in terms of an openness [*Offenheit*] or clearing [*Lichtung*], stressing that it is not a product of human consciousness but nothing less than the 'supporting ground of our humanity', as Heidegger writes in a lecture course from 1938 (Heidegger 2004, 179). And as such it reigns over us, being 'apparently nothing of our own doing', he continues (Heidegger 2004, 179). It is an openness that indeed opens us toward beings and grants us access to them but that is not under our control. With Stiegler, however, I will claim to the contrary that this openness *is* dependent in some sense on our 'doing', since it does have an anthropogenic or rather (to use a term by Sloterdijk again) antropo*techno*genic origin (one in which man as being-there and being as unconcealment arise co-originally from a process of technogenesis).

2 The essence of modern technology as enframing

Modern technology, and that is to say machine or industrial technology, must also be considered as a way of revealing, says Heidegger, but unlike traditional technology it is a revealing in the sense of a challenging-forth [*Herausfordern*] which forces nature, more or less violently, to supply resources and energy (and nothing besides). This revealing takes place on the basis of an understanding of the unconcealment of beings in terms of a standing reserve [*Bestand*]. Modern technology understands nature as a reservoir of matter and energy to be exploited by man, while man himself appears as the one that is challenged to reveal nature as a standing reserve, i.e., to order it as such (Heidegger 1977, 18).

It is in this challenging, provocative, ordering mode of revealing that the ontological-aletheialogical essence of modern technology consists. The name Heidegger gives to this essence is of course enframing [*Gestell*] and he understands it explicitly as an *imperative*, that is to say as a call [*Anspruch*] in the sense of a claim of being upon the 'essence' of man (Heidegger 1977, 19). This imperative provokes man to the exploitation but also generalized planning and calculation of all beings, which are revealed solely with a view to their mastery, manageability and calculability (Heidegger 2002a, 35). Enframing is as such more real [*seiender*], as Heidegger contends in another essay of the same period, than all technical equipment and all the processes of technologization, rationalization, computerization and automation together, but it is not itself a being and does not stand in front of us as a being, and it is precisely in this strange and uncanny [*unheimlich*] nature that the liberating the potential of modern technology also resides (Heidegger 2002a, 35).

Enframing itself results from the metaphysical destining [*Geschick*] of revealing which reigns over Western culture since the end of the great Greek commencement [*Anfang*], i.e., since the thought of Plato and Aristotle, and which Heidegger describes elsewhere as a history of being characterized by a growing forgetfulness of being but that is nevertheless the onto-historical unfolding of the freedom of man or rather of the being-there in man, which is the most original freedom of man according to Heidegger and lies in the 'belongingness to' the destining or *Ge-schickhaft* happening or event of being (Heidegger 1977, 25). I will speak here of the ontological freedom of man or the being-there in man.

Insofar as the destiny of being reigns in the metaphysical mode of forgetfulness, man remains caught as it were in his essence as mere 'exploiter of the standing reserve' [*Besteller des Bestandes*]. This is for Heidegger the so-called danger of technology, which I will address more extensively below. What Heidegger emphasizes, however, is that in this movement of ordering enframing man nevertheless always remains the 'administrator' [*Verwalter*] of the original ontological freedom which is granted to him by being. An explicit hearing of the call of enframing as the experiencing of the claim that being lays on our being (our ontological freedom) thus bears in itself the possibility of a liberation from this claim in such a way that, if explicitly heard, it can be experienced *as* a liberating call that can thus liberate us to our ontological freedom or our originally free essence, which she has always already claimed throughout the destiny. This explicit hearing of the call of enframing as the veritable, ontological-aletheialogical essence of technology would mean as much as a renewed awakening in the awareness of our original and – according to Heidegger – also *indestructible* belongingnes [*unzerstörbare Zugehörigkeit*] to the revealing-event of being (Heidegger 1977, 32) and would as such initiate what he calls the turning [*Kehre*], understood here as a 'recollection' [*Einkehr*] of the essence of technology. This would open the free relationship to technology Heidegger talks about at the beginning of his essay. And therein lies exactly the saving power immanent in the danger of technology.

3 The danger and the saving power of technology in Heidegger

Neither the famous danger [*Gefahr*] of technology sensu Heidegger has, any more than the essence of technology, anything to do with concrete technical media. It is also onto-aletheialogical in nature. It must be understood essentially as the *tendency*, inherent in any kind of reveling but radicalized in technical revealing, to forget or ignore itself *as* revealing and only focus on that which is thereby revealed. The danger of technology in this sense is nothing else than the most explicit essence of technology as enframing. It lies in the most fundamental sense in the *in-sistent* turning away from itself of the free *ek-sistent* essence of man and 'enacts' with it the turning away from itself of enframing of its own essence, such that it thereby realizes its own totalization or hegemonization in the sense that the technical, ordering mode of revealing becomes exclusive and beings tendentially appear *only* in a technical way.

The *highest* danger of technology, according to Heidegger, consists in the fact that through this hegemony of technical revealing man is led to understand also himself, like any other being, exclusively in ontic terms of an exploitable (and technically perfectionable) standing reserve and thus loses any sense of his own (ontological) openness as essential belongingness to the revealing dynamic of being[1]. The danger residing in the essence of technology therefore lies in the possibility of a total closure of the openness to being, which would be tantamount for Heidegger to the liquidation of man's ontological freedom, i.e., to the complete abandonment of the free essence of man (Heidegger 1977, 32).

However, precisely in this highest danger of technology is also sheltered its saving power, understood as that which can bring us again into connection with our innermost revealing being. Referring to the famous phrase from Hölderlin's hymn *Patmos* 'But where danger is, Grows the saving power also', Heidegger suggests that the power that could save us from the threat that the full reign of the essence of technology represents for our free being, can be found in that very threat itself. And the kind of salvation Heidegger is referring to here is not something like a rescuing of humanity from the dangers of technologies in order to secure its survival. Saving here means precisely allowing the danger to come to itself, to let it be confronted by itself as it were, by explicitly bringing it into its own essence, *liberating* it to its own essence so that it can appear and shine *as*

---

1 We might think here of the current aspirations and projections of 'human enhancement' promoted mainly by so-called transhumanists, who understand the human purely technologically as a 'work in progress', according to an expression by Nick Bostrom (Bostrom 2005, 4).

such and that is to say: can come to light *as* the danger that it is in the first place (Heidegger 1977, 42).

The saving power is immanent in the *experience* of the danger *as* danger, since the danger as the essence of enframing is the very coming to presence of being (as event of disclosure) itself, namely in its self-forgetful being, i.e., turned-away from itself and 'pursuing' or chasing after [*nachstellen*] itself with its own forget-fulness ('pursuing' being the meaning of the *Nachstellen* that Heidegger reads in the fara of *Ge-fahr* as the most fundamental trait of all framing-ordering activity of enframing: its 'ensnaring' turning away from its own essence). As he writes: 'What essences of danger is beyng itself insofar as it pursues the truth of its essence with the forgetting of this essence' (Heidegger 2012, 59). The saving power of technology is rooted and thrives *in* and *as* the danger to the extent that it, as the very ontological essence of enframing, 'is nothing less than being itself' (Heidegger 2012, 59). Being *itself* is the danger, and it is this *always*, we might say, to the extent that any destining of revealing tends to forget itself *as* such a revealing and merely pursues that which is being revealed. Unfolding in the mode of enframing, however, this danger is at its highest, since it threatens with the loss of the event of revealing altogether and hence threatens the human being with the danger of completely losing his ontological essence, i.e., his ontological freedom.

It should be clear by now that the essence of technology as the essence of being itself must be understood 'dynamically' and 'verbally' as a 'coming to presence' [*Wesung*] or a 'presencing' [*Anwesen*], which Heidegger further interprets in the sense of an 'enduring' and also a 'preserving' of that which is. And this enduring and preserving of beings takes place *in* and *through* the being-there of man, *as* his ek-sistence. And it does so, Heidegger emphasizes, even when it reigns as enframing and thus in the form of the extreme danger (characteristic of modern technology), because even then it persists in granting human beings their share in the event of revealing and exactly herein lies and thrives the saving power: the possibility man experiences the danger *as* danger and as such becomes 'aware' or 'conscious' of the fact that he is 'needed' [*gebraucht*] for this event to happen and essentially belongs to it. As Heidegger puts it very beautifully in the technology essay: 'It is precisely in Enframing, which threatens to sweep man away into ordering as the supposed single way of revealing, and so thrusts man into the danger of the surrender of his free essence – it is precisely in this extreme danger that the innermost indestruc-tible belongingness of man within granting may come to light, provided that we, for our part, begin to pay heed to the coming to presence of technology' (Heidegger 1977, 32).

As the coming to presence of being itself modern technology is in its essence thus *both*, and that is to say *simultaneously*, danger and saving power. On the one hand it threatens to subject the free essence of man fully to the technical challenging-forth and exploitation of beings, on the other hand, it is therefore precisely in modern technology that the (according to Heidegger indestructible) involvement of the human in the 'enduring-preserving' event of revealing manifests itself. As such, man is simultaneously the 'challenged one' [*Herausgeforderte*] (Heidegger 1977, 23) of enframing and the 'used one' [*Gebrauchte*] (Heidegger 1977, 33) of the event of revealing or disclosure of being. Being the 'used one' of the destining of revealing however is a more original destination of man than being the 'challenged one' of the exploitative ordering of beings that reigns as enframing. It is in the growing of this awareness, which only a kind of reflection or meditation [*Besinnung*] on the essence of technology in the manner of Heidegger can make one sensitive to, that the saving power accrues (Heidegger 1977, 34).

4 The ambiguity of technology in Heidegger

Understood in this way, and here I touch upon the central theme of this chapter, the essence of modern technology as the enframing coming to presence of being is 'in a lofty sense ambiguous', [*in einem Hohen Sinne zweideutig*], Heidegger writes (Heidegger 1977, 33). It unfolds after all simultaneously as an 'overhearing' [*Überhören*] by man of the appeal of being (manifesting as the imperative to set upon and order beings in their totality) and, inevitably as it were, as a 'belonging-together' [*Zusammengehören*] of man and being. The essence of modern technology thus consists both in a blind 'pursuing' of its own forgetfulness *and* as a prelude to or a possible transition towards an explicit experiencing of the 'event of appropriation' [*Ereignis*] in which man knowingly 'enacts' and takes upon himself as it were his 'indestructible belongingness' to being.

Since the project of technical revealing of beings in fact dominates the West since the Greek commencement, enframing is understood by Heidegger both as the completion of metaphysics as the history of forgetfulness and abandonment of being [*Seinsverlassenheit*] *and* as the beginning of a rapprochement of being and man or in other words as a 'giving oneselves over to one another' [*Übereignen*] of man and being, through which the reign of metaphysics would be overcome. In 'The principle of identity', an essay from 1957, he writes in this regard: 'Within the framework there prevails a strange ownership [*Vereignen*] and a strange appropriation [*Zueignen*]' (Heidegger 2002a, 36). Heidegger understands enframing thus in terms of an onto-historical passage in which the transition can take place from the dominance [*Herrschaft*] by man *over beings* toward a servitude [*Dienstschaft*] by man *for being*. Here too, the ambiguity of enframing is in play, its 'double appearance' or 'dual gaze' which Heidegger in a text from 1962 compares with a 'Janus head' (Heidegger 2002b, 53).

In a 1955 address to his fellow citizens at Messkirch entitled 'Releasement' [*Gelassenheit*] Heidegger states, advertent of the ambiguity of modern technology, that on the one hand we become more and more dependent on technical media and feel challenged to constantly improve them (think here of the imperative of innovation nowadays, which has become the most obvious, most self-evident thing in the world), while on the other hand we become so deeply attached to them almost to the extent of merging with them, that we seem to be subjected to these media more and more, even tending to become their servants instead of the other way around (Heidegger 1969, 54). We recognize here all too easy the well-known pattern that characterizes any debate between proponents and opponents about the advantages and disadvantages of new technical media, both present and in the past: again and again these technical media are evaluated and judged for their beneficial and/or dangerous consequences, their positive or negative effects on man and his world, and it is always the current human reality in its present-at-hand-ness that is used as the 'measure stick'. In doing so, technical media are considered only in a technical sense and that is to say only ontically and calculatively, in complete ignorance of their ontological essence.

From a reflection on the essence of technology, from what in this address is called 'meditative thinking' [*besinnendes Denken*] as opposed to the purely 'calculative thinking' [*rechnendes Denken*] of technology, Heidegger suggests that we can also deal differently with this ambiguity, namely by simultaneously affirming and distancing ourselves from the impact technical media have on our lives, i.e., by saying both 'yes' and 'no' to them. We can use them as they ought to be used, but can do so in such a way that we can always release ourselves from them at any moment so as not to let ourselves be *determined* by them. This is of course reminiscent of the free relationship to technology mentioned in the technology essay. From a relationship to technology that is not exclusively calculative but also meditative – and this in fact means considering it onto-logically as a horizon of understanding – we can properly use technical media (i.e., instrumentally) but let them at the same time rest in their own, Heidegger suggests, as 'something which does not affect our inner and real core' (Heidegger 1969, 54). And he continues: 'We can affirm the unavoidable use of technical media, and also deny them the right to dominate us, and so to warp, confuse, and lay waste our nature' (Heidegger 1969, 54).

In this way, we allow technical media entrance in our world but leave them at the same time outside of it, namely as things that do not have an absolute status but can only be what they are thanks to 'something higher'. This attitude of a simultaneous Yes and No to technology and the increasing invasiveness of technical media into our world – an attitude that perhaps opens the free relationship to technology Heidegger alludes to in the technology essay, as already said – is called 'releasement toward things' here (Heidegger 1969, 54). This attitude opens us to that 'higher thing' upon which all technical media remain dependent according to Heidegger and that he describes here as a certain 'meaning' or 'sense' [*Sinn*] which seizes us in all our doings when we are engaged in technical activity, a 'meaning' which is not devised or invented by man but that nevertheless summons him to the technical ordering of the world, to speak again in the terms of the technology essay.

This 'sense' is of course nothing other than being, coming to presence as enframing, which itself originates from the destining of metaphysics, of which the modern technical world is the ultimate realization according to Heidegger, but which from his onto-historical perspective is to be understood as the 'seizure' of the ontological freedom of man by being or the '*Inanspruchnahme*' by being of the free essence of man. The 'sense' of the technical world, the imperative of enframing in which the call of being manifests itself in the modern age, hides itself precisely in the exclusive orientation on the technical ordering of beings but it can as such also 'show' (and thereby open) itself if we only learn, as Heidegger teaches, to open ourselves for this hiddenness, which he refers to in this address with the word *Geheimnis*, which is difficult to render in English but can be translated as 'secret' or 'mystery' (Heidegger 1969, 56). This 'openness to the mystery', coupled with 'the releasement toward things', can guard man for the 'great danger' that he fully surrenders his free essence to the essence of technology such that its rule becomes total and safeguard him from this by 'retrieving' him into his own free essence, a 'retrieval' in the sense of a reversal of the forgetfulness of being and a return to the belongingness to the truth of being, a return that Heidegger in earlier remarks from 1938 to 1939 has called 'man's fundamental remembrance' [*Wesenserinnering des Menschen*] and that would inaugurate another commencement of being (Heidegger 2006, 109).

What I would like to draw attention to here, and this kicks off my Stieglerian interpretation of Heidegger's notion of the danger of technology, is that Heidegger in his address on releasement (as in many other texts, but here in the most simple and concrete terms) suggests that technical media do 'not affect our inner and real core' and that an exclusive preoccupation with them does 'warp, confuse, and lay waste our nature', as he puts it. Technical media are ultimately things that do not *really* concern us, that in the most fundamental sense – and that means for Heidegger: with respect to our being-there and existence – remain outside of us insofar as they are not essential to our being. It is precisely this view that I want to challenge here with Stiegler and subsequently show the consequences of this for thinking about the danger of technology. For that purpose I will first explain Stiegler's conception of the 'original technicity' of being-there, through which I will show that the relationship between man and technology is indeed a very intimate and substantial, yes essential one, and this from the very beginning.

5 Stiegler on the original technicity of being-there

For Stiegler, in contrast to Heidegger, the 'free essence' of man does not exist without an intimate and original coupling with concrete technical media. Being-there as the being capable of questioning both his own being and the being of other beings can in his opinion not exist without technology, and that is to say technology in a concrete sense: technical media. The 'who' of being-there – and as for Heidegger, this 'who' is for Stiegler an entity that is essentially (but essentially understood in a thoroughly accidental way) 'in question' and must therefore actually always be designated as 'who?' (with a question mark) – cannot exist without the 'what' of technology. Yet this latter view seems to be held by Heidegger, at least implicitly, despite his 'practicist' emphasis on the essential role of the 'readiness-to-hand' [*Zuhandene*] or utensils [*Zeug*] in both the projection and thrownness of being-there as being-in-the-world. For Heidegger, the free essence of man seems to be conceived as an ontological purity, totally unaffected and in no sense constituted by technology, without any foundation in the ontic and this not only in *Being and Time*, but throughout his work. In this sense Heidegger presents himself as a transcendentalist and more precisely as a 'transcendentalist of being' (my term) and this makes him in the eyes of Stiegler, for whom the essence of metaphysics consists in the forgetfulness of technology rather than in the forgetfulness of being (as it does for Heidegger), a metaphysician (Stiegler 2009 5).

Stiegler elaborates this thesis of the original technicity of being-there in great detail in the first volume of *Technics and Time*, both from an anthropological and anthropogenetic perspective based on the work of the French paleoanthropologist André Leroi-Gourhan on hominization as the effect of a process of technical exteriorization, which I can discuss only briefly here, and from a phenomenological perspective based on a critical analysis of the thought of Husserl and Heidegger, respectively, on inner time consciousness and on the existential (ecstatic-horizontal) temporality of being-there.

Like Heidegger, Stiegler characterizes man as an ek-sistent being, which has his own being outside of himself due to his 'standing-out' in the clearing of being, but unlike Heidegger, Stiegler understands this ek-sistent essence of man not as an irretrievable 'gift' of being[2], but as the effect of a process of technical exteriorization. As such, it should also be seen as something that – in the course of a long process of techno-cultural evolution and history, mainly through interiorization of the technically exteriorized – has been acquired largely by man himself. That the human is a being that is 'burdened' with 'having to be' and having to care for its own being and is therefore 'in its being [...] concerned *about* its very being', as famously stated in *Being and Time* (Heidegger 2010, 11), is only possible because of the fundamental technicity of that being in the sense of an intimate relation between the human and technology. As Stiegler puts it in an interview from 2004 with Élie During '[Humans] have to "invent" their "being-there", their existence. It is for this reason that what Heidegger calls "having to be" [*Zu-sein*], i.e., freedom and self-responsibility is, in contrast to Heidegger's own viewpoint, not alienated by technology, but is on the contrary constituted by it, that is to say it is only made possible by technology' (Stiegler 2004, 45).

For Stiegler, the possibilities of the 'what' fundamentally constitute those of the 'who?' as being-there (Stiegler 2009, 76). Human *ek*-sistence as described for the first time by Heidegger in *Being and Time* is always already *pros*-thetic, i.e., being-there's ek-sistence as standing-out in the openness or unconcealment of being is only possible on the basis of technical prostheses, i.e., of an intimate and original relationship between the 'who?' ('man' as being-there) and the 'what' (technical media). Human existence sensu Heidegger is *essentially* constituted and conditioned, as Stiegler shows, by a technical exteriority, a milieu of technical media. And since that milieu, to put it paradoxically, is 'essentially accidental' and also constantly changing and only exists as a compensation for an *original* lack of natural qualities, as I will explain below, the existence of man is characterized by what Stiegler calls an 'original disorientation', an original wandering or erring of man in his 'own' essence, something that is repeatedly emphasized by Heidegger as well (Stiegler 2009, 2).

---

2   Or as an '*Urfaktum* in the metaphysical sense', as he writes in a lecture course on Leibniz and the metaphysical foundations of logic from 1928, in which he designates the event of 'entering into the world' of beings *as* and *through* being-there also as an 'original event' [*Urereignis*] (Heidegger 1984, 245, 247).

6 Retentional finitude and the original technicity of time

Technical media are also constitutive for the human relation to time, in the sense of the ecstatic-horizontal structure of temporality of being-there as described in *Being and Time*. Again in the first volume of *Technics and Time* for example, Stiegler shows in great detail that what Heidegger in his seminal work called 'facticity' [*Faktizität*] or the 'already there' [*schon da*] of being-there, its historial 'having-been-ness' [*Gewesenheit*] or the ecstasis of the 'past', is only accessible thanks to the technical artefacts originating from that past. These function as artificial memories which give being-there access to a past that it has never been itself and has never experienced itself, but that nevertheless fundamentally determines it, and it does so through the way that past is appropriated in being-there's future, which is typical of the historial mode of being of being-there, as Heidegger stresses (Heidegger 2010, 19).

Although Heidegger in his analytic of the historiality of being-there explicitly mentions technical media when he speaks of 'antiquities' which can be found for example in museums as relics of the past and which he describes with the term 'world historial' [*Weltgeschichtliches*], he does in no way attribute to them any role in the constitution of the ecstatic-horizontal structure of being-there's being. They are for Heidegger just innerworldly beings that are only historial because they belong to the world of being-there, entirely constituted by that world and thus in no way constitutive of it (Stiegler 1998, 204). The (historiality of) the world is grounded purely in being-there; it is an *existential* that being-there has independent of any relation to technical media, yes independent of any relation to beings (or in other words: the empirical) at all. Here, Heidegger's said 'transcendentalism of being' shows itself, which is still a transcendentalism of being-there in *Being and Time*, but develops in his later thinking on technology into a genuine transcendentalism of being. Stiegler, however, shows that technical media are not only empirical and intra-temporal but are constitutive of the temporality of being-there in the strict sense (Stiegler 1998, 27).

Also the ecstasis of the future as the projecting of being-there on its own possibilities is only possible, as Stiegler shows, because of being-there's fundamental prostheticity. This means that also the understanding [*Verstehen*] of being-there, which is nothing else than the projection of being-there on its own possibilities of being and which is founded primarily in the *ecstasis* of the future, is fundamentally constituted and conditioned technically and prosthetically. In Husserlian terminology Stiegler expresses this by saying that every *noesis* is fundamentally a *technesis* (Stiegler 2005, 31). Moreover, and this is what Heidegger firmly denies of technology in an ontic sense (but of course affirms of the ontological-aletheic essence of technology as a specific mode of revealing beings), we must according to Stiegler acknowledge an autonomous ontic dynamic of technology (of the 'what') that is somehow more original and 'older' than the ecstatic-temporal ontological dynamic of being-there (the 'who?').

The human is characterized by what Stiegler calls, echoing Derrida, 'retentional finitude', which means that our capacity to remember, i.e., to retain (experiences from) the past is limited or finite due to the fragility and finitude of our biology (Stiegler 1998, 17). However, it is technical media functioning as external memory supports that have always 'compensated' for this fact, since the very beginning of human evolution – which starts for Stiegler with the production of the first stone tools, which from the outset have implicitly acted as memory vectors because they retain in their durable materiality (technical) experience which can thus be transferred to the offspring. Although Stiegler never speaks like Heidegger of the essence of technology, we can nevertheless state that technology for him is to be understood in its most essential sense in terms of memory, i.e., an artificial memory or in other words, an artificial material retention (Stiegler 2011a, 131).

The word 'retention' is derived from Husserl, who in his phenomenological analysis of inner time consciousness from 1928, executed on the basis of repeatedly listening to a melody via a grammophone, distinguished between primary and secondary retentions or memories. Primary retention refers to the retention of a perception (e.g., a just heard sequence of sounds), secondary retention on the other hand refers to a memory and accordingly a product of the imagination (for example, when the same sequence of sounds is called up from one's memory or spontaneously presents itself during a second listening to the same piece of music, which in turn has an effect on the primary retentions, and this explains of course why we always hear something else with each new listening experience, but also reading and seeing new things of course on repeated readings of a book or watching a movie more frequently). Stiegler adds to these a third form of retention, the tertiary retention, which is technical and artificial, like a record or a CD, and shows that only these kinds of external retentions allowed Husserl to distinguish between primary and secondary retentions at all. What Stiegler claims more generally however is that tertiary retentions are original in the sense that they are from the outset constitutive and conditional for the production of primary and secondary retentions. The technical milieu as the retentional medium of the human mind is a milieu that consists of tertiary retentions and this milieu is essential for the human mind, since without such substrates it would be no more than an ephemeral 'vapor' (Stiegler 2011a, 80).

These tertiary retentions therefore act as an artificial, extra-biological memory that supplements and compensates for the finite retentionality (and protentionality) of the defective biological memory of man as a mortal 'being-towards-death' [*Sein zum Tode*]. Heidegger's understanding of being, as a form of *at*-tention, can be understood from Stiegler's point of view as built of pro-tentions and *re*-tentions which are themselves always 'overdetermined' as Stiegler claims by artificial tertiary retentions (Stiegler 2010, 18). Now, according to Stiegler it is also only because of its artificial or accidental constitution by tertiary retentions (the domain of the 'what') that being-there (the 'who?') can be a questioning and reflexive being in the first place. But even more original than granting it this possibility of questioning, as Stiegler corrects Heidegger, what technology first of all does is *putting into* question the being of being-there, it's own questioning being only a response to this *more original* being-put-into-question. I will elaborate upon this below.

7 Being-there as individuation and man as an organological being

The production of tertiary retentions results in evolutionary terms in what Stiegler calls, with Leroi-Gourhan, a process of technical *exteriorization* which is co-originally accompanied by a process of *interiorization* of technical skills, know-how and knowledge. This process is responsible for the emergence or coming-into-being of what is thought by Heidegger as being-there's understanding of being, an understanding that becomes rational in nature with the advent of alphabetic writing (or the ortothetic literary retention as Stiegler calls it). It is this process of technical exteriorization that thus lies at the basis of the genesis of the human mode of being, which Stiegler conceptualizes with a term from the French philosopher of technology Gilbert Simondon as a process of *individuation*, more precisely as a process of psychic and collective individuation, emphasizing that this process can only take place in relation to a process of technical individuation (an insight lacking remarkably enough in Simondon himself (Stiegler 2014a, 51)) of which the motor is obviously located foremost in technical exteriorization.

It is the process of technical exteriorization that has led slowly, in the human species, to the transformation from a merely subsistent way of being (that of life) to an existent way of being (that of being-there), a transformation that is not thought by Heidegger, let alone deemed possible, but that Stiegler aims to conceive with Freud and psychoanalysis but also with the tradition of philosophical anthropology of, for example, Arnold Gehlen, as the transition from

an instinctive (animal) economy to a libidinal economy or an economy of
desire (and passions). And in this respect there are also many parallels with the
way Peter Sloterdijk thinks the technogenesis of being-there (Sloterdijk 2017,
89–148). This actually creates the transcendence as the being-in-the-world
sensu Heidegger and opens what he called the ontological difference (i.e., the
difference between being and beings), which Stiegler incidentally does not think
only as existence but also as consistence: as the domain of ideality, of the projection of ideas and ideals.

Just as the 'conscious', intrinsically temporal and ek-sistent being of being-
there can be interpreted in Husserlian terms as a play of primary and secondary (individual and collective) re-tentions and pro-tentions which are
themselves constituted by tertiary retentions and which form in their mutual
dynamic the at-tention that Heidegger calls understanding of being, so can
the Heideggerian history of being as destining be understood as a retentional-
protentional dynamic that is also originally supported by tertiary retentions, in
which the mnemotechnology of writing (and in particular the book) is crucial.
Thus Stiegler interprets the Western process of psychosocial individuation that
Heidegger thinks as the history of being with a term coined by the French lin-
guist Sylvain Auroux as conditioned by an ongoing process of *grammatization*,
i.e., the discretization and formalization of the continuity of speaking in the form
of letters, which in the form of writing, then printing and still later the invention
of digital technology, permits the in principle infinite reproduction (and subsequently interpretation) of that which has been grammatized. The invention of
the technology of writing as the first phase of grammatization forms the technological condition of all forms of knowledge and also inaugurates the history
of being, something that is completely ignored by Heidegger (Stiegler 2014a,
53–54).

Tertiary retentions accumulate over time and collectively form what Stiegler
calls a 'technical system' or 'technical milieu'. This milieu has its own evolutionary dynamic. In a very general sense he considers these tertiary retentions,
i.e., technical media, as belonging to an ontological domain *sui generis*, that of the
organized inorganic beings (possessing a quasi-autonomous status next to the
organized organic beings of life and the unorganized inorganic beings of lifeless
nature) (Stiegler 1998, 49). These organized inorganic beings are indeed created
by man as a living being, but man is in his turn re-organized and transformed
by these organized inorganic beings and in a very profound manner such that
Stiegler, following Georges Canguilhem, argues that the human life form is effectively a technical life form.

Stiegler thinks this re-organization and transformation of the human under the influence of techno-evolution in terms of a *general organology*. In the ek-sistent individuation process of man there are always three organ systems involved which co-individuate (or co-evolve) with each other and form as such a dynamic *transductive* relationship with each other, which means that they only are what or who they are *in* and *through* their relationship or articulation to each other: the psychic or psycho-somatic organs, the social organizations and the technical organs. The evolution of the technical organs, which is always in structural advance according to Stiegler, constantly induces de- and refunctionalizations of the other two organ systems place, which in their turn obviously influence the evolution of the technical organs again, and so on (Stiegler 2015a, 120). This is for instance why the 'oral brain' functions in a different way than the 'literary' or 'reading brain', as Stiegler suggests following the example of Walter Ong and Jack Goody; and this 'literary brain' is being replaced in our time more and more with the 'digital brain', as he emphasizes with Maryanne Wolf (Stiegler 2013b, 35). Psycho-somatic organs and social organizations evolve in direct interaction with technical media and the human psyche and spirit exist only thanks to the intimate link between the brain and its technical media.

Man is therefore not so much an organic as an organo-logical being and it is precisely his organological constitution which makes him into a noetic (knowing) and that is to say a symbolic creature that is sensitive to meaning and significance and able to express and produce this himself. It also makes him a libidinal (desiring) being: organological configurations are also circuits of libidinal energy and always instantiate a libidinal economy that is fundamentally different from the instinctive economy of animals, but which can always regress into a drive-based diseconomy. I would like to suggest here that what Heidegger identifies with concepts like being-there, but also ontological difference, clearing and the openness of being, can in a certain sense be understood from Stiegler's thesis of the original technicity of man in a in terms of a libidinal economy and one that is always constituted and conditioned by an organological configuration. From such a point of view we can then also understand what Heidegger refers to as the essence and danger of technology not only merely ontologically and onto-historically but also in an organological, organogenetical and (to coin a neologism) 'libidological' sense. But before elaborating upon this we first need to explain in some more detail the core insight of Stiegler's conception of technology, which is his idea, developed on the basis of an interpretation of the tragic myth of Prometheus and Epimetheus, that technical media are accidental 'compensations' for the original lack of qualities or the original absence of a natural origin in humans. And *as such* Stiegler understands technical media as *pharmaka*.

8 The human condition as original default and man as a pharmacological being

A basic insight of Stiegler's thinking, which he has developed in the first volume of *Technics and Time*, primarily on the basis of an original interpretation of the Prometheus myth which I cannot discuss here unfortunately, is that man is characterized essentially by what he calls an 'original default of origin', a *défaut d'origine* (Stiegler 1998, 16). Simply put, this means that the human does not possess natural properties like the animal. To 'compensate' for this, he is forced to provide these properties himself as it were, and as a consequence they are always accidental, i.e., technical and as such they are never really his 'own', i.e., 'proper' to himself. Instead, they always need to be appropriated, again and again, which means that the human being is constantly involved in a process Stiegler calls *adoption*, which is also always and necessarily a process 'exappropriation'. This continuous appropriation and exappropriation must be understood organologically, as already said, as a process of de- and re-functionalization of the psychic organs and social organizations under the influence of the evolution of the technical organs. The technical milieu functions for humans as an 'original supplement' (in Derrida's terminology) that 'compensates' for the default of origin that marks the original (technical) condition of being-there.

This original absence of origin – and this is crucial for understanding the stakes of Stiegler's thinking of technology insofar as they are analogous, in my view, to those of Heidegger's questioning of technology – means for Stiegler nothing less than the very condition of possibility for being-there as existence and consistence, and this is the reason why he thinks this original default is something that *ought* to be, both in the sense of a necessity, without which there could not be something like the human in the first place, and in the sense of an imperative to which the human is obliged as it were and that therefore has to be instituted as a right or a law: the *défaut d'origine* is thus a *défaut qu'il faut*, as it can be expressed this strikingly only in French.

Whilst the aim of Heidegger's questioning of technology is the preparation of a free relationship to technology, the goal of Stiegler's thinking of technology as I see it is also motivated by a concern for the 'preservation' of the kind of openness and freedom that has come into being with the emergence of the human-technology coupling and is in danger of disappearing due to the exclusive dominance of enframing. This is most evident in a chapter on the 'pharmacology of the question' that is included in his 2010 treatise *What Makes Life Worth Living. On Pharmacology*, his theoretically most fundamental book on the notion of *pharmakon*. In it Stiegler offers a pharmacological re-interpretation of what is addressed by Heidegger as the question of being (of being-there) and also implicitly, as I will try to demonstrate, of his thought of the danger of technology. But this of course presupposes some explanation of what the notion of *pharmakon* means for Stiegler and what he understands by pharmacology.

The concept of the *pharmakon* is probably the core concept of Stiegler's thought as it forms the crux of his understanding of technology. According to him, all technial media, from the simplest to the most complex, have to be understood as *pharmaka*. The Greek word *pharmakon* originally means both poison and medicine. Applied to the human condition as technical condition it means for Stiegler that technical media, as compensations for the original default, can both support *and* undermine human existence in all its dimensions[3]. They 'remedy' or 'cure' as it were the human default in all kinds of ways but simultaneously deepen it and as such can also frustrate human existence. Herein lies the essential – and for that reason insurmountable – ambiguity of technology: it is *at once* poisonous and beneficial to humans. This 'at once' is the core meaning of the pharmacological nature of technical media: they are curative or healing precisely insofar as they are *also always* toxic or destructive (Stiegler 2013a, 4). Think for instance of writing or computer software which can both support the elevation and emancipation of human individuals and collectives as well as facilitate their manipulation and disciplining, they can both foster their self-realization as well as their alienation from themselves and from each-other. Or think of a GPS device that both supports topographical orientation and at the same time erodes that ability in humans.

The technical organs that constitute the organological configurations discussed above are thus *pharmaka* and that means every organology is also always a pharmacology. And as such, it aims to study the consistently ambiguous effects of various artificial organs on the other two organ systems. Man is a pharmacological being that needs to take care of his fundamental 'deficiency' through technical *pharmaka*. What Heidegger theorized as care [*Sorge*], meaning the ontological structure of being of being-there, and what the later Foucault analyzed as care of the self and others, is only possible according to Stiegler through *pharmaka*. Every human culture is supported by a system of *pharmaka* and cultures for

---

3   Stiegler derives this notion first of all from Derrida but it goes back to Plato, who famously characterizes writing as a *pharmakon* in his dialogue *Phaedrus*.

Stiegler are therefore to be understood as *systems of care*, namely as care *through* and *for* the *pharmaka* (Stiegler 2010, 35).

9 Loss of the original default: organo-pharmacological reinterpretation of the danger

From the perspective of Stiegler, and this is finally the thesis that I want to defend in this chapter, the Heideggerian danger of technology appears as an organo-pharmacological phenomenon and that is to say, as an ontic condition: it is for Stiegler the technical milieu in a concrete sense that first of all enables being-there's understanding of being and openness for the truth of being – the level of the ontological and aletheialogical – i.e., constitutes and conditions it. And it is also the *pharmakon*, as Stiegler shows in *What Makes Life Worth Living*, on the basis of which being-there can question both its own being and that of other beings. But more originally still, Stiegler claims, is the *putting into question* of being-there itself by technology, as a result of pharmacological mutations caused by the arrival of a new technical system. For Stiegler, the human as being-there *is* only insofar as he is constantly and always challenged and put into question by technology, i.e., by the process of technical exteriorization that pervades his 'essence' and as such constitutes it in an accidental manner as both their default and their excess (Stiegler 2013a, 104).

Although Stiegler endorses Heidegger's characterization of the human as an essentially questioning being, he reproaches him for failing to recognize that every questioning of being-there is technically and therefore pharmacologically conditioned. What Heidegger did not see is that every question is necessarily preceded by what Stiegler calls a 'pharmacological situation': the being put into question of the human by a new pharmacological regime, as for example happens in the present time with the advent of the digital media which pervade all domains of society and thereby disrupt all existing ways of life and habits, both individually and collectively. To a more extreme extent still is this the case with the new nano-, bio-, info and cognitive or the so-called NBIC technologies that Stiegler describes as transformational technologies, which have laid open even the biological constitution of man for technical intervention. But it has in the past also been the advent of the medium of writing which had a disruptive effect on the oral and mythical culture of ancient Greece and which put that culture into question in a radical sense, but subsequently enabled a wholly new form of questioning, namely that of philosophy, politics and science (this event is commonly known as the transition from *mythos* to *logos*, but has never been interpreted explicitly as a technological mutation). It is a pharmacological situation that underlies any questioning according to Stiegler. And it can always be traced back to the originally being-put-into-question of man *through* and *as* the original lack of origin, a lack that also constitutes his original disorientation (Stiegler 2013a, 106).

It is the technical genesis or the process of technical exteriorization that incessantly puts the human into question. As for Heidegger, the question concerning technology for Stiegler is not in the first instance a question posed by man with respect to the technology, but the question that technology imposes upon us, namely by putting us into question. Heidegger thinks here of the ontological essence of technology and thus of being but for Stiegler it is technology in its concrete, ontic guise which puts the human in question and thereby makes all questioning of being first of all possible. Technology, he writes, '*is not a question that is posed by the questioning being itself*, but *that which puts this being into question*, what forms the *condition* of *every* question, and in that sense I do not believe that Heidegger himself really understood the question of technology in this 'questioning' radicalism – despite the fact that what he called "revealing" exists only under that condition' (Stiegler 2014b, 156). All revealing is technical revealing, unlike what Heidegger suggests in the technology essay, namely that there exists a more original way of revealing that would not be technical but would 'obey' a more initial (self)revelation of the truth of being (Heidegger 1977, 28).

The primacy of the *pharmakon* and the pharmacological situation as the heteronomous – and as such 'traumatic' – source of all understanding of being and any questioning of being is the unthought in Heidegger. As Stiegler shows, however, the lack of origin and the being put into question by the *pharmakon* is older and more original than any question of being (Stiegler 2013a, 109). What is more, the being put into question by technology is in the first instance always toxic, and therefore traumatic, causing an injury or a wound, since every appearance of a new *pharmakon* undermines and suspends the existing technical milieu or organological configuration that lies at the basis of the current understanding of being (think for example of today's 'digital revolution' which totally disrupts the traditional culture of writing).

Now Stiegler shows that being-there as the questioning being is put into question by technology precisely when technology puts the very possibility of questioning itself into question. Technology is for the human being the *uncanny* other that nevertheless forms the hidden ground of its most 'proper' being, namely as that which exteriorizes it and thereby both enables and disables its existent being-in-the-world. This 'other' that is technical exteriority, the *heteros-*'what' of technology, can open the question of the *autos-*'who' of the human – of what Heidegger called the 'innermost and authentic' of being-there above – but as a *pharmakon* it can also block and thereby disable this question (Stiegler 2013a, 107–108). Stiegler claims that the condition of any real question of being-there consists precisely in the possibility of this questioning itself to be put into question. And this happens, when being-there is exposed to a new pharmacological situation, one resulting from the technical process of becoming that structurally and quasi-autonomously precedes the process of psychic and collective individuation as a kind of 'inorganic drift', thereby *pro*-jecting being-there in a *pros*-thetic manner in a becoming [*devenir*] that precedes any possibility of questioning and puts into question precisely in making every questioning *im*possible, and that can be transformed into a meaningful existential future [*avenir*] solely through the processes of psychic and collective individuation through the *invention* of a *new way* of questioning – or in Heidegger's terms: a new understanding of being under the condition of the new *pharmakon* (Stiegler 2013a, 108).

Being-there is, in the interpretation of Stiegler, an originally 'defective' being (originally without origin) which can only question because it has more originally been put into question by the technical *pharmakon*. And it can only question and be put into question because and insofar as it is prosthetic. It is being-there's prostheticity which puts it – pro-jectively – into question and it does so since and due to its (absent) as originally without origin: as a being that is *always* not yet 'there [*Da*]' but elsewhere, outside of itself and far from itself and that as such will always remain unfinished and in becoming (Stiegler 2013a, 108). The *pharmaco*logical, essentially ambiguous nature of this consists herein that this prostheticity, during the process of technical exteriorization as production of ever new prostheses which compensate each time again for the original default, periodically generates situations in which, on the one hand, an established possibility of questioning (an existing understanding of bein) is interrupted and put out of order, *but* in which, but on the other hand, and precisely *through* this provocation, necessitates but also possibilizes a new mode of questioning. The former aspect of the *pharmakon* Stiegler calls the toxic aspect, the latter the healing aspect (Stiegler 2013a, 109–10).

The *pharmakon* as that which puts being-there into question, can at the same time also close it off from questioning and thus put it into a situation that we might call with a term from Heidegger, the 'absence of questioning' [*Fraglosigkeit*], in which the human being does not ask questions anymore in the sense that he no longer questions being (i.e., his own being and the being of other beings) and therefore loses or abandons his innermost 'free essence'. Stiegler also speaks in this regard of the possibility of the human of losing his being-there, of being no longer 'there' [*Da*] anymore (Stiegler 2013a, 111). And he believes that the current pharmacological situation, which in his view is characterized by a generalized toxicity of today's technical milieu of the mind through the digital *pharmakon*, carries the threat of causing a complete blockage of the opportunity to ask questions and therefore of a disappearance of being-there, or in his own terms of a complete reduction of human existence and consistence to the level of subsistence (Stiegler 2011b, 86). This situation is engendered predominantly through the global annexation by the capitalist economy of the digital networks for the organization and control of production and consumption and currently realizes itself mainly through the generalization of (digital) automation and robotics which increasingly short-circuit the psychic and collective processes of individuation, including the scientific-intellectual and political ones. Another aspect of this is the emergence of so-called transformational technologies such as the already mentioned NBIC technologies, which introduce a wholly new pharmacological regime which is no longer one of technical exteriorization but of technical interiorization and thus of direct re-organization of the biological domain. I will not go into this here but it is clear that this involves a radically new mode of putting-into-question of the human, one that is completely neglected in many contemporary debates around what is called 'human enhancement', especially by so-called transhumanists (Stiegler 2013a, 116–17)[4].

The question Stiegler poses, and that is his way to point to the danger of technology in the quasi-Heideggerian sense, is whether the era of integrated automation which we now enter and which he also characterizes as the 'automatic condition' (Stiegler 2014b, 157), will short-circuit the processes of psychic and collective individuation and frustrate the adoption and appropriation of technologies and the invention of new forms of freedom, autonomy and criticism based on it, to such an extent that only a blind and threfore uncritical permanent adaptation to a market-driven technological innovation remains. This would mean nothing less than a *de facto* liquidation of the freedom, openness and indeterminacy of being-there, which is only guaranteed by the original default as a *necessary* default or as a 'default that should be' [*défaut qu'il faut*]. The horizon of an undetermined and free future would thereby be 'neutralized' as Jean-François Lyotard once put it (Lyotard 1991, 66). Instead, a purely adaptive process of sheer survival would be installed and we would see a regression of the existent, free, world-forming essence of man to the level of subsistence, in which drives rather

---

4   See for a Stieglerian organo-pharmacological interpretation and critique of the idea of cognitive enhancement in transhumanism: Lemmens 2015.

than desires would dominate and any long-term perspective would be destroyed by the dictates of the short term, i.e., of short-term speculative capitalism (Stiegler 2010, 182). Here the short circuiting of the processes of psychic and collective individuation by mechanical and digital automatisms would transform them into processes of disindividuation (Stiegler 2013a, 123), engendering a situation Stiegler often designates as 'symbolic misery' (Stiegler 2011b, 12).

10 The danger of technology as proletarianization and the ruination of the original default

Using a term Stiegler derives from the Marxist tradition but interprets more in a Simondonian sense as a loss of knowledge, expertise and intelligence due to the short-circuiting of psycho-collective individuation by a technical individuation that is not properly interiorized and appropriated and thus engenders disindividuation, I would argue that what Heidegger indicates as he points to the danger of technology can be understood in a more concrete and perhaps more fruitful sense in terms of a dynamic of *proletarianization* – and more precisely as the generalization of it – in which the toxicity of the technical milieu brings about a loss of openness and freedom and therefore of the possibilities of existence and consistence. This means a loss of ontological freedom, which can also be understood with Stiegler as a reduction of existence and consistence to the level of subsistence resulting from the toxic pharmacological situation.

Proletarianization for Stiegler also means the collapse of the libidinal economy due to the total mobilization of libidinal energy (i.e., desire in all its forms) of individuals and collectives for the economy of subsistence by subjecting them to a systematic calculation and exploitation, causing a regression into a desublimatory (dis)economy of drives. In such an economy human life is in fact reduced to survival and instead of a desiring-libidinal orientation toward motives, goals and ideals, drive-based addictions and automatisms reign, inevitably resulting in 'desymbolization', 'symbolic misery' and 'systemic stupidity' (Stiegler 2013a, 22). Stiegler does not hesitate to associate this situation with Nietzsche's diagnosis of nihilism, which is currently reaching its pinnacle in his view (Stiegler 2011b, 55). Our time is that of a *total nihilism* in the sense that it currently achieves its completion, as the 'philosopher with the hammer' predicted about one and a half century ago in his unfinished magnum opus *The Will to Power* (Stiegler 2011b, 53; Stiegler 2015b, 25).

Of relevance in relation to Heidegger is that Stiegler reinterprets his notion of ontological difference as the difference between existence and consistence (Stiegler 2011b, 91). Both are for Stiegler fundamentally constituted by tertiary retentions, something that remains unthought in Heidegger. And it is precisely *this* difference that is threatened with disappearence in what Stiegler quite recently has called our 'automatic society' (Stiegler 2015b, 33). Instead of the ontological difference, which according to Heidegger 'reigns, without us taking heed' (Heidegger 2004, 207), there reigns an ontological *in*difference (Stiegler 2011a, 5) in which the Heideggerian care, which Stiegler associates with the Roman notion of *otium*, fully regresses to concern, or in other words *otium* is completely absorbed into *negotium*, i.e., into economic activity. In contrast to Heidegger, Stiegler argues that the ontological difference requires a cultivation through practices of care based on tertiary retentions in order to keep it open. However, the current hyperindustrial control and automation of the tertiary retentions that constitute the technical milieu of the mind renders such a cultivation almost impossible.

This cultivation of the ontological difference sensu Stiegler is actually the safeguarding and taking care of the original lack of origin which, as he writes, 'keeps people going' since it is the very condition of possibility for the human as being-there (Stiegler 2005, 82). This condition of possibility is itself technically-accidentally conditioned and in contrast to Heidegger, for whom the belonging-ness of human beings to the revealing-event of being is said to be 'indestructible' (Heidegger 1977, 32), Stiegler claims it *can* disappear. Moreover, what Heidegger thinks only in ontological terms, Stiegler also understands as a libidinal and politico-economic phenomenon and therefore as something that is and always should be the stakes of a 'struggle', i.e., a pharmacological struggle, waged with the *pharmaka* of technology.

For although Stiegler describes the current pharmacological situation as that of an extreme toxicity and therefore as extremely 'dangerous' for being-there as original default, it is nothing other than that toxicity itself which also carries the possible saving power, since it can become the curative through which being-there, to put it in the words of Heidegger, can transfrom the 'absence of questioning' in which it is imprisoned by the pathological toxicity of the phar-macological regime into a a new 'question-worthiness' [*Fragwürdigkeit*], i.e., in a renewed questioning of its own being and that of the other beings. Such a 'phar-macological turn', the therapeutic moment through which the poison becomes the medicine, would mark the beginning, again in Heidegger's words, of a new disclosure of being, and that means in practice of new forms of existence and consistence, of new practices of self and freedom, of new forms of knowledge and know-how, of a new 'faith' and above all of new questions that are truly 'worthy to be asked', as Stiegler writes (Stiegler 2013a, 115). It would establish a new pharmacological epoch and a new organological configuration, and with it a new 'con-stellation of Being and man' (Heidegger 2002a, 34).

11 By way of a conclusion

In conclusion, I would like to argue that since the 'reign' of technology as that which constitutes and conditions all dimensions of human existence is interpreted by Stiegler in an ontico-ontological sense as a technical milieu, the danger and saving power of technology can be understood from his perspective in terms of an ecology: an ecology of the technical milieu which conditions the milieu of the mind from the outset and which could also be called an 'ecology of mind', to use a term of Gregory Bateson. According to Stiegler this technical milieu of the mind currently suffers from poisoning and pollution to the same extent (or even more so) as the natural environment does and it is this poisoning that constitutes the danger of technology sensu Stiegler.

In Heideggerian terms, we could say that Stiegler's pharmacological view of technology teaches us that technology simultaneously supports and endangers human existence, that the danger lies precisely in the dependence on technical supports or media but that it is only through these supports that this danger can be taken care of. For Heidegger being-there's way of being is most fundamentally characterized by an openness to being, through what I call the ontological freedom of man. With Stiegler, we have seen that man 'possesses' this openness thanks to his original technicity. As *pharmakon*, however, technology also constitutes a threat to this openness. It opens man's 'world openness' as openness to the being of beings, but it can also close off that openness. Technology is at once the condition of possibility and the condition of impossibility for the free essence or the ontological openness/freedom of man. Heidegger, who would obviously reject the idea of an original technical constitution of man as being-there, tends to perceive in technology, at least in the technology essay, only an occulting and alienating dynamic of destitution (Stiegler 1998, 204).

As such, the Heideggerian danger of technology can be seen from Stiegler's more ontico-ontological perspective as a pharmacological situation and that is to say a situation of generalized toxicity of the technical *pharmakon*, one that might be described by Heidegger himself as one of 'absence of questioning' [*Fraglosigkeit*], 'absence of thought' [*Gedankenlosigkeit*], 'forgetfulness of being', 'abandonment of being' [*Seinsverlassenheit*] and 'nihilism', and which Stiegler often identifies with terms like 'adaptation', 'disindividuation', 'systemic stupidity' and very recently 'entropization', as the most fundamental feature of the hyper-industrialization that characterizes the era of the anthropocene (Stiegler 2015b,

19f). Heidegger's idea of salvation as immanent in the danger of technology as the possibility of a re-turn towards being and an overcoming of the forgetfulness of being could again be interpreted more ontico-ontologically as a 'pharmacological turn', understood as the healing potential of the becoming-therapeutic of the *pharmakon*, a turn that would consist in a process of *adoption*, which would in turn lead to a new understanding of being as well as a new question of being.

In practice, a pharmacological turn sensu Stiegler would be tantamount as it were to a 're-invention' of ourselves based on the condition of the new (digital) organo-pharmacological regime that momentarily, at least according to Stiegler, in many ways frustrates and blocks this through an extreme, in his view even total proletarianization – which is currently mainly realized by an integral and generalized automation of our individual and collective lives (think of 'big data') and what Antoinette Rouvroy and Thomas Berns designate as 'algorithmic governance', with reference to Michel Foucault (Berns & Rouvroy 2013). Dealing with the risk of a complete loss of being-there recognized here by Stiegler would entail in his view by no means the adoption of an attitude of Heideggerian releasement but rather that we should develop a politics, i.e., a techno-politics of *pharmaka* that he explicitly conceives as a therapy (and politics in his view most originally means *pharmaco*therapy), a socio-therapy which involves the collective invention and design, within the new organological configuration, of new forms of living and living-together, of science, economy, art, etc., i.e., a new mode of *Sorge* in the Heideggerian sense, but also forms of care in the sense Foucault: care for the self and care for others, based on the new digital *pharmaka*.

What can save us from the technological juggernaut that is currently rolling over us and seems to wholly overwhelm and imprison us, which is undermining all our familiar habits, realities and truths, which puts all existing forms of freedom, autonomy and sovereignty into question, is precisely this juggernaut itself, which must be pharmacologically transformed and turned into a positive force, changed from something that makes us weaker into something that makes us stronger, to paraphrase a famous phrase by Friedrich Nietzsche. The 'salvation' from technology's 'danger' in the sense of a more free relationship to it will not be achieved through a practice and attitude of releasement or separation [*Abgeschiedenheit*], as Heidegger proclaimed. It will not come from being itself or through the grace of a god, as he once suggested in his famous interview with *Der Spiegel* from 1968. If it is possible at all to speak of 'salvation' in a Stieglerian sense it would consist, most generally, in the willingness to affirm the *patho*genesis that all *techno*genesis of man as an ontological being fundamentally is and to assume a readiness to become 'sick' in order to acquire a new 'health' (Stiegler 2013a, 28). In a recent interview Stiegler very nicely says that what is most important for the fundamentally technical creature that the human being is, is to be 'worthy' to technology, also where, and *precisely* where she puts this worthiness fundamentally in question. For philosophy this means, to use a typically Heideggerian word, to consider technology explicitly as the most 'question worthy' [*fragwürdig*] or 'dignifying' (Heidegger 2012, 57). Like no other contemporary thinker, Stiegler has practiced this in the wake of Heidegger, in thinking both *with* and *against* Heidegger, by 'dignifying' the technical accident or medium as the most fundamental issue of philosophy.

Bibliography

Berns, Thomas & Rouvroy, Antoinette. 'Gouvernementalité algorithmique et Perspectives d'Émanicaption. Le disparate comme condition d'individuation par la relation?' in *La Découverte | Réseaux*, Nr. 177, 2013, pp. 163–196.

Bostrom, Nick. 'Transhumanist Values', *Review of Contemporary Philosophy*, Vol. 4, May 2005, pp. 3–14.

Heidegger, Martin. *Discourse on Thinking*. New York: Harper & Row, 1969.

Heidegger, Martin. *The Question Concerning Technology and Other Essays*. New York: Harper & Row, 1977.

Heidegger, Martin. *The Metaphysical Foundations of Logic*. Bloomington: Indiana University Press, 1984.

Heidegger, Martin. *Nietzsche: The Will to Power as Knowledge and as Metaphysics/Nihilism*, Volumes 3 & 4. New York: Harper & Row, 1991.

Heidegger, Martin. *The Fundamental Concepts of Metaphysics: World, Finitude, Solitude*. Bloomington: Indiana University Press, 1995.

Heidegger, Martin. *Identity and Difference*. Chicago: University of Chicago Press, 2002a.

Heidegger, Martin. *On Time and Being*. Chicago: University of Chicago Press, 2002b.

Heidegger, Martin. *Basic Questions of Philosophy: Selected Problems of Logic*. Bloomington: Indiana University Press, 2004.

Heidegger, Martin. *Mindfulness*. London: Continuum, 2006.

Heidegger, Martin. *Being and Time*. New York: State University of New York Press, 2010.

Heidegger, Martin. *Bremen and Freiburg Lectures: Insight into that which is and Basic Principles of Thinking*. Bloomington: Indiana University Press, 2012.

Lemmens, Pieter. 'Cognitive Enhancement and Anthropotechnological Change: Towards an Organology and Pharmacology of Cognitive

Enhancement Technologies', *Techné. Research in Philosophy and Technology* 19/2, Spring 2015, pp. 168–192.

Lyotard, Jean-François. *The Inhuman, Reflections on Time.* Cambridge: Polity, 1991.

Sloterdijk, Peter. *Not Saved. Essays after Heidegger.* Cambridge–Malden: Polity, 2017.

Stiegler, Bernard. *Technics and Time 1. The Fault of Epimetheus.* Stanford: Stanford University Press, 1998.

Stiegler, Bernard. *Philosopher par accident. Entretiens avec Élie During.* Paris: Galilée, 2004.

Stiegler, Bernard. *Constituer l'Europe 2. Le motif européen.* Paris: Galilée, 2005.

Stiegler, Bernard. *Technics and Time 2. Disorientation.* Stanford: Stanford University Press, 2009.

Stiegler, Bernard. *Taking Care of Youth and the Generations.* Stanford: Stanford University Press, 2010.

Stiegler, Bernard. *Technics and Time 3. Cinematic Time and the Question of Malaise.* Stanford: Stanford University Press, 2011a.

Stiegler, Bernard. *The Decadence of Industrial Democracies. Disbelief and Discredit 1.* Cambridge-Malden: Polity, 2011b.

Stiegler, Bernard. *What Makes Life Worth Living. On Pharmacology.* Cambridge-Malden Polity, 2013a.

Stiegler, Bernard, 'Die Aufklärung in the Age of Philosophical Engineering'. In: *Digital Enlightenment Yearbook 2013*, Hildebrandt M et al. Fairfax, VA: IOS press, Inc.2013b, pp. 29-39.

Stiegler, Bernard. *Symbolic Misery 1. The Hyperindustrial Epoch.* Cambridge–Malden: Polity, 2014a.

Stiegler, Bernard. *Per toeval filosoferen. Gesprekken met Élie During.* Zoetermeer: Klement, 2014b.

Stiegler, Bernard. *Symbolic Misery 2. The katastrophe of the sensible.* Cambridge-Malden: Polity, 2015a.

Stiegler, Bernard. *La société automatique 1. L'Avenir du travail.* Paris: Fayard, 2015b.

Author Biographies

Justin Michael Battin – University of Silesia in Katowice
Justin Michael Battin is an Assistant Professor of English Cultures and Literatures in the Department of American and Canadian Studies at the University of Silesia in Katowice. His research focuses on intersecting various strands of Heidegger's philosophy with the everyday uses of mobile media technologies and mobile social media.

German A. Duarte – University of Bolzano
German A. Duarte is Assistant Professor of Film and Media Studies at the Free University of Bozen-Bolzano. His research interests include history of media, film history, cybernetics, cognitive-cultural economy, and philosophy.

Leighton Evans – Swansea University
Dr Leighton Evans is a Senior Lecturer in Media Theory, College of Arts and Humanities, Swansea University, UK. His research interests are in phenomenology, digital media, mobile media, and virtual reality.

Eve Forrest – Independent Scholar
Eve Forrest is an ethnographer and writer. Her wider research interests include everyday media practices, photography, and phenomenology.

Heidi Herzogenrath-Amelung – University of Westminster
Heidi Herzogenrath-Amelung is a Senior Lecturer at the University of Westminster, UK, and a member of the Communication and Media Research Institute (CAMRI). She gained her PhD on Martin Heidegger's philosophy of technology and digital surveillance from University of Leeds in 2015. She has researched and written about digital surveillance (governmental & corporate use of citizens' data), technological determinism and digital media, and more recently she has been interested in philanthrocapitalism and digital media.

Pieter Lemmens – Radbound University Nijmegen
Pieter Lemmens teaches philosophy and ethics at the Radboud University in Nijmegen, Netherlands. He has published on themes in the philosophy of technology and innovation, on the work of Martin Heidegger, Peter Sloterdijk, and Bernard Stiegler, on post-autonomist Marxism, and on themes in philosophical anthropology and (post)phenomenology. Current interests are the political and ecological potentials of new digital media, the politics of human (cognitive) enhancement technologies, and philosophy of technology in the age of the Anthropocene.

Dimitra V. Pavlakou – Architect at K-Studio
Dimitra Pavlakou has been working as an architect at K-studio since July 2017 and previously worked as an adjunct professor in the University of Patras, School of Engineering, Department of Architecture (2015-2017). She earned her diploma from the same institution in 2009.

Sascha Rashof – Goldsmiths College, University of London
Sascha Rashof completed her PhD thesis in media philosophy at the Centre for Cultural Studies at Goldsmiths College, University of London, for which she received support from the Arts and Humanities Research Council. She has a background in cultural journalism, taught media and cultural theory at a number of UK universities, including Goldsmiths, the University for the Creative Arts, Southampton Solent and others, and is currently coordinating research projects across the University of the Arts London.

Tony Richards – University of Lincoln
Tony Richards is a Senior Lecturer in Media Theory and Production at the Lincoln School of Film and Media, University of Lincoln, UK. As well as being a filmmaker his research is mainly based around the work of Derrida, Heidegger, and Bataille in relation to digital and emergent media.

Camilo Salazar Prince – University of Bogotá Jorge Tadeo Lozano
Camilo Salazar Prince majored in Philosophy at UC Berkeley where he was mentored by Hubert L. Dreyfus. In 2012 he received an M.F.A. from UCLA and has since worked as a screenwriter and director. Since 2017 he has been an Associate Professor in the Department of Film and Television at University Jorge Tadeo Lozano in Bogotá, Colombia.

Philippe Theophanidis – York University
Philippe Theophanidis is an Assistant Professor in the Communications program at Glendon College, a campus of York University, in Toronto. His research is concerned with philosophies of communication, media studies, and visual culture. He has published academic articles and book chapters in French and English on a variety of topics, ranging from cinema to contemporary political issues. His current research examines the concept of media through the prisms of space and community.

Georgios Tsagdis – University of Greenwich
Georgios Tsagdis is Fellow at the Westminster Law & Theory Lab and teaches at the University of Greenwich. His work operates across theoretical and disciplinary intersections drawing on 20th Century, Contemporary, and Ancient

Greek Philosophy. His current research examines the function of the negative in the ontology of matter from Plato to New Materialisms. In other recent research, he has explored various themes in the historic encounters of philosophy and nature, from the figure of the animal in the Platonic corpus to post-humanism and parasitism.

LITERARY AND CULTURAL THEORY

General editor: Wojciech H. Kalaga

Vol. 1   Wojciech H. Kalaga: Nebulae of Discourse. Interpretation, Textuality, and the Subject. 1997.

Vol. 2   Wojciech H. Kalaga / Tadeusz Rachwał (eds.): Memory – Remembering – Forgetting. 1999.

Vol. 3   Piotr Fast: Ideology, Aesthetics, Literary History. Socialist Realism and its Others. 1999.

Vol. 4   Ewa Rewers: Language and Space: The Poststructuralist Turn in the Philosophy of Culture. 1999.

Vol. 5   Floyd Merrell: Tasking Textuality. 2000.

Vol. 6   Tadeusz Rachwał / Tadeusz Slawek (eds.): Organs, Organisms, Organisations. Organic Form in 19th-Century Discourse. 2000.

Vol. 7   Wojciech H. Kalaga / Tadeusz Rachwał: Signs of Culture: Simulacra and the Real. 2000.

Vol. 8   Tadeusz Rachwal: Labours of the Mind. Labour in the Culture of Production. 2001.

Vol. 9   Rita Wilson / Carlotta von Maltzan (eds.): Spaces and Crossings. Essays on Literature and Culture in Africa and Beyond. 2001.

Vol. 10   Leszek Drong: Masks and Icons. Subjectivity in Post-Nietzschean Autobiography. 2001.

Vol. 11   Wojciech H. Kalaga / Tadeusz Rachwał (eds.): Exile. Displacements and Misplacements. 2001.

Vol. 12   Marta Zajac: The Feminine of Difference. Gilles Deleuze, Hélène Cixous and Contempora-ry Critique of the Marquis de Sade. 2002.

Vol. 13   Zbigniew Bialas / Krzysztof Kowalczyk-Twarowski (eds.): Alchemization of the Mind. Literature and Dissociation. 2003.

Vol. 14   Tadeusz Slawek: Revelations of Gloucester. Charles Olsen, Fitz Hugh Lane, and Writing of the Place. 2003.

Vol. 15   Carlotta von Maltzan (ed.): Africa and Europe: En/Countering Myths. Essays on Literature and Cultural Politics. 2003.

Vol. 16   Marzena Kubisz: Strategies of Resistance. Body, Identity and Representation in Western Culture. 2003.

Vol. 17   Ewa Rychter: (Un)Saying the Other. Allegory and Irony in Emmanuel
Levinas's Ethical Language. 2004.

Vol. 18   Ewa Borkowska: At the Threshold of Mystery: Poetic Encounters
with Other(ness). 2005.

Vol. 19   Wojciech H. Kalaga / Tadeusz Rachwał (eds.): Feeding Culture: The
Pleasures and Perils of Appetite. 2005.

Vol. 20   Wojciech H. Kalaga / Tadeusz Rachwał (eds.): Spoiling the Cannibals'
Fun? Cannibalism and Cannibalisation in Culture and Elsewhere. 2005.

Vol. 21   Katarzyna Ancuta: Where Angels Fear to Hover. Between the
Gothic Disease and the Meataphysics of Horror. 2005.

Vol. 22   Piotr Wilczek: (Mis)translation and (Mis)interpretation: Polish
Literature in the Context of Cross-Cultural Communication. 2005.

Vol. 23   Krzysztof Kowalczyk-Twarowski: Glebae Adscripti. Troping Place,
Region and Nature in America. 2005.

Vol. 24   Zbigniew Białas: The Body Wall. Somatics of Travelling and
Discursive Practices. 2006.

Vol. 25   Katarzyna Nowak: Melancholic Travelers. Autonomy, Hybridity
and the Maternal. 2007.

Vol. 26   Leszek Drong: Disciplining the New Pragmatism. Theory, Rhetoric,
and the Ends of Literary Study. 2007.

Vol. 27   Katarzyna Smyczyńska: The World According to Bridget Jones.
Discourses of Identity in Chicklit Fictions. 2007.

Vol. 28   Wojciech H. Kalaga / Marzena Kubisz (eds.): Multicultural Dilemmas.
Identity, Difference, Otherness. 2008.

Vol. 29   Maria Plochocki: Body, Letter, and Voice. Construction Knowledge
in Detective Fiction. 2010.

Vol. 30   Rossitsa Terzieva-Artemis: Stories of the Unconscious: Sub-Versions
in Freud, Lacan and Kristeva. 2009.

Vol. 31   Sonia Front: Transgressing Boundaries in Jeanette Winterson's Fiction. 2009.

Vol. 32   Wojciech Kalaga / Jacek Mydla / Katarzyna Ancuta (eds.): Political
Correctness. Mouth Wide Shut? 2009.

Vol. 33   Paweł Marcinkiewicz: The Rhetoric of the City: Robinson Jeffers
and A. R. Ammons. 2009.

Vol. 34   Wojciech Małecki: Embodying Pragmatism. Richard Shusterman's
Philosophy and Literary Theory. 2010.

Vol. 35   Wojciech Kalaga / Marzena Kubisz (eds.): Cartographies of Culture.
            Memory, Space, Representation. 2010.

Vol. 36   Bożena Shallcross / Ryszard Nycz (eds.): The Effect of Pamplisest.
            Culture, Literature, History. 2011.

Vol. 37   Wojciech Kalaga / Marzena Kubisz / Jacek Mydla (eds.): A Culture
            of Recycling / Recycling Culture? 2011.

Vol. 38   Anna Chromik: Disruptive Fluidity. The Poetics of the Pop Cogito. 2012.

Vol. 39   Paweł Wojtas: Translating Gombrowicz´s Liminal Aesthetics. 2014.

Vol. 40   Marcin Mazurek: A Sense of Apocalypse. Technology, Textuality,
            Identity. 2014.

Vol. 41   Charles Russell / Arne Melberg / Jarosław Płuciennik / Michał Wróblewski
            (eds.): Critical Theory and Critical Genres. Contemporary Perspectives
            from Poland. 2014.

Vol. 42   Marzena Kubisz: Resistance in the Deceleration Lane. Velocentrism, Slow
            Culture and Everyday Practice. 2014.

Vol. 43   Bohumil Fořt: An Introduction to Fictional Worlds Theory. 2016.

Vol. 44   Agata Wilczek: Beyond the Limits of Language. Apophasis and
            Transgression in Contemporary Theoretical Discourse. 2016.

Vol. 45   Witold Sadowski / Magdalena Kowalska / Magdalena Maria Kubas (eds.):
            Litanic Verse I. Origines, Iberia, Slavia et Europa Media. 2016.

Vol. 46   Witold Sadowski / Magdalena Kowalska / Magdalena Maria Kubas (eds.):
            Litanic Verse II. Britannia, Germania et Scandinavia. 2016.

Vol. 47   Julia Szołtysek: A Mosaic of Misunderstanding: Occident, Orient,
            and Facets of Mutual Misconstrual. 2016.

Vol. 48   Manyaka Toko Djockoua: Cross-Cultural Affinities. Emersonian
            Transcendentalism and Senghorian Negritude. 2016.

Vol. 49   Ryszard Nycz: The Language of Polish Modernism. Translated by
            Tul'si Bhambry. 2017.

Vol. 50   Alina Silvana Felea: Aspects of Reference in Literary Theory. Poetics,
            Rhetoric and Literary History. 2017.

Vol. 51   Jerry Xie: Mo Yan Thought. Six Critiques of Hallucinatory Realism. 2017.

Vol. 52   Paweł Stachura / Piotr Śniedziewski / Krzysztof Trybuś (eds.):
            Approaches to Walter Benjamin's The Arcades Project. 2017.

Vol. 53   Ricardo Namora: Before the Trenches. A Mapping of Problems
            in Literary Interpretation. 2017.

Vol. 54   Kerstin Eksell / Gunilla Lindberg-Wada (eds.): Studies of Imagery
          in Early Mediterranean and East Asian Poetry. 2017.

Vol. 55   Justin Michael Battin / German A. Duarte (eds.): We Need to Talk About
          Heidegger. Essays Situating Martin Heidegger in Contemporary Media
          Studies. 2018.

www.peterlang.com

**Die folgenden Bände erscheinen als Reihe „Litanic Verse"
in der Reihe „Literary and Cultural Theory":**

Sadowski, Litanic Verse I: Origines, Iberia, Slavia et
Europa Media (ISBN: 978-3-631-66350-9)
Sadowski, Litanic Verse II: Britannia, Germania et
Scandinavia (ISBN: 978-3-631-66349-3).
Kowalska, Litanic Verse III: Francia (ISBN: 978-3-631-75622-5).
Kubas, Litanic Verse IV: Italia (978-3-631-74805-3).
Sadowski, European Litanic Verse. A Different Space-Time (ISBN: 978-3-631-75624-9).